Best Ever
Indian
Cookbook

Best Ever
Indian
Cookbook

325 famous step-by-step recipes for
the greatest spicy and aromatic dishes

Mridula Baljekar, Rafi Fernandez, Shehzad Husain & Manisha Kanani

METRO BOOKS
NEW YORK

Contents

Introduction to
Indian Cooking

INDIAN COOKING displays a remarkable range of influences, as befits a subcontinent that has been subject to British, Italian, Dutch, Portuguese, and French colonial rule, and which remains home to a vast number of religious practices. As new migrants of all nationalities flock into the streets of Mumbai, Delhi, and Kolkata, and neighbors, such as China and Myanmar, exert their influence on ingredients and cooking techniques, the evolution and diversification of this popular cuisine may never be complete.

Within these pages, you'll find familiar classics, simple country dishes little known outside their area of origin, contemporary recipes that utilize convenience ingredients, and even fusion foods. Indian cooking also boasts the world's greatest array of vegetarian dishes, with flavorful dishes based on lentils, dried beans and peas, and vegetables. All are delicious, and equally suited to entertaining friends, or cooking for the family.

Principles of Indian Cooking

Until recently, no written record of Indian recipes has existed in India itself. Recipes have traditionally been handed down from one generation to another. Far from being a disadvantage, this has actually helped to fire the imagination of the creative cook, and many dishes that first started out as experiments in spice blends and flavor combinations have now become world classics.

Spices and aromatics
The key to successful Indian cooking lies in the art of blending spices and herbs instead of sophisticated cooking techniques. The traditional Indian cook relies on instinct rather than written recipes when measuring and combining spices, and, in this way, unique and personal tastes can be created. This is one reason why the same dish from one region can look and taste different, depending on who has cooked it.

Herbs are added to a dish during the cooking time to add flavor and aroma, but spices, including those used mainly for taste or for aroma, perform a more complex role.

Spices are divided into two main groups: those that are integrated into a dish by the end of the cooking process, and those that are later removed. Those in the first group add taste, texture, and color. Different combinations are used, and no single spice is allowed to dominate the final flavor. Useful spices in this group include coriander, cumin, turmeric, and garam masala, all in ground form.

Spices from the second group add aroma to a dish. They remain identifiable at the end of cooking because most of them are used whole. Once these spices have released their aroma, their function is complete and they are not eaten, but removed from the dish before serving or simply left on one side of the plate. Examples of this type of spice are whole cloves, cardamom pods, cinnamon sticks, and bay leaves. These spices can also be ground, in which case they blend into the sauce during cooking and are eaten in the dish in the same way as any other ground spice.

Adding flavor
Having chosen which spices to use, you can then decide what kind of flavors you would like to create. For instance, dry-roasting and grinding flavoring ingredients before adding them to a dish creates a completely different taste and aroma from frying the raw ground spices in hot fat before adding the main ingredients. The flavor of a dish will also vary according to the sequence in which the spices are added, and the length of time each spice is fried and allowed to release its flavor.

Indian cooking lends itself to being personalized by different cooks, and with even just two or three spices, you can create distinctly varied dishes.

Below: Spices and seasonings are what gives Indian food its unique character.

What is a curry?

In India, the word curry refers to a sauce or gravy that is used as an accompaniment to moisten grains of chawal (rice) or to make rotis (bread) more enjoyable. The rice or bread is considered the main dish of the meal.

The word curry is generally believed to be an anglicized version of the south Indian word kaari. It belongs to the Tamil language, which is spoken in the state of Tamil Nadu, of which Madras is the capital. In Tamil, the word means sauce and it is thought that when the British were active in this area, the spelling was changed to curry. Other theories suggest that the word cury has existed in English in the context of cooking since the fourteenth century, and that it was originally derived from the French verb cuire (to cook).

The main ingredients of a curry can vary enormously, and two highly dissimilar dishes can be equally deserving of the name. Even the lentil dish known as dhal, which bears no resemblance to a sauce, falls under the definition of a curry; in India, dhal-chawal and dhal-roti are eaten on a daily basis.

A vegetable curry usually consists of a selection of fresh vegetables cooked in a sauce, which can have a thick or a thin consistency, depending on the style of cooking in the region. The sauces for meat, poultry, and fish curries also vary in consistency, and are all designed to be served with rice or bread. Gujarat in the west and Punjab in the north also make spiced curries using just yogurt mixed with a little besan (gram) flour. Made without meat, poultry, or vegetables, these dishes are known as khadis.

Above: Most of the key ingredients needed for Indian dishes are now available from large supermarkets, but Indian food stores will usually stock a wider selection.

What to eat with a curry

In south and eastern India, curries are always served with rice, which, as the region's main crop, is the staple food of the area and is eaten daily. Wheat grows abundantly in north India, and in most northern regions, breads, such as nan, chapatis, and parathas, are eaten with curries and with dry, spiced vegetable and lentil dishes. In the Punjab region, however, breads made from besan flour and makki (cornmeal) are more usually served. In western India, curries are eaten with breads made with flour from jowar (millet) and bajra (milo), a form of sorghum.

Preparing an Indian Curry

While there may be no such thing as a definitive curry recipe, there certainly is an established procedure to follow when preparing a curry. Deciding what type of curry you are going to make is the first step. Choose your main ingredient, and select your cooking pan accordingly, because this will affect the ultimate success of the dish. A deep-sided pan will be necessary if the curry will contain a lot of liquid, while a wide, flat pan is needed for fish so that the pieces can be laid flat, side by side, in a single layer.

Cooking fats
You need to decide whether you want to use ghee, which is clarified butter, or oil as your cooking medium. Traditionally, the Indian housewife would use ghee, not just for its rich flavor, but also because dairy products are believed to be more nutritious. Modern Indian families are now deviating from this practice, however, because of a growing awareness of the dangers of eating too much saturated fat. Sunflower, vegetable, and corn oils will all make suitable alternatives. Olive oil is not normally used, although a basic cooking version (not virgin or extra virgin) will work perfectly well. Ghee can be reserved for special occasion dishes, if you like.

Cooking liquids
Most curries are water-based. Stock is sometimes used in Indian cooking, but it is not a common practice because meat is always cooked on the bone, and this creates a sufficiently robust flavor. Whether you use stock or water as your cooking liquid, it is important to make sure the liquid is at least lukewarm. Adding cold liquid to carefully blended spices will impair the flavors.

Adding salt
Be careful when using salt in an Indian dish. Do not be afraid to use the amount specified in a recipe; even if it seems like a lot, it will have been worked out to achieve an overall balance of flavors. There are now

Above: *Fresh and dried herbs provide color, flavor, aroma, and texture to Indian food.*

several brands of low-sodium salt on the market, which can be substituted, if you prefer.

Thickening agents
Indian cooking does not rely on flour to thicken sauces. Instead, the correct consistency is more often achieved by adding ingredients, such as dairy cream or coconut cream, nut pastes, onion paste, tomatoes, or ground seeds, such as poppy, sesame, and sunflower.

Adding color
Some of the ingredients added to curries not only determine their texture and consistency, but also their color. In Mughlai sauces and curries, the onions are softened but not browned, which gives the dishes their distinctive pale color. Bhoona (stir-fried) curries, on the other hand, use browned onions, making the final dishes reddish brown in color.

Souring agents
Some of the souring agents used in curries also affect their color and consistency. Tamarind, for instance, darkens and thickens a sauce at the same time. Lime, lemon, and white vinegar, however, will neither alter the color of a curry nor thicken it, and a thickening agent, such as coconut milk or a nut or seed paste, will need to be used, too. Ingredients, such as dried

COLORING INGREDIENTS
The depth of the curry's color will depend on the amount of colorant used in relation to other ingredients.
turmeric: bright yellow
saffron: pale apricot
red chiles: reddish brown
fresh cilantro leaves: green
tomatoes: reddish, if used alone; pinkish if combined with yogurt
onions: brown
ground coriander: deep brown if fried for 5–6 minutes
garam masala: deep brown if fried for 1 minute

mango powder (amchur), dried pomegranate seeds (known as anardana), as well as tomatoes and yogurts, are all used to lend a distinctive tangy flavor to a curry, and they will also affect the color to varying degrees.

Adding heat

The most important ingredient for achieving a fiery flavor and appearance is chile. Although chiles were unknown in India before the Portuguese settlers introduced them in the 15th century, it is difficult to imagine Indian food without them today. It is chile in its powdered form that contributes to the color of a curry, and chili powder is readily available in a range of heat levels. Always be sure to check the label carefully. If you want the curry to be appealing to the eye without scorching the taste buds, choose a chili powder made from either Kashmiri or Byadigi chiles. This will lend a rich color to the dish, but the flavor will be fairly mild. You can always use a mild powder with a hot chili powder if you prefer to give the curry some kick. Another way to achieve both color and heat in the same dish is to combine chili powder with fresh chiles: fresh chiles are always hotter than dried.

When buying fresh chiles, try to find the ones used in Indian cooking instead of the Mexican varieties. Those used in Indian cooking are long and slim, and are sometimes labeled "finger chiles". Thai chiles make a good substitute, and are available from Asian food stores.

Paste made from dried red chiles also provides a good color and a flavor different from that of chili powder. To make it, all you need to do is to soak the chiles for 15–20 minutes in hot water and then purée them. The paste will keep well in an airtight jar in the refrigerator for 4–5 days.

Cooking a curry

Several factors will influence the making of a good curry, and one of the most important of these is the cooking temperature. The fat should be heated to the right temperature and maintained at a steady heat until the spices have released their flavor. A heavy pan, such as a karahi, wok, or large pan, will help to maintain the temperature, so that the spices can cook without burning. While recipes may vary, the usual procedure is to start by cooking the onions over a medium heat. Once the onions have softened, the ground spices are added and the temperature is lowered.

Another important factor is how the onions are chopped. The finer an onion is chopped, the better it will blend

Below: The secret of Indian cooking lies in the use of spices, and blending spices at home will give more flavorsome curries.

into the sauce. In many recipes, onion, ginger, and garlic are puréed to make a wet spice paste, which is fried until all the moisture has evaporated, before the ground spices are added. It is crucial to follow the timings specified in a recipe for each of these cooking stages.

Adding spices in the correct sequence is also vital. While some spices take only a few seconds to release their flavor, others need a few minutes, and if you add spices that require less cooking time together with those that need more, some will burn and others will remain raw. The simplest way to avoid this is to stick to the order in which the spices are listed in the recipe, and to be diligent about following the specified cooking time for each ingredient.

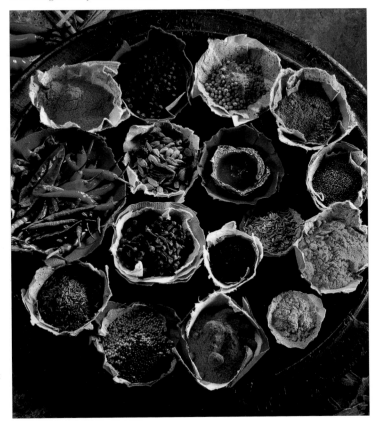

Planning an Indian Meal

When planning your menu, always bear in mind that an everyday Indian meal features only three items: the main dish, a side dish, and a staple, which would be rice or bread. Chutneys, salads, and raitas can also be served to add a tangy taste.

Planning the menu

When deciding which foods to serve, consider the main dish. Is it going to be highly spiced, such as a vindaloo or a bhoona? Or will it have subtle flavors, such as a korma or a pasanda? A little careful planning will ensure that the flavors of the dishes complement, rather than compete with, each other. Choose the side dish according to the strength of the main one. A lightly spiced side dish is more enjoyable when the main dish is spicier. This does not apply in

Below: There is no rigid structure to an Indian meal, but there should always be a good balance of dry and moist dishes.

reverse, however, and a side dish with complex spicing is not the ideal accompaniment to a mild main dish.

Dishes with a drier consistency are generally accompanied by a vegetable curry or a lentil dish. Biryanis and pilaus are traditionally served with a simple raita, although they are more usually served with a vegetable curry in Indian restaurants in the West.

How to serve

An Indian meal is not served as separate courses, with an appetizer, followed by a main dish and one or two side dishes. Although the meal will usually consist of several dishes, all complement each other and are brought to the table at the same time, with diners helping themselves to each dish in any order.

For entertaining and more lavish occasions, you can add other dishes to the standard three-dish Indian menu. One or two dry meat dishes, such as a kebab or tandoori chicken, in addition

USEFUL STANDBYS

- Use bottled ginger and garlic paste instead of peeling and chopping the fresh aromatics.
- Canned chopped tomatoes can be used instead of fresh tomatoes, although you may need to increase the quantities of souring agent, salt, and chile to compensate for the depleted flavor.
- Canned or packaged coconut cream is a convenient replacement for fresh coconut. Follow the manufacturer's instructions.

to some chutneys, pickles, raitas, and poppadums, with a dessert to follow, can turn an ordinary family meal into dinner-party fare.

Indian desserts

In India, a meal will usually end with fresh fruit, rather than elaborate fresh or

cooked desserts. Fruits are served with real flair, however, and are often combined with other ingredients to create imaginative and exciting flavors. Choose one or two exotic fruits, such as papaya, pomegranate, or carambola, and combine them with everyday fruits in a fruit salad. Serve with strained plain yogurt flavored with rose water and a little ground cardamom.

Indian candies are heavy and are served as a snack with tea and coffee, in the same way as cakes and cookies are eaten in the West.

Freezing curries

In today's busy world, it is not always possible to serve a meal while it is still sizzling in the pan. If you are cooking for guests, you may prefer to cook the curry in advance to save yourself time

COOKING FOR A PARTY

It is a good idea to cook the curry dishes a day ahead of the party, storing them in the refrigerator until you are ready to reheat them. Accompanying dhal dishes can also be prepared 24 hours in advance, although the seasonings should not be added until just before serving. You can prepare vegetables in advance, but do not cook them more than a few hours ahead. Likewise, you can prepare ingredients for raitas a day ahead, but do not assemble them until a few hours before they are needed; the yogurt for raitas should always be fresh. Pickles and chutneys will benefit from advance preparation, but follow individual recipes for timing guides, because some will deteriorate more quickly than others. The bread dough for rotis can be made the day before. The rotis can be made 2 hours before you serve them. Spread them with butter and wrap in aluminum foil to keep warm, then set them aside; reheat in the oven before serving.

on the day, or you may like to cook a larger quantity than you will need and freeze some for another meal; you may even have leftovers.

Spicy food is ideal for freezing because the flavors seem to improve when the food is thawed and reheated. Most of the spices used in Indian cooking have natural preservative qualities, as does the acid in souring agents. However, you should bear in mind the following factors if cooking specifically for the freezer:
• Prepare the food slightly underdone.
• Cool the food rapidly. The best way to do this is to tip it into a large tray (a large roasting pan is ideal) and let it stand in a cool place.
• Once the food has cooled completely, spoon it into plastic containers, cover, label, and chill it in the refrigerator for a couple of hours, then transfer it to the freezer. The food will keep in the freezer for 6–8 months, depending on your freezer.

Food that you did not plan to freeze, such as leftovers, should not be kept in the freezer for longer than 2–3 months, again, depending on the efficiency of your freezer. Meat and poultry curries freeze successfully, as do curries made from vegetables, lentils, beans, and peas. Fish curries can be frozen, but they are generally less successful because changes in the water balance may damage the more delicate texture of cooked fish.

Thawing and reheating

It is important to thaw frozen food thoroughly and slowly. Let it stand in the refrigerator for 18–24 hours before reheating. After reheating, always make sure the food is piping hot before serving. These steps are crucial in order to ensure that any potentially harmful bacteria are destroyed. If you have a temperature probe, check that the reheated food is at least 185°F all the way through before serving.

A certain amount of water separation is to be expected as a frozen dish thaws out. The dish will return to its normal

REHEATING LEFTOVERS

This method will make leftover food that has been frozen taste really fresh. The method can also be used to reheat food that has been stored for a day or two in the refrigerator.

Heat about 2 teaspoons vegetable oil in a karahi, wok, or large pan over a medium heat. Add up to ¼ teaspoon garam masala, depending on the quantity of food, and let bubble gently for 10–15 seconds. Add the thawed food to the pan and increase the heat to high. Let the food bubble or sizzle in the pan until it is heated through, stirring from time to time to make sure the heat is well distributed. Add a little water if the food looks particularly dry. Stir in 1 tablespoon chopped fresh cilantro. Remove from the heat, transfer to a warmed platter, and serve immediately.

consistency when it is reheated, because the water will be reabsorbed by the meat or vegetables.

Thawed food can be reheated in the microwave or in a covered casserole on the stovetop. If using a microwave, cover the food with microwave plastic wrap. Stir the food from time to time as it is heated to ensure the heat passes all the way through. You may need to add a small amount of water when reheating to ensure that the dish does not dry out.

Aromatics, Spices, and Herbs

Spices are integral to both the flavor and aroma of a dish. Some spices are used principally for the taste they impart, while ingredients known as aromatics are used mainly for their aroma. One individual spice can completely alter the taste of a dish and a combination of several spices will also affect its color and texture.

The quantities of spices and salt specified in recipes are measured to achieve a balance of flavors, although you may prefer to increase or decrease the quantities according to taste. This is particularly true of fresh chiles and chili powder—experiment with quantities, adding less or more than specified.

Fresh and dried herbs also play an important part in the combinations of color, flavor, aroma, and texture that make up a curry. Because herbs require

only a minimal amount of cooking, they retain a marvelous intensity of flavor and fragrance.

Garlic

Widely available fresh and dried, garlic is used for its strong, aromatic flavor, and is a standard ingredient, along with ginger, in most curries. Fresh garlic can be puréed, crushed, or chopped, or the cloves can be used whole. Garlic powder is mainly used in spice mixtures.

Ginger

One of the most popular spices in India and also one of the oldest, fresh ginger root is an important ingredient in many Indian curries. Its refreshing scent is reminiscent of citrus and it has a pleasant, sharp flavor. The root should be plump with a fairly smooth skin, which is peeled off before use. Young ginger root is tender and mild, whereas older roots are fibrous, with a more pungent flavor. Dried powdered ginger is a useful standby, but the flavor is not identical. Ginger is often blended with other spices to make curry powder.

PURÉEING GARLIC

Fresh garlic is used so regularly in Indian cooking that you may find it more practical to prepare garlic in bulk and store it in the refrigerator or freezer until needed.

Separate the garlic bulb into cloves and peel off the papery skin. Process the whole cloves in a food processor until smooth. Freeze the garlic paste in ice-cube trays used especially for the purpose. Put 1 teaspoon in each compartment, freeze, remove from the tray, and store in the freezer in a sealed plastic bag. Alternatively, store the paste in an airtight container in the refrigerator for 3–4 weeks.

Below: Fresh ginger root

Below: Ground ginger

PREPARING FRESH GINGER ROOT

Fresh ginger root has a delightfully clean and pungent taste, and is easy to prepare. It is widely available from supermarkets and grocers.

To grate ginger, carefully remove the skin, using a sharp knife or vegetable peeler. Grate the peeled ginger using the fine side of a metal cheese grater. To chop, slice the ginger into fine strips, then chop as required.

PURÉEING FRESH GINGER ROOT

Puréed fresh ginger root is time-consuming to prepare for each individual recipe. Instead, prepare a large quantity and store in the freezer until needed.

Peel off the tough outer skin, using a sharp knife or a vegetable peeler. Roughly chop, then process in a food processor, adding a little water to get a smooth consistency. Store the paste in the refrigerator for 3–4 weeks or freeze in ice-cube trays used for the purpose.

Chiles

These hot peppers belong to the genus capsicum, along with bell peppers. Some varieties are extremely fiery and all chiles should be used with caution. Much of the severe heat of fresh chiles is contained in the seeds, and the heat can be toned down by removing these before use. Like other spicy foods, chiles are perfect for hot climates because they cause blood to rush to the surface of the skin, promoting instant cooling.

Chiles vary in size and color, but as a rule, dark green chiles tend to be hotter than light green ones. Red chiles are usually hotter still, and some will darken to brown or black when fully ripe. Shape and color give no sure indication of the hotness, and it is wise to be wary of any unfamiliar variety. Dried chiles can be used whole or coarsely crushed. Chili powder is a fiery ground spice that should be used with great caution. The heat varies from brand to brand, so adjust quantities to suit your taste buds. Some brands include other spices and herbs, as well as ground chiles, and these may not be appropriate for the dish you are cooking. Always check the label carefully.

PREPARING DRIED CHILES

Dried chiles are available from good supermarkets and Indian food stores.

To prepare the chiles, remove the stems and seeds, then break each chile into two or three pieces. Put the pieces in a small bowl and cover with hot water. Let stand for 30 minutes, then drain (using the soaking water in the recipe, if appropriate). Use the chile pieces as they are, or chop them finely.

WARNING

All chiles contain capsaicin, an oily substance, that can cause intense irritation to sensitive skin. If you get capsaicin on your hands and transfer it to your eyes by rubbing, you will experience considerable pain. Wash hands with soapy water after handling. Dry your hands and rub a little oil into the skin to remove any stinging juices. Many cooks prefer to wear latex gloves to avoid such problems.

Above: The color of chiles gives no sure indication of heat, although red chiles are usually hotter.

PREPARING FRESH CHILES

Using two or more fresh chiles will make a dish very hot. If you prefer a milder flavor, reduce the amount of chile used, and make sure you remove the seeds and pithy membrane, which contains the most heat. If you have sensitive skin, you may prefer to wear latex gloves to protect your hands when preparing the chiles.

1 Cut the chiles in half lengthwise. Remove the membranes and seeds.

2 Cut the chile flesh lengthwise into long, thin strips.

3 If required, cut the strips of chile crosswise into tiny dice.

Below: *From left, cloves, ground cinnamon, and cinnamon sticks*

Aniseed

These liquorice-flavored seeds are used in many fried and deep-fried Indian dishes as an aid to digestion.

Cinnamon

One of the earliest known spices, cinnamon has a highly aromatic, sweet, warm flavor. It is sold already ground and as sticks, which are quill-like shapes rolled from the bark of the cinnamon tree. Use cinnamon sticks whole or broken, and remove them from the food before serving. Finely ground cinnamon is a useful pantry staple, but, for a finer flavor, grind stick cinnamon in a mill or coffee grinder kept exclusively for spices.

Cloves

The unopened flower buds of a tree that belongs to the myrtle family, cloves have an aromatic and sometimes fiery flavor and an intense fragrance, and are used to flavor many sweet and savory dishes. Cloves are usually added whole to recipes. Their warm flavor complements all rich meats, and they need no preparation. Ground cloves are one of the ingredients added to spice mixtures.

Above: *From left, cumin seeds, fenugreek, and ground cumin*

Cumin

White cumin seeds are oval, ridged, and greenish brown in color. They have a strong aroma and flavor and can be used whole or ground. Prepared ground cumin powder is widely available, but it should be bought in small quantities because it loses its flavor rapidly. Black cumin seeds are dark and aromatic. This is one of the ingredients used in garam masala.

Left: *Ground and fresh turmeric*

Turmeric

A member of the ginger family but without ginger's characteristic heat, turmeric is a rhizome that is indigenous to Asia. Turmeric is sometimes referred to as Indian saffron, because it shares saffron's ability to color food yellow, although it lacks that spice's subtlety. Fresh turmeric adds a warm and slightly musky flavor to food, but it has a strong, bitter flavor and should be used sparingly. Turmeric has a natural affinity with fish, and is also used in rice, dhal, and vegetable dishes.

Dhania jeera powder

This spice mixture is made from ground roasted coriander and cumin seeds. The proportions are generally two parts coriander to one part cumin.

Fennel seeds

Similar in appearance to cumin, fennel seeds have a sweet taste and are used to flavor curries. They can be chewed as a mouth freshener after a spicy meal.

Mustard seeds

Whole black and brown mustard seeds are indigenous to India and appear often in Indian cooking. The seeds have no aroma in their raw state, but when roasted or fried in ghee or hot oil they release a rich, nutty flavor and aroma. Mustard seeds are commonly used with vegetables and dhal dishes.

Nigella seeds

Also known as kalonji or wild onion seeds, this aromatic spice has a sharp and tingling taste and is frequently used in Indian vegetarian dishes.

Onion seeds

Black, triangular shaped, and aromatic, onion seeds are used in pickles and to flavor vegetable curries and lentil dishes.

Garam masala

This is a mixture of spices that can be made at home from freshly ground spices, or purchased prepared. There is no set recipe, but a typical mixture might include black cumin seeds, peppercorns, cloves, cinnamon, and black cardamom pods. Many variations of garam masala are sold commercially, as prepared pastes in jars. These can be subtituted for homemade garam masala.

Below: From left, paprika, whole nutmeg, and grated nutmeg

Left: Small green cardamom pods and the larger brown variety

Asafetida

This seasoning is a resin with an acrid and bitter taste and a strong odor. It is used primarily as an anti-flatulent, and only minute quantities are used in recipes. Store in a glass jar with a strong airtight seal to prevent the smell from contaminating other ingredients in the pantry.

Cardamom pods

This spice is native to India, where it is considered the most prized spice after saffron. The pods can be used whole or the husks can be removed to release the seeds; whole pods should always be removed from the dish before serving. They have a slightly pungent but very aromatic taste. They come in three colors: green, white, and black or brown. The green and white pods can be used for both sweet and savory dishes or to flavor rice. Black or brown pods are used only for savory dishes.

Nutmeg

Whole nutmeg should be grated to release its sweet, nutty flavor. Ground nutmeg imparts a similar, although less intense, flavor, and is a very useful pantry standby.

DRY-FRYING MUSTARD SEEDS

Mustard seeds release their aroma when heated so should be dry-fried before being added to a dish.

Heat a little ghee or vegetable oil in a karahi, wok, or large pan, and add the mustard seeds. Shake the pan over the heat until the seeds start to change color. Stir the seeds from time to time. Use the pan lid to stop the seeds from jumping out of the pan when they start to splutter and pop.

Peppercorns

Black peppercorns are native to India, and are an essential ingredient in garam masala. White peppercorns are less aromatic. Use peppercorns whole or ground. Pink peppercorns are an unrelated spice used in some contemporary Indian dishes. Treat with caution because they are mildly toxic.

Paprika

A mild, sweet red powder, paprika is often used in place of or alongside chiles in westernized Indian cooking to add color to a dish.

Saffron

The dried stigmas of the saffron crocus, which is native to Asia Minor, is the world's most expensive spice. To produce 1 pound of saffron requires 60,000 stigmas. Fortunately, only a small quantity of saffron is needed to flavor and color a dish. Saffron is sold as threads and as a powder. It has a beautiful flavor and aroma.

Above: From left, white, black, and pink peppercorns

Below: From left, saffron powder and threads

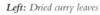
Left: Dried curry leaves

Curry leaves

Bright green and shiny, curry leaves are similar in appearance to bay leaves, but they have a different flavor. The leaves of a hardwood tree that is indigenous to India, they are widely used in Indian cooking, particularly in southern and western India (although not in Goa) and in Sri Lanka. Curry leaves have a warm fragrance with a subtle hint of sweet, green pepper or tangerine. They release their full flavor when bruised, and impart a highly distinctive flavor to curries. Curry leaves are sold dried and occasionally fresh in Indian food stores. Fresh leaves freeze well, but the dried leaves make a poor substitute, because they rapidly lose their fragrance.

Bay leaves

Indian bay leaves come from the cassia tree, which is similar to the tree from which cinnamon is taken. Bay leaves sold in the West are taken from the laurel tree. When used fresh, bay leaves have a deliciously sweet flavor, but they keep well in dried form if stored in a cool, dark place in an airtight jar. Bay leaves are used in meat and rice dishes.

Below: Bay leaves

Below: Fresh cilantro

Coriander and cilantro

There is no substitute for fresh cilantro, and the more that is used in Indian cooking the better. Cilantro imparts a wonderful aroma and flavor, and it is used both as an ingredient in cooking and sprinkled over dishes as a garnish. Chopped cilantro can be frozen successfully; the frozen herb does not need to be thawed before use. Coriander seeds and ground coriander powder are used for flavoring. The seeds have a pungent, slightly lemony flavor, and they are used coarsely ground in meat, fish, and poultry dishes. Ground coriander, a brownish powder, is an important constituent of any curry spice mixture.

Mint

There are many varieties of mint available, and the stronger flavored types tend to be used in Indian cooking. These taste slightly sweet and have a cool aftertaste. Mint has a fresh, stimulating aroma and is traditionally used with lamb, as well as for flavoring some vegetables, and for making chutneys and refreshing raitas. Mint is added at the end of cooking time in order to retain the flavor.

Fenugreek

Fresh fenugreek is generally sold in bunches. It has very small leaves and is used to flavor meat and vegetarian dishes. Always discard the stalks, which will impart an unpleasant bitterness to a dish if used. The seeds are hard, pungent, and slightly bitter. They can be used whole, often in rice, lentil, and vegetable dishes, or ground to a yellow powder. They have a tangy flavor and powerful scent, and, for this reason, they should be used moderately. Dried fenugreek leaves are sold in Indian food stores. Store them in an airtight jar in a cool, dark place; they will keep for about 12 months.

Below: Aromatic fresh fenugreek leaves are widely used in savory Indian dishes.

Curry Powders and Pastes

Powders and pastes are blends of spices, chiles, and herbs that are used as the basis of a curry. Traditional Indian households blend individual spices as needed, but for convenience you may prefer to prepare a quantity in advance.

Curry powder

This is a basic recipe for a dry spice blend. It is a mild recipe, but you can increase the quantity of dried chile.

INGREDIENTS

Makes ½ cup
½ cup coriander seeds
4 tablespoons cumin seeds
2 tablespoons fennel seeds
2 tablespoons fenugreek seeds
4 dried red chiles
5 curry leaves
1 tablespoon chili powder
1 tablespoon ground turmeric
½ teaspoon salt

1 Dry-roast the whole spices in a karahi, wok, or large pan for 8–10 minutes, shaking the pan until the spices darken and release a rich aroma. Let cool.

2 Put the dry-roasted whole spices in a spice mill and grind to a fine powder.

3 Add the ground, roasted spices to the chili powder, turmeric, and salt in a large glass bowl and mix well. Store the curry powder in an airtight container.

Garam masala

Garam means hot and masala means spices, and this mixture uses spices that are known to heat the body, such as black peppercorns and cloves. Garam masala is used mainly for meat, although it can be used in poultry and rice dishes. It is generally too strong for fish or vegetables.

INGREDIENTS

Makes ¼ cup
10 dried red chiles
3 × 1-inch pieces cinnamon stick
2 curry leaves
2 tablespoons coriander seeds
2 tablespoons cumin seeds
1 teaspoon black peppercorns
1 teaspoon cloves
1 teaspoon fenugreek seeds
1 teaspoon black mustard seeds
¼ teaspoon chili powder

1 Dry-roast the whole dried red chiles, cinnamon sticks, and curry leaves in a karahi, wok, or large pan over a low heat for about 2 minutes.

2 Add the coriander and cumin seeds, black peppercorns, cloves, fenugreek, and mustard seeds, and dry-roast for 8–10 minutes, shaking the pan from side to side, until the spices begin to darken in color and release a rich aroma. Let the mixture cool.

3 Using either a spice mill or a stainless steel mortar and pestle, grind the roasted spices to a fine powder.

4 Transfer the powder to a glass bowl and mix in the chili powder. Store in an airtight container.

COOK'S TIP

Both the curry powder and the garam masala will keep for 2–4 months in an airtight container in a cool, dark place. Once opened, store in the refrigerator.

VARIATIONS

For convenience, you can buy prepared garam masala, or try any of the following pastes in alternative flavors:
• Tandoori masala   • Kashmiri masala
• Madras masala   • Sambhar masala
• Dhansak masala   • Green masala

Curry paste

A curry paste is a wet blend of spices, herbs, and chiles cooked with oil and vinegar, which help to preserve the spices during storage. It is a quick and convenient way of adding a spice mixture to a curry, and different blends will produce different flavors. Only a small amount of paste is added at a time, so a little lasts a long time. Store in the refrigerator and use as required.

INGREDIENTS

Makes 2½ cups

½ cup coriander seeds
4 tablespoons cumin seeds
2 tablespoons fennel seeds
2 tablespoons fenugreek seeds
4 dried red chiles
5 curry leaves
1 tablespoon chili powder
1 tablespoon ground turmeric
⅔ cup wine vinegar
1 cup vegetable oil

1 Grind the whole spices to a powder in a spice mill. Transfer to a bowl and add the remaining ground spices.

2 Mix the spices until well blended. Add the wine vinegar and stir. Add 5 tablespoons water; stir to form a paste.

3 Heat the oil in a karahi, wok, or large pan and stir-fry the spice paste for about 10 minutes, or until all the water has been absorbed. When the oil rises to the surface, the paste is cooked. Let cool slightly in the pan before spooning the paste into airtight jars.

COOK'S TIP

Curry pastes will keep for 3–4 weeks after opening if stored in the refrigerator.

Tikka paste

This is a delicious, versatile paste. It has a slightly sour flavor and can be used in a variety of Indian dishes, including chicken tikka, tandoori chicken, and tikka masala. Use sparingly because a little bit goes a long way. Store the paste in airtight glass jars in the refrigerator until required.

INGREDIENTS

Makes 2 cups

2 tablespoons coriander seeds
2 tablespoons cumin seeds
1½ tablespoons garlic powder
2 tablespoons paprika
1 tablespoon garam masala
1 tablespoon ground ginger
2 teaspoons chili powder
½ teaspoon ground turmeric
1 tablespoon dried mint
¼ teaspoon salt
1 teaspoon lemon juice
few drops of red food coloring
few drops of yellow food coloring
⅔ cup wine vinegar
⅔ cup vegetable oil

1 Grind the coriander and cumin seeds to a fine powder using a spice mill or mortar and pestle. Spoon the mixture into a bowl and add the remaining spices, the mint, and salt, stirring well.

2 Mix the spice powder with the lemon juice, food colorings, and wine vinegar and add 2 tablespoons of water to form a thin paste.

3 Heat the oil in a large pan, karahi, or wok, and stir-fry the paste for 10 minutes, until all the water has been absorbed. When the oil rises to the surface, the paste is cooked. Let cool before spooning into airtight jars.

22

Additional Ingredients

Besides the essential spices, aromatics, and herbs, there are several other ingredients that are central to Indian cooking. Among the additional ingredients listed here are popular thickening and souring agents, flavorings, and Indian cheese.

Above: *Cashew nuts*

Almonds
In the West, almonds are readily available whole, sliced, ground, and as thin slivers. The whole kernels should be soaked in boiling water before use to remove the thin red skin; once blanched, they can be eaten raw. Almonds have a uniqe aroma and they impart a sumptuous richness to curries. They make an effective thickener for sauces, and they are also used for garnishing. Almonds are considered a delicacy in India and, because they are not indigenous, they are very expensive to buy.

Left: *Whole almond kernels*

Cashew nuts
These full-flavored nuts can be used raw and roasted in Indian cooking. Cashews are ground and used in korma dishes to enrich and thicken the sauce,

or they can also be toasted and sprinkled over pilaus and biryanis as a garnish. In India, cashews are often used in vegetable and rice dishes as a substitute for the more expensive almonds.

Pistachio nuts
These small, greenish purple nuts are not indigenous to India, but they are frequently used as a thickening agent and to add their characteristic rich and creamy flavor. Raw or toasted pistachio nuts also make an attractive garnish.

Poppy seeds
These seeds are usually toasted to bring out their full, nutty flavor. They can be sprinkled over dry meat and vegetable dishes, or ground and added to curries to thicken sauces.

Sesame seeds
These small, flat, pear-shaped seeds probably originated in Africa, but they have been cultivated in India since ancient times. They are usually white but can be cream to brown, red, or black. Raw sesame seeds have little aroma and taste until they have been roasted or dry-fried, when they take on a slightly nutty taste. They can be ground with a mortar and pestle, or in a spice mill, and used to enrich curries. They are also added to chutneys. The high fat content of sesame seeds means that they do not keep well: buy them in small quantities and store in a cool, dark place.

Pomegranate seeds
These can be extracted from fresh pomegranates or, for convenience, they can be bought in jars from Asian food stores. Pomegranate seeds impart a delicious tangy flavor.

Dried mango powder
Mangoes are indigenous to India, and they have many uses in Indian cooking. The fruit is used in curries at different stages of ripeness, but the unripe fruit is also sun-dried and ground into a dry powder called amchur. The powder has a sour taste and is sprinkled over dishes as a garnish; it is seldom used in cooking.

Above: *White and black poppy seeds*

Above: *Black sesame seeds and white sesame seeds*

Above: *Fresh coconut*

Coconut

Used in both sweet and savory Indian dishes, fresh coconut is available from Indian food stores and supermarkets. Dry unsweetened shredded coconut and coconut cream, which are made from grated coconut, will make acceptable substitutes in most recipes if fresh coconut is out of season. Coconut milk is used in Indian curries to thicken and enrich sauces. In Western supermarkets, it is sold in cans and in powdered form as a convenient alternative to the fresh fruit; the powdered milk has to be blended with hot water before use. Coconut milk can be made at home from dry unsweetened shredded coconut. Coconut cream is used to add fragrance and aroma to dishes.

Below: *Clockwise from left, coconut cream, coconut milk, and dry unsweetened shredded coconut*

MAKING COCONUT MILK

You can make as much of the milk as you like from this recipe by adapting the quantities accordingly, although the method is more practical for larger quantities.

Tip 2⅔ cups dry unsweetened shredded coconut into a food processor and pour over scant 2 cups boiling water. Process for 20–30 seconds, then cool. Place a strainer lined with cheesecloth over a bowl in the sink. Ladle some of the softened coconut into the cheesecloth. Bring up the ends of the cloth and twist it over the strainer to extract the liquid. Use the milk as directed in recipes. Coconut milk keeps for 1–2 days in the refrigerator, or it can be frozen for use on a later occasion.

Yogurt

In India, yogurt is known as curd. It can be added to sauces to give a thick and creamy texture, although it is most often used as a souring agent, particularly in the dairy-dominated north. Yogurt will curdle quickly when heated, so it should be used carefully in recipes. Add only a spoonful at a time, stir well, and let the sauce simmer for 5 minutes before adding the next spoonful. In India, yogurt is made at home on a daily basis, although prepared plain yogurt is an acceptable substitute. Always choose live yogurt because of its beneficial effect on the digestive system.

Below: Fresh paneer

Paneer

This traditional North Indian cheese is made from rich dairy milk. Paneer is white in color and smooth-textured. It is usually available from Indian food stores and supermarkets, but tofu is an adequate substitute.

MAKING PANEER

Paneer is very easy to make, and adventurous cooks may prefer to make their own at home.

Bring 4 cups milk to a boil over a low heat. Add 2 tablespoons lemon juice and stir gently until the milk thickens and begins to curdle. Strain the curdled milk through a strainer lined with cheesecloth. Set the curd aside for 1½–2 hours, under a heavy weight to press it into a flat shape, about ½-inch thick. Cut into wedges and use as required. Paneer will keep for up to 1 week in the refrigerator.

Tamarind

The brown fruit pods of the tamarind tree are 6–8 inches long. Inside, the seeds are surrounded by a sticky brown pulp. Tamarind is cultivated in India, as well as in other parts of Southeast Asia, East Africa, and the West Indies, and it is undoubtably one of the natural treasures of the East. The high tartaric acid content makes tamarind an excellent souring agent, and for this purpose it has no substitute. It doesn't have a strong aroma but the flavor is wonderful—tart without being bitter, fruity and refreshing. Tamarind is sold compressed in blocks and dried in slices. Fresh tamarind and concentrate and paste are also available.

PREPARING COMPRESSED TAMARIND

Asian food stores and supermarkets sell compressed tamarind in a solid block, and in this form it looks like a package of dried dates.

To prepare compressed tamarind, tear off a piece that is roughly equivalent to 1 tablespoon. Put the tamarind in a pitcher and add ⅔ cup warm water. Let soak for 10 minutes. Swirl the tamarind around with your fingers so that the pulp is released from the seeds. Using a nylon strainer, strain the juice into a bowl. Discard the contents of the strainer, and use the liquid as required. Store any leftover liquid in the refrigerator for use in another recipe.

Below: Tamarind, compressed into a block

Fruits

Indians love fruit and, as well as eating fresh fruits raw as a dessert at the end of a meal, they will also cook them with spices, chile, and coconut milk in savory dishes. The exotic fruits listed here are all native to India, and they are as diverse in color and shape as they are in flavor.

Mangoes

Ripe, fresh mangoes grow in India throughout the summer months and are used in sweet dishes. Unripe green mangoes, sold in the springtime, are used to make tangy pickles and chutneys, and they are added to curries as a souring agent for seasoning.

Papayas

Also known as pawpaws, these pear-shaped fruits are native to tropical America, and were not introduced to Asia until the 17th century. When ripe, the green skin turns a speckled yellow and the pulp is a vibrant orange-pink. The edible small black seeds taste peppery when dried. Peel off the skin using a sharp knife and eat the creamy flesh of the ripe fruit raw. The unripe green fruit is used in cooking. One of the unique properties of papaya is that it will help to tenderize meat.

Pineapples

These distinctive-looking fruits have a sweet, golden, and juicy flesh. Unlike most other fruits, pineapples do not ripen after picking, although leaving a slightly unripe fruit at room temperature will help to reduce its acidity. Pineapples are cultivated in India, mainly in the South, and are gently cooked with spices to make palate-cleansing side dishes.

Bananas

The soft and creamy flesh of bananas is high in starch, and is an excellent source of energy. Indians use several varieties of banana in vegetarian curries, including plantains, green bananas, and the sweet red-skinned variety.

Lemons and limes

These citrus fruits are indigenous to India, although limes, which in India are confusingly called lemons, are the most commonly available of the two. Both fruits are used as souring agents and are added to curries at the end of the cooking process; adding them any sooner would prevent any meat in the dish from becoming tender while it cooks.

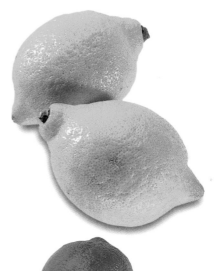

Above: Lemons (top) and limes are used as souring agents in Indian curries.

Above: A whole papaya, with the cut fruit showing the small black, edible seeds.

Right: Sweet, red-skinned bananas and the more familiar large and small yellow-skinned varieties.

Vegetables

Indian cooking specializes in a huge range of excellent vegetable dishes, using everything from cauliflower, potatoes, and peas to the more exotic and unusual varieties, such as okra, bottle gourds, and eggplant. When it comes to Indian cooking, vegetables are simply indispensable.

Right: Small and large onions

Eggplants
Available in different varieties, the shiny deep purple eggplant is the most common and widely used variety in Indian cooking. Eggplants have a strong flavor and some have a slightly bitter taste. The cut flesh can be sprinkled with salt to extract these bitter juices.

Bottle gourds
One of the many bitter vegetables used in Indian cooking, this long, knobbly green vegetable comes from Kenya and has a strong, bitter taste. It is known to have properties that purify the blood. To prepare a gourd, peel the ridged skin with a sharp knife, scrape away and discard the seeds, and chop the flesh.

Okra
Also known as ladies' fingers, okra are among the most popular vegetables in Indian cooking. These small green five-sided pods are indigenous to India. They have a very distinctive flavor and a sticky, pulpy texture when they are cooked.

Left: Various sizes of purple eggplants

Onions
A versatile vegetable belonging to the allium family, onions have a strong pungent flavor and aroma. Globe onions are the most commonly used variety for Indian cooking. Scallions are also used in some dishes to add color and for their mild taste.

Bell peppers
Large, hollow pods belonging to the capsicum family, bell peppers are available in a variety of colors. Red peppers are sweeter than green peppers. They are used in a wide variety of dishes, adding both color and flavor.

Left: Bell peppers

Spinach
Available all year round, this leafy green vegetable has a mild, delicate flavor. The leaves vary in size and only the large thick leaves need to be trimmed of their stalks. Spinach is a favorite vegetable in Indian cooking, and it is cooked in many ways, with meat, other vegetables, and with beans, peas, and lentils.

Corn
Although it originated in South America, corn is now grown worldwide, and is widely cultivated in North India. It has a delicious sweet, juicy flavor, which is at its best just after picking.

Tomatoes
These are an essential ingredient, and are used to make sauces for curries, chutneys, and relishes. The type of tomatoes used in salads are adequate but are usually peeled. Use canned tomatoes in sauces and curries for their rich color.

Beans, Peas, and Lentils

These play an important role in Indian cooking and are an excellent source of protein and fiber. Some are cooked whole, some are puréed and made into soups or dhals, and some are combined with vegetables or meat. Beans and chickpeas should be soaked before cooking. Lentils do not need to be soaked. Red and green split lentils cook to a soft mush when left to simmer, and whole lentils hold their shape when cooked.

Black-eyed peas
These are small and cream-colored, with a black spot or "eye". When cooked, black-eyed peas have a tender, creamy texture and a mild, smoky flavor. They are used widely in Indian cooking.

PREPARING AND COOKING BEANS AND PEAS
Beans and chickpeas should be boiled for at least 10 minutes at the start of cooking to destroy harmful toxins that may be present.

Wash the beans or chickpeas under cold running water, then place in a large bowl of fresh cold water and let soak overnight. Discard any that float to the surface, drain, and rinse again. Put in a large pan and cover with plenty of fresh cold water. Bring to a boil and boil rapidly for 10–15 minutes. Reduce the heat and simmer until tender. Drain and use as required.

Above: *Chickpeas*

Chana dhal
This round, yellow split lentil is similar in appearance to the yellow split pea, which will make a good substitute. It is cooked in a variety of vegetable dishes and can be deep-fried and mixed with spices for the Indian snack Bombay mix. Chana dhal is often used as a binding agent in Indian curries.

Chickpeas
These round, beige peas have a strong, nutty flavor when cooked. As well as being used for curries, they are also ground into besan flour (also known as chickpea or gram flour), which is used in many Indian dishes, such as pakoras and bhajias, and are also added to Indian snacks.

Left: *From left, navy beans, red kidney beans, and pinto beans*

Flageolet beans
These white or pale green oval beans have a very mild, refreshing flavor.

Green lentils
Also known as continental lentils, these have a strong flavor, and they retain their shape during cooking.

Navy beans
These small, white, oval beans come in different varieties. Known as haricot beans in some places, these are ideal for Indian cooking because they retain their shape and absorb flavors.

Kidney beans
These red-brown, kidney-shaped beans have a distinctive flavor. They belong to the same family as the pinto bean.

Mung beans
These small, round green beans have a sweet flavor and creamy texture. They are the most commonly used bean for sprouting. Split mung beans are also used, often with rice.

Red split lentils
Another lentil that can be used for making dhal. Use instead of tuvar dhal.

Tuvar dhal
A dull orange-colored split pea with a distinctive earthy flavor. Tuvar dhal is available plain and in an oily variety.

Urid dhal
This lentil is available split, either with the blackish hull retained or removed. It has a dry texture when cooked.

Above: *Red lentils*

Rice

This staple grain is served with almost every meal in some parts of India, so it is no surprise that the Indians have created a variety of ways of cooking it, each one being distinctive. Plain boiled rice is an everyday accompaniment; for special occasions and entertaining, it is often combined with other ingredients.

There is no definitive way to cook plain rice, but whatever the recipe, the aim is to produce dry, separate-grained rice that is cooked through yet still retains some bite. The secret is the amount of water added—the rice must be able to absorb it all.

Basmati rice

Known as the prince of rices, basmati is the recommended rice for Indian curries, not only because it is easy to cook and produces an excellent finished result, but because it has a cooling effect on hot and spicy curries. Basmati is a slender, long grain, milled rice grown in northern India, the Punjab, parts of Pakistan, and in the foothills of the Himalayas. Its name means "fragrant," and it has a distinctive and appealing aroma. After harvesting, it is aged for a year, which gives it the characteristic flavor and a light, fluffy texture. Basmati can be used in almost any savory dish, particularly curries or pilaus, and is the essential ingredient in biryanis. White and brown basmati rice are widely available from supermarkets and Indian food stores.

Above: White basmati, probably the most commonly eaten rice in India.

COOKING PLAIN BOILED RICE

Always make sure you use a tight-fitting lid for your rice pan. If you do not have a lid that fits tightly, you can either wrap a dish towel around the lid or put some aluminum foil between the lid and the pan to make a snug fit. Try not to remove the lid until the rice is cooked. (The advantage of using just a lid is that you can tell when the rice is ready because steam begins to escape, visibly and rapidly.)

As a rough guide, allow scant ½ cup rice per person.

1 Put the dry rice in a colander and rinse it under cold running water until the water runs clear.

2 Place the rice in a large, deep pan and pour in enough cold water to come ¾ inch above the surface of the rice. Add a pinch of salt and, if you like, 1 teaspoon vegetable oil, stir once, and bring to a boil.

3 Stir once more, reduce the heat to the lowest possible setting, and cover the pan with a tight-fitting lid.

4 Cook the rice for 12–15 minutes, then turn off the heat and let the rice stand, still tightly covered, for about 10 minutes.

5 Before serving, gently fluff up the rice with a fork or slotted rice spoon—the slotted spoon will help you to avoid breaking up the grains, which would make the rice mushy.

Below: Patna rice, a long-grain rice native to eastern India.

Patna rice

This rice takes its name from Patna in eastern India. At one time, most of the long grain rice sold in Europe came from Patna, and the term was used loosely to mean any long-grain rice, whatever its origin. The custom still persists in parts of the United States, but elsewhere Patna is used to describe the specific variety of rice grown in the eastern state of Bihar. Patna rice is used in the same way as other long-grain rices, and it is suitable for use wherever plain boiled rice is called for.

Breads

Breads are an important part of any Indian meal. Most traditional Indian breads are unleavened, that is, made without any raising agent, and are made with whole-wheat flour, which is known as chapati flour or atta.

Throughout India, breads vary from region to region, depending on local ingredients. Some breads are cooked dry on a hot griddle, while some are fried with a little oil, and others are deep-fried to make small savory puffs. To enjoy Indian breads at their best, they should be made just before you are ready to serve the meal, so that they can be eaten hot.

Above: *Chapatis and parathas*

Below: *Poppadums*

Nan

Probably the most well-known Indian bread outside India is nan, from the north of the country. Nan is made with all-purpose flour, yogurt, and yeast; some contemporary recipes favor the use of a chemical raising agent, such as baking soda or self-raising flour, as a leaven in place of yeast. The yogurt is important for the fermentation of the dough, and some nan are made entirely using a yogurt fermentation. Fermentation gives the bread its characteristic light, puffy texture and soft crust. The flavor comes partly from the sour yogurt and partly from the tandoor, which is the the clay oven, sunk into the ground, in which the bread is traditionally cooked. The bread is flattened against the blisteringly hot walls of the oven and the pull of gravity produces the characteristic teardrop shape. As the dough scorches and puffs up, it produces a bread that is soft and crisp. Nan can be eaten with almost any meat or vegetable dish. There are many types of flavored nan sold commercially, including plain, cilantro and garlic, and masala nan.

Chapatis

The favorite bread of central and southern India is the chapati, a thin, flat, unleavened bread made from ground whole-wheat flour. Chapatis are cooked on a hot tava, a concave-shaped Indian griddle. Chapatis have a light texture and bland flavor, which makes them an ideal accompaniment for highly spiced curry dishes. Spices can be added to the flour to give more flavor.

Rotis

There are many variations of chapatis, including rotis and dana rotis. These are unleavened breads, made using chapati flour to which ghee, oil, celery seeds and/or fresh cilantro are added. They are rolled out thinly and cooked like chapatis.

Parathas

A paratha is similar to a chapati except that it contains ghee, which gives the bread a richer flavor and flakier texture. Parathas are much thicker than chapatis and are shallow-fried. Plain parathas are often eaten for lunch, and they go well with most vegetable dishes. They can be stuffed with various fillings, the most popular being spiced potato. Stuffed parathas are served as a snack.

Pooris

Another popular variation on the chapati is the poori, which is a small, deep-fried puffy bread made from chapati flour. Pooris are best eaten hot and are traditionally served for breakfast. They can be plain or flavored with spices, such as cumin, turmeric, and chili powder, which are mixed into the dough. Pooris are often served with fish or vegetable curries.

Poppadums

These are now widely available outside of India. These are large, thin crisp disks, which can be bought already cooked or ready-to-cook. In India, they are served with vegetarian meals. They are sold in markets and by street vendors, and are available plain, flavored with spices, or seasoned with ground red or black pepper. The dough is generally made from dried beans, but it can also be made from potatoes or sago. It is thinly rolled and left to dry in the sun. Poppadums are cooked either by deep-frying or placing under a hot broiler.

Above: *Nan*

Equipment and Utensils

While a reasonably stocked kitchen will provide most of the equipment needed for cooking Indian curries, it may still be necessary to invest in one or two more special items for perfect results.

Chapati griddle
Known in India as a *tava,* the chapati griddle allows chapatis and other breads to be cooked without burning. The heavy wrought-iron pan can also be used to dry-roast spices. Traditionally, the griddle would be set over an open fire, but it will work equally well on a gas flame or electric stovetop.

Chapati rolling board
This round wooden board on short stubby legs is used to mold breads into shape; the extra height provided by the legs helps to disperse excess dry flour. A wooden pastry board makes an appropriate substitute.

Chapati rolling pin
The traditional chapati rolling pin is thinner in shape than Western rolling pins and comes in many different sizes. Use whichever size feels the most comfortable in your hands.

Chapati spoon
The square, flat-headed chapati spoon is used for turning roasting breads on the hot chapati griddle. A metal spatula can also be used.

Grinding stone and roller
The traditional oblong grinding stone is the Indian equivalent of the Western food processor. Fresh and dry ingredients are placed on the heavy slate stone, which is marked with notches to hold ingredients in place. The heavy roller is then used to pulverize the ingredients against the stone.

Table sizzler
This heated appliance allows food that is still cooking to be brought to the dinner table ready for serving. It is very useful for entertaining.

Slotted spoon
Stirring cooked, drained rice with a slotted spoon will make the rice soft and fluffy by introducing air between the grains; slots in the spoon prevent the grains from breaking as the rice is moved around the pan. The spoon is also used to remove foods from hot oil or other cooking liquids.

Heat diffuser
Many curries are left to simmer slowly over a low heat, and a heat diffuser will help to prevent food from burning on the bottom of the karahi or wok. Check that the diffuser can be used on your type of stovetop.

Above: *Chapati griddle and chapati rolling pin*

Left: *Grinding stone and roller, tongs, and stainless steel mortar and pestle*

Below right: *Heat diffuser*

Below:
A traditional
cast-iron karahi

Karahi
Basically an Indian frying pan, the karahi is similar to a wok but is more rounded in shape and is made of heavier metal. Originally, the karahi would be cast iron, although a variety of metals are now used. Karahis are available in various sizes, including small ones for single portions. Serving food from a karahi at the table adds an authentic touch to the meal.

Wok
This is a good substitute for a karahi for cooking most types of Indian food. Buy the appropriate wok for your stovetop. Round-bottom woks can be used on gas stovetops only; flat-bottom woks are for use on electric stovetops.

Stainless steel pans
Quality kitchen pans in various sizes are essential for cooking rice, vegetables, meats, and other ingredients. A heavy nonstick skillet can be used in place of a karahi or wok.

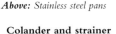

Above: Stainless steel pans

Spice mill
An electric spice mill is useful for grinding small quantities of ingredients, such as spices. A coffee grinder—used solely for spices—makes a good substitute.

Stainless steel mortar and pestle
These are ideal for grinding small amounts of wet ingredients, such as fresh ginger, chiles, and garlic. Stainless steel is durable and will not retain the strong flavors of the spices.

Stone mortar and pestle
A heavy granite mortar and pestle is used to grind small amounts of ingredients, both wet and dry.

Pastry brush
Use for brushing and basting meats and vegetables lightly with oil before and during broiling.

Handheld whisk
A metal whisk is useful for beating yogurt and dairy or coconut cream before adding to recipes.

Knives
Kitchen knives in a range of sizes are essential. Keep knives sharp to make it easier to chop ingredients and to ensure neat edges when cutting.

Colander and strainer
Use for draining boiled rice and vegetables, and for straining ingredients. Choose long-handled, sturdy utensils made from stainless steel—the handles let you stand back to pour steaming rice out of a pan, and the utensils will not discolor like plastic ones.

Food processor
This is essential for blending the ingredients. Smaller quantities can be ground in a mortar and pestle.

Right:
From left,
stainless steel
colander and
strainer

Soups
and Appetizers

THE CONCEPT of starting a meal with a tempting morsel to whet the appetite is not widely adopted in India, where it is usual for most of the dishes to be brought to the table at the same time. Snacks, on the other hand, are extremely popular, and a samosa or spiced potato cake are appreciated at any time of day.

India has only a few soups, but those that exist are famous the world over. South Indian Pepper Water and Chicken Mulligatawny are substantial enough to be served solo, or with deliciously warmed nan as an accompaniment. Both of these soups are highly spiced, whereas Tomato and Cilantro Soup is simply soothing and a perfect antidote to summer heat. Also included in this chapter are delicious fish, chicken, and meaty appetizers, from koftas to kebabs, bhajias to Indian-style pancakes, tikka to tandoori. All are ideal for serving either as Western-style first courses, snacks, or light suppers.

Tomato and Cilantro Soup

Although soups are not often eaten in India or Pakistan, tomato soup bucks the trend and is popular. This is excellent on a cold winter's day.

INGREDIENTS

Serves 4

1½ pounds tomatoes, peeled and chopped
1 tablespoon oil
1 bay leaf
4 scallions, chopped
1 teaspoon salt
½ teaspoon crushed garlic
1 teaspoon crushed black peppercorns
2 tablespoons chopped fresh cilantro
generous 3 cups water
1 tablespoon cornstarch
2 tablespoons light cream, to garnish (optional)

NUTRITIONAL NOTES	
Per Portion	
Energy	76cal
Fat	3.40g
Saturated Fat	0.43g
Carbohydrate	10.10g
Fiber	1.90g

COOK'S TIP

If the only fresh tomatoes available look a little pale and under ripe, you can add 1 tablespoon tomato paste to the pan with the chopped tomatoes to enhance the color and flavor of the soup.

1 To peel the tomatoes, plunge them in hot water, let stand for 30 seconds, then take them out. The skin should now peel off easily. If not, put the tomatoes back in the water for a little longer. Once they have been peeled, roughly chop the tomatoes.

2 In a medium heavy pan, heat the oil and fry the tomatoes, bay leaf, and scallions for a few minutes, until soft.

3 Gradually add the salt, garlic, peppercorns, and cilantro. Pour in the water. Stir, then simmer gently over a low heat for 15–20 minutes.

4 Meanwhile, dissolve the cornstarch in a little cold water to form a thick creamy paste.

5 Remove the soup from the heat and let cool slightly for a few minutes. Press through a strainer, or purée in a blender or food processor.

6 Return the puréed soup to the pan, add the cornstarch mixture, and stir over a gentle heat for about 3 minutes, until thickened.

7 Pour the soup into individual serving dishes and garnish with a swirl of cream, if using. Serve hot.

Spiced Cauliflower Soup

Light and tasty, this creamy, mildly spicy vegetable soup has multipurposes. It makes a wonderful warming first course, an appetizing quick meal, and is delicious chilled.

INGREDIENTS

Serves 4–6
1 large potato, diced
1 small cauliflower, chopped
1 onion, chopped
1 tablespoon oil
1 garlic clove, crushed
1 tablespoon grated fresh ginger root
2 teaspoons ground turmeric
1 teaspoon cumin seeds
1 teaspoon black mustard seeds
2 teaspoons ground coriander
4 cups vegetable stock
1¼ cups plain low-fat yogurt
salt and black pepper
fresh cilantro or parsley, to garnish

NUTRITIONAL NOTES	
Per Portion (4)	
Energy	188cal
Fat	5.40g
Saturated Fat	0.77g
Carbohydrate	24.60g
Fiber	3.00g

----- COOK'S TIP -----

To make homemade vegetable stock, add 15 cups of water, 2 sliced leeks, 3 chopped celery stalks, 1 chopped onion, 1 chopped parsnip, 1 seeded and chopped yellow bell pepper, 3 crushed garlic cloves, fresh herbs, and 3 tablespoons light soy sauce to a pan. Season, then slowly bring to a boil. Lower the heat and simmer for 30 minutes, stirring from time to time. Let the stock cool. Pour the stock through a strainer, discard the vegetables, and use the stock as indicated in the recipe.

1 Put the potato, cauliflower, and onion into a large heavy pan with the oil and 3 tablespoons water. Heat until hot and bubbling, then stir well, cover the pan and turn the heat down. Continue cooking the mixture for about 10 minutes.

2 Add the garlic, ginger, and spices. Stir well, and cook for another 2 minutes, stirring occasionally. Pour in the stock and season well. Bring to a boil, then cover and simmer for about 20 minutes. Purée in a food processor and return to the pan. Stir in the yogurt, adjust the seasoning, and serve garnished with cilantro or parsley.

Yogurt and Chili Soup

Hot chiles, cool yogurt—this is
an unusual and tasty soup.

INGREDIENTS

Serves 2–3

scant 2 cups plain low-fat yogurt,
   beaten
4 tablespoons besan flour
½ teaspoon chili powder
½ teaspoon ground turmeric
salt, to taste
2 fresh green chiles, finely chopped
2 tablespoons vegetable oil
4 whole dried red chiles
1 teaspoon cumin seeds
3–4 curry leaves
3 garlic cloves, crushed
2-inch piece of fresh ginger
   root, crushed
fresh cilantro leaves, chopped,
   to garnish

NUTRITIONAL NOTES	
Per Portion	
Energy	321cal
Fat	13.7g
Saturated Fat	2.5g
Carbohydrate	33.8g
Fiber	1.5g

1 Mix the yogurt, besan flour, chili
powder, turmeric, and salt in a
bowl. Press the mixture through a
strainer into a pan. Add the green
chiles and simmer for 10 minutes,
without boiling, stirring occasionally.

2 Heat the oil in a heavy pan and
fry the remaining spices, crushed
garlic, and fresh ginger until the dried
chiles turn black.

_____ COOK'S TIP _____

For a lower fat version, drain off some of
the oil before adding it to the yogurt.
Adjust the amount of chiles, according to
how hot you want the soup to be.

3 Pour the oil and the spices over
the yogurt soup, cover the pan,
and let rest for 5 minutes off the heat.
Mix well and gently reheat for another
5 minutes. Ladle into warmed soup
bowls and serve hot, garnished with
the cilantro leaves.

Spicy Chicken and Mushroom Soup

This creamy chicken soup has just enough spice to make it a great winter warmer, but not so much that it overwhelms the flavor of the mushrooms.

INGREDIENTS

Serves 4

8 ounces boneless chicken, skinned
6 tablespoons ghee or unsalted butter
½ teaspoon crushed garlic
1 teaspoon garam masala
1 teaspoon crushed black peppercorns
1 teaspoon salt
¼ teaspoon grated nutmeg
1 medium leek, sliced
1 cup mushrooms, sliced
⅓ cup corn
1¼ cups water
1 cup light cream
1 tablespoon chopped fresh cilantro
1 teaspoon crushed dried red chiles (optional)

1 Cut the chicken pieces into very fine strips.

2 Melt the ghee or butter in a medium pan. Lower the heat slightly and add the garlic and garam masala. Lower the heat even more and add the black peppercorns, salt, and nutmeg. Finally, add the chicken pieces, sliced leek, mushrooms, and corn, and cook, stirring constantly, for 5–7 minutes, or until the chicken is cooked through.

VARIATION

For a vegetarian version of this soup, you can omit the chicken and use 4½ cups mushrooms instead.

3 Remove from the heat and let cool slightly. Transfer three-quarters of the mixture into a food processor or blender. Add the water and process for about 1 minute.

4 Pour the resulting paste back into the pan and stir with the rest of the mixture. Bring to a boil over a medium heat. Lower the heat and stir in the cream.

5 Add the fresh cilantro and taste the soup for seasoning. Serve hot, garnished with the crushed red chiles, if you like.

NUTRITIONAL NOTES	
Per Portion	
Energy	342cal
Fat	28.5g
Saturated Fat	17.6g
Carbohydrate	4.8g
Fiber	1g

Chicken and Almond Soup

This soup makes an excellent appetizer and served with naan bread will also make a satisfying lunch or supper dish.

INGREDIENTS

Serves 4
6 tablespoon ghee or unsalted butter
1 medium leek, chopped
½ teaspoon shredded fresh ginger root
1 cup ground almonds
1 teaspoon salt
½ teaspoon crushed black
  peppercorns
1 fresh green chile, chopped
1 medium carrot, sliced
½ cup frozen peas
¾ cup cubed skinless chicken
  breast fillet
1 tablespoon chopped fresh cilantro,
  plus extra to garnish
scant 2 cups water
1 cup light cream

1 Melt the ghee or butter in a large karahi, wok, or deep pan, and sauté the leek with the ginger until softened.

2 Lower the heat and add the ground almonds, salt, peppercorns, chile, carrot, peas, and chicken. Fry for about 10 minutes, or until the chicken is completely cooked, stirring constantly. Add the chopped fresh cilantro.

3 Remove from the heat and let cool slightly. Transfer the mixture to a food processor or blender and process for about 1½ minutes. Pour in the water and blend for another 30 seconds.

NUTRITIONAL NOTES	
Per Portion	
Energy	429cal
Fat	39.2g
Saturated Fat	18.4g
Carbohydrate	5.5g
Fiber	2.7g

4 Pour back into the pan and bring to a boil, stirring. Lower the heat and gradually stir in the cream. Cook gently for another 2 minutes, stirring occasionally. Serve garnished with more cilantro.

South Indian Pepper Water

This soothing broth is perfect for winter evenings. The quantity of lemon juice can be adjusted to taste, but this dish should be distinctly sour.

INGREDIENTS

Serves 4–6
2 tablespoons vegetable oil
½ teaspoon black pepper
1 teaspoon cumin seeds
½ teaspoon mustard seeds
¼ teaspoon asafetida
½ teaspoon ground turmeric
2 dried red chiles
4–6 curry leaves
2 garlic cloves, crushed
1¼ cups tomato juice
juice of 2 lemons
½ cup water
salt, to taste
fresh cilantro, to garnish

1 Heat the oil in a large pan and fry the next eight ingredients until the chiles are nearly black and the garlic is golden brown.

2 Lower the heat and pour in the tomato juice, lemon juice, and water. Bring to a boil, then simmer for 10 minutes. Season to taste with salt. Pour into heated bowls, garnish with the chopped cilantro if you like, and serve.

NUTRITIONAL NOTES *Per Portion*	
Energy	60cal
Fat	5.5g
Saturated Fat	0.7g
Carbohydrate	2.3g
Fiber	0.5g

Chicken Mulligatawny

This world famous broth hails from the days of the British Raj.

INGREDIENTS

Serves 4–6
2 pounds boneless chicken portions, skinned
2½ cups water
6 green cardamom pods
2-inch piece cinnamon stick
4–6 curry leaves
1 tablespoon ground coriander
1 teaspoon ground cumin
½ teaspoon ground turmeric
3 garlic cloves, crushed
1 onion, finely chopped
½ cup coconut cream
juice of 2 lemons
deep-fried onions, to garnish

1 Place the chicken in a large pan with the water. Bring to a boil, then simmer for about 1 hour, or until the chicken is tender.

2 Skim the surface, then remove the chicken pieces with a slotted spoon and keep warm.

3 Reheat the stock in the pan. Add all the remaining ingredients, except the chicken and deep-fried onions. Simmer for 10–15 minutes, then strain and return the chicken to the soup. Reheat the soup and serve garnished with the deep-fried onions.

NUTRITIONAL NOTES *Per Portion*	
Energy	444cal
Fat	22.3g
Saturated Fat	17.7g
Carbohydrate	5g
Fiber	0.5g

Onion Bhajias

A favorite snack in India, Bhajias consist of a savory vegetable mixture in a spicy batter. They can be served as an appetizer or as a side dish with curries.

INGREDIENTS

Makes 20-25

2 cups besan flour
½ teaspoon chili powder
1 teaspoon ground turmeric
1 teaspoon baking powder
¼ teaspoon asafetida
salt, to taste
½ teaspoon each, nigella, fennel, cumin, and onion seeds, coarsely crushed
2 large onions, finely sliced
2 fresh green chiles, finely chopped
2 cups fresh cilantro, chopped
water, to mix
vegetable oil, for deep-frying

2 In a bowl mix together the flour, chili powder, ground turmeric, baking powder, and asafetida. Add salt to taste. Sift the mixture into a large mixing bowl.

3 Add the coarsely crushed seeds, onion slices, green chiles, and fresh cilantro and toss together well.

4 Add enough cold water to make a paste, then stir in more water to make a thick batter that coats the onions and spices.

5 Heat enough oil in a karahi or wok for deep-frying. Drop spoonfuls of the mixture into the hot oil and fry the bhajias until they are golden brown. Leave enough space to turn the bhajias. Drain well and serve hot.

_____ VARIATION _____

This versatile batter can be used with other vegetables, including okra, cauliflower, and broccoli.

1 Using a sharp knife, slice the onions into thin slices. Separate the slices and set them aside on a plate.

NUTRITIONAL NOTES	
Per Portion	
Energy	157cal
Fat	12.7g
Saturated Fat	1.5g
Carbohydrate	8.2g
Fiber	0.9g

Vegetable Samosas

A selection of highly spiced vegetables in a pastry casing makes these samosas a delicious snack at any time of the day.

INGREDIENTS

Makes 28

14 sheets of phyllo pastry, thawed and wrapped in a damp dish towel
oil for brushing the pastries

For the filling

3 large potatoes, boiled and roughly mashed
¾ cup frozen peas, thawed
⅓ cup canned corn, drained
1 teaspoon ground coriander
1 teaspoon ground cumin
1 teaspoon dried mango powder (amchur)
1 small onion, finely chopped
2 fresh green chiles, finely chopped
2 tablespoons cilantro leaves, chopped
2 tablespoons fresh mint leaves, chopped
juice of 1 lemon
salt, to taste

NUTRITIONAL NOTES	
Per Samosa	
Energy	50cal
Fat	0.78g
Saturated Fat	0.10g
Carbohydrate	9.40g
Fiber	0.50g

1 Preheat the oven to 400°F. Cut each sheet of phyllo pastry in half lengthwise and fold each piece in half lengthwise to make 28 thin strips. Lightly brush with oil.

--- COOK'S TIP ---

Work with one or two sheets of phyllo pastry at a time; cover the rest with a damp dish towel to prevent them from drying out.

2 Toss all the filling ingredients together in a large mixing bowl until they are well blended. Adjust the seasoning with salt and lemon juice if necessary.

3 Using one strip of the pastry at a time, place 1 tablespoon of the filling mixture at one end and fold the pastry diagonally over. Continue folding to form a triangle shape. Brush the samosas with oil. Bake for 10–15 minutes, until golden brown.

Curried Lamb Samosas

Phyllo pastry is perfect for making samosas. Once you've mastered folding them, you'll be amazed how quick they are to make.

INGREDIENTS

Makes 12
2 tablespoons butter
1 cup ground lamb
2 tablespoons mild curry paste
12 sheets of phyllo pastry, thawed and wrapped in a damp dish towel
salt and black pepper

1 Heat a little of the butter in a large pan and add the lamb. Fry for 5–6 minutes, stirring occasionally, until browned. Stir in the curry paste and cook for another 1–2 minutes. Season and set aside. Preheat the oven to 400°F.

2 Melt the remaining butter in a pan. Cut the pastry sheets in half lengthwise. Brush one strip of pastry with butter, then lay another strip on top and brush with more butter.

3 Place a spoonful of lamb in the corner of the strip and fold over to form a triangle at one end. Keep folding over in the same way to form a triangular package.

4 Brush with butter and place on a baking sheet. Repeat using the remaining pastry and filling. Bake for 10–15 minutes, until golden. Serve hot.

NUTRITIONAL NOTES	
Per Portion	
Energy	81cal
Fat	5.2g
Saturated Fat	2.4g
Carbohydrate	4.9g
Fiber	0.2g

Spiced Potato Cakes with Chickpeas

This is a typical Mumbai street snack, the kind that locals would happily eat while walking along the beach or watching a cricket match. It is the type of food that unites different communities.

INGREDIENTS

Makes 10–12
2 tablespoons vegetable oil
2 tablespoons ground coriander
2 tablespoons ground cumin
½ teaspoon ground turmeric
½ teaspoon salt
½ teaspoon sugar
2 tablespoons besan flour, mixed with a little water to make a paste
3 cups cooked chickpeas, drained
2 fresh green chiles, chopped
2-inch piece fresh ginger root, crushed
1½ cups fresh cilantro, chopped
2 firm tomatoes, chopped
fresh mint sprigs, to garnish

For the potato cakes

1 pound potatoes, boiled and mashed
4 fresh green chiles, finely chopped
1 cup fresh cilantro, finely chopped
1½ teaspoons ground cumin
1 teaspoon dried mango powder (amchur)
vegetable oil, for shallow-frying
salt

1 To prepare the chickpeas, heat the oil in a karahi, wok, or large pan. Add the coriander, cumin, turmeric, salt, sugar, and besan flour paste and cook until the water has evaporated and the oil has separated.

2 Add the chickpeas to the spices in the pan, and stir in the chopped chiles, ginger, fresh cilantro, and tomatoes. Toss the ingredients well and simmer gently for about 5 minutes. Transfer to a serving dish and keep warm.

3 To make the potato cakes, place the mashed potato in a large bowl and add the green chiles, chopped fresh cilantro, cumin, dried mango powder, and salt. Mix together until all the ingredients are well blended.

4 Using your hands, shape the potato mixture into little cakes. Heat the oil in a shallow skillet and fry the cakes on both sides until golden brown. Transfer to a serving dish, garnish with mint sprigs, and serve with the spicy chickpeas.

NUTRITIONAL NOTES	
Per Portion	
Energy	91cal
Fat	3.3g
Saturated Fat	0.4g
Carbohydrate	11.9g
Fiber	2.2g

Crisp Fried Eggplant

The spicy besan flour coating on these slices is deliciously crisp, providing the perfect contrast to the succulent eggplant. Choose a large eggplant with an unblemished, glossy skin.

INGREDIENTS

Serves 4
½ cup besan flour
1 tablespoon semolina or ground rice
½ teaspoon onion seeds
1 teaspoon cumin seeds
½ teaspoon fennel seeds or aniseeds
½–1 teaspoon hot chili powder
½ teaspoon salt, or to taste
1 large eggplant
vegetable oil, for deep-frying

NUTRITIONAL NOTES	
Per Portion	
Energy	288cal
Fat	25.4g
Saturated Fat	3.1g
Carbohydrate	13.7g
Fiber	1.4g

1 Sift the besan flour into a large mixing bowl and add all the remaining ingredients except the eggplant and the vegetable oil.

------ COOK'S TIP ------

Fennel and aniseeds aid digestion, and most deep-fried Indian recipes use them.

2 Halve the eggplant lengthwise and cut each half into ¼-inch thick slices. Rinse them and shake off the excess water, but do not pat dry. With some of the water still clinging to the slices, add them to the spiced besan flour mixture. Toss them around until they are evenly coated with the flour. Use a spoon if necessary to ensure that all the flour is used.

3 Heat the oil in a deep-fat fryer or other suitable pan over a medium-high heat. If you have a thermometer, check that the oil has reached 375°F. Alternatively, drop a small piece of day-old bread into the oil. If it floats immediately, the oil has reached the right temperature.

4 Fry the spice-coated eggplant slices in a single layer. Avoid over-crowding the pan because this lowers the oil temperature, resulting in a soggy texture. Fry until the eggplant slices are crisp and well browned. Drain on paper towels and serve with a chutney.

Glazed Garlic Shrimp

It is best to shell the shrimp for this dish because it helps them to absorb maximum flavor. Serve with salad as a first course or with rice and accompaniments for a more substantial meal.

INGREDIENTS

Serves 4
1 tablespoon oil
3 garlic cloves, roughly chopped
15–20 cooked jumbo shrimp
3 tomatoes, chopped
½ teaspoon salt
1 teaspoon crushed red chiles
1 teaspoon lemon juice
1 tablespoon mango chutney
1 fresh green chile, chopped
fresh cilantro sprigs, to garnish

NUTRITIONAL NOTES	
Per Portion	
Energy	73cal
Fat	3.30g
Saturated Fat	0.38g
Carbohydrate	4.90g
Fiber	0.80g

1 Heat the oil in a medium heavy pan. Add the garlic and cook gently for a few minutes.

COOK'S TIP

Use a skewer or the point of a knife to remove the black intestinal vein running down the back of the shrimp.

2 Set aside four whole shrimp for the garnish. Shell the remainder. Lower the heat and add the chopped tomatoes to the pan with the salt, crushed red chiles, lemon juice, mango chutney, and fresh green chile. Stir gently to mix and cook for 2–3 minutes.

3 Add the peeled shrimp, increase the heat, and stir-fry until heated through. Transfer the shrimp to a serving dish. Serve garnished with fresh cilantro sprigs. Add a whole cooked shrimp, in the shell, to each portion.

Shrimp and Vegetable Kebabs

This light and refreshing first course, with its delicate tang of cilantro and lemon juice, looks great on a bed of lettuce, and makes a perfect summer appetizer at a barbecue. To upgrade the recipe to a light lunch dish, simply add some Peshwari nan and follow with a mango sherbet.

INGREDIENTS

Serves 4

2 tablespoons chopped
    fresh cilantro
1 teaspoon salt
2 fresh green chiles
3 tablespoons lemon juice
2 tablespoons oil
20 cooked jumbo shrimp, shelled
1 medium zucchini,
    thickly sliced
1 medium onion, cut into
    8 chunks
8 cherry tomatoes
8 baby corn
mixed salad greens, to serve

NUTRITIONAL NOTES	
Per Portion	
Energy	183cal
Fat	7.70g
Saturated Fat	1.04g
Carbohydrate	4.50g
Fiber	1.30g

1 Place the chopped cilantro, salt, chiles, lemon juice, and oil in a food processor and process for a few seconds to form a paste.

2 Scrape the spice paste from the food processor and transfer it to a medium mixing bowl.

3 Add the peeled shrimp to the spices and stir to coat well. Cover the bowl and set aside to marinate for about 30 minutes.

4 Preheat the broiler to very hot. Arrange the vegetables and shrimp alternately on four skewers.

5 Reduce the temperature of the broiler to medium and broil the shrimp kebabs for 5–7 minutes, until cooked and browned, turning once.

6 Serve immediately on a bed of mixed salad greens.

COOK'S TIP

Jumbo shrimp are a luxury, but well worth buying for a special dinner. Because they are a large size, they remain succulent when broiled. The spice marinade will provide extra protection.

Shrimp and Spinach Pancakes

Serve these delicious filled pancakes hot. They can be eaten by hand, but they can be messy, so provide plenty of paper napkins if you choose the casual approach. Try to use red onions for this recipe, although they are not essential.

INGREDIENTS

Makes 4–6 pancakes
For the pancakes
1½ cups all-purpose flour
½ teaspoon salt
3 eggs
1½ cups low-fat milk
1 tablespoon low-fat spread
1 tomato, quartered,
   fresh cilantro sprigs
   and lemon wedges,
   to garnish

For the filling
2 tablespoons oil
2 medium red onions,
   sliced
½ teaspoon crushed garlic
1-inch piece fresh ginger root,
   shredded
1 teaspoon chili powder
1 teaspoon garam masala
1 teaspoon salt
2 tomatoes, sliced
8 ounces frozen leaf spinach,
   thawed and drained
1 cup frozen cooked shelled
   shrimp, thawed
2 tablespoons chopped fresh
   cilantro

NUTRITIONAL NOTES	
Per Portion (6)	
Energy	389cal
Fat	14.70g
Saturated Fat	2.83g
Carbohydrate	48.80g
Fiber	4.00g

1 To make the pancakes, sift the flour and salt together. Beat the eggs and add to the flour, beating continuously. Gradually stir in the milk. Let the batter stand for 1 hour.

2 Make the filling. Heat the oil in a deep skillet and fry the sliced onions until golden.

3 Gradually add the garlic, ginger, chili powder, garam masala, and salt, followed by the tomatoes and spinach, stirring constantly.

4 Add the shrimp and chopped cilantro. Cook for another 5–7 minutes, or until any excess liquid has been absorbed. Keep warm.

5 Heat about ½ teaspoon of the low fat margarine in a 10-inch nonstick skillet or pancake pan. Pour in about one-quarter of the pancake batter, tilting the pan so that the batter spreads well, coats the bottom of the pan, and is evenly distributed.

6 When fine bubbles begin to appear on the surface, flip the pancake over, using a spatula, and cook for another minute or so. Transfer to a plate and keep warm. Cook the remaining pancakes in the same way.

7 Fill the pancakes with the spinach and shrimp. Serve warm, garnished with the tomato, cilantro sprigs, and lemon wedges.

COOK'S TIP

To keep the pancakes warm while cooking the remainder, pile them one on top of another on a plate with a sheet of waxed paper between each one to prevent them from sticking. Place in a low oven.

Shrimp with Pomegranate Seeds

This pretty dish makes an impressive appetizer, and is delicious served with a mixed salad.

INGREDIENTS

Serves 4
1 teaspoon crushed garlic
1 teaspoon grated fresh ginger root
1 teaspoon coarsely ground
    pomegranate seeds
1 teaspoon ground coriander
1 teaspoon salt
1 teaspoon chili powder
2 tablespoons tomato paste
4 tablespoons water
3 tablespoons chopped fresh
    cilantro
2 tablespoons corn oil
12 large cooked shrimp
1 medium onion, sliced
    into rings

1 Put the garlic, ginger, pomegranate seeds, ground coriander, salt, chili powder, tomato paste, and water into a bowl. Stir in 2 tablespoons of the chopped cilantro. Add the oil and mix well.

2 Shell the shrimp, rinse them gently, and pat dry on paper towels. Using a sharp knife, make a small slit at the back of each shrimp and remove the black vein. Open out each shrimp to make a butterfly shape.

NUTRITIONAL NOTES	
Per Portion	
Energy	88cal
Fat	5.8g
Saturated Fat	0.8g
Carbohydrate	4g
Fiber	0.7g

3 Add the shrimp to the spice mixture, making sure they are all well coated. Let marinate for about 2 hours.

4 Meanwhile, cut four squares of aluminum foil, about 8 × 8 inches. Preheat the oven to 450°F. When the shrimp are ready, place three shrimp and a few onion rings on each square of foil, garnish each with a little fresh cilantro, and fold up into little packages. Bake for 12–15 minutes and open up the foil to serve.

Broiled Shrimp

Shrimp taste delicious when broiled, especially if they are first flavored with spices.

INGREDIENTS

Serves 4–6
18 large cooked shrimp
4 tablespoons lemon juice
1 teaspoon salt
1 teaspoon chili powder
1 teaspoon crushed garlic
1½ teaspoons light brown sugar
3 tablespoons corn oil, plus extra
    for basting
2 tablespoons chopped fresh
    cilantro
1 fresh green chile, sliced
1 tomato, sliced
1 small onion, cut into rings
lemon wedges

1 Shell the shrimp and rinse them gently under cold water. Pat dry. Make a slit at the back of each shrimp and remove the black vein. Open each shrimp out into a butterfly shape.

2 Mix the remaining ingredients, except for the chile, tomato, onion, and lemon wedges, in a bowl. Stir in the shrimp and let marinate for 1 hour.

3 Preheat the broiler to the maximum setting. Place the green chile, tomato slices, and onion rings in a flameproof dish. Add the shrimp mixture.

4 Broil for 10–15 minutes, basting several times with a brush dipped in oil. Serve immediately, garnished with the lemon wedges.

NUTRITIONAL NOTES	
Per Portion	
Energy	122cal
Fat	8.7g
Saturated Fat	1.3g
Carbohydrate	1.9g
Fiber	0.4g

Quick-fried Shrimp with Spices

These spicy shrimp are stir-fried in moments to make a wonderful appetizer. This is fabulous finger food, so be sure to provide your guests with finger bowls.

INGREDIENTS

Serves 4
1 pound large shrimp
1-inch fresh ginger root, grated
2 garlic cloves, crushed
1 teaspoon hot chili powder
1 teaspoon ground turmeric
2 teaspoons black mustard seeds
seeds from 4 green cardamom
  pods, crushed
4 tablespoons ghee or butter
½ cup coconut milk
salt and black pepper
2–3 tablespoons chopped fresh cilantro,
  to garnish
nan bread, to serve

1 Shell the shrimp carefully, leaving the tails attached.

2 Using a small sharp knife, make a slit along the back of each shrimp and remove the dark vein. Rinse under cold running water, drain, and pat dry.

3 Put the ginger, garlic, chili powder, turmeric, mustard seeds, and cardamom seeds in a bowl. Add the shrimp and toss to coat completely in the spice mixture.

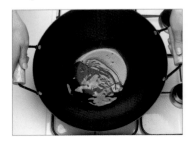

4 Heat a karahi or wok until hot. Add the ghee or butter and swirl it around until foaming.

5 Add the marinated shrimp and stir-fry for 1–1½ minutes, until they are just turning pink.

6 Stir in the coconut milk and simmer for 3–4 minutes, until the shrimp are just cooked through. Season to taste with salt and pepper. Sprinkle with the cilantro and serve immediately with nan bread.

NUTRITIONAL NOTES	
Per Portion	
Energy	196cal
Fat	11.5g
Saturated Fat	7g
Carbohydrate	2.1g
Fiber	0g

Spicy Fried Fish Cubes

Firm white fish cubes, coated in a spicy tomato mixture and deep-fried, make an excellent appetizer. They are slightly messy for eating with the fingers, but taste so good that guests will waste no time in popping them into their mouths. Have plenty of paper napkins handy.

INGREDIENTS

Serves 4-6

1½ pounds cod fillet, or any other firm, while fish
1 medium onion
1 tablespoon lemon juice
1 teaspoon salt
1 teaspoon grated garlic
1 teaspoon crushed dried red chiles
1½ teaspoons garam masala
2 tablespoons chopped fresh cilantro
2 medium tomatoes
2 tablespoons cornstarch
⅔ cup corn oil

1 Skin the fish and remove any remaining bones. Cut it into small cubes. Place in a bowl, cover, and put into the refrigerator to chill.

2 Using a sharp knife, cut the onion into thin slices. Put into a bowl and add the lemon juice and salt.

3 Add the garlic, crushed red chiles, garam masala, and fresh cilantro. Mix well.

4 Peel the tomatoes by dropping them into boiling water for a few seconds. Remove with a slotted spoon and gently peel off the skins. Chop the tomatoes roughly and add to the onion mixture in the bowl.

5 Tip the contents of the bowl into a food processor or blender and process for about 30 seconds. Remove the fish from the refrigerator. Pour the contents of the food processor or blender over the fish and mix well.

6 Add the cornstarch and mix again until the fish pieces are well coated.

7 Heat the oil in a wok, karahi, or deep pan. Lower the heat slightly and add the fish pieces, a few at a time. Turn them gently with a slotted spoon as they are liable to break easily. Cook for about 5 minutes, until the fish is lightly browned.

8 Remove the fish pieces from the pan and drain on paper towels. Keep warm and continue frying the remaining fish. This dish is delicious served with apricot chutney and parathas.

NUTRITIONAL NOTES	
Per Portion	
Energy	434cal
Fat	26.5g
Saturated Fat	3.2g
Carbohydrate	18.2g
Fiber	1g

Goan-style Mussels

Mussels make a marvelous appetizer. Serve them Goan-style, in a fragrant coconut sauce. They take only minutes to cook, and the wonderful aroma will stimulate the most jaded appetite.

INGREDIENTS

Serves 4

2 pounds live mussels
½ cup coconut cream
1¾ cups boiling water
3 tablespoons oil
1 onion, finely chopped
3 garlic cloves, crushed
1-inch piece fresh ginger root, peeled and finely chopped
½ teaspoon ground turmeric
1 teaspoon ground cumin
1 teaspoon ground coriander
¼ teaspoon salt
chopped fresh cilantro, to garnish

1 Scrub the mussels under cold water and pull off any beards that remain attached to the shells. Discard any mussels that are open, or which fail to snap shut when tapped.

NUTRITIONAL NOTES	
Per Portion	
Energy	339cal
Fat	29.5g
Saturated Fat	18.3g
Carbohydrate	5g
Fiber	0.5g

2 Put the coconut cream in a measuring cup and pour in the boiling water. Stir with a wooden spoon until all the coconut has dissolved, then set aside until required. Heat the oil in a karahi, wok, or heavy pan. Add the onion and fry for 5 minutes, stirring frequently.

3 Add the garlic and ginger and fry for 2 minutes. Stir in the turmeric, cumin, coriander, and salt and fry for 2 minutes. Pour in the coconut liquid, stir well, and bring to a boil. Reduce the heat and simmer for 5 minutes.

4 Add the mussels, cover the pan, and cook over medium heat for 6–8 minutes, by which time all the mussels should have opened. Spoon the mussels onto a serving platter. If any of the mussels have failed to open, discard them immediately.

5 Pour the sauce over the mussels, garnish with the chopped fresh cilantro, and serve.

Chile Crabs

The ingredients of this delicious dish owe more to Southeast Asia than India, and it is not surprising to discover that it comes from the eastern part of the country, close to the border with Myanmar.

INGREDIENTS

Serves 4

2 cooked crabs, about 1½ pounds
½-inch cube shrimp paste
2 garlic cloves
2 fresh red chiles, seeded, or
   1 teaspoon chopped chili from a jar
½-inch fresh ginger root, peeled
   and sliced
4 tablespoons sunflower oil
1¼ cups ketchup
1 tablespoon molasses sugar
⅔ cup warm water
4 scallions, chopped
cucumber chunks and hot toast,
   to serve (optional)

1 Remove the large claws of one crab and turn onto its back, with the head facing away from you. Use your thumbs to push the body up from the main shell. Discard the stomach sac and "dead men's fingers"—the lungs and any green matter. Leave the creamy brown meat in the shell and cut the shell in half with a cleaver or strong knife. Cut the body section in half and crack the claws with a sharp blow from a hammer or cleaver. Avoid splintering the claws. Repeat with the other crab.

2 Grind the shrimp paste, garlic, chiles, and ginger to a paste in a food processor or with a mortar and pestle.

3 Heat a karahi or wok and add the oil. Fry the spice paste, stirring constantly, without browning.

4 Stir in the ketchup, sugar, and water and mix the sauce well. When just boiling, add all the crab pieces and toss in the sauce until well-coated and hot. Serve in a large bowl, sprinkled with the scallions. Place in the center of the table for everyone to help themselves. Accompany this dish with cool cucumber chunks and hot toast for mopping up the sauce, if you like.

NUTRITIONAL NOTES	
Per Portion	
Energy	276cal
Fat	14.3g
Saturated Fat	1.7g
Carbohydrate	25.4g
Fiber	0.7g

Spicy Crab with Coconut

This simple appetizer looks pretty and tastes delicious. Have all the ingredients ready and cook it just before calling your guests to the table. It needs no accompaniment other than some plain warm nan bread.

INGREDIENTS

Serves 4
½ cup dry unsweetened
    shredded coconut
2 garlic cloves
2-inch piece fresh ginger root,
    peeled and grated
½ teaspoon cumin seeds
1 small cinnamon stick
½ teaspoon ground turmeric
2 dried red chiles
1 tablespoon coriander seeds
½ teaspoon poppy seeds
1 tablespoon vegetable oil
1 medium onion, sliced
1 small green bell pepper,
    seeded and cut into strips
16 crab claws
fresh cilantro sprigs,
    to garnish
⅔ cup plain low-fat yogurt,
    to serve

2 Heat the oil in a karahi, wok, or heavy pan. Add the onion slices and fry over a medium heat for 2–3 minutes, until softened but not colored.

3 Stir in the green bell pepper strips and toss over the heat for 1 minute. Using a slotted spoon, remove the vegetables from the pan and place them in a bowl.

4 Place the pan over a high heat. When it is hot, add the crab claws and stir-fry for 2 minutes. Return the vegetables to the pan with the coconut mixture. Toss over the heat until the mixture is fragrant and the crab claws and vegetables are coated in the spices. Serve on individual plates, garnished with the cilantro. Serve the cooling yogurt separately.

NUTRITIONAL NOTES	
Per Portion	
Energy	186cal
Fat	10.1g
Saturated Fat	5.8g
Carbohydrate	4.8g
Fiber	2.6g

COOK'S TIP

The heat of this dish will depend upon the type of dried chiles you use. To make them somewhat less fiery, remove the seeds before processing the chiles with the coconut and other spices.

1 Put the shredded coconut in a food processor and add the garlic, ginger, cumin seeds, cinnamon stick, turmeric, red chiles, and coriander and poppy seeds. Process until well blended.

Fish Cakes

Goan fish and shellfish are skillfully prepared with spices to make cakes of all shapes and sizes, while the rest of India makes fish kababs. Although haddock is used in this recipe, you can use other less expensive white fish, such as coley or whiting.

INGREDIENTS

Makes 20

1 pound skinned haddock or cod
2 potatoes, peeled, boiled, and
   coarsely mashed
4 scallions, finely chopped
4 fresh green chiles, finely
   chopped
2-inch piece fresh ginger root,
   crushed
a few fresh cilantro and mint
   sprigs, chopped
2 eggs
bread crumbs, for coating
vegetable oil, for shallow-frying
salt and black pepper
lemon wedges and chili sauce,
   to serve

—————— COOK'S TIP ——————

For a quick version, used canned tuna in brine and omit step 1. Make sure the tuna is thoroughly drained before use.

NUTRITIONAL NOTES	
Per Portion	
Energy	56cal
Fat	3.3g
Saturated Fat	0.5g
Carbohydrate	1.5g
Fiber	0.1g

1 Place the skinned fish in a lightly greased steamer and steam gently until cooked. Remove the steamer from the stovetop but let the fish stand on the steaming tray until cool.

2 When the fish is cool, crumble it coarsely into a large bowl, using a fork. Mix in the mashed potatoes.

3 Add the scallions, chiles, crushed ginger, chopped cilantro and mint, and one of the eggs. Mix well and season to taste with salt and pepper.

4 Shape into cakes. Beat the remaining egg and dip the cakes in it, then coat with the bread crumbs. Heat the oil and fry the cakes until brown on all sides. Serve as an appetizer or as a side dish, with the lemon wedges and chili sauce.

Ginger Chicken Wings

Many people regard chicken wings as the best part of the bird. Served this way, they are certainly delicious.

INGREDIENTS

Serves 4

10–12 chicken wings, skinned
³/₄ cup plain low-fat yogurt
1½ teaspoons crushed fresh ginger root
1 teaspoon salt
1 teaspoon Tabasco sauce
1 tablespoon ketchup
1 teaspoon crushed garlic
1 tablespoon lemon juice
1 tablespoon fresh cilantro leaves
1 tablespoon oil
2 medium onions, sliced
1 tablespoon shredded fresh ginger root

1 Place the chicken wings in a glass or china bowl. Pour the yogurt into a separate bowl along with the ginger pulp, salt, Tabasco sauce, ketchup, garlic pulp, lemon juice, and half the fresh cilantro leaves. Whisk everything together, then pour the mixture over the chicken wings and stir gently to coat the chicken.

2 Heat the oil in a wok or heavy skillet and fry the onions until soft.

3 Pour in the chicken wings and cook over a medium heat, stirring occasionally, for 10–15 minutes.

4 Add the remaining cilantro and the shredded ginger and serve hot.

COOK'S TIP

You can substitute drumsticks or other chicken portions for the wings in this recipe, but remember to increase the cooking time.

NUTRITIONAL NOTES	
Per Portion	
Energy	224cal
Fat	9.00g
Saturated Fat	2.23g
Carbohydrate	12.64g
Fiber	1.24g

Chicken Tikka

This extremely popular Indian first course is quick and easy to cook. The dish can also be served as a main course for four.

INGREDIENTS

Serves 6 as an appetizer
1 pound boneless chicken, skinned and cubed
1 teaspoon crushed fresh ginger root
1 teaspoon crushed garlic
1 teaspoon chili powder
¼ teaspoon ground turmeric
1 teaspoon salt
⅔ cup plain low-fat yogurt
4 tablespoons lemon juice
1 tablespoon chopped fresh cilantro
1 tablespoon oil

For the garnish
mixed salad greens
1 small onion, cut into rings
lime wedges
fresh cilantro

NUTRITIONAL NOTES
Per Portion

Energy	134cal
Fat	5.50g
Saturated Fat	1.49g
Carbohydrate	3.90g
Fiber	0.30g

— COOK'S TIP —

To make the turning and basting of the chicken easier, thread the chicken pieces onto six wooden skewers before placing under the broiler.

1 In a medium bowl, mix together the chicken pieces, ginger, garlic, chili powder, turmeric, and salt.

2 Stir in the yogurt, lemon juice, and fresh cilantro and let marinate for at least 2 hours.

3 Place in a broiler pan or in a flameproof dish lined with aluminum foil and baste with the oil.

4 Preheat the broiler to medium, then broil the chicken for 15–20 minutes, until cooked, turning and basting several times. Serve on a bed of mixed salad greens, garnished with onion rings, lime wedges, and cilantro.

Chicken Kofta Balti with Paneer

This unusual appetizer looks most elegant when served in small individual karahis.

INGREDIENTS

Serves 6

For the koftas
1 pound boneless chicken,
  skinned and cubed
1 teaspoon crushed garlic
1 teaspoon shredded fresh ginger root
1½ teaspoons ground coriander
1½ teaspoons chili powder
1½ teaspoons ground fenugreek
¼ teaspoon turmeric
1 teaspoon salt
2 tablespoons chopped fresh
  cilantro
2 fresh green chiles, chopped
2½ cups water
corn oil, for frying

For the paneer mixture
1 medium onion, sliced
1 red bell pepper, seeded
  and cut into strips
1 green bell pepper, seeded
  and cut into strips
6 ounces paneer, cubed
1 cup corn
fresh mint sprigs
1 dried red chile, crushed (optional)

1 Put all the kofta ingredients, apart from the oil, into a medium pan. Bring to a boil slowly, over a medium heat, and cook until all the liquid has evaporated.

2 Remove from the heat and let cool slightly. Put the mixture into a food processor or blender and process for 2 minutes, stopping once or twice to loosen the mixture with a spoon.

3 Scrape the mixture into a large mixing bowl, using a wooden spoon. Taking a little of the mixture at a time, shape it into small balls, using your hands. You should be able to make about 12 koftas.

4 Heat the oil in a karahi, wok, or deep pan over a high heat. Reduce the heat slightly and drop the koftas carefully into the oil. Move them around gently to ensure that they cook evenly.

5 When the koftas are lightly browned, remove them from the oil with a slotted spoon and drain on paper towels. Set aside.

6 Heat the oil still remaining in the karahi, and flash fry all the ingredients for the paneer mixture. This should take about 3 minutes over a high heat.

7 Divide the paneer mixture evenly between six individual karahis. Add two koftas to each serving, and garnish with mint sprigs. Add the crushed red chile, if you like.

NUTRITIONAL NOTES	
Per Portion	
Energy	235cal
Fat	10.3g
Saturated Fat	2.1g
Carbohydrate	12.3g
Fiber	1.9g

Pineapple Chicken Kebabs

This chicken dish has a delicate tang and the meat is tender. The pineapple not only tenderizes the chicken but also gives it a slight sweetness.

INGREDIENTS

Serves 6

8-ounce can pineapple chunks
1 teaspoon ground cumin
1 teaspoon ground coriander
1 teaspoon chili powder
½ teaspoon crushed garlic
1 teaspoon salt
2 tablespoons plain low-fat yogurt
1 tablespoon chopped fresh
  cilantro
few drops of orange food
  coloring, optional
10 ounces boneless chicken, skinned
½ red bell pepper, seeded
½ yellow or green bell pepper, seeded
1 large onion
6 cherry tomatoes
1 tablespoon oil
salad greens, to serve

NUTRITIONAL NOTES	
Per Portion	
Energy	183cal
Fat	6.60g
Saturated Fat	1.47g
Carbohydrate	15.40g
Fiber	1.80g

1 Drain the pineapple juice into a bowl. Reserve eight large chunks of pineapple and squeeze the juice from the remaining chunks into the bowl and set aside. You should have about ½ cup pineapple juice.

2 In a large bowl, mix together the spices, garlic, salt, yogurt, fresh cilantro, and food coloring, if using. Mix in the reserved pineapple juice.

3 Cut the chicken into bitesize cubes, add to the yogurt and spice mixture, cover, and let marinate in a cool place for about 1–1½ hours.

4 Cut the peppers and onion into bitesize chunks.

5 Preheat the broiler to medium. Meanwhile, arrange the chicken pieces, vegetables, and reserved pineapple chunks alternately onto six metal skewers.

6 Brush the kebabs lightly with the oil, then place the skewers on a flameproof dish or in a broiler pan, turning the chicken pieces and basting with the marinade regularly, for about 15 minutes, until cooked through. Serve with salad greens.

COOK'S TIPS

• If possible, use a mixture of chicken breast and thigh meat for this recipe.
• Use wooden skewers, if you prefer, but soak them in water for at least 30 minutes first to prevent them from scorching under the broiler.

Mini Koftas in a Spicy Sauce

This kofta curry is very popular in most Indian homes. It is also extremely easy to make.

INGREDIENTS

Serves 4

8 ounces lean ground lamb
2 teaspoons poppy seeds
1 medium onion, chopped
1 teaspoon crushed fresh ginger root
1 teaspoon crushed garlic
1 teaspoon salt
1 teaspoon chili powder
1½ teaspoons ground coriander
2 tablespoons fresh cilantro leaves
1 small egg

For the sauce

⅓ cup plain low-fat yogurt
2 tablespoons tomato paste
1 teaspoon chili powder
1 teaspoon salt
1 teaspoon crushed garlic
1 teaspoon crushed fresh ginger root
1 teaspoon garam masala
2 teaspoons oil
1 cinnamon stick
1⅔ cups water

1 Place the lamb in a food processor and grind it further for about 1 minute. Remove from the processor, scrape into a bowl, put the poppy seeds on top, and set aside.

2 Place the onion in the food processor, with the crushed ginger, garlic, salt, chili powder, ground coriander, and half the fresh cilantro. Grind this spice mixture for about 30 seconds, then add it to the lamb. Mix well.

3 Whisk the egg and thoroughly mix it into the spiced lamb. Let stand for about 1 hour.

4 For the sauce, whisk together the yogurt, tomato paste, chili powder, salt, crushed garlic, ginger, and garam masala.

5 Heat the oil with the cinnamon stick in a karahi or wok for about 1 minute, then pour in the prepared sauce. Lower the heat and cook for about 1 minute. Remove the karahi or wok from the heat and set aside.

6 Break off small balls of the meat mixture and make the koftas, using your hands. When all the koftas are ready, return the sauce to the heat and stir in the water. Drop in the koftas one by one. Place the remaining fresh cilantro on top, cover with a lid, and cook for 7–10 minutes, stirring gently several times to turn the koftas around. Serve hot.

NUTRITIONAL NOTES	
Per Portion	
Energy	155cal
Fat	9.24g
Saturated Fat	2.79g
Carbohydrate	7.56g
Fiber	1.16g

Stuffed Eggplant with Lamb

Lamb and eggplant go really well together. This dish uses different colored bell peppers in the lightly spiced filling mixture.

INGREDIENTS

Serves 4

2 medium eggplants
1 tablespoon oil, plus extra
   for brushing
1 medium onion, sliced
1 teaspoon crushed fresh ginger root
1 teaspoon chili powder
1 teaspoon crushed garlic
¼ teaspoon ground turmeric
1 teaspoon salt
1 teaspoon ground coriander
1 medium tomato, chopped
12 ounces lean leg of lamb,
   ground
1 medium green bell pepper, seeded
   and roughly chopped
1 medium orange bell pepper, seeded
   and roughly chopped
2 tablespoons chopped fresh
   cilantro
plain rice, to serve

For the garnish

½ onion, sliced
2 cherry tomatoes, quartered
fresh cilantro

1 Cut the eggplants in half lengthwise and scoop out most of the flesh and discard.

2 Preheat the oven to 350°F. Meanwhile, place the eggplant shells, cut-side up, in a lightly greased ovenproof dish.

3 In a medium heavy pan, heat the oil and fry the onion until golden brown.

4 Gradually stir in the ginger, chili powder, garlic, turmeric, salt, and ground coriander. Add the chopped tomato, lower the heat, and cook for about 5 minutes, stirring frequently.

5 Add the ground lamb and cook for 7–10 minutes more.

NUTRITIONAL NOTES	
Per Portion	
Energy	238cal
Fat	11.70g
Saturated Fat	4.08g
Carbohydrate	12.60g
Fiber	5.90g

6 Add the chopped bell peppers and chopped fresh cilantro to the lamb mixture and stir well.

7 Spoon the lamb mixture into the eggplant shells and brush the edge of the shells with a little oil. Bake in the oven for 1 hour, or until cooked through and browned on top.

8 Serve with the garnish ingredients on a bed of plain rice.

COOK'S TIP

For that special occasion, stuffed baby eggplants look particularly attractive. Instead of the medium eggplants, you can use 4 small eggplants, leaving the stalks intact, and prepare and cook them as described above, reducing the baking time slightly. Large tomatoes or zucchini will make an excellent alternative to eggplants.

Tandoori Masala Spring Lamb Chops

These spicy, lean and trimmed lamb chops are marinated for three hours and then cooked in the oven using very little oil. They make a tasty appetizer, served with a salad garnish, and would also serve three as a main course if served with rice.

INGREDIENTS

Serves 6 as an appetizer
6 small lean spring lamb chops
2 tablespoons plain low-fat
   yogurt
1 tablespoon tomato paste
2 teaspoons ground coriander
1 teaspoon crushed fresh ginger root
1 teaspoon crushed garlic
1 teaspoon chili powder
few drops of red food
   coloring (optional)
1 teaspoon salt
1 tablespoon oil, plus extra
   for basting
3 tablespoons lemon juice

For the salad garnish
lettuce (optional)
lime wedges
1 small onion, sliced
fresh cilantro

NUTRITIONAL NOTES	
Per Portion	
Energy	117cal
Fat	6.60g
Saturated Fat	2.42g
Carbohydrate	3.10g
Fiber	0.30g

1 Rinse the chops and pat dry. Trim off all excess fat.

2 In a medium bowl, mix together the yogurt, tomato paste , ground coriander, ginger, garlic, chili powder, food coloring (if using), salt, oil, and lemon juice.

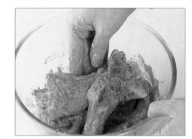

3 Rub this spice mixture over the lamb chops, using your hands, and let the chops marinate in a cool place for at least 3 hours.

4 Preheat the oven to 475°F. Place the marinated chops in an ovenproof dish.

5 Using a brush, baste the chops with about 1 teaspoon oil and cook in the oven for 15 minutes. Lower the heat to 350°F and cook for another 10–15 minutes.

6 Check that the chops are cooked and serve immediately on a bed of lettuce, if you like, and garnish with lime wedges, sliced onion, and fresh cilantro.

--- COOK'S TIP ---

This bright red tandoori masala mixture is used to color and spice both meat and chicken and give the effect of a tandoori-style dish without the need to cook it in a traditional clay oven (tandoor).

Lamb Kebabs

First introduced by the Muslims, kebabs have now become a favorite Indian dish.

INGREDIENTS

Serves 8

For the kebabs

2 pounds lean ground lamb
1 large onion, roughly chopped
2-inch piece fresh ginger root, chopped
2 garlic cloves, crushed
1 fresh green chile, finely chopped
1 teaspoon chili powder
2 tablespoons chopped fresh cilantro
1 teaspoon garam masala
2 teaspoons ground coriander
1 teaspoon ground cumin
1 teaspoon salt
1 egg
1 tablespoon plain low-fat yogurt
1 tablespoon oil
mixed salad, to serve

For the raita

1 cup plain low-fat yogurt
½ cucumber, finely chopped
2 tablespoons chopped fresh mint
¼ teaspoon salt

1 Put all the ingredients for the kebabs, except the yogurt and oil, into a food processor or blender and process until the mixture binds together. Spoon into a bowl, cover, and let marinate for 1 hour.

2 For the raita, mix together all the ingredients and chill for at least 15 minutes in a refrigerator.

3 Preheat the broiler. Divide the lamb mixture into eight equal portions with lightly floured hands and mold into long sausage shapes. Thread onto skewers and chill.

4 Brush the kebabs lightly with the yogurt and oil and cook under a hot broiler for 8–10 minutes, turning occasionally, until brown all over. Serve the kebabs on a bed of mixed salad accompanied by the raita.

NUTRITIONAL NOTES	
Per Portion	
Energy	249cal
Fat	12.75g
Saturated Fat	5.30g
Carbohydrate	7.00g
Fiber	0.60g

Shammi Kabab

These Indian treats are derived from the kebabs of the Middle East, but Indian cooks changed the spelling, dispensed with the skewers, and formed the mixture into large patties, which they deep-fried. Kababs can be served either as appetizers or side dishes with an accompanying raita or chutney.

INGREDIENTS

Serves 5–6

2 onions, finely chopped
9 ounces lean lamb, boned
　and cubed
⅓ cup chana dhal or yellow split peas
1 teaspoon cumin seeds
1 teaspoon garam masala
4–6 fresh green chiles
2-inch piece fresh ginger root, grated
¾ cup water
a few fresh cilantro and mint leaves,
　chopped, plus extra cilantro sprigs
　to garnish
juice of 1 lemon
1 tablespoon besan flour
2 eggs, beaten
vegetable oil, for shallow-frying
salt

1 Put the first seven ingredients and the water into a large pan with salt, and bring to a boil. Simmer, covered, until the meat and dhal are cooked. Remove the lid and continue to cook for a few more minutes to reduce the excess liquid. Set aside to cool.

2 Transfer the cooled meat and dhal mixture to a food processor or blender and process well until the mixture becomes a rough, gritty paste.

3 Put the paste into a large mixing bowl and add the chopped cilantro and mint leaves, lemon juice, and besan. Knead well with your fingers for a good couple of minutes to ensure that all ingredients are evenly distributed through the mixture and any excess liquid has been thoroughly absorbed. When the color appears even throughout, and the mixture has taken on a semisolid, sticky rather than powdery consistency, the kababs are ready for shaping into portions.

4 Divide the kabab mixture into 10–12 even-size portions and use your hands to roll each into a ball, then flatten slightly. Chill for 1 hour. Dip the kabab in the beaten egg and shallow fry each side until golden brown. Pat dry on paper towels.

| NUTRITIONAL NOTES | |
Per Portion	
Energy	179cal
Fat	8.5g
Saturated Fat	3.4g
Carbohydrate	10.4g
Fiber	1.3g

Fish
and Shellfish

SURROUNDED ON three sides by sea, India has a vast coastline. The waters of the Arabian Sea, the Indian Ocean, and the Bay of Bengal lap its shores, so it is not at all surprising that some of the most delectable Indian dishes are based on fish and shellfish.

Freshwater rivers and lakes contribute their own bounty, and the resulting catch is cooked in a variety of ways, some of which are unique to this land. This chapter invites you to try a vast range of specialities, such as Kerala's famous Marinated Fried Fish, a delightfully unusual Monkfish and Okra Curry, and a hearty Fish Stew that hails from Eastern India.

Also on the menu are shellfish dishes, such as Curried Shrimp in Coconut Milk and Jumbo Shrimp Bhoona. Fish has the advantage of being quick and easy to cook—many of the following dishes can be prepared in no time at all. For the most part, spicing is subtle to allow the full flavor to shine.

Marinated Fried Fish

Fish and shellfish are a strong feature of the cuisine in the coastal region of southern India. Kerala, in the southernmost part of the country, produces some of the finest fish and shellfish dishes. These are flavored with local spices, grown in the fabulous spice plantation that is the pride and joy of the state.

INGREDIENTS

Serves 4–6

1 small onion, coarsely chopped
4 garlic cloves, crushed
2-inch piece fresh ginger root, chopped
1 teaspoon ground turmeric
2 teaspoons chili powder
4 red snappers
vegetable oil, for shallow-frying
1 teaspoon cumin seeds
3 fresh green chiles, finely sliced
salt
lemon or lime wedges,
    to serve

_____ COOK'S TIP _____

To enhance the flavor, add 1 tablespoon chopped fresh cilantro leaves to the spice paste in step 1.

NUTRITIONAL NOTES
Per Portion

Energy	336cal
Fat	20.1g
Saturated Fat	1.5g
Carbohydrate	1.2g
Fiber	0.2g

1 In a food processor, grind the first five ingredients with salt to a smooth paste. Make several slashes on both sides of the fish and rub them with the paste. Let rest for 1 hour. Excess fluid will be released as the salt dissolves, so lightly pat the fish dry with paper towels without removing the paste.

2 Heat the oil and fry the cumin seeds and sliced chiles for 1 minute. Add the fish, in batches if necessary, and fry on one side. When the first side is sealed, turn them over gently to ensure they do not break. Fry until golden brown on both sides and fully cooked. Drain and serve hot, with lemon or lime wedges.

Fish with Mango Sauce

This salad is best served during the summer months, preferably outdoors. The dressing combines the flavor of rich mango with those of hot chile, ginger, and lime.

INGREDIENTS

Serves 4

1 French loaf
4 redfish, red snapper, or porgy, each about 10 ounces
1 tablespoon vegetable oil
1 mango
½-inch fresh ginger root
1 fresh red chile, seeded and finely chopped
2 tablespoons lime juice
2 tablespoons chopped fresh cilantro
6 ounces young spinach
5 ounces bok choy
6 ounces cherry tomatoes, halved

1 Preheat the oven to 350°F. Cut the French loaf into 8-inch lengths. Slice lengthwise, then cut into thick fingers. Place the bread on a baking sheet and let dry in the oven for 15 minutes.

2 Preheat the broiler or light the barbecue and allow the embers to settle. Slash the fish deeply on both sides and moisten with oil. Broil the fish or grill it on the barbecue for 6 minutes, turning once.

3 Peel the mango and cut in half, discarding the pit. Thinly slice one half and set aside. Place the other half in a food processor. Peel the ginger, grate finely, then add to the mango with the chile, lime juice, and cilantro. Process until smooth. Adjust to a pouring consistency with 2–3 tablespoons water.

4 Wash the spinach and bok choy leaves and spin dry, then distribute them among four serving plates. Place the fish on the leaves. Spoon on the mango dressing and finish with the reserved slices of mango and the tomato halves. Serve with the fingers of crisp French bread.

NUTRITIONAL NOTES	
Per Portion	
Energy	512cal
Fat	12.3g
Saturated Fat	0.8g
Carbohydrate	50g
Fiber	4.9g

Braised Whole Fish in Chili and Garlic Sauce

Although every region of
India has its own cuisine, and
traditional dishes are what
Western visitors expect to find,
there is in India, as elsewhere in
the world, an increasing number
of dishes that borrow from other
cultures. The vinegar in the
sauce for this fish dish is typical
of Goa, but the rice wine and
bean sauce reveal a distinct
Szechuan influence.

INGREDIENTS

Serves 4–6
1 carp, red snapper, sea bass, trout,
  grouper or pompano, about
  1½ pounds, gutted
1 tablespoon light soy sauce
1 tablespoon rice wine or
  dry sherry
vegetable oil, for deep-frying

For the sauce
2 garlic cloves, finely chopped
2–3 scallions, finely chopped,
  the white and green parts
  separated
1 teaspoon finely chopped fresh
  ginger root
2 tablespoons chili bean sauce
1 tablespoon tomato paste
2 teaspoons light brown sugar
1 tablespoon rice vinegar
½ cup chicken stock
1 tablespoon cornstarch, mixed to a
  paste with 2 teaspoons water
few drops of sesame oil

NUTRITIONAL NOTES	
Per Portion	
Energy	292cal
Fat	16.1g
Saturated Fat	2.5g
Carbohydrate	10.7g
Fiber	0.4g

1 Rinse and dry the fish well. Using
a sharp knife, score both sides
of the fish down to the bone with
diagonal cuts about 1 inch apart. Rub
both sides of the fish with the soy sauce
and rice wine or sherry. Set aside for
10–15 minutes to marinate.

2 Heat sufficient oil for deep-frying
in a wok. When it is hot, add the
fish and fry for 3–4 minutes on both
sides, until golden brown.

3 To make the sauce, pour away all
but about 1 tablespoon of the oil.
Push the fish to one side of the wok
and add the garlic, the white part of the
scallions, the ginger, chili bean sauce,
tomato paste, sugar, vinegar, and stock.
Bring to a boil and braise the fish in the
sauce for 4–5 minutes, turning it over
once. Add the green of the scallions.
Stir in the cornstarch paste to thicken
the sauce. Sprinkle over a little sesame
oil and serve.

Spicy Broiled Fish Fillets

The good thing about fish is that it can be marvelous broiled without sacrificing any flavor.

INGREDIENTS

Serves 4

4 medium flatfish fillets, such as sole, or flounder, about 4 ounces each
1 teaspoon crushed garlic
1 teaspoon garam masala
1 teaspoon chili powder
¼ teaspoon ground turmeric
½ teaspoon salt
1 tablespoon finely chopped fresh cilantro
1 tablespoon oil
2 tablespoons lemon juice
tomato wedges, lime slices, and grated carrot, to garnish

1 Line a flameproof dish or broiler pan with aluminum foil. Rinse the fish fillets, pat dry, and put them in the foil-lined dish or pan.

2 In a bowl, mix the garlic, garam masala, chili powder, turmeric, salt, cilantro, oil, and lemon juice.

3 Brush the fish fillets evenly all over with the spice mixture.

4 Preheat the broiler to very hot, then lower the heat. Broil the fish for about 10 minutes, basting it with the spice mixture, until the fish is cooked.

5 Serve immediately with a garnish of tomato wedges, lime slices, and grated carrot.

NUTRITIONAL NOTES	
Per Portion	
Energy	152cal
Fat	5.90g
Saturated Fat	0.88g
Carbohydrate	3.70g
Fiber	0.70g

_____ COOK'S TIP _____

Use lime juice instead of lemon to give the dish a slightly more sour flavor.

Sweet and Sour Fish

When fish is cooked in this way the skin becomes crispy on the outside while the flesh remains moist and juicy inside. The sweet and sour sauce, with its colorful cherry tomatoes, complements the fish wonderfully.

INGREDIENTS

Serves 4–6
1 large or 2 medium-size fish,
   such as snapper, heads removed
4 teaspoons cornstarch
½ cup vegetable oil
1 tablespoon chopped garlic
1 tablespoon chopped fresh
   ginger root
2 tablespoons chopped shallots
8 ounces cherry tomatoes
2 tablespoons red wine vinegar
2 tablespoons sugar
2 tablespoons ketchup
3 tablespoons water
salt and black pepper
cilantro leaves, to garnish
shredded scallions, to garnish

1 Thoroughly rinse and clean the fish. Score the skin diagonally on both sides of the fish.

2 Coat the fish lightly on both sides with 3 teaspoons of the cornstarch. Shake off any excess.

3 Heat the oil in a karahi or wok and slide the fish into the pan. Reduce the heat to medium and fry the fish 6–7 minutes on both sides, until crisp and brown.

4 Remove the fish with a spatula and place on a large platter.

5 Pour off all but 2 tablespoons of the oil and add the garlic, ginger, and shallots. Fry until golden.

6 Add the cherry tomatoes and cook until they burst open. Stir in the vinegar, sugar, and ketchup. Simmer gently for 1–2 minutes and adjust the seasoning.

7 Mix the remaining 1 teaspoon cornstarch with the water. Stir into the sauce and heat until it thickens. Pour the sauce over the fish and garnish with cilantro leaves and shredded scallions.

NUTRITIONAL NOTES	
Per Portion	
Energy	297cal
Fat	21.5g
Saturated Fat	2.8g
Carbohydrate	6g
Fiber	0.7g

Vinegar Fish

Fish cooked in a spicy mixture that includes chiles, ginger, and vinegar is delicious. The method lends itself particularly well to strong-flavored, oily fish, such as the mackerel that are regularly caught off the coast of Goa.

INGREDIENTS

Serves 2–3
2–3 mackerel, filleted
2–3 fresh red chiles, seeded
4 macadamia nuts or 8 almonds
1 red onion, quartered
2 garlic cloves, crushed
½-inch piece fresh ginger root, peeled
   and sliced
1 teaspoon ground turmeric
3 tablespoons coconut oil or
   vegetable oil
3 tablespoons wine vinegar
⅔ cup water
salt
deep-fried onions and finely chopped
   fresh chile, to garnish
boiled rice or coconut rice,
   to serve, optional

1 Rinse the mackerel fillets in cold water and dry well on paper towels. Set aside.

----- COOK'S TIP -----

To make coconut rice, put 2 cups washed long grain rice in a heavy pan with ½ teaspoon salt, a 2-inch piece of lemongrass, and 2 tablespoons coconut cream. Add 3 cups boiling water and stir once to prevent the grains from sticking together. Simmer over a medium heat for 10–12 minutes. Remove the pan from the heat, cover, and set aside for 5 minutes. Fluff the rice with a fork or chopsticks before serving.

2 Put the chiles, macadamia nuts or almonds, onion, garlic, ginger, turmeric, and 1 tablespoon of the oil in a food processor and process to form a paste. Alternatively, pound them together in a mortar with a pestle to form a paste. Heat the remaining oil in a karahi or wok. Add the paste and cook for 1–2 minutes without browning. Stir in the vinegar and water and season with salt to taste. Bring to a boil, then lower the heat.

NUTRITIONAL NOTES	
Per Portion	
Energy	659cal
Fat	54.8g
Saturated Fat	8.1g
Carbohydrate	7.7g
Fiber	2.9g

3 Add the mackerel fillets to the sauce and simmer for 6–8 minutes, or until the fish is tender and cooked.

4 Transfer the fish to a warm serving dish. Bring the sauce to a boil and cook for 1 minute, or until it has reduced slightly. Pour the sauce over the fish, garnish with the deep-fried onions and chopped chile, and serve with rice, if desired.

Stuffed Fish

Every community in India prepares stuffed fish, but the Parsi version must rank top of the list. The most popular fish in India is the porgy. These are available from Indian and Chinese stores or large supermarkets.

INGREDIENTS

Serves 4

2 large porgy, or Dover or lemon sole
2 teaspoons salt
juice of 1 lemon

For the masala

1⅓ cups dry unsweetened shredded coconut
4 cups fresh cilantro, including the tender stalks
8 fresh green chiles (or to taste)
1 teaspoon cumin seeds
6 garlic cloves
2 teaspoons sugar
2 teaspoons lemon juice

1 Scale the fish and cut off the fins. Gut the fish and remove the heads, if desired. Using a sharp knife, make two diagonal gashes on each side, then pat dry with paper towels.

NUTRITIONAL NOTES	
Per Portion	
Energy	247cal
Fat	14.3g
Saturated Fat	10g
Carbohydrate	1.2g
Fiber	2.6g

2 Rub the fish inside and out with salt and lemon juice. Cover and let stand in a cool place for about 1 hour. Pat dry thoroughly.

3 For the masala, grind all the ingredients together using a mortar and pestle or food processor. Stuff the fish with most of the masala mixture. Rub the rest into the gashes and all over the fish on both sides.

4 Place each fish on a separate piece of greased aluminum foil. Tightly wrap the foil over each fish. Place in a steamer and steam for 20 minutes, or bake in a preheated oven for 30 minutes at 400°F, or until cooked. Remove the fish from the foil and serve hot.

COOK'S TIP

In India, this fish dish is always steamed wrapped in banana leaves. Banana leaves are generally available from Indian or Chinese grocery stores.

Pickled Fish Steaks

This dish is served cold, often as an appetizer. It also makes an ideal lunch when served with salad on a hot summer's day. Prepare it a day or two in advance to let the flavors blend.

INGREDIENTS

Serves 4–6
juice of 4 lemons
1-inch piece fresh ginger root, finely sliced
2 garlic cloves, crushed
2 fresh red chiles, finely chopped
3 fresh green chiles, finely chopped
4 thick firm fish steaks
4 tablespoons vegetable oil
4–6 curry leaves
1 onion, finely chopped
½ teaspoon ground turmeric
1 tablespoon ground coriander
⅔ cup pickling vinegar
1 tablespoon sugar
salt, to taste
salad greens and ½ tomato, to garnish

1 In a bowl, mix the lemon juice with the ginger, garlic, and chiles. Pat the fish dry and rub the mixture on all sides of the fish. Cover and marinate for 3–4 hours in the refrigerator.

2 Heat the oil in a skillet and fry the curry leaves, onion, turmeric, and coriander until the onion is translucent.

3 Place the fish steaks and their marinade in the skillet and spoon the onion mixture over them. Cook for 5 minutes, then turn the fish over gently to avoid damaging the steaks.

4 Pour in the vinegar and add the sugar and salt. Bring to a boil, then lower the heat and simmer until the fish is cooked. Carefully transfer the steaks to a large platter or individual serving dishes and pour over the vinegar mixture. Cool, then chill for 24 hours before serving, garnished with the salad greens and tomato.

NUTRITIONAL NOTES	
Per Portion	
Energy	233cal
Fat	12.1g
Saturated Fat	1.5g
Carbohydrate	3g
Fiber	0.5g

Fish and Vegetable Skewers

Threading firm fish cubes and
colorful vegetables on skewers
scores on several fronts. Not only
does the food look good, but it is
also easy to cook and serve.

INGREDIENTS

Serves 4

10 ounces firm white fish fillets,
    such as cod
3 tablespoons lemon juice
1 teaspoon grated fresh ginger root
2 fresh green chiles, very
    finely chopped
1 tablespoon very finely chopped
    fresh cilantro
1 tablespoon very finely chopped
    fresh mint
1 teaspoon ground coriander
1 teaspoon salt
1 red bell pepper
1 green bell pepper
½ medium cauliflower
8–10 white mushrooms
8 cherry tomatoes
1 tablespoon oil
1 lime, quartered, to garnish (optional)
yellow rice, to serve

NUTRITIONAL NOTES	
Per Portion	
Energy	131cal
Fat	4.40g
Saturated Fat	0.51g
Carbohydrate	7.20g
Fiber	3.00g

1 Cut the fish fillets into large and
even-size chunks.

2 In a large mixing bowl, stir
together the lemon juice, ginger,
chopped green chiles, fresh cilantro,
mint, ground coriander, and salt. Add
the fish chunks, cover, and let marinate
for about 30 minutes.

3 Cut the red and green bell peppers
into large squares and divide the
cauliflower into individual florets.

4 Preheat the broiler to hot. Arrange
the bell peppers, cauliflower
florets, white mushrooms, and cherry
tomatoes alternately with the fish
pieces on four skewers.

5 Brush the kebabs with the oil and
any remaining marinade. Transfer
to a flameproof dish and broil for
7–10 minutes, turning occasionally, or
until the fish is cooked right through.

6 Garnish with lime quarters, if
desired, and serve the kebabs
on a bed of yellow rice.

COOK'S TIP

Try baby corn instead of mushrooms and
broccoli or one of the new cultivated
cabbages in place of the cauliflower.

Cod in a Tomato Sauce

Dusting cod with spices before cooking gives it a delectable coating. The spices are echoed in the tomato sauce. Creamy mashed potatoes are the perfect accompaniment, although pilau rice is the traditional choice.

INGREDIENTS

Serves 4

2 tablespoons cornstarch
1 teaspoon salt
1 teaspoon garlic powder
1 teaspoon chili powder
1 teaspoon ground ginger
1 teaspoon ground fennel seeds
1 teaspoon ground coriander
2 medium cod fillets, each cut
  into 2 pieces
1 tablespoon oil
mashed potatoes, to serve

For the sauce

2 tablespoons tomato paste
1 teaspoon garam masala
1 teaspoon chili powder
1 teaspoon crushed garlic
1 teaspoon grated fresh ginger root
½ teaspoon salt
¾ cup water
1 tablespoon oil
1 bay leaf
3–4 black peppercorns
½-inch piece cinnamon stick
1 tablespoon chopped fresh
  cilantro
1 tablespoon chopped fresh mint

NUTRITIONAL NOTES	
Per Portion	
Energy	122cal
Fat	6.65g
Saturated Fat	0.89g
Carbohydrate	4.73g
Fiber	0.48g

1 Mix together the cornstrach, salt, garlic powder, chili powder, ground ginger, ground fennel seeds, and ground coriander.

2 Spoon the mixture over the four cod pieces and make sure that they are well coated in the spices.

3 Preheat the broiler to very hot, then reduce the heat slightly and place the fish fillets under the heat. After about 5 minutes spoon the oil over the cod. Turn the cod over and repeat the process. Cook for another 5 minutes, check that the fish is cooked through, and set aside.

4 Make the sauce by mixing together the tomato paste, garam masala, chili powder, garlic, ginger, salt, and water. Set aside.

5 Heat the oil in a karahi or wok and add the bay leaf, peppercorns, and cinnamon. Pour the sauce into the pan and reduce the heat to low. Bring slowly to a boil, stirring occasionally, then simmer for about 5 minutes. Gently slide the pieces of fish into this mixture and cook for another 2 minutes.

6 Finally, add the chopped fresh cilantro and mint and serve the dish with mashed potatoes.

Green Fish Curry

This dish combines all the flavors
of the East.

INGREDIENTS

Serves 4

¼ teaspoon ground turmeric
2 tablespoons lime juice
pinch of salt
4 cod fillets, skinned and cut
   into 2-inch chunks
1 onion, chopped
1 fresh green chile, sliced
1 garlic clove, crushed
¼ cup cashew nuts
½ teaspoon fennel seeds
2 tablespoons dry unsweetened
   shredded coconut
2 tablespoons oil
¼ teaspoon cumin seeds
¼ teaspoon ground coriander
¼ teaspoon ground cumin
¼ teaspoon salt
⅔ cup water
¾ cup plain low-fat yogurt
3 tablespoons finely chopped
   fresh cilantro, plus extra
   to garnish

1 Mix together the turmeric, lime
juice, and salt and rub over the fish.
Cover and marinate for 15 minutes.

2 Meanwhile, grind the onion, chile,
garlic, cashew nuts, fennel seeds,
and coconut to a paste. Spoon the paste
into a bowl and set aside.

3 Heat the oil in a large heavy pan
and fry the cumin seeds for
2 minutes, or until they begin to
splutter. Add the paste and fry for
5 minutes, then stir in the ground
coriander, cumin, salt, and water and
cook for about 2–3 minutes.

4 Stir in the yogurt and chopped
fresh cilantro. Simmer gently for
5 minutes. Add the fish pieces and
gently stir in. Cover and cook gently
for 10 minutes, until the fish is tender.
Garnish with more cilantro. This is
good served with a vegetable pilau.

NUTRITIONAL NOTES	
Per Portion	
Energy	244cal
Fat	14.30g
Saturated Fat	5.21g
Carbohydrate	5.40g
Fiber	1.70g

Cod with a Spicy Mushroom Sauce

Broiling fish before adding it to a sauce helps to prevent it from breaking up during the cooking process.

INGREDIENTS

Serves 4

4 cod fillets
1 tablespoon lemon juice
1 tablespoon oil
1 medium onion, chopped
1 bay leaf
4 black peppercorns, crushed
1 cup mushrooms
³/₄ cup plain low-fat yogurt
1 teaspoon grated fresh ginger root
1 teaspoon crushed garlic
½ teaspoon garam masala
½ teaspoon chili powder
1 teaspoon salt
1 tablespoon fresh cilantro leaves,
    to garnish
lightly cooked green beans,
    to serve

COOK'S TIP

If you can find tiny white mushrooms, they look very attractive in this fish dish. Alternatively, choose from the many other pretty colored varieties, such as cremini and oyster mushrooms.

2 Heat the oil in a karahi or wok and fry the onion with the bay leaf and peppercorns for 2–3 minutes. Lower the heat, then add the whole mushrooms and stir-fry for another 4–5 minutes.

3 In a bowl, mix together the yogurt, ginger, garlic, garam masala, chili, and salt. Pour this over the onions and stir-fry for 3 minutes.

1 Remove the skin and any bones from the cod fillets. Sprinkle with lemon juice, then par-cook under a preheated broiler for 5 minutes on each side. Remove the fillets from the heat and set aside.

NUTRITIONAL NOTES
Per Portion

Energy	170cal
Fat	4.32g
Saturated Fat	0.79g
Carbohydrate	7.67g
Fiber	1.00g

---

4 Add the cod fillets to the sauce and cook for another 2 minutes. Serve garnished with the fresh cilantro and accompanied by lightly cooked green beans.

Fish Fillets with a Chili Sauce

For this recipe, the fish fillets are first marinated with fresh cilantro and lemon juice, then cooked quickly before being served with a chili sauce.

INGREDIENTS

Serves 4

4 flatfish fillets, such as sole, or
 flounder, about 4 ounces each
2 tablespoons lemon juice
1 tablespoon finely chopped fresh
 cilantro
1 tablespoon oil
lime wedges and a fresh cilantro sprig,
 to garnish
yellow rice, to serve

For the sauce

1 teaspoon grated fresh ginger root
2 tablespoons tomato paste
1 teaspoon sugar
1 teaspoon salt
1 tablespoon chili sauce
1 tablespoon malt vinegar
1¼ cups water

NUTRITIONAL NOTES
Per Portion

Energy	149cal
Fat	5.40g
Saturated Fat	0.81g
Carbohydrate	3.90g
Fiber	0.20g

COOK'S TIP

Fresh cilantro and lemon juice are popular marinade ingredients for Indian fish dishes. For a subtle change in flavor, you can substitute an equal quantity of lime juice for the lemon juice in the marinade, and then garnish the dish with lemon wedges rather than lime.

1 Rinse and pat dry the fish fillets and place in a medium bowl. Add the lemon juice, cilantro, and oil and rub into the fish. Let marinate for at least 1 hour.

2 Make the sauce. Mix the grated ginger, tomato paste, sugar, salt, and chili sauce in a bowl. Stir in the vinegar and water.

3 Pour into a small pan and simmer gently over a low heat for about 6 minutes, stirring occasionally.

4 Meanwhile, preheat the broiler to medium. Lift the fish fillets out of the marinade and place them in a broiler pan. Broil for 5–7 minutes.

5 When the fish is cooked, arrange it on a warmed serving dish.

6 The chili sauce should now be fairly thick—about the consistency of a thick chicken soup.

7 Spoon the sauce over the fish fillets, garnish with the lime wedges and cilantro sprig, and serve immediately with yellow rice.

Fish Stew

Cooking fish with vegetables is a tradition in eastern regions of India. This hearty dish with potatoes, bell peppers, and tomatoes is perfect served with chapatis or parathas. You can try other combinations, such as green beans and spinach, but you need a starchy vegetable to thicken the sauce.

INGREDIENTS

Serves 4
2 tablespoons vegetable oil
1 teaspoon cumin seeds
1 onion, chopped
1 red bell pepper, thinly sliced
1 garlic clove, crushed
2 fresh red chiles, finely chopped
2 bay leaves
½ teaspoon salt
1 teaspoon ground cumin
1 teaspoon ground coriander
1 teaspoon chili powder
14-ounce can chopped tomatoes
2 large potatoes, cut into
   1-inch chunks
1¼ cups fish stock
4 cod fillets
chapatis, to serve

2 Add the salt, ground cumin, ground coriander, and chili powder to the onion and red pepper mixture. Cook for 1–2 minutes, stirring occasionally.

4 Add the fish fillets. Cover the pan and let simmer for 5–6 minutes, until the fish is just cooked. Serve hot with chapatis, if desired.

1 Heat the oil in a karahi, wok, or large pan over a medium heat and fry the cumin seeds for 30–40 seconds, until they begin to splutter. Add the onion, red pepper, garlic, chilies, and bay leaves and fry for 5–7 minutes more, until the onions have browned.

3 Stir in the tomatoes, potatoes, and fish stock. Bring to a boil, then lower the heat and simmer for another 10 minutes, or until the potatoes are almost tender.

NUTRITIONAL NOTES	
Per Portion	
Energy	251cal
Fat	7.2g
Saturated Fat	0.9g
Carbohydrate	8.4g
Fiber	1.8g

Fish in a Rich Tomato and Onion Sauce

It is difficult to imagine the cuisine of eastern India without fish. Bengal is as well known for its fish and shellfish dishes as Goa on the west coast. In both regions, coconut is used extensively, and the difference in the taste, as always, lies in the spicing. This onion-rich dish is known as kalia in Bengal, and a firm-fleshed fish is essential.

INGREDIENTS

Serves 4

1½ pounds steaks of firm-textured
   fish, such as tuna or monkfish,
   skinned
2 tablespoons lemon juice
1 teaspoon salt
1 teaspoon ground turmeric
vegetable oil, for shallow-frying
⅓ cup all-purpose flour
¼ teaspoon ground black pepper
4 tablespoons vegetable oil
2 teaspoons sugar
1 large onion, finely chopped
1 tablespoon grated fresh ginger root
1 tablespoon crushed garlic
1 teaspoon ground coriander
½–1 teaspoon hot chili powder
6-ounce can chopped tomatoes,
   including the juice
1¼ cups warm water
2 tablespoons chopped fresh cilantro
   leaves, to garnish
plain boiled rice, to serve

1 Cut the fish into 3-inch pieces and put into a large bowl. Add the lemon juice and sprinkle with half the salt and half the turmeric. Mix gently with your fingertips, then cover and set aside for 15 minutes.

2 Pour enough oil into a 9-inch skillet to cover the bottom to a depth of ½ inch and heat over a medium setting. Mix the flour and pepper and dust the fish in the seasoned flour. Add to the oil in a single layer and fry until browned on both sides and a light crust has formed. Drain on paper towels.

3 In a karahi, wok or large pan, heat 4 tablespoons oil. When the oil is hot, but not smoking, add the sugar and let it caramelize. As soon as the sugar is brown, add the onion, ginger, and garlic and fry for 7–8 minutes, until just beginning to colour. Stir regularly.

4 Add the ground coriander, chili powder, and the remaining turmeric. Stir-fry for about 30 seconds and add the tomatoes. Cook until the tomatoes are mushy and the oil separates from the spice paste, stirring regularly.

5 Pour the warm water and remaining salt into the pan, and bring to a boil. Carefully add the fried fish, reduce the heat to low, and simmer, uncovered, for 5–6 minutes.

6 Transfer to a serving dish and garnish with the cilantro leaves. Serve with plain boiled rice.

NUTRITIONAL NOTES	
Per Portion	
Energy	435cal
Fat	30.7g
Saturated Fat	3.8g
Carbohydrate	12.5g
Fiber	1.2g

Tuna Fish Curry

This not-very-authentic fish curry can be made in minutes. It's the ideal dish for a wannabe Bollywood star on a tight schedule.

Ingredients

Serves 4

1 onion
1 red bell pepper
1 green bell pepper
2 tablespoons oil
¼ teaspoon cumin seeds
½ teaspoon ground cumin
½ teaspoon ground coriander
½ teaspoon chili powder
¼ teaspoon salt
2 garlic cloves, crushed
14-ounce can tuna in brine, drained
1 fresh green chile, finely chopped
1-inch piece fresh ginger root, grated
¼ teaspoon garam masala
1 teaspoon lemon juice
2 tablespoons chopped fresh cilantro
fresh cilantro sprig, to garnish
pita bread and cucumber raita, to serve

_____ Cook's Tip _____

Place the pita bread on a broiler rack and broil until it just puffs up. It will be easy to split with a sharp knife.

Nutritional Notes
Per Portion

Energy	165cal
Fat	6.80g
Saturated Fat	0.97g
Carbohydrate	8.70g
Fiber	1.80g

1 Thinly slice the onion and the red and green bell peppers, discarding the seeds from the peppers.

2 Heat the oil in a karahi, wok, or heavy pan and stir-fry the cumin seeds for 2–3 minutes, until they begin to spit and splutter.

3 Add the ground cumin, coriander, chili powder, and salt and cook for 2–3 minutes. Then add the garlic, onion, and bell peppers.

4 Fry the vegetables, stirring from time to time, for 5–7 minutes, until the onion has browned.

5 Stir in the tuna, green chile, and ginger and cook for 5 minutes.

6 Add the garam masala, lemon juice, and chopped fresh cilantro and continue to cook the curry for another 3–4 minutes. Serve in warmed, split pita bread with the cucumber raita, garnished with a cilantro sprig.

Monkfish and Okra Curry

An interesting combination of flavors and textures is used in this delicious fish dish.

INGREDIENTS

Serves 4

1 pound monkfish
1 teaspoon ground turmeric
½ teaspoon chili powder
½ teaspoon salt
1 teaspoon cumin seeds
½ teaspoon fennel seeds
2 dried red chiles
2 tablespoons oil
1 onion, finely chopped
2 garlic cloves, crushed
4 tomatoes, peeled and finely chopped
⅔ cup water
8 ounces okra, trimmed and cut into 1-inch lengths
1 teaspoon garam masala
plain rice, to serve

1 Remove the membrane and bones from the monkfish, cut into 1-inch cubes, and place in a dish. Mix together the turmeric, chili powder, and ¼ teaspoon of the salt and rub the mixture all over the fish. Cover and marinate for 15 minutes.

COOK'S TIP

Coconut rice would also go very well with this fish curry, making a very attractive presentation. Or serve it with plain rice, if you prefer.

2 Put the cumin seeds, fennel seeds, and chiles in a large heavy pan and dry-roast the spice mixture for 3–4 minutes. Put the spices into a blender or use a pestle and mortar to grind to a coarse powder.

3 Heat 1 tablespoon of the oil in the pan and fry the monkfish cubes for 4–5 minutes. Remove with a slotted spoon and drain on paper towels.

NUTRITIONAL NOTES	
Per Portion	
Energy	193cal
Fat	8.80g
Saturated Fat	1.31g
Carbohydrate	9.40g
Fiber	3.60g

4 Add the remaining oil to the pan and fry the onion and garlic for about 5 minutes. Add the roasted spice powder and remaining salt and fry for 2–3 minutes. Stir in the tomatoes and water and simmer for 5 minutes.

5 Add the prepared okra and cook for 5–7 minutes.

6 Return the fish to the pan together with the garam masala. Cover and simmer for 5–6 minutes, or until the fish is tender. Serve immediately with plain rice.

Goan Fish Casserole

The cooking of Goa is a mixture of Portuguese and Indian; the addition of tamarind gives a slightly sour note to the spicy coconut sauce.

INGREDIENTS

Serves 4

1½ teaspoons ground turmeric
1 teaspoon salt
1 pound monkfish fillet, cut into
   8 pieces
1 tablespoon lemon juice
1 teaspoon cumin seeds
1 teaspoon coriander seeds
1 teaspoon black peppercorns
1 garlic clove, chopped
2-inch piece fresh ginger root,
   finely chopped
1 ounce tamarind paste
⅔ cup hot water
2 tablespoons vegetable oil
2 onions, halved and sliced lengthwise
1⅔ cups coconut milk
4 mild fresh green chiles, seeded and
   cut into thin strips
16 large shrimp, shelled
2 tablespoons chopped fresh cilantro
   leaves, to garnish

1 Mix together the ground turmeric and salt in a small bowl. Place the monkfish in a shallow dish and sprinkle over the lemon juice, then rub the turmeric and salt mixture over the fish fillets to coat them completely. Cover and chill until ready to cook.

2 Put the cumin seeds, coriander seeds, and black peppercorns in a blender or small food processor and grind to a powder. Add the garlic and ginger and process for a few seconds more.

3 Preheat the oven to 400°F. Mix the tamarind paste with the hot water and set aside.

4 Heat the oil in a skillet, add the onions, and cook for 5–6 minutes, until softened and golden. Transfer the onions to a shallow earthenware dish.

5 Add the fish fillets to the oil remaining in the skillet, and fry briefly over a high heat, turning them to seal on all sides. Remove the fish from the skillet and place on top of the onions.

6 Add the ground spice mixture to the skillet and cook over a medium heat, stirring constantly, for 1–2 minutes. Stir in the tamarind liquid, coconut milk, and chile strips and bring to a boil. Pour the sauce into the earthenware dish to coat the fish completely.

7 Cover the earthenware dish and cook the fish casserole in the oven for about 10 minutes.

8 Add the shrimp, pushing them into the liquid, then cover the dish again and return it to the oven for 5 minutes, or until the shrimp turn pink. Do not overcook them or they will toughen. Check the seasoning, sprinkle with cilantro leaves, and serve.

NUTRITIONAL NOTES	
Per Portion	
Energy	211cal
Fat	6.7g
Saturated Fat	1g
Carbohydrate	10.8g
Fiber	1.1g

Stir-fried Monkfish with Vegetables

Monkfish is an expensive fish, but it is ideal to use in stir-fry recipes because it is robust and will hold its shape when cooked.

INGREDIENTS

Serves 4
2 tablespoons oil
2 medium onions, sliced
1 teaspoon crushed garlic
1 teaspoon ground cumin
1 teaspoon ground coriander
1 teaspoon chili powder
6 ounces monkfish, cut into cubes
2 tablespoons fresh fenugreek leaves
2 tomatoes, seeded and sliced
1 zucchini, sliced
salt
1 tablespoon lime juice

1 Heat the oil in a karahi, wok, or heavy pan and fry the onions over a low heat until soft.

2 Meanwhile mix together the garlic, cumin, coriander, and chili powder. Add this spice mixture to the onions and stir-fry for about 1 minute.

3 Add the fish and continue to stir-fry for 3–5 minutes, until the fish is well cooked through.

NUTRITIONAL NOTES	
Per Portion	
Energy	86cal
Fat	2.38g
Saturated Fat	0.35g
Carbohydrate	8.32g
Fiber	1.87g

4 Add the fenugreek, tomatoes, and zucchini, followed by salt to taste, and stir-fry for another 2 minutes. Sprinkle with lime juice before serving.

_____ COOK'S TIP _____

Try to use monkfish for this recipe, but if it is not available, either cod or shrimp make a suitable substitute.

Fish and Shrimp in Herb Sauce

Bengalis are famous for their seafood dishes and like to use mustard oil in recipes because it imparts a unique taste, flavor, and aroma. No feast in Bengal is complete without one of these celebrated fish dishes.

INGREDIENTS

Serves 4–6

3 garlic cloves
2-inch piece fresh ginger root
1 large leek, roughly chopped
4 fresh green chiles
4 tablespoons mustard oil, or
  vegetable oil
1 tablespoon ground coriander
½ teaspoon fennel seeds
1 tablespoon crushed yellow
  mustard seeds, or 1 teaspoon
  mustard powder
¾ cup thick coconut milk
8 ounces huss or monkfish fillets,
  cut into thick chunks
8 ounces jumbo shrimp, shelled and
  deveined, with tails intact
salt, to taste
4 cups fresh cilantro, chopped
2 fresh green chiles, to garnish

1 In a food processor, grind the garlic, ginger, leek, and chiles to a coarse paste. Add a little vegetable oil if the mixture is too dry and process the mixture again.

2 In a large skillet, heat the mustard or vegetable oil with the paste until it is well blended. Keep a window open and take care not to overheat the mixture because any smoke from the mustard oil will sting the eyes.

3 Stir in the ground coriander, fennel seeds, mustard, and coconut milk. Gently bring the mixture to a boil, then lower the heat and simmer, uncovered, for about 5 minutes.

4 Add the fish chunks. Simmer for 2 minutes, then fold in the shrimp and cook until the shrimp turn a bright orange/pink color. Season with salt, fold in the fresh cilantro, and serve hot. Garnish with the fresh green chiles, if desired.

NUTRITIONAL NOTES	
Per Portion	
Energy	204cal
Fat	12.1g
Saturated Fat	1.6g
Carbohydrate	3.7g
Fiber	1.4g

Shrimp with Chayote in Turmeric Sauce

This delicious, attractively colored dish reveals the influence of Malaysian immigrants.

INGREDIENTS

Serves 4
1–2 chayotes or 2–3 zucchini
2 fresh red chiles, seeded
1 onion, quartered
1 teaspoon grated fresh
   ginger root
1 lemongrass stem, lower 2 inches
   sliced, top bruised
1 inch fresh turmeric, peeled
scant 1 cup water
lemon juice
14 fluid ounce can coconut milk
1 pound cooked, shelled shrimp
salt
fresh red chile shreds, to garnish
boiled rice, to serve

1 Peel the chayotes, remove the seeds, and cut into strips. If using zucchini, cut into 2-inch strips.

2 Grind the fresh red chiles, onion, ginger, sliced lemongrass, and the fresh turmeric to a paste in a food processor or with a mortar and pestle. Add the water to the paste mixture, with a squeeze of lemon juice, and salt to taste.

3 Pour into a pan. Add the top of the lemongrass stem. Bring to a boil and cook for 1–2 minutes. Add the chayote or zucchini pieces and cook for 2 minutes. Stir in the coconut milk. Taste and adjust the seasoning.

4 Stir in the shrimp and cook gently for 2–3 minutes. Remove the lemon grass stem. Garnish with shreds of chile and serve with rice.

NUTRITIONAL NOTES	
Per Portion	
Energy	132cal
Fat	1.3g
Saturated Fat	0.4g
Carbohydrate	9g
Fiber	1.1g

Mackerel in Tamarind

A delicious dish originating from Western India.

INGREDIENTS

Serves 6–8
2¼ pounds fresh mackerel
   fillets, skinned
2 tablespoons tamarind pulp,
   soaked in scant 1 cup water
1 onion
½-inch piece fresh ginger root
2 garlic cloves
1–2 fresh red chiles, seeded, or
   1 teaspoon chili powder
1 teaspoon ground coriander
1 teaspoon ground turmeric
½ teaspoon ground fennel seeds
1 tablespoon brown sugar
6–7 tablespoons oil
scant 1 cup coconut cream
fresh chile shreds, to garnish

1 Rinse the fish fillets in cold water and dry them well on paper towels. Put into a shallow dish and sprinkle with a little salt. Strain the tamarind and pour the juice over the fish fillets. Let stand for 30 minutes.

2 Quarter the onion, peel and slice the ginger, and peel the garlic. Grind the onion, ginger, garlic, and chiles or chili powder to a paste in a food processor or with a pestle and mortar. Add the ground coriander, turmeric, fennel seeds, and sugar.

3 Heat half of the oil in a skillet. Drain the fish fillets and fry for 5 minutes, or until cooked. Set aside.

4 Wipe out the pan and heat the remaining oil. Fry the spice paste, stirring all the time, until it gives off a spicy aroma. Do not let it brown. Add the coconut cream and simmer gently for a few minutes. Add the fish fillets and gently heat through.

5 Taste for seasoning and serve sprinkled with shredded chile.

NUTRITIONAL NOTES	
Per Portion	
Energy	482cal
Fat	38g
Saturated Fat	6.9g
Carbohydrate	3.6g
Fiber	0.4g

Pineapple Curry with Shrimp and Mussels

The delicate sweet and sour flavor of this curry comes from the pineapple and, although it seems an odd combination, it is delicious. Use the freshest shellfish that you can find.

INGREDIENTS

Serves 4–6

2½ cups coconut milk
2 tablespoons curry paste
1 tablespoon sugar
8 ounces jumbo shrimp,
  shelled and deveined
1 pound mussels, cleaned and
  beards removed
6 ounces fresh pineapple, finely crushed
  or chopped
2 bay leaves
2 fresh red chiles, chopped,
  to garnish
cilantro leaves, to garnish

1 In a large pan, bring half the coconut milk to a boil and heat, stirring, until it separates.

2 Add the curry paste and cook until fragrant. Add the sugar and continue to cook for 1 minute.

3 Stir in the rest of the coconut milk and bring back to a boil. Add the jumbo shrimp, mussels, pineapple, and bay leaves.

4 Reheat until boiling and then simmer for 3–5 minutes, until the shrimp are cooked and the mussels have opened. Remove any mussels that have not opened and throw them away. Discard the bay leaves if you like. Serve the curry garnished with chopped red chiles and cilantro leaves.

NUTRITIONAL NOTES	
Per Portion	
Energy	125cal
Fat	1.7g
Saturated Fat	0.5g
Carbohydrate	12.8g
Fiber	0.5g

Curried Shrimp in Coconut Milk

This is a currylike dish where the shrimp are cooked in a spicy coconut gravy.

INGREDIENTS

Serves 4–6

2½ cups coconut milk
2 tablespoons yellow curry paste
½ teaspoon salt
1 teaspoon sugar
1 pound jumbo shrimp, shelled, tails
  left intact, deveined
8 ounces cherry tomatoes
juice of ½ lime, to serve
red chile strips, to garnish
cilantro leaves, to garnish

1 Put half the coconut milk into a pan or wok and bring to a boil.

2 Add the curry paste to the coconut milk, stir until it disperses, then simmer for about 10 minutes.

3 Add the salt, sugar, and remaining coconut milk. Simmer for another 5 minutes.

NUTRITIONAL NOTES	
Per Portion	
Energy	129cal
Fat	1.4g
Saturated Fat	0.5g
Carbohydrate	9g
Fiber	0.6g

4 Add the shrimp and cherry tomatoes. Simmer very gently for about 5 minutes, until the shrimp are pink and tender.

5 Serve sprinkled with lime juice and garnish with the chiles and cilantro.

Red and White Shrimp with Green Vegetables

Reflecting the influence of
neighboring mainland China,
this colorful dish has a fresh and
pleasing flavor.

INGREDIENTS

Serves 4–6
1 pound shrimp
½ egg white
1 tablespoon cornstarch,
    mixed to a paste with
    2 teaspoons water
6 ounces snow peas
about 2½ cups vegetable oil
1 teaspoon light brown sugar
1 tablespoon finely chopped
    scallion
1 teaspoon finely chopped
    fresh ginger root
1 tablespoon light soy sauce
1 tablespoon Chinese rice wine
    or dry sherry
1 teaspoon chili bean sauce
1 tablespoon tomato paste
salt

1 Shell the shrimp and remove the
black intestinal vein that runs
down the back of each one. Place in
a bowl and mix with the egg white,
cornstarch paste, and a pinch of salt.

2 Trim the snow peas. If necessary,
string them, but keep the
pods whole.

3 Heat 2–3 tablespoons of the oil in
a preheated wok and stir-fry the
snow peas for about 1 minute.

4 Add the sugar and a little salt and
continue stirring for 1 more
minute. Remove and place in the
center of a warmed serving platter.

5 Add the remaining oil to the wok
and cook the shrimp for 1 minute.
Remove and drain.

6 Pour off all but about 1 tablespoon
of the oil. Add the scallion and
ginger to the wok.

NUTRITIONAL NOTES	
Per Portion	
Energy	551cal
Fat	50.7g
Saturated Fat	6.1g
Carbohydrate	1.8g
Fiber	1g

7 Return the shrimp to the wok and
stir-fry for 1 minute, then add the
soy sauce and rice wine or dry sherry.
Blend the mixture thoroughly. Transfer
half the shrimp to one end of the
serving platter.

8 Add the chili bean sauce and
tomato paste to the remaining
shrimp in the wok, blend well, and
place the "red" shrimp at the other
end of the platter. Serve.

_____ COOK'S TIP _____

All uncooked shrimp have an intestinal
tract that runs just beneath the outside
curve of the tail. The tract is not poisonous,
but it can taste unpleasant. It is, therefore,
best to remove it—devein. To do this, shell
the shrimp, leaving the tail intact. Score
each shrimp lightly along its length to
expose the tract. Remove the tract by lifting it out with the tip of a small knife.

Jumbo Shrimp with Onions and Curry Leaves

An excellent partner for this mildly spiced shrimp dish would be a basmati rice with vegetables.

INGREDIENTS

Serves 4
3 medium onions
1 tablespoon oil
6–8 curry leaves
¼ teaspoon onion seeds
1 fresh green chile, seeded and diced
1 fresh red chile, seeded and diced
12–16 frozen cooked jumbo shrimp, thawed and shelled
1 teaspoon shredded fresh ginger root
1 teaspoon salt
1 tablespoon fresh fenugreek leaves

1 Cut the onions into thin slices, using a sharp knife.

2 Heat the oil in a karahi, wok, or heavy pan and fry the onions with the curry leaves and onion seeds for about 3 minutes.

3 Add the diced green and red chiles, followed by the shrimp. Cook for about 5–7 minutes before adding the ginger and salt.

4 Finally, add the fenugreek leaves, cover, and cook for another 2–3 minutes before serving.

COOK'S TIP

For a quicker and less-expensive meal, you can use the prepared small shrimp sold in most supermarkets. Allow 4 ounces shrimp per person, and cook the shrimp for slightly less time than the larger ones.

NUTRITIONAL NOTES	
Per Portion	
Energy	97cal
Fat	3.29g
Saturated Fat	0.45g
Carbohydrate	9.39g
Fiber	1.58g

Shrimp and Snow Pea Stir-fry

Keep some shrimp in the freezer, because they are handy for a quick stir-fry, such as this one. Serve with rice or chapatis.

INGREDIENTS

Serves 4

1 tablespoon oil
2 medium onions, diced
1 tablespoon tomato paste
1 teaspoon Tabasco sauce
1 teaspoon lemon juice
1 teaspoon grated fresh ginger root
1 teaspoon crushed garlic
1 teaspoon chili powder
1 teaspoon salt
1 tablespoon chopped fresh
   cilantro
1½ cups frozen cooked shelled shrimp,
   thawed
12 snow peas, halved

1 Heat the oil in a karahi, wok, or heavy pan and fry the onions until golden brown.

2 Mix the tomato paste with 2 tablespoons water in a bowl. Stir in the Tabasco sauce, lemon juice, ginger, garlic, chili powder, and salt.

4 Add the cilantro, shrimp, and snow peas to the pan and stir-fry for 5–7 minutes, or until the sauce is thick. Serve immediately.

3 Lower the heat, pour the sauce over the onions, and stir-fry for a few seconds, until well mixed in.

NUTRITIONAL NOTES	
Per Portion	
Energy	108cal
Fat	3.48g
Saturated Fat	0.49g
Carbohydrate	7.96g
Fiber	1.60g

_____ COOK'S TIP _____

Snow peas, being small and almost flat, are perfect for stir-frying and are a popular ingredient in Indian cooking. They are particularly good stir-fried with shrimp, which need only minutes to heat through.

Jumbo Shrimp Bhoona

The unusual and delicious flavor of this dish is achieved by broiling the marinated shrimp to give them a chargrilled taste and then adding them to stir-fried onions and bell peppers.

Ingredients

Serves 4

3 tablespoons plain low-fat yogurt
1 teaspoon paprika
1 teaspoon grated fresh ginger root
salt
12–16 frozen cooked jumbo shrimp,
  thawed and shelled
1 tablespoon oil
3 medium onions, sliced
½ teaspoon fennel seeds,
  crushed
1 piece cinnamon stick
1 teaspoon crushed garlic
1 teaspoon chili powder
1 medium yellow bell pepper,
  seeded and roughly chopped
1 medium red bell pepper,
  seeded and roughly chopped
1 tablespoon fresh cilantro leaves,
  to garnish

COOK'S TIP

Although frozen cilantro is convenient and good to use in cooking, the fresh herb is more suitable for garnishes.

NUTRITIONAL NOTES
Per Portion

Energy	132cal
Fat	3.94g
Saturated Fat	0.58g
Carbohydrate	15.95g
Fiber	3.11g

1 In a bowl, mix the yogurt, paprika, ginger, and salt to taste. Pour this mixture over the shrimp and let marinate for 30–45 minutes.

2 Heat the oil in a karahi, wok, or heavy pan and fry the onions with the fennel seeds and the piece of cinnamon stick.

3 Lower the heat and add the garlic and chili powder. Stir over the heat until well mixed.

4 Add the peppers and stir-fry gently for 3–5 minutes.

5 Remove from the heat and transfer to a warm serving dish, discarding the cinnamon.

6 Preheat the broiler to medium. Put the shrimp in a broiler pan or flameproof dish and place under the heat to darken their tops and get a chargrilled effect. Add to the onion mixture, garnish with the cilantro, and serve.

Shrimp with Fenugreek and Seeds

Tender shellfish, crunchy vegetables, and a thick curry sauce combine to produce a dish rich in flavor and texture.

INGREDIENTS

Serves 4

2 tablespoons oil
1 teaspoon mixed fenugreek, mustard, and onion seeds
2 curry leaves
½ medium cauliflower, cut into small florets
8 baby carrots, halved lengthwise
6 new potatoes, thickly sliced
½ cup frozen peas
2 medium onions, sliced
2 tablespoons tomato paste
1½ teaspoons chili powder
1 teaspoon ground coriander
1 teaspoon grated fresh ginger root
1 teaspoon crushed garlic
1 teaspoon salt
2 tablespoons lemon juice
1 pound frozen, cooked, shelled shrimp, thawed
2 tablespoons chopped fresh cilantro
1 fresh red chile, seeded and sliced
½ cup plain low-fat yogurt

1 Heat the oil in a karahi, wok, or heavy pan. Lower the heat slightly and add the fenugreek, mustard, and onion seeds and the curry leaves.

2 Increase the heat and add the cauliflower, carrots, potatoes, and peas. Stir-fry quickly until browned, then remove the vegetables from the pan with a slotted spoon and drain on paper towels.

3 Add the onions to the oil left in the pan and fry over a medium heat until golden brown.

4 While the onions are cooking, mix together the tomato paste, chili powder, ground coriander, ginger, garlic, salt, and lemon juice and pour the paste onto the onions.

5 Add the shrimp and stir-fry over a low heat for about 5 minutes, or until they are heated through.

6 Add the fried vegetables to the pan and mix together well. Add the fresh cilantro and red chile and pour in the yogurt. Warm through and serve.

NUTRITIONAL NOTES	
Per Portion	
Energy	288cal
Fat	9.20g
Saturated Fat	1.34g
Carbohydrate	20.10g
Fiber	3.10g

Parsi Shrimp Curry

This dish comes from the west coast of India, where fresh shellfish are eaten in abundance. Fresh jumbo shrimp are ideal for this recipe.

INGREDIENTS

Serves 4–6

4 tablespoons vegetable oil
1 medium onion, finely sliced
6 cloves garlic, finely crushed
1 teaspoon chili powder
1½ teaspoons turmeric
2 medium onions, finely chopped
4 tablespoons tamarind juice
1 teaspoon mint sauce
1 tablespoon raw sugar
salt, to taste
1 pound fresh jumbo shrimp, shelled and deveined
3 cups fresh cilantro, chopped

2 Add the chopped onions to the skillet and fry until they become translucent, stirring frequently. Stir in the tamarind juice, mint sauce, sugar, and salt and gently simmer for a further 3 minutes.

3 Pat the shrimp dry with paper towels. Add to the spice mixture with a small amount of water and stir-fry until the shrimp turn a bright orange/pink color.

1 Heat the oil in a skillet and fry the sliced onion until golden brown. In a bowl, mix the garlic, chili powder, and turmeric with a little water to form a paste. Add to the browned onion and simmer for 3 minutes.

NUTRITIONAL NOTES	
Per Portion	
Energy	244cal
Fat	12g
Saturated Fat	1.4g
Carbohydrate	13.2g
Fiber	1.6g

4 When the shrimp are cooked, add the fresh cilantro and stir-fry over a high heat for a few minutes to thicken the sauce. Serve hot.

Cod and Shrimp Green Coconut Curry

This quick curry involves very little preparation, and takes just minutes to cook, so it's ideal if friends spring a surprise visit. If you can't find green masala curry paste at your local grocer or supermarket, simply substitute another variety—the curry will taste just as good.

INGREDIENTS

Serves 4

1½ pounds cod fillets, skinned
6 tablespoons green masala
   curry paste
¾ cup canned coconut milk
   or scant 1 cup coconut cream
6 ounces uncooked or cooked,
   shelled shrimp
fresh cilantro, to garnish
basmati rice, to serve

VARIATION

Any firm fish, such as monkfish, can be used instead of cod. Whole fish steaks can be cooked in the sauce, but allow an extra 5 minutes' cooking time and baste them with the sauce from time to time.

1 Using a sharp knife, cut the skinned cod fillets into 1½-inch pieces.

2 Put the green masala curry paste and the coconut milk or cream into a skillet. Heat to simmering and simmer gently for 5 minutes, stirring occasionally.

3 Add the cod pieces and shrimp (if uncooked) to the cream mixture and cook gently for 5 minutes. If using already cooked shrimp instead, add them to the pan after this time has elapsed, and heat through.

4 Spoon into a serving dish, garnish the curry with fresh cilantro, and serve immediately with basmati rice.

NUTRITIONAL NOTES	
Per Portion	
Energy	227cal
Fat	7.1g
Saturated Fat	1g
Carbohydrate	2.2g
Fiber	0g

Goan Shrimp Curry

The cuisine of Goa is well known for its excellent range of fish and shellfish-based recipes, such as this one for shrimp. Numerous varieties of fish and shellfish are found along the extended coastline and the network of inland waterways.

INGREDIENTS

Serves 4

1 tablespoon ghee or butter
2 garlic cloves, crushed
1 pound small shrimp, shelled
   and deveined
1 tablespoon peanut oil
4 cardamom pods
4 cloves
2-inch piece cinnamon stick
1 tablespoon mustard seeds
1 large onion, finely chopped
½–1 fresh red chile, seeded
   and sliced
4 tomatoes, peeled, seeded,
   and chopped
¾ cup fish stock or water
1½ cups coconut milk
3 tablespoons Fragrant Spice Mix
   (see Cook's Tip)
2–4 teaspoons chili powder
salt
turmeric-colored basmati rice,
   to serve

1 Melt the ghee or butter in a wok, karahi, or large pan, add the garlic, and stir over a low heat for a few seconds. Add the shrimp and stir-fry briskly to coat. Transfer to a plate and set aside.

2 In the same pan, heat the oil and fry the cardamom, cloves, and cinnamon for 2 minutes. Add the mustard seeds and fry for 1 minute.

3 Add the onion and chile and fry for 7–8 minutes, or until softened and lightly browned.

4 Add the remaining ingredients and bring to a slow simmer. Cook gently for 6–8 minutes and add the shrimp. Simmer for 5–8 minutes until the shrimp are cooked through. Serve the curry with basmati rice cooked with turmeric so that it is tinted a pale yellow color and is lightly flavored with the spice.

NUTRITIONAL NOTES	
Per Portion	
Energy	187cal
Fat	7g
Saturated Fat	2.8g
Carbohydrate	10.5g
Fiber	1.3g

COOK'S TIP

To make a Fragrant Spice Mix, dry-fry 1½ tablespoons coriander seeds, 1 tablespoon mixed peppercorns, 1 teaspoon cumin seeds, ¼ teaspoon fenugreek seeds, and ¼ teaspoon fennel seeds until aromatic, then grind finely in a spice mill.

Jumbo Shrimp Korma

This korma has a light, mild, creamy texture, and makes a good introduction to Indian cuisine for people who claim not to like spicy food.

INGREDIENTS

Serves 4

12–16 frozen cooked jumbo shrimp, thawed and shelled
3 tablespoons plain low-fat yogurt
3 tablespoons low-fat ricotta cheese
1 teaspoon ground paprika
1 teaspoon garam masala
1 tablespoon tomato paste
3 tablespoons coconut milk
1 teaspoon chili powder
⅔ cup water
1 tablespoon oil
1 teaspoon crushed garlic
1 teaspoon grated fresh ginger root
½ piece cinnamon stick
2 green cardamom pods
salt
1 tablespoon chopped fresh cilantro, to garnish

NUTRITIONAL NOTES	
Per Portion	
Energy	93cal
Fat	4.10g
Saturated Fat	0.57g
Carbohydrate	7.20g
Fiber	0.40g

COOK'S TIPS

• Paprika gives a good rich color to the curry without adding extra heat.
• Do not let the shrimp overcook in the sauce or they will toughen.

1 Drain the shrimp to ensure that all excess liquid is removed.

2 Place the yogurt, ricotta, paprika, garam masala, tomato paste, coconut milk, chili powder, and water in a bowl.

3 Blend all the ingredients together well and set aside.

4 Heat the oil in a karahi, wok, or heavy pan, add the garlic, ginger, cinnamon, cardamoms, and salt to taste and fry over a low heat.

5 Increase the heat and pour in the spice mixture. Bring to a boil, stirring occasionally.

6 Add the shrimp to the spices and continue to stir-fry until the shrimp have heated through and the sauce is thick. Serve garnished with the chopped fresh cilantro.

Rich Shrimp Curry

This is a rich, flavorful curry made with shrimp and a delicious blend of aromatic spices.

INGREDIENTS

Serves 4

1½ pounds shrimp
4 dried red chiles
½ cup dry unsweetened shredded
  coconut
1 teaspoon black mustard seeds
1 large onion, chopped
2 tablespoons oil
4 bay leaves
1-inch piece fresh ginger root,
  finely chopped
2 garlic cloves, crushed
1 tablespoon ground coriander
1 teaspoon chili powder
1 teaspoon salt
4 tomatoes, finely chopped
plain rice, to serve

1 Shell the shrimp and discard the shells. Run a sharp knife along the center back of each shrimp to make a shallow cut and carefully remove the thin black intestinal vein.

___ COOK'S TIP ___

Serve extra jumbo shrimp, unshelled, on the edge of each plate, for an attractive garnish. Cook them with the shelled shrimp until they turn pink.

2 Put the dried red chiles, coconut, mustard seeds, and onion in a large heavy skillet and dry-fry for 8–10 minutes, or until the spices begin to brown. The onion should turn a deep golden brown, but do not let it burn or it will taste bitter.

3 Tip the mixture into a food processor or blender and process to a coarse paste.

4 Heat the oil in the skillet and fry the bay leaves for 1 minute. Add the chopped ginger and the garlic and fry for 2–3 minutes.

NUTRITIONAL NOTES	
Per Portion	
Energy	289cal
Fat	12.13g
Saturated Fat	4.18g
Carbohydrate	12.77g
Fiber	2.65g

5 Add the coriander, chili powder, salt, and the coconut paste and fry gently for 5 minutes.

6 Stir in the chopped tomatoes and about ¾ cup water and simmer gently for 5–6 minutes, or until the sauce has thickened.

7 Add the shrimp and cook for about 4–5 minutes, or until they turn pink and the edges are curling slightly. Serve with plain boiled rice.

Basmati Mushroom Rice with Shrimp

Although mushrooms are not a particularly popular vegetable in India, they go well with the shrimp in this dish.

INGREDIENTS

Serves 4
⅔ cup basmati rice
1 tablespoon oil
1 medium onion, chopped
4 black peppercorns
1-inch cinnamon stick
1 bay leaf
¼ teaspoons cumin seeds
2 cardamom pods
1 teaspoon crushed garlic
1 teaspoon grated fresh ginger root
1 teaspoon garam masala
1 teaspoon chili powder
1½ teaspoons salt
1 cup frozen shelled shrimp, thawed
1½ cups mushrooms, cut into large pieces
2 tablespoons chopped fresh cilantro
½ cup plain low-fat yogurt
1 tablespoon lemon juice
½ cup frozen peas
1 cup water
1 fresh red chile, seeded and sliced, to garnish

1 Wash the rice well and let it soak in water for 30 minutes.

2 Heat the oil in a heavy pan and add the chopped onion, peppercorns, cinnamon, bay leaf, cumin seeds, cardamom pods, garlic, ginger, garam masala, chili powder, and salt. Lower the heat and stir-fry the mixture for 2–3 minutes.

3 Add the shrimp to the spice mixture and cook for 2 minutes, then add the mushrooms.

_____ COOK'S TIP _____

Basmati rice grows in the foothills of the Himalayas. The delicate, slender grains have a unique aroma and flavor. The rice cooks to light, separate, fluffy grains, making it perfect for a dish such as this.

<table>
<tr><td colspan="2" align="center">NUTRITIONAL NOTES
Per Portion</td></tr>
<tr><td>Energy</td><td>248cal</td></tr>
<tr><td>Fat</td><td>5.20g</td></tr>
<tr><td>Saturated Fat</td><td>0.99g</td></tr>
<tr><td>Carbohydrate</td><td>40.04g</td></tr>
<tr><td>Fiber</td><td>1.85g</td></tr>
</table>

4 Stir in the cilantro and yogurt, followed by the lemon juice and peas, and cook for another 2 minutes.

5 Drain the rice and add it to the shrimp mixture. Pour in the water, cover the pan, and cook over a medium heat for about 15 minutes, checking once to make sure that the rice has not stuck to the bottom of the pan.

6 Remove the pan from the heat and let stand, still covered, for about 5 minutes. Transfer to a serving dish and serve garnished with the sliced red chile.

Ragout of Shellfish with Coconut Milk

Green curry paste, made with green chiles and plenty of fresh cilantro, is what gives this seafood dish its unique flavor. This recipe recalls the days when the French were influential in India, first through their trading interests, and later, when they ruled Pondicherry.

INGREDIENTS

Serves 4–6

1 pound mussels in their shells
4 tablespoons water
8 ounces medium cuttlefish or squid
1⅔ cups coconut milk
1¼ cups chicken or vegetable stock
12 ounces monkfish, hoki, or red
   snapper, skinned
5 ounces uncooked or cooked shrimp
   tails, shelled and deveined
3 ounces green beans, trimmed
   and cooked
1 tomato, peeled, seeded, and
   roughly chopped
torn basil leaves, to garnish
boiled rice, to serve

For the green curry paste

2 teaspoons coriander seeds
½ teaspoon cumin seeds
3–4 medium fresh green chiles,
   finely chopped
4 teaspoons sugar
2 teaspoons salt
¾-inch fresh ginger root, peeled and
   finely chopped
3 garlic cloves, crushed
1 medium onion, finely chopped
2 cups fresh cilantro leaves,
   finely chopped
½ teaspoon grated nutmeg
2 tablespoons vegetable oil

1 Scrub the mussels in cold running water and pull off the "beards." Discard any mussels that do not shut when sharply tapped. Put them in a pan with the water, cover, and cook for 6–8 minutes. Discard any mussels that remain closed and remove three-quarters of the mussels from their shells. Set aside. Strain the cooking liquid and set aside.

2 To prepare the cuttlefish or squid, trim off the tentacles and discard the gut. Remove the cuttle shell from inside the body and rub off the skin. Cut the body open and score in a crisscross pattern with a sharp knife. Cut into strips and set aside.

3 To make the green curry paste, dry-fry the coriander and cumin seeds in a karahi or wok. Grind the chiles with the sugar and salt in a mortar with a pestle or in a food processor. Add the coriander and cumin seeds, ginger, garlic, and onion and grind to a paste. Add the fresh cilantro, nutmeg, and oil and combine thoroughly.

4 Strain the coconut milk and pour the thin liquid into a karahi or wok with the stock and reserved cooking liquid from the mussels. Reserve the thick part of the coconut milk. Add 4–5 tablespoons of the green curry paste to the wok and bring the mixture to a boil. Boil rapidly for a few minutes, until the liquid has reduced completely.

5 Add the thick part of the coconut milk. Stir well, then add the cuttlefish or squid and monkfish, hoki, or red snapper. Simmer for 15–20 minutes. Then add the shrimp, mussels, beans, and tomato. Simmer for 2–3 minutes until heated through. Transfer to a warmed serving dish, garnish with torn basil leaves, and serve immediately with boiled rice.

NUTRITIONAL NOTES	
Per Portion	
Energy	270cal
Fat	8.6g
Saturated Fat	1.5g
Carbohydrate	9g
Fiber	0.9g

Shrimp Salad with Curry Dressing

Curry spices add an unexpected twist to this salad. The warm flavors combine especially well with the sweet shellfish and grated apple. Curry paste is needed here instead of curry powder because there is no cooking, which is necessary for bringing out the flavors of powdered spices.

INGREDIENTS

Serves 4

1 ripe tomato
½ iceberg lettuce
1 small onion
1 small bunch fresh cilantro
1 tablespoon lemon juice
1 pound shelled, cooked shrimp
1 apple
salt
8 whole cooked shrimp,
　8 lemon wedges, and 4 fresh
　coriander sprigs, to garnish

For the curry dressing

5 tablespoons mayonnaise
1 teaspoon mild curry paste
1 tablespoon ketchup

1 To peel the tomato, cut a cross in the skin with a knife and immerse in boiling water for 30 seconds. Drain and cool under cold water. Peel off the skin. Cut the tomato in half and squeeze each half gently to remove the seeds. Discard them, then cut each tomato half into large dice.

2 Wash the lettuce leaves, place them in a soft dish towel, and gently pat them dry. Shred the leaves finely and put in a large bowl.

3 Finely chop the onion and cilantro. Add to the bowl together with the tomato, moisten with lemon juice, and season with salt.

4 To make the dressing, combine the mayonnaise, curry paste, and ketchup in a small bowl. Add 2 tablespoons water to thin the dressing and season to taste with salt.

5 Combine the shrimp with the dressing and stir gently so that all the shrimp are evenly coated with the dressing.

6 Quarter and core the apple and grate into the shrimp and dressing mixture.

7 Distribute the shredded lettuce mixture among four serving plates or bowls. Pile the shrimp mixture in the center of each and decorate each with two whole shrimp, two lemon wedges, and a sprig of cilantro.

NUTRITIONAL NOTES	
Per Portion	
Energy	73cal
Fat	0.6g
Saturated Fat	0.1g
Carbohydrate	6.8g
Fiber	1.3g

COOK'S TIP

Fresh cilantro is inclined to wilt if it is kept out of water for too long. Put it in a jar of water, cover with a plastic bag, and place in the refrigerator, and it will stay fresh for several days.

Poultry Dishes

SOME OF the most deliciously spiced Indian dishes are based on chicken. Perhaps because this bird is such a familiar (and inexpensive) ingredient, chicken curries have become the mainstay of menus at Indian restaurants the world over.

Curiously, some of the most popular poultry dishes in the West, such as Chicken Tikka Masala, are little known in what many assume to be their country of origin, but are now being introduced to India by travelers from Great Britain. More authentic Indian dishes include Chicken Dopiaza, Chicken Jalfrezi, and the milder kormas, whose rich content can be adapted by using low-fat yogurt instead of cream.

All of these, plus some less well known—but equally sumptuous—dishes, are to be found in the pages that follow. Whether you favor a Red Hot Chicken Curry or a quick and easy one-pot Chicken Pilau, these flavorful dishes are equally suited to family meals or more formal occasions.

Tandoori Chicken

This is a delicious Indian/Pakistani chicken dish that is cooked in a clay oven called a tandoor. It is extremely popular in the West and appears on the majority of restaurant menus. Although the authentic tandoori flavor is difficult to achieve in a conventional oven, this version still makes a very tasty dish.

INGREDIENTS

Serves 4
4 chicken quarters, skinned
¾ cup plain low-fat yogurt
1 teaspoon garam masala
1 teaspoon grated fresh ginger root
1 teaspoon crushed garlic
1½ teaspoons chili powder
¼ teaspoon ground turmeric
1 teaspoon ground coriander
1 tablespoon lemon juice
1 teaspoon salt
few drops of red food coloring
1 tablespoon oil
mixed salad greens and lime wedges, to garnish

1 Rinse and pat dry the chicken quarters. Make two deep slits in the flesh of each piece, place in a dish, and set aside.

COOK'S TIP

The traditional bright red color is derived from food coloring. This is only optional and may be omitted if you prefer.

2 Mix together the yogurt, garam masala, ginger, garlic, chili powder, turmeric, coriander, lemon juice, salt, red food coloring, and oil, and beat so that all the ingredients are well combined.

NUTRITIONAL NOTES	
Per Portion	
Energy	300cal
Fat	12.00g
Saturated Fat	3.39g
Carbohydrate	5.90g
Fiber	0.20g

3 Cover the chicken quarters with the spice mixture, cover, and let marinate for about 3 hours.

4 Preheat the oven to 475°F. Transfer the chicken pieces to an ovenproof dish.

5 Bake the chicken in the oven for 20–25 minutes, or until the chicken is cooked all the way through and evenly browned on top.

6 Remove from the oven, transfer to a serving dish, and garnish with the salad greens and lime wedges.

Chicken Nan Pockets

This quick-and-easy dish is ideal for a light snack, lunch, or supper. For speed, use the ready-to-bake nans available in many supermarkets and Asian stores, but beware that because they are larger than home-cooked nan, they will contain more fat.

INGREDIENTS

Serves 4

4 small nan, about 3½ ounces each
3 tablespoons plain low-fat yogurt
1½ teaspoons garam masala
1 teaspoon chili powder
1 teaspoon salt
3 tablespoons lemon juice
1 tablespoon chopped fresh
  cilantro
1 fresh green chile, chopped
1 pound boneless chicken,
  skinned and cubed
8 onion rings
2 tomatoes, quartered
½ white cabbage, shredded

For the garnish
mixed salad greens
2 small tomatoes, halved
lemon wedges
fresh cilantro

NUTRITIONAL NOTES
Per Portion

Energy	472cal
Fat	15.30g
Saturated Fat	6.46g
Carbohydrate	53.40g
Fiber	4.20g

COOK'S TIP

For a version that is even lower in fat, substitute whole-wheat or plain pita bread for the nan. Warm the pita in the oven, split to form a pocket, and then follow the recipe from step 2.

1 Cut into the middle of each nan to make a pocket, then set aside.

2 Mix together the yogurt, garam masala, chili powder, salt, lemon juice, fresh cilantro, and chopped green chile. Pour the marinade over the chicken, cover, and let marinate for about 1 hour.

3 Preheat the broiler to very hot, then lower to medium. Put the chicken in a pan or flameproof dish lined with aluminum foil. Broil for 15–20 minutes, until tender and fully cooked, turning the chicken twice.

4 Remove from the heat and fill each nan with the chicken and then with the onion rings, tomatoes, and cabbage. Serve garnished with mixed salad greens, tomato halves, lemon wedges, and cilantro.

Goan Chicken Curry

Lines of swaying palm trees
and the raised borders of a vast
patchwork of paddy fields are
just two of the features typical
of the superb landscape of Goa.
Not surprisingly, coconut, in all
of its forms, is widely used to
enrich Goan cuisine.

INGREDIENTS

Serves 4

1½ cups dry unsweetened shredded
　coconut
2 tablespoons vegetable oil
½ teaspoon cumin seeds
4 black peppercorns
1 tablespoon fennel seeds
1 tablespoon coriander seeds
2 onions, finely chopped
½ teaspoon salt
8 small chicken pieces, such as thighs
　and drumsticks, skinned
fresh cilantro sprigs and lemon wedges,
　to garnish

1 Put the shredded coconut in a
bowl with 3 tablespoons water.
Let soak for 15 minutes.

2 Heat 1 tablespoon of the oil in a
karahi, wok, or large pan. Fry the
cumin seeds, peppercorns, and fennel
and coriander seeds over a low heat for
3–4 minutes, until they begin to splutter.

3 Add the finely chopped onions
and fry for about 5 minutes,
stirring occasionally, until the onion
has softened and turned opaque.

4 Stir in the coconut, along with
the soaking water and salt, and
continue to fry for another 5 minutes,
stirring occasionally to prevent the
mixture from sticking to the pan.

5 Put the coconut mixture into a
food processor or blender and
process to form a coarse paste. Spoon
into a bowl and set aside until required.

6 Heat the remaining oil and fry the
chicken for 10 minutes. Add the
coconut paste and cook over a low heat
for 15–20 minutes, or until the coconut
mixture is golden brown and the
chicken is tender.

7 Transfer the curry to a warmed
serving plate, and garnish with
sprigs of fresh cilantro and lemon
wedges. Mint and coconut chutney,
plain boiled rice, or a lentil dish would
all make good accompaniments.

_____ COOK'S TIP _____

If you prefer, make the spiced coconut
mixture the day before and chill it in the
refrigerator, then continue from step 6.

NUTRITIONAL NOTES
Per Portion

Energy	305cal
Fat	21.4g
Saturated Fat	12.1g
Carbohydrate	1.2g
Fiber	2.6g

Chicken Dopiaza

Dopiaza translates literally as "two onions" and describes this chicken dish in which two types of onion—large and small—are used at different stages during the cooking process.

INGREDIENTS

Serves 4

2 tablespoons oil
8 small onions, halved
2 bay leaves
8 green cardamom pods
4 cloves
3 dried red chiles
8 black peppercorns
2 onions, finely chopped
2 garlic cloves, crushed
1-inch piece fresh ginger root, finely chopped
1 teaspoon ground coriander
1 teaspoon ground cumin
½ teaspoon ground turmeric
1 teaspoon chili powder
½ teaspoon salt
4 tomatoes, peeled and finely chopped
½ cup water
8 chicken pieces, such as thighs and drumsticks, skinned
plain rice, to serve

COOK'S TIP

Soak the small onions in boiling water for 2–3 minutes to make them easier to peel.

NUTRITIONAL NOTES
Per Portion

Energy	352cal
Fat	15.10g
Saturated Fat	3.67g
Carbohydrate	22.60g
Fiber	3.90g

1 Heat half the oil in a large heavy pan or wok and fry the small onions for 10 minutes, or until golden brown. Remove and set aside.

3 Add the tomatoes and water and simmer for 5 minutes, until the sauce thickens. Add the chicken and cook for about 15 minutes.

2 Add the remaining oil and fry the bay leaves, cardamoms, cloves, chiles, and peppercorns for 2 minutes. Add the onions, garlic, and ginger and fry for 5 minutes. Stir in the ground spices and salt and cook for 2 minutes.

4 Add the reserved small onions, then cover and cook for another 10 minutes, or until the chicken is cooked through. Spoon the mixture onto a serving dish or individual plates. Serve with plain boiled rice.

Chicken Dhansak

Dhansak curries originate from the Parsee community and traditionally include lentils.

INGREDIENTS

Serves 4

½ cup green lentils
2 cups chicken stock
1 tablespoon oil
1 teaspoon cumin seeds
2 curry leaves
1 onion, finely chopped
1-inch piece fresh ginger
    root, chopped
1 fresh green chile, finely chopped
1 teaspoon ground cumin
1 teaspoon ground coriander
¼ teaspoon salt
¼ teaspoon chili powder
14-ounce can chopped tomatoes
8 chicken pieces, skinned
6 tablespoons chopped fresh
    cilantro
1 teaspoon garam masala
plain and yellow rice, to serve

1 Rinse the lentils under cold running water. Put into a pan with the stock. Bring to a boil, cover, and simmer for about 15–20 minutes. Put the lentils and stock to one side.

NUTRITIONAL NOTES	
Per Portion	
Energy	328cal
Fat	10.80g
Saturated Fat	2.54g
Carbohydrate	19.70g
Fiber	3.50g

2 Heat the oil in a large heavy pan and fry the cumin seeds and curry leaves for 2 minutes. Add the onion, ginger, and chile and fry for about 5 minutes. Stir in the cumin, ground coriander, salt and chili powder with 2 tablespoons water.

3 Add the tomatoes and the chicken pieces to the spices. Cover and cook for 10–15 minutes.

4 Add the lentils and stock, half the chopped fresh cilantro, and the garam masala. Cook for another 10 minutes, or until the chicken is tender. Garnish with the remaining fresh cilantro and serve with spiced plain and yellow rice.

Hot Chile Chicken

Not for the faint-hearted, this fiery, hot curry is made with a spicy chili masala paste.

INGREDIENTS

Serves 4

2 tablespoons tomato paste
2 garlic cloves, roughly chopped
2 fresh green chiles, roughly chopped
5 dried red chiles
½ teaspoon salt
¼ teaspoon sugar
1 teaspoon chili powder
½ teaspoon paprika
1 tablespoon curry paste
1 tablespoon oil
½ teaspoon cumin seeds
1 onion, finely chopped
2 bay leaves
1 teaspoon ground coriander
1 teaspoon ground cumin
¼ teaspoon ground turmeric
14-ounce can chopped tomatoes
⅔ cup water
8 chicken thighs, skinned
1 teaspoon garam masala
sliced fresh green chiles, to garnish
chapatis and plain low-fat yogurt,
    to serve

1 Put the tomato paste, chopped garlic cloves, fresh green chiles, and the dried red chiles into a food processor or blender.

2 Add the salt, sugar, chili powder, paprika, and curry paste. Process all the ingredients to a smooth paste, stopping once or twice to scrape down any of the mixture that has stuck to the sides of the bowl.

3 Heat the oil in a large heavy pan and fry the cumin seeds for 2 minutes. Add the onion and bay leaves and fry for about 5 minutes.

4 Add the chili paste and fry for 2–3 minutes. Add the ground coriander, cumin, and turmeric and cook for 2 minutes. Tip in the tomatoes.

5 Pour in the water and stir to mix. Bring to a boil and simmer for 5 minutes, until the sauce thickens.

6 Add the chicken and garam masala. Cover and simmer for 25–30 minutes, until the chicken is tender. Garnish with sliced green chiles and serve with chapatis and plain low-fat yogurt.

NUTRITIONAL NOTES	
Per Portion	
Energy	290cal
Fat	13.00g
Saturated Fat	3.50g
Carbohydrate	11.60g
Fiber	1.40g

Chicken Saag

A mildly spiced dish using a popular combination of spinach and chicken. This recipe is best made using fresh spinach.

INGREDIENTS

Serves 4

8 ounces fresh spinach leaves,
    washed but not dried
1-inch piece fresh ginger root, grated
2 garlic cloves, crushed
1 fresh green chile,
    roughly chopped
scant 1 cup water
1 tablespoon oil
2 bay leaves
1/4 teaspoon black peppercorns
1 onion, finely chopped
4 tomatoes, peeled and
    finely chopped
2 teaspoons curry powder
1 teaspoon salt
1 teaspoon chili powder
3 tablespoons plain low-fat yogurt
8 chicken thighs, skinned
nan bread, to serve
plain low fat-yogurt and chili powder,
    to garnish

1 Cook the spinach leaves, without extra water, in a tightly covered pan for 5 minutes. Put the cooked spinach, ginger, garlic, and chile with 1/4 cup of the measured water into a food processor or blender and process to a thick paste. Set aside.

2 Heat the oil in a large heavy pan, add the bay leaves and black peppercorns, and fry for 2 minutes. Stir in the onion and fry for another 6–8 minutes, or until the onion has browned.

3 Add the tomatoes and simmer for about 5 minutes.

4 Stir in the curry powder, salt, and chili powder. Cook for 2 minutes over a medium heat, stirring once or twice.

NUTRITIONAL NOTES	
Per Portion	
Energy	283cal
Fat	12.70g
Saturated Fat	3.48g
Carbohydrate	9.70g
Fiber	3.10g

5 Stir in the spinach paste and the remaining measured water, then simmer for 5 minutes.

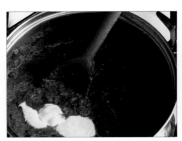

6 Add the yogurt, 1 tablespoon at a time, and simmer for 5 minutes.

7 Add the chicken thighs and stir to coat them in the sauce. Cover and cook for 25–30 minutes, until the chicken is tender. Serve on nan bread, drizzle over some yogurt, and dust with chili powder.

Jeera Chicken

Here is an aromatic dish with
a delicious, distinctive taste of
cumin. Serve simply with a
cooling cucumber raita.

INGREDIENTS

Serves 4
3 tablespoons cumin seeds
1 tablespoon oil
½ teaspoon black peppercorns
4 green cardamom pods
2 fresh green chiles, finely
   chopped
2 garlic cloves, crushed
1-inch piece fresh ginger root, grated
1 teaspoon ground coriander
2 teaspoons ground cumin
½ teaspoon salt
8 chicken pieces, skinned
1 teaspoon garam masala
fresh cilantro and chili powder,
   to garnish
cucumber raita, to serve

1 Dry-roast 1 tablespoon of the
cumin seeds for 5 minutes and
then set aside.

___ COOK'S TIP ___

Dry-roast the cumin seeds in a small, heavy
skillet over a medium heat, stirring them
until they turn a few shades darker and give
off a wonderful roasted aroma.

2 Heat the oil in a large heavy pan
or wok and fry the remaining
cumin seeds, black peppercorns, and
cardamoms for about 2–3 minutes.

3 Add the chiles, garlic, and ginger
and fry for about 2 minutes.

4 Add the ground coriander, ground
cumin, and salt. Stir well, then
cook for another 2–3 minutes.

5 Add the chicken and stir to coat
the pieces in the sauce. Cover and
simmer for 20–25 minutes.

6 Add the garam masala and reserved
toasted cumin seeds and cook for
another 5 minutes. Garnish with fresh
cilantro and chili powder and serve
with cucumber raita.

NUTRITIONAL NOTES	
Per Portion	
Energy	286cal
Fat	14.10g
Saturated Fat	3.19g
Carbohydrate	7.60g
Fiber	0.10g

Chicken in Cashew Nut Sauce

This strongly flavored chicken dish has a deliciously thick and nutty sauce, and is best served with plain boiled rice.

INGREDIENTS

Serves 4

2 medium onions
2 tablespoons tomato paste
½ cup cashew nuts
1½ teaspoons garam masala
1 teaspoon crushed garlic
1 teaspoon chili powder
1 tablespoon lemon juice
¼ teaspoon ground turmeric
1 teaspoon salt
1 tablespoon plain low-fat yogurt
2 tablespoons oil
2 tablespoons chopped fresh cilantro
1 tablespoon golden raisins
1 pound boneless chicken, skinned and cubed
2½ cups white mushrooms
1¼ cups water

1 Cut the onions into quarters, place in a food processor or blender, and process for about 1 minute.

_____ COOK'S TIP _____

Cut the chicken into small, equal-size cubes for quick and even cooking.

2 Add the tomato paste, cashew nuts, garam masala, garlic, chili powder, lemon juice, turmeric, salt, and yogurt to the processed onions.

3 Process the spiced onion mixture in the food processor for another 1–1½ minutes.

4 In a heavy pan or karahi, heat the oil, lower the heat to medium, and pour in the spice mixture from the food processor. Fry for 2 minutes, lowering the heat more if necessary.

5 When the spice mixture is lightly cooked, add half the chopped fresh cilantro, the golden raisins, and the chicken cubes and continue to stir-fry for another 1 minute.

6 Add the mushrooms, pour in the water, and bring to a simmer. Cover the pan and cook over a low heat for about 10 minutes.

7 After this time, check that the chicken is cooked through and the sauce is thick. Cook for a little longer if necessary, then spoon into a serving bowl. Garnish with the remaining fresh cilantro and serve.

NUTRITIONAL NOTES	
Per Portion	
Energy	286cal
Fat	13.30g
Saturated Fat	2.39g
Carbohydrate	12.90g
Fiber	2.10g

Chicken with Green Mango

Green, unripe mango is used for making various dishes on the Indian subcontinent, including pickles, chutneys, and some meat, chicken, and vegetable dishes. This is a simple chicken dish to prepare and is good served with rice and dhal.

INGREDIENTS

Serves 4

1 medium green mango
1 pound boneless chicken, skinned and cubed
¼ teaspoon onion seeds
1 teaspoon grated fresh ginger root
½ teaspoon crushed garlic
1 teaspoon chili powder
¼ teaspoon ground turmeric
1 teaspoon salt
1 teaspoon ground coriander
2 tablespoons oil
2 medium onions, sliced
4 curry leaves
1¼ cups water
2 medium tomatoes, quartered
2 fresh green chiles, chopped
2 tablespoons chopped fresh cilantro

1 To prepare the mango, peel the skin and slice the flesh thickly. Discard the pit from the middle. Place the mango slices in a small bowl, cover, and set aside.

2 Place the chicken cubes in a bowl and add the onion seeds, ginger, garlic, chili powder, turmeric, salt, and ground coriander. Mix to coat the chicken with the spices, then add half the mango slices.

3 In a medium heavy pan, heat the oil and fry the sliced onions until golden brown. Add the curry leaves and stir lightly.

4 Gradually add the chicken pieces and mango, stirring all the time.

5 Pour in the water, lower the heat, and cook for about 12–15 minutes, stirring occasionally, until the chicken is cooked through and the water has been absorbed.

6 Add the remaining mango slices, the tomatoes, green chiles, and fresh cilantro and serve hot.

VARIATION

A good, firm cooking apple can be used instead of unripe green mango, if you like. Prepare and cook in the same way.

NUTRITIONAL NOTES
Per Portion

Energy	281cal
Fat	11.20g
Saturated Fat	2.44g
Carbohydrate	20.60g
Fiber	3.60g

Chicken Tikka Masala

This is another of those dishes that is celebrated in the West but less well known in India. It is said to be Great Britain's favorite chicken dish. In this version, tender chicken pieces are cooked in a creamy, spicy tomato sauce and served on nan bread.

INGREDIENTS

Serves 4

1½ pounds chicken breast
   fillets, skinned
6 tablespoons tikka paste
½ cup plain low-fat yogurt
1 tablespoon oil
1 onion, chopped
1 garlic clove, crushed
1 fresh green chile, seeded
   and chopped
1-inch piece fresh ginger root, grated
1 tablespoon tomato paste
1 cup water
a little melted ghee or butter
1 tablespoon lemon juice
fresh cilantro sprigs, plain low-fat
   yogurt and toasted cumin seeds,
   to garnish
nan bread, to serve

NUTRITIONAL NOTES	
Per Portion	
Energy	315cal
Fat	12.50g
Saturated Fat	4.00g
Carbohydrate	7.50g
Fiber	0.60g

COOK'S TIPS

• Make your own paste, using the basic recipe in the introduction to this book, or use a good-quality store-bought paste.
• Soak the wooden skewers in cold water before using to prevent them from burning while under the broiler.

1 Remove any visible fat from the chicken and cut the meat into 1-inch cubes. Mix 3 tablespoons of the tikka paste and 4 tablespoons of the yogurt into a bowl. Add the chicken and let marinate for 20 minutes.

2 Heat the oil in a heavy pan and fry the onion, garlic, chile, and ginger for 5 minutes. Add the remaining tikka paste and fry for 2 minutes. Stir in the tomato paste and water, bring to a boil, and simmer for 15 minutes.

3 Meanwhile, thread the chicken pieces onto wooden kebab skewers. Preheat the broiler.

4 Brush the chicken pieces lightly with melted ghee or butter and cook under a medium heat for 15 minutes, turning the skewers occasionally.

5 Put the tikka sauce into a food processor or blender and process until smooth. Return to the pan.

6 Add the remaining low-fat yogurt and the lemon juice to the pan, then remove the broiled chicken from the skewers and add to the pan. Let simmer for about 5 minutes. Garnish with the fresh cilantro, yogurt, and toasted cumin seeds and serve on nan bread.

Spicy Masala Chicken

These tender chicken pieces have a sweet-and-sour taste. Serve cold with a salad and rice or hot with potatoes.

INGREDIENTS

Serves 6

12 chicken thighs, skinned
6 tablespoons lemon juice
1 teaspoon grated fresh ginger root
1 teaspoon crushed garlic
1 teaspoon crushed dried red chiles
1 teaspoon salt
1 teaspoon brown sugar
2 tablespoons honey
2 tablespoons chopped fresh
 cilantro
1 fresh green chile, finely chopped
2 tablespoons vegetable oil
fresh cilantro, to garnish
yellow rice and salad, to serve

1 Prick the chicken thighs with a fork, rinse them, pat dry with paper towels, and set aside in a bowl.

2 In a large mixing bowl, mix together the lemon juice, ginger, garlic, crushed dried red chiles, salt, sugar, and honey.

3 Transfer the chicken thighs to the spice mixture and coat well. Cover and set aside for about 45 minutes.

4 Preheat the broiler to medium. Add the fresh cilantro and chopped chile to the chicken and place them in a flameproof dish.

5 Pour any remaining marinade over the chicken and brush with the oil.

6 Broil the chicken thighs for 15–20 minutes, turning and basting with the marinade occasionally, until cooked through and browned.

7 Serve cold, garnished with fresh cilantro and accompanied by yellow rice and salad.

NUTRITIONAL NOTES	
Per Portion	
Energy	243cal
Fat	12.00g
Saturated Fat	3.18g
Carbohydrate	5.30g
Fiber	0.00g

Chicken in Orange and Black Pepper Sauce

A low-fat version of a favorite
Indian dish, this is very creamy.

INGREDIENTS

Serves 4

8 ounces low-fat ricotta cheese
¼ cup plain low-fat yogurt
½ cup orange juice
1½ teaspoons grated fresh
  ginger root
1 teaspoon crushed garlic
1 teaspoon ground black pepper
1 teaspoon salt
1 teaspoon ground coriander
1 small chicken, about 1½ pounds,
  skinned and cut into 8 pieces
1 tablespoon oil
1 bay leaf
1 large onion, chopped
1 tablespoon fresh mint leaves
1 fresh green chile, seeded
  and chopped

1 In a small mixing bowl, whisk the
ricotta cheese with the yogurt,
orange juice, ginger, garlic, pepper,
salt, and coriander.

2 Pour this over the chicken, cover,
and set aside for 3–4 hours.

3 Heat the oil with the bay leaf in a
wok or heavy skillet and fry the
chopped onion until soft.

NUTRITIONAL NOTES	
Per Portion	
Energy	199cal
Fat	5.11g
Saturated Fat	1.06g
Carbohydrate	14.40g
Fiber	1.02g

4 Pour in the chicken mixture and
stir-fry for 3–5 minutes over a
medium heat. Lower the heat, cover,
and cook for 7–10 minutes, adding a
little water if the sauce is too thick.
Add the fresh mint and chile and serve.

_____ COOK'S TIP _____

If you prefer the taste of curry leaves, you
can use them instead of the bay leaf, but
you will need to double the quantity.

Chicken Korma

Although kormas are traditionally rich and high in fat, this recipe uses low-fat yogurt instead of cream, which gives the sauce a delicious flavor while keeping down the fat content. To prevent the yogurt from curdling, add it very slowly to the sauce and keep stirring until it is incorporated.

INGREDIENTS

Serves 4

1½ pounds chicken breast
    fillets, skinned
2 garlic cloves, crushed
1-inch piece fresh ginger root,
    roughly chopped
1 tablespoon oil
3 green cardamom pods
1 onion, finely chopped
2 teaspoons ground cumin
¼ teaspoon salt
1¼ cups plain low-fat yogurt
toasted sliced almonds (optional)
    and a fresh cilantro sprig,
    to garnish
plain rice, to serve

1 Using a sharp knife, remove any visible fat from the chicken breast portions and cut the meat into 1-inch cubes.

2 Put the garlic and ginger into a food processor or blender with 2 tablespoons water and process to a smooth, creamy paste.

3 Heat the oil in a large heavy pan and cook the chicken cubes for 8–10 minutes, until browned on all sides. Remove the chicken cubes with a slotted spoon and set aside.

4 Add the cardamom pods and fry for 2 minutes. Add the onion and fry for another 5 minutes.

NUTRITIONAL NOTES	
Per Portion	
Energy	288cal
Fat	9.30g
Saturated Fat	2.54g
Carbohydrate	9.80g
Fiber	0.50g

5 Stir in the garlic and ginger paste, cumin, and salt and cook, stirring, for another 5 minutes.

6 Add half the yogurt, stirring in a tablespoonful at a time, and cook over a low heat, until it has all been absorbed.

7 Return the chicken to the pan. Cover and simmer over a low heat for 5–6 minutes, or until the chicken is tender.

8 Add the remaining yogurt and simmer for another 5 minutes. Garnish with toasted almonds and cilantro and serve with rice.

_____ COOK'S TIP _____

Traditionally, kormas are spicy dishes with a rich, creamy texture. They are not meant to be very hot curries.

Mild Chicken Curry with Lentils

In this dish, the mildly spiced sauce is thickened using low-fat lentils instead of the traditional onions fried in ghee.

INGREDIENTS

Serves 4–6

½ cup red lentils
2 tablespoons mild curry powder
2 teaspoons ground coriander
1 teaspoon cumin seeds
2 cups vegetable stock
8 chicken thighs, skinned
8 ounces fresh spinach, shredded,
  or frozen spinach, thawed and
  well drained
1 tablespoon chopped fresh cilantro,
  plus extra to garnish
salt and black pepper
white or brown basmati rice and
  broiled poppadums, to serve

1 Put the lentils in a large heavy pan and add the curry powder, ground coriander, cumin seeds, and the stock.

2 Bring the mixture to a boil, then lower the heat. Cover and simmer for 10 minutes, stirring often.

3 Add the chicken and spinach. Replace the cover and simmer gently for another 40 minutes, or until the chicken is cooked through.

4 Stir in the chopped cilantro and season to taste. Serve garnished with fresh cilantro sprigs and accompanied by white or brown basmati rice and poppadums.

NUTRITIONAL NOTES	
Per Portion (4)	
Energy	296cal
Fat	10.20g
Saturated Fat	2.83g
Carbohydrate	15.10g
Fiber	3.80g

_____ COOK'S TIP _____

Lentils are an excellent low-fat source of vitamins and fiber, as well as being ideal for adding subtle color and texture to dishes. Yellow and red lentils, in particular, are very popular in Indian cooking.

Chicken Jalfrezi

A Jalfrezi is a stir-fried curry that features onions, ginger, and garlic in a rich bell pepper sauce.

INGREDIENTS

Serves 4

1½ pounds chicken breast fillets
1 tablespoon oil
1 teaspoon cumin seeds
1 onion, finely chopped
1 green bell pepper, seeded and
    finely chopped
1 red bell pepper, seeded and
    finely chopped
1 garlic clove, crushed
¾-inch piece fresh ginger root,
    finely chopped
1 tablespoon curry paste
¼ teaspoon chili powder
1 teaspoon ground coriander
1 teaspoon ground cumin
½ teaspoon salt
14-ounce can chopped tomatoes
2 tablespoons chopped fresh cilantro,
    plus extra to garnish
plain rice, to serve

1 Skin the chicken breast portions and remove any visible fat. Cut the meat into 1-inch cubes.

NUTRITIONAL NOTES	
Per Portion	
Energy	291cal
Fat	9.80g
Saturated Fat	2.24g
Carbohydrate	11.70g
Fiber	3.50g

2 Heat the oil in a karahi, wok, or heavy pan and fry the cumin seeds for 2 minutes, until they splutter. Add the onion, peppers, garlic, and ginger and fry for 6–8 minutes.

3 Add the curry paste and fry for about 2 minutes. Stir in the chili powder, ground coriander, cumin, and salt and add 1 tablespoon water; fry for another 2 minutes.

4 Add the chicken cubes and fry for about 5 minutes. Add the canned tomatoes and chopped fresh cilantro. Cover the pan tightly with a lid and cook for about 15 minutes, or until the chicken cubes are tender. Garnish with sprigs of fresh cilantro and serve with rice.

Karahi Chicken with Fresh Fenugreek

Fresh fenugreek is a flavor that not many people are familiar with and this recipe is a good introduction to this delicious herb. Once again, the chicken is boiled before it is quickly stir-fried to make sure it is cooked through.

INGREDIENTS

Serves 4

4 ounces boneless chicken thigh meat, skinned and cut into strips
4 ounces chicken breast fillet, skinned and cut into strips
½ teaspoon crushed garlic
1 teaspoon chili powder
½ teaspoon salt
2 teaspoons tomato paste
2 tablespoons oil
1 bunch fresh fenugreek leaves
1 tablespoon chopped fresh cilantro
1¼ cups water
pilau rice and whole-wheat chapatis, to serve (optional)

1 Bring a pan of water to a boil, add the chicken strips, and cook for about 5–7 minutes. Drain the chicken and set aside.

2 In a mixing bowl, combine the garlic, chili powder, and salt with the tomato paste.

3 Heat the oil in a large heavy pan. Lower the heat and stir in the tomato paste and spice mixture.

4 Add the chicken pieces to the spices and stir-fry for 5–7 minutes, then lower the heat again.

5 Add the fenugreek leaves and fresh cilantro. Continue to stir-fry for 5–7 minutes, until all the ingredients are mixed well together.

6 Pour in the water, cover, and cook for about 5 minutes, stirring several times, until the dish is simmering. Serve hot with some pilau rice and warm whole-wheat chapatis, if you like.

NUTRITIONAL NOTES	
Per Portion	
Energy	127cal
Fat	7.90g
Saturated Fat	1.51g
Carbohydrate	1.20g
Fiber	0.10g

Karahi Chicken with Mint

Another herb that goes well with spicy chicken is mint, which has cooling qualities to counter the heat of ginger and chiles.

INGREDIENTS

Serves 4

10 ounces chicken breast fillets,
    skinned and cut into strips
1¼ cups water
2 tablespoons oil
2 small bunches scallions,
    roughly chopped
1 teaspoon shredded fresh ginger root
1 teaspoon crushed dried red chiles
2 tablespoons lemon juice
1 tablespoon chopped fresh
    cilantro
1 tablespoon chopped fresh mint
3 tomatoes, peeled, seeded, and
    roughly chopped
1 teaspoon salt
mint and cilantro sprigs,
    to garnish

1 Put the chicken and water into a pan, bring to a boil, and lower the heat to medium. Cook for about 10 minutes, or until the water has evaporated and the chicken is cooked. Remove from the heat and set aside.

2 Heat the oil in a heavy pan and stir-fry the scallions for 2 minutes, until soft but not browned.

3 Add the cooked chicken strips and stir-fry for about 3 minutes over a medium heat.

4 Gradually add the shredded ginger, dried red chiles, lemon juice, chopped cilantro and mint, tomatoes, and salt and gently stir to blend all the flavors together.

5 Transfer the spicy chicken mixture to a serving dish and garnish with a few sprigs of fresh mint and cilantro before serving.

NUTRITIONAL NOTES	
Per Portion	
Energy	157cal
Fat	8.20g
Saturated Fat	1.50g
Carbohydrate	4.20g
Fiber	1.40g

Aromatic Chicken Curry

Tender pieces of chicken are lightly cooked with fresh vegetables and aromatic spices.

INGREDIENTS

Serves 4

1½ pounds chicken breast
  fillets, skinned
1 tablespoon oil
½ teaspoon cumin seeds
½ teaspoon fennel seeds
1 onion, thickly sliced
2 garlic cloves, crushed
1-inch piece fresh ginger root,
  finely chopped
1 tablespoon curry paste
8 ounces broccoli, broken
  into florets
4 tomatoes, cut into thick wedges
1 teaspoon garam masala
2 tablespoons chopped fresh cilantro
nan bread, to serve

1 Remove any visible fat from the chicken and cut the meat into 1-inch cubes.

NUTRITIONAL NOTES	
Per Portion	
Energy	286cal
Fat	9.80g
Saturated Fat	2.19g
Carbohydrate	8.50g
Fiber	3.70g

2 Heat the oil in a karahi, wok, or heavy pan and fry the cumin and fennel seeds for 2 minutes, until the seeds begin to splutter. Add the onion, garlic, and ginger and cook for 5–7 minutes. Stir in the curry paste and cook for another 2–3 minutes.

3 Add the broccoli florets and fry for about 5 minutes. Add the chicken cubes and fry for 5–8 minutes.

4 Add the tomato wedges to the pan with the garam masala and the chopped fresh cilantro. Cook the curry for another 5–10 minutes, or until the chicken cubes are tender. Serve with the nan bread.

Traditional Chicken Curry

Chicken curry is always popular, whether served at a family dinner or a banquet. This version is cooked with a lid on, producing a thin consistency. If you prefer a thick curry, cook uncovered for the last 15 minutes.

INGREDIENTS

Serves 4-6

4 tablespoons vegetable oil
4 cloves
4–6 green cardamom pods
2-inch piece cinnamon stick
3 whole star anise
6–8 curry leaves
1 large onion, finely chopped
2-inch piece fresh ginger root,
    crushed
4 garlic cloves, crushed
4 tablespoons mild curry paste
1 teaspoon ground turmeric
3½-pound chicken, skinned
    and jointed
14-ounce can chopped tomatoes
½ cup coconut cream
½ teaspoon sugar
salt, to taste
2 cups fresh cilantro,
    chopped

2 Add the onion, ginger, and garlic and fry until the onion turns brown. Add the curry paste and turmeric and fry until the oil separates.

3 Add the chicken pieces and mix well. When all the pieces are evenly sealed, cover the pan and cook until the meat is nearly cooked.

4 Add the canned chopped tomatoes and the coconut cream. Simmer gently until the mixture thickens. Mix well and add the sugar and salt. Fold in the chopped fresh cilantro, then reheat briefly. Spoon into a dish and serve hot.

NUTRITIONAL NOTES	
Per Portion	
Energy	647cal
Fat	49.3g
Saturated Fat	17g
Carbohydrate	8.7g
Fiber	1.9g

1 Heat the oil in a pan and fry the cloves, cardamoms, cinnamon stick, star anise, and curry leaves over a medium heat for about 5 minutes, until the cloves swell and the curry leaves are slightly burned.

Red Hot Chicken Curry

This curry has a satisfyingly thick sauce, and uses red and green peppers for extra color.

INGREDIENTS

Serves 4

2 medium onions
½ red bell pepper
½ green bell pepper
2 tablespoons oil
¼ teaspoon fenugreek seeds
¼ teaspoon onion seeds
½ teaspoon crushed garlic
½ teaspoon grated fresh ginger root
1 teaspoon ground coriander
1 teaspoon chili powder
1 teaspoon salt
14-ounce can tomatoes
2 tablespoons lemon juice
12 ounces chicken, skinned
  and cubed
2 tablespoons chopped fresh cilantro
3 fresh green chiles, chopped
fresh cilantro, to garnish

NUTRITIONAL NOTES	
Per Portion	
Energy	214cal
Fat	10.00g
Saturated Fat	2.08g
Carbohydrate	11.00g
Fiber	2.20g

1 Using a sharp knife, dice the onions. Seed the bell peppers and cut them into chunks.

2 In a medium heavy pan, heat the oil and fry the fenugreek and onion seeds until they turn a shade darker. Add the chopped onions, garlic, and ginger. Fry for about 5 minutes, until the onions turn golden brown. Reduce the heat to very low.

3 In a bowl, mix together the ground coriander, chili powder, salt, canned tomatoes, and lemon juice. Stir well.

4 Pour this mixture into the pan and increase the heat to medium. Stir-fry for about 3 minutes.

5 Add the chicken cubes and stir-fry for 5–7 minutes.

6 Add the chopped fresh cilantro and green chiles and the red and green bell pepper chunks.

7 Lower the heat, cover the pan, and let simmer for about 10 minutes until the chicken cubes are cooked.

8 Serve the curry hot, garnished with fresh cilantro.

VARIATION
For a milder version of this delicious curry, simply omit some, or even all, of the green chiles.

Mughlai-style Chicken

The cuisine of Andhra Pradesh is renowned for its pungency because the hottest variety of chile is grown there. In sharp contrast, however, the region is also home to the subtle flavors of a style of cooking known as nizami, which has a distinct Mogul influence. This recipe, with the heady aroma of saffron and the captivating flavor of a silky almond and cream sauce, is a typical example.

INGREDIENTS

Serves 4–6
1 large onion
2 eggs
4 chicken breast fillets
1–2 tablespoons garam masala
6 tablespoons ghee or
   vegetable oil
2-inch piece fresh ginger root,
   finely crushed
4 garlic cloves, finely crushed
4 cloves
4 green cardamom pods
2-inch piece cinnamon stick
2 bay leaves
15–20 saffron threads
⅔ cup plain yogurt, beaten with
   1 teaspoon cornstarch
⅓ cup heavy cream
½ cup ground almonds
salt and pepper

2 Rub the chicken fillets with the garam masala, then brush with the beaten egg. In a karahi, wok, or large pan, heat the ghee or vegetable oil and fry the chicken until cooked through and browned on both sides. Remove from the pan and keep warm.

3 In the same pan, fry the chopped onion, ginger, garlic, cloves, cardamom pods, cinnamon, and bay leaves. When the onion turns golden, remove the pan from the heat, let the contents cool a little, and add the saffron and yogurt mixture. Stir well to prevent the yogurt from curdling.

4 Return the chicken to the pan, along with any juices, and gently cook until the chicken is tender. Adjust the seasoning if necessary.

5 Just before serving, pour in the cream. Fold it in, then repeat the process with the ground almonds. Make sure the curry is piping hot before serving.

1 Chop the onion finely. Break the eggs into a bowl and season with salt and pepper.

NUTRITIONAL NOTES	
Per Portion	
Energy	514cal
Fat	32.3g
Saturated Fat	9.9g
Carbohydrate	7.9g
Fiber	0.9g

_____ COOK'S TIP _____

The whole spices used in this curry look attractive and are usually left in for serving, but you can remove the cloves, cinnamon stick, and bay leaves if you like.

Kashmiri Chicken Curry

Surrounded by the snow-capped Himalayas, Kashmir is popularly known as the "Switzerland of the East." The state is also renowned for its rich culinary heritage, and this aromatic dish is one of the simplest among the region's repertoire.

INGREDIENTS

Serves 4–6

4 teaspoons Kashmiri masala paste
4 tablespoons ketchup
1 teaspoon Worcestershire sauce
1 teaspoon five-spice powder
1 teaspoon sugar
8 chicken joints, skinned
2-inch piece fresh ginger root
3 tablespoons vegetable oil
4 garlic cloves, crushed
juice of 1 lemon
1 tablespoon cilantro leaves,
    finely chopped
salt

1 To make the marinade, mix the masala paste, ketchup, Worcestershire sauce, and five-spice powder with the sugar and a little salt. Let the mixture rest in a warm place until the sugar has dissolved.

_____ COOK'S TIP _____

You can buy specialty masala pastes, including Kashmiri paste, from some Indian stores. Alternatively, make your own paste or use an all-purpose curry paste.

2 Rub the chicken pieces with the marinade and set aside in a cool place for another 2 hours, or in the refrigerator overnight. Bring to room temperature before cooking.

3 Thinly peel the ginger, using a sharp knife or vegetable peeler. Grate the peeled root finely.

4 Heat the oil in a karahi, wok, or large pan and fry half the ginger and all the garlic until golden.

5 Add the chicken and fry until both sides are sealed. Cover and cook until the chicken is tender and the oil has separated from the sauce.

6 Sprinkle the chicken with the lemon juice, remaining ginger, and chopped cilantro leaves, and mix in well. Serve hot. Plain boiled rice makes a good accompaniment.

NUTRITIONAL NOTES	
Per Portion	
Energy	483cal
Fat	34.9g
Saturated Fat	8.2g
Carbohydrate	5.7g
Fiber	0.2g

Chicken Curry with Sliced Apples

This mild yet flavorsome dish is given a special lift by the addition of sliced apples.

INGREDIENTS

Serves 4

2 teaspoons oil
2 medium onions, diced
1 bay leaf
2 cloves
1-inch cinnamon stick
4 black peppercorns
1 baby chicken, about 1½ pounds,
   skinned and cut into 8 pieces
1 teaspoon garam masala
1 teaspoon grated fresh ginger root
1 teaspoon crushed garlic
1 teaspoon salt
1 teaspoon chili powder
1 tablespoon ground almonds
⅔ cup plain low-fat yogurt
2 green apples, peeled, cored, and
   roughly sliced
1 tablespoon chopped fresh
   cilantro
½ ounce sliced almonds, lightly
   toasted, and fresh cilantro leaves,
   to garnish

2 Add the chicken pieces to the onions and continue to stir-fry for at least another 3 minutes.

4 Pour in the yogurt and stir for a couple more minutes.

3 Lower the heat and add the garam masala, ginger, garlic, salt, chili powder, and ground almonds and cook, stirring constantly, for 2–3 minutes.

5 Add the apples and chopped cilantro, cover, and cook for about 10–15 minutes.

NUTRITIONAL NOTES	
Per Portion	
Energy	237cal
Fat	8.25g
Saturated Fat	1.31g
Carbohydrate	17.21g
Fiber	2.88g

----- COOK'S TIP -----

To keep the fat content of this dish to a minimum, you can omit the ground and sliced almonds. Serve the dish with plain rice and it will be delicious.

1 Heat the oil in a karahi, wok, or heavy pan and fry the onions with the bay leaf, cloves, cinnamon, and peppercorns for about 3–5 minutes, until the onions are beginning to soften but have not yet begun to brown.

6 Check that the chicken is cooked through and serve immediately, garnished with the sliced almonds and whole cilantro leaves.

Rice Layered with Chicken and Potatoes

This dish, Murgh Biryani, is mainly prepared for important occasions, and is truly fit for royalty. Every cook in India has a subtle variation that is kept a closely guarded secret.

INGREDIENTS

Serves 4-6

3 pounds chicken breast fillets,
  skinned and cut into large pieces
4 tablespoons biryani masala paste
2 fresh green chiles, chopped
1 tablespoon grated fresh ginger root
1 tablespoon crushed garlic
2 cups fresh cilantro, chopped
6–8 fresh mint leaves, chopped
⅔ cup plain yogurt, beaten
2 tablespoons tomato paste
4 onions, finely sliced,
  deep-fried, and crushed
salt, to taste
2¼ cups basmati rice,
  washed and drained
1 teaspoon black cumin seeds
2-inch piece cinnamon stick
4 green cardamom pods
2 black cardamom pods
vegetable oil, for shallow-frying
4 large potatoes, peeled, and quartered
¾ cup milk, mixed with
  6 tablespoons water
1 envelop saffron powder, mixed with
  6 tablespoons milk
2 tablespoons ghee or unsalted butter
1 tomato, sliced

For the garnish
ghee or unsalted butter,
  for shallow-frying
½ cup cashew nuts
⅓ cup golden raisins

1 Mix the chicken pieces with the next ten ingredients in a large bowl and marinate, covered, in a cool place for about 2 hours. Place in a large heavy pan and cook over a low heat for about 10 minutes. Set aside.

2 Boil a large pan of water and soak the rice with the cumin seeds, cinnamon stick, and green and black cardamom pods for about 5 minutes. Drain well. If you prefer, some of the whole spices may be removed at this stage and discarded.

3 Heat the oil for shallow-frying and fry the potatoes until they are evenly browned on all sides. Drain the potatoes and set aside.

4 Place half the rice on top of the chicken in the pan in an even layer. Then make an even layer with the potatoes. Put the remaining rice on top of the potatoes and spread to make an even layer.

5 Sprinkle the water mixed with milk all over the rice. Make random holes through the rice with the handle of a spoon and pour into each a little saffron milk. Place a few knobs of ghee or butter on the surface, cover the pan, and cook over a low heat for 35–45 minutes.

6 While the biryani is cooking, make the garnish. Heat a little ghee or butter and fry the cashew nuts and golden raisins until they swell. Drain and set aside. When the biryani is ready, gently toss the rice, chicken, and potatoes together, garnish with the nut mixture, and serve hot.

NUTRITIONAL NOTES	
Per Portion	
Energy	1,032cal
Fat	9.8g
Saturated Fat	2.4g
Carbohydrate	131.1g
Fiber	2.9g

Chicken Pilau

Like biryanis, pilaus that include
cooked meat and poultry make
a convenient one-pot meal. A
vegetable curry makes a good
accompaniment, although for a
simpler meal, such as supper, you
could serve the pilau with a simple
raita, combining plain yogurt with
any uncooked vegetable, such as
white cabbage, grated carrots, or
cauliflower florets.

INGREDIENTS

Serves 4

2 cups basmati rice
6 tablespoons ghee or
    unsalted butter
1 onion, sliced
¼ teaspoon mixed onion
    and mustard seeds
3 curry leaves
1 teaspoon grated fresh ginger root
1 teaspoon crushed garlic
1 teaspoon ground coriander
1 teaspoon chili powder
1½ teaspoons salt
2 tomatoes, sliced
1 potato, cubed
½ cup frozen peas, thawed
6 ounces chicken breast fillets,
    skinned and cubed
4 tablespoons chopped fresh
    cilantro
2 fresh green chiles, chopped
3 cups water

NUTRITIONAL NOTES	
Per Portion	
Energy	603cal
Fat	16.8g
Saturated Fat	10g
Carbohydrate	91.9g
Fiber	2.1g

1 Wash the rice thoroughly under
running water, then let soak for
30 minutes. Drain in a strainer or
colander and set aside.

2 In a pan, melt the ghee or butter
and fry the sliced onion until golden.

3 Add the onion and mustard seeds,
the curry leaves, ginger, garlic,
ground coriander, chili powder, and
salt. Stir-fry for about 2 minutes over
a low heat.

4 Add the sliced tomatoes, cubed
potato, peas, and chicken cubes
and mix everything together well.

_____ COOK'S TIP _____

There's no need to have the heat high
when stir-frying the spices. When ground,
spices require only gentle warmth to release
their flavors.

5 Add the rice and stir gently
to combine with the other
ingredients.

6 Add the cilantro and chiles. Mix
and stir-fry for 1 minute. Pour in
the water, bring to a boil and then
lower the heat. Cover tightly and cook
for 20 minutes. Remove from the heat,
leaving the lid in place, and let the
pilau stand for 6–8 minutes. Serve.

Chicken Biryani

Biryani is a meal in itself and needs no accompaniment, except for a raita and some poppadums. It is a dish that is equally at home on the family dining table or as a dinner-party centerpiece.

INGREDIENTS

Serves 4

1½ cups basmati rice
10 whole green cardamom pods
½ teaspoon salt
2–3 whole cloves
2-inch piece cinnamon stick
3 tablespoons vegetable oil
3 onions, sliced
4 chicken breast fillets, each about
   6 ounces, skinned and cubed
¼ teaspoon ground cloves
¼ teaspoon hot chili powder
1 teaspoon ground cumin
1 teaspoon ground coriander
½ teaspoon ground black pepper
3 garlic cloves, chopped
1 teaspoon finely chopped fresh
   ginger root
juice of 1 lemon
4 tomatoes, sliced
2 tablespoons chopped fresh
   cilantro
⅔ cup plain yogurt, plus extra
   to serve
4–5 saffron threads, soaked in
   2 teaspoons warm milk
⅔ cup water
toasted sliced almonds and fresh
   cilantro sprigs, to garnish

NUTRITIONAL NOTES	
Per Portion	
Energy	548cal
Fat	11.1g
Saturated Fat	1.7g
Carbohydrate	67.5g
Fiber	2.2g

1 Wash the rice well and let soak in water for 30 minutes.

2 Preheat the oven to 375°F. Remove the seeds from half the cardamom pods and grind them finely, using a mortar and pestle. Set aside the ground seeds.

3 Bring a pan of water to a boil. Drain the rice and add it with the salt, whole cardamom pods, cloves, and cinnamon stick. Boil for 2 minutes, then drain, leaving the whole spices in the rice. Keep the rice hot in a covered pan.

4 Heat the oil in a karahi, wok, or large pan, and fry the onions for 8 minutes, until softened and browned.

5 Add the chicken and the ground spices, including the ground cardamom seeds. Mix well, then add the garlic, ginger, and lemon juice. Stir-fry for about 5 minutes.

6 Transfer the chicken mixture to a casserole and arrange the tomatoes on top. Sprinkle on the fresh cilantro, spoon the yogurt evenly on top, and cover with the drained rice.

7 Drizzle the saffron milk over the rice and pour over the water. Cover, then bake in the oven for 1 hour. Transfer to a serving platter and discard the whole spices. Garnish with the toasted sliced almonds and cilantro sprigs and serve immediately.

Chicken with Spicy Onions

Chunky onion slices infused with toasted cumin seeds and shredded ginger add a delicious contrast to the flavor of the chicken.

INGREDIENTS

Serves 4–6
3-pound chicken, jointed
   and skinned
½ teaspoon turmeric
½ teaspoon chili powder
salt, to taste
4 tablespoons oil
4 small onions, finely chopped
6 cups fresh cilantro, coarsely chopped
2-inch piece fresh ginger root,
   finely shredded
2 fresh green chiles, finely chopped
2 teaspoons cumin seeds, dry-roasted
5 tablespoons plain yogurt
5 tablespoons heavy cream
½ teaspoon cornstarch

1 Rub the chicken joints with the turmeric, chili powder, and salt. Heat the oil in a large skillet and fry the chicken pieces in batches until both sides are sealed. Remove to a plate and keep hot.

COOK'S TIP

Make a few slashes in the chicken joints before rubbing them with the spice mixture to encourage the flavors to penetrate the meat.

---

2 Reheat the oil remaining in the skillet and add three of the chopped onions, most of the fresh cilantro, half the ginger, the green chiles, and the cumin seeds and fry until the onions are translucent.

3 Return the chicken to the skillet with any juices and mix well. Cover and cook gently for 15 minutes.

NUTRITIONAL NOTES	
Per Portion	
Energy	819cal
Fat	65.4g
Saturated Fat	23.4g
Carbohydrate	8.2g
Fiber	0.9g

4 Remove the skillet from the heat and let cool a little. Mix the yogurt, cream, and cornstarch in a bowl and gradually fold into the chicken, mixing well.

5 Return the skillet to the heat and cook gently until the chicken is tender. Just before serving, stir in the reserved onion, cilantro, and ginger. Spoon into a bowl and serve hot.

Hot Sweet and Sour Duck Casserole

This recipe can be made with any game bird, or even rabbit. It is a distinctively sweet, sour, and hot dish best eaten with rice as an accompaniment.

INGREDIENTS

Serves 4–6

3-pound duck, jointed and skinned
4 bay leaves
2 teaspoons salt
5 tablespoons vegetable oil
juice of 5 lemons
8 medium onions, finely chopped
4–5 garlic cloves, crushed
1 tablespoon chili powder
1¼ cups pickling vinegar
2-inch piece fresh ginger root, peeled and shredded
½ cup sugar
1 tablespoon garam masala

1 Place the duck, bay leaves, and salt in a large pan and cover with cold water. Bring to a boil, then simmer for 30–45 minutes, or until the duck is fully cooked. Remove the pieces of duck and keep warm. Reserve the liquid as a base for stock or soup.

NUTRITIONAL NOTES
Per Portion

Energy	444cal
Fat	17.5g
Saturated Fat	3.3g
Carbohydrate	53.8g
Fiber	4.2g

2 In a large pan, heat the oil and lemon juice until it reaches smoking point. Add the onions, garlic, and chili powder and fry the onions until they are golden brown.

3 Add the vinegar, ginger, and sugar and simmer until the sugar dissolves and the oil has separated from the mixture.

4 Return the duck to the pan and add the garam masala. Mix well, then reheat until the masala clings to the pieces of duck and the sauce is thick. Adjust the seasoning if necessary. If you prefer a thinner sauce, add a little of the reserved stock.

COOK'S TIP

Be very careful when adding the onions and garlic to the oil and lemon juice mixture. Stand well back and use a spoon to scrape the onions into the pan, a few at a time. The hot mixture is likely to spit or splutter.

Meat Dishes

INDIAN COOKS have perfected the art of tenderizing meat, thanks to their use of marinades and slow, careful cooking. Lamb is a popular choice for dishes, since it can be enjoyed by all those whose religion permits them to eat meat. Many Hindus avoid pork, and this meat is forbidden to those of the Muslim faith. Only in Goa, and other parts of India with significant Christian populations, can pork be found on the menu. Beef is forbidden to Hindus, although Muslims enjoy it.

Vegetables, beans, and lentils are used effectively in meat dishes. Lamb with Spinach, Hot and Sour Lamb and Lentil Curry, and Beef with Green Beans are typical examples of these hearty combinations, rich in flavor and texture. The most important addition to any meat dish, however, is the spices. The types and quantities used, and the time at which they are added, are two of the variables that contribute to making Indian meat dishes among the very best in the world.

Spicy Lamb Tikka

One of the best ways of tenderizing meat is to marinate it in papaya, which must be unripe or it will lend its sweetness to what should be a savory dish. Papaya, or paw-paw, is readily available from most large supermarkets.

INGREDIENTS

Serves 4

1½ pounds lean lamb, cubed
1 unripe papaya
3 tablespoons plain yogurt
1 teaspoon grated fresh ginger root
1 teaspoon chili powder
1 teaspoon crushed garlic
¼ teaspoon turmeric
2 teaspoons ground coriander
1 teaspoon ground cumin
1 teaspoon salt
2 tablespoons lemon juice
1 tablespoon chopped fresh cilantro,
    plus extra to garnish
¼ teaspoon red food coloring
1¼ cups corn oil
lemon wedges
onion rings

1 Place the lamb in a large mixing bowl. Peel the papaya, cut it in half, and scoop out the seeds. Cut the flesh into cubes and place in a food processor or blender. Process in bursts until the papaya forms a paste, adding about 1 tablespoon water if necessary.

2 Pour 2 tablespoons of the papaya pulp over the lamb cubes and rub it in well with your fingers. Cover and set aside for at least 3 hours.

3 Meanwhile, mix the yogurt, ginger, chili powder, garlic, turmeric, ground coriander, ground cumin, salt, and lemon juice in a bowl. Add the fresh cilantro, red food coloring, and 2 tablespoons of the oil and mix well.

4 Pour the spicy yogurt mixture over the lamb and mix well.

5 Heat the remaining oil in a karahi, wok, or deep pan. Lower the heat slightly and add the lamb cubes, a few at a time.

6 Deep-fry each batch for 5-7 minutes, or until the lamb is thoroughly cooked and tender. Keep the cooked pieces warm while frying the remainder.

7 Transfer to a serving dish and garnish with lemon wedges, onion rings, and fresh cilantro. Serve with raita and freshly baked nan bread.

COOK'S TIP

A good-quality meat tenderizer, available from supermarkets, can be used in place of the papaya. However, the meat will need a longer marinating time and should ideally be left to tenderize overnight.

NUTRITIONAL NOTES
Per Portion

Energy	438cal
Fat	32.7g
Saturated Fat	10.4g
Carbohydrate	2.4g
Fiber	0.7g

Indian Lamb Burgers

Serve this Indian burger in a roll with chili sauce and salad or unaccompanied as an appetizer.

INGREDIENTS

Serves 4–6

¼ cup chickpeas, soaked
   overnight in water
2 onions, finely chopped
9 ounces lean lamb, cut into small cubes
1 teaspoon cumin seeds
1 teaspoon garam masala
4–6 fresh green chiles,
   roughly chopped
2-inch piece fresh ginger root, crushed
salt, to taste
¾ cup water
few fresh cilantro and mint leaves,
   chopped
juice of 1 lemon
1 tablespoon besan flour
2 eggs, beaten
vegetable oil, for shallow-frying
half a lime

1 Drain the chickpeas and cook them in a pan of boiling water for 1 hour. Drain again, return to the pan, and add the next eight ingredients. Bring to a boil. Simmer, covered, until the meat and chickpeas are cooked.

2 Remove the lid and cook uncovered to reduce the excess liquid. Cool, and grind to a paste in a food processor.

3 Scrape the mixture into a mixing bowl and add the fresh cilantro and mint, lemon juice, and flour. Knead well. Divide into 10–12 portions and roll each into a ball, then flatten slightly. Chill for 1 hour. Dip the burgers in the beaten egg and shallow-fry each side until golden brown. Serve hot with the lime.

NUTRITIONAL NOTES	
Per Portion	
Energy	357cal
Fat	25.1g
Saturated Fat	6g
Carbohydrate	15.6g
Fiber	1.5g

Lamb Meatballs

The word "meatballs" conjures up something humdrum, but these spicy little patties, with their delectable sauce, are exciting and full of flavor.

INGREDIENTS

Serves 6

For the meatballs
1½ pounds lean ground lamb
1 fresh green chile, roughly
   chopped
1 garlic clove, chopped
1-inch piece fresh ginger root, chopped
¼ teaspoon garam masala
¼ teaspoon salt
3 tablespoons chopped fresh cilantro,
   plus extra to garnish
pilau rice, to serve

For the sauce
1 tablespoon oil
¼ teaspoon mustard seeds
½ teaspoon cumin seeds
1 onion, chopped
1 garlic clove, chopped
1-inch piece fresh ginger root,
   finely chopped
1 teaspoon ground cumin
1 teaspoon ground coriander
½ teaspoon salt
½ teaspoon chili powder
1 tablespoon tomato paste
14-ounce can chopped tomatoes

1 To make the meatballs, put all the ingredients into a food processor or blender and process until the mixture binds together. Shape the mixture into 18 balls. Cover and chill for 10 minutes.

2 To make the sauce, heat the oil in a heavy pan and fry the mustard and cumin seeds until they splutter.

NUTRITIONAL NOTES	
Per Portion	
Energy	231cal
Fat	12.30g
Saturated Fat	5.00g
Carbohydrate	5.40g
Fiber	0.90g

3 Add the onion, garlic, and ginger and fry for 5 minutes. Stir in the remaining sauce ingredients and simmer for 5 minutes.

4 Add the meatballs to the sauce. Bring to a boil, cover, and simmer for 25–30 minutes or until the meatballs are cooked through. Serve on a bed of pilau rice and garnish with fresh cilantro.

Lamb Chops Kashmiri-style

These chops are cooked in a unique way, being first boiled in milk, and then fried. Despite the large number of spices used in this recipe, the actual dish has a mild flavor and is delicious served with fried rice and a lentil dish.

INGREDIENTS

Serves 4
8-12 lamb chops, about
  2–3 ounces each
1 piece cinnamon bark
1 bay leaf
½ teaspoon fennel seeds
½ teaspoon black peppercorns
3 green cardamom pods
1 teaspoon salt
2½ cups milk
⅔ cup unsweetened condensed milk
⅔ cup plain yogurt
2 tablespoons all-purpose flour
1 teaspoon chili powder
1 teaspoon grated fresh ginger root
½ teaspoon garam masala
½ teaspoon crushed garlic
pinch of salt
1¼ cups corn oil
fresh mint sprigs
lime quarters

1 Trim the lamb chops to remove any excess fat, and place them in a large pan.

2 Add the cinnamon bark, bay leaf, fennel seeds, peppercorns, cardamoms, and salt. Pour in the milk. Bring to a boil over a high heat.

3 Lower the heat and cook for 12–15 minutes, or until the milk has reduced to about half its original volume. At this stage, pour in the condensed milk and lower the heat again. Simmer until the chops are cooked through and all the milk has evaporated.

4 While the chops are cooking, blend together the yogurt, flour, chili powder, ginger, garam masala, crushed garlic, and a pinch of salt in a mixing bowl.

5 Remove the chops from the pan and discard the whole spices. Add the chops to the spicy yogurt mixture.

6 Heat the oil in a deep pan, wok, or medium karahi. Lower the heat slightly and add the chops. Fry until they are golden brown, turning them once or twice as they cook.

7 Transfer the chops to a serving dish, and garnish with mint sprigs and lime quarters. Serve immediately.

NUTRITIONAL NOTES	
Per Portion	
Energy	484cal
Fat	29g
Saturated Fat	9.3g
Carbohydrate	17.6g
Fiber	0.2g

Spring Lamb Chops

Tender spring lamb is perfect for this quick and easy dish.

INGREDIENTS

Serves 4

8 small lean spring lamb chops
1 large fresh red chile, seeded
2 tablespoons chopped
    fresh cilantro
1 tablespoon chopped
    fresh mint
1 teaspoon salt
1 teaspoon brown sugar
1 teaspoon garam masala
1 teaspoon crushed garlic
1 teaspoon grated fresh ginger root
3/4 cup plain low-fat yogurt
2 teaspoons oil
mixed salad, to serve

NUTRITIONAL NOTES	
Per Portion	
Energy	207cal
Fat	10.29g
Saturated Fat	4.26g
Carbohydrate	6.63g
Fiber	0.27g

1 Trim the lamb chops of any excess fat. Place them in a large bowl.

2 Finely chop the chile, then place in a bowl and mix with the cilantro, mint, salt, brown sugar, garam masala, garlic, and ginger.

3 Pour the yogurt into the chili mixture and, using a small whisk or a fork, mix together thoroughly. Pour this mixture over the top of the chops and turn them with your fingers to make sure that they are completely covered. Cover and marinate overnight in the refrigerator.

4 Heat the oil in a karahi, wok, or heavy pan and add the chops. Cook over a medium heat for about 20 minutes, or until cooked all the way through, turning the chops from time to time. Alternatively, broil the chops, basting often with oil. Serve with the mixed salad.

Lamb Korma with Mint

Cutting the lamb into strips for this lovely dish makes it easier and quicker to cook.

INGREDIENTS

Serves 4

2 fresh green chiles
½ cup plain low-fat yogurt
¼ cup coconut milk
1 tablespoon ground almonds
1 teaspoon salt
1 teaspoon crushed garlic
1 teaspoon grated fresh ginger root
1 teaspoon garam masala
¼ teaspoon ground cardamom
large pinch of ground cinnamon
1 tablespoon chopped fresh mint
1 tablespoon oil
2 medium onions, diced
1 bay leaf
4 black peppercorns
8 ounces lean lamb,
    cut into strips
⅔ cup water
fresh mint leaves, to garnish

1 Finely chop the chiles. Whisk the yogurt with the chiles, coconut milk, ground almonds, salt, garlic, ginger, garam masala, cardamom, cinnamon, and mint.

2 Heat the oil in a karahi, wok, or heavy pan and fry the onions with the bay leaf and peppercorns for about 5 minutes.

3 When the onions are soft and golden brown, add the lamb and stir-fry for about 2 minutes.

4 Pour in the yogurt mixture and water, lower the heat, cover, and cook for about 15 minutes, or until the lamb is cooked through, stirring occasionally. Using two spoons, toss over the heat for another 2 minutes. Serve garnished with fresh mint leaves.

NUTRITIONAL NOTES	
Per Portion	
Energy	193cal
Fat	10.14g
Saturated Fat	2.91g
Carbohydrate	11.50g
Fiber	1.60g

___ COOK'S TIP ___

Rice with peas and curry leaves goes very well with this korma.

Stir-fried Lamb with Pearl Onions

The pearl onions are stir-fried whole before being added to the lamb and pepper mixture in this recipe. Serve this dish with rice, lentils, or nan bread.

INGREDIENTS

Serves 4

1 tablespoon oil
8 pearl onions
8 ounces boned lean lamb, cut
   into strips
1 teaspoon ground cumin
1 teaspoon ground coriander
1 tablespoon tomato paste
1 teaspoon chili powder
1 teaspoon salt
1 tablespoon lemon juice
½ teaspoon onion seeds
4 curry leaves
1¼ cups water
1 small red bell pepper, seeded
   and roughly sliced
1 small green bell pepper, seeded
   and roughly sliced
1 tablespoon chopped fresh
   cilantro
1 tablespoon chopped fresh mint

1 Heat the oil in a karahi, wok, or heavy pan and stir-fry the whole pearl onions for about 3 minutes. Using a slotted spoon, remove the onions from the pan and set aside to drain. Set the pan aside, with the oil remaining in it.

2 Mix together the lamb, cumin, ground coriander, tomato paste, chili powder, salt, and lemon juice in a bowl and set aside.

3 Reheat the oil and briskly stir-fry the onion seeds and curry leaves for 2–3 minutes.

COOK'S TIP

This dish benefits from being cooked a day in advance and kept in the refrigerator overnight, making it a very good choice to serve for a relaxed dinner party.

NUTRITIONAL NOTES
Per Portion

Energy	155cal
Fat	9.48g
Saturated Fat	2.82g
Carbohydrate	5.74g
Fiber	1.49g

4 Add the lamb and spice mixture and stir-fry for about 5 minutes, then pour in the water, lower the heat, and cook gently for about 10 minutes, until the lamb is cooked through.

5 Add the peppers and half the fresh cilantro and mint. Stir-fry for another 2 minutes.

6 Finally, add the pearl onions and the remaining chopped fresh cilantro and mint and serve.

Lamb with Spinach

Lamb with Spinach, or Saag Gosht, is a well-known recipe from the Punjab. It is important to use red bell peppers because they add such a distinctive flavor to the dish. Serve with plain boiled rice, nan bread, or parathas.

INGREDIENTS

Serves 4-6

1 teaspoon grated fresh ginger root
1 teaspoon crushed garlic
1½ teaspoons chili powder
1 teaspoon salt
1 teaspoon garam masala
6 tablespoons corn oil
2 medium onions, sliced
1½ pounds lean lamb, cut into
   2-inch cubes
2½–3¾ cups water
14 ounces fresh spinach
1 large red bell pepper, seeded
   and chopped
3 fresh green chiles, chopped
3 tablespoons chopped
   fresh cilantro
1 tablespoon lemon juice
   (optional)

1 Mix together the ginger, garlic, chili powder, salt, and garam masala in a bowl. Set to one side.

2 Heat the oil in a medium pan. Add the onions and fry for 10–12 minutes, or until well browned.

3 Add the cubed lamb to the sizzling onion slices and fry for about 2 minutes, stirring frequently.

4 Tip in the spice mixture and stir thoroughly until the meat pieces are well coated.

5 Pour in the water and bring to a boil. As soon as it is boiling, cover the pan and lower the heat. Cook gently for 25–35 minutes, without letting the contents of the pan burn.

6 If there is still a lot of water in the pan when the meat has become tender, remove the lid and boil briskly to evaporate any excess.

7 Meanwhile, wash and chop the spinach roughly, then blanch it for about 1 minute in a pan of boiling water. Drain well.

8 As soon as the water has evaporated, add the spinach to the lamb. Fry over a medium heat for 7–10 minutes, using a wooden spoon in a semicircular motion, scraping the bottom of the pan as you stir.

9 Add the red bell pepper, green chiles, and fresh cilantro to the pan and stir over a medium heat for 2 minutes. Sprinkle on the lemon juice (if using) and serve immediately.

COOK'S TIP

Frozen spinach can also be used for the dish, but try to find whole-leaf spinach instead of the chopped kind. Let the frozen spinach thaw, then drain well; there is no need to blanch it.

NUTRITIONAL NOTES	
Per Portion	
Energy	500cal
Fat	36.4g
Saturated Fat	11.3g
Carbohydrate	6.8g
Fiber	3.2g

Zucchini with Lamb

For this simple supper dish, lamb is cooked first with yogurt, and then the sliced zucchini, which have already been browned, are added to the mixture.

INGREDIENTS

Serves 4

1 tablespoon oil
2 medium onions, chopped
8 ounces lean lamb steaks,
   cut into strips
½ cup plain low-fat yogurt
1 teaspoon garam masala
1 teaspoon chili powder
1 teaspoon crushed garlic
1 teaspoon grated fresh ginger root
½ teaspoon ground coriander
2 medium zucchini, sliced
1 tablespoon chopped fresh cilantro,
   to garnish

NUTRITIONAL NOTES
Per Portion

Energy	178cal
Fat	8.36g
Saturated Fat	2.78g
Carbohydrate	10.83g
Fiber	1.99g

_____ COOK'S TIP _____

Frying onions in very little oil needs to be done over a low heat and requires some patience. They will take a little longer to brown and should be gently stirred only occasionally. Excessive stirring will draw the moisture out of the onions and make them even more difficult to fry.

1 Heat the oil in a karahi, wok, or heavy pan and fry the onions until golden brown.

2 Add the lamb strips and stir-fry for 1 minute to seal the meat.

3 Put the yogurt, garam masala, chili powder, garlic, ginger, and ground coriander into a bowl. Whisk the mixture together.

4 Pour the yogurt mixture over the lamb and stir-fry for 2 minutes. Cover and cook over a medium to low heat for 12–15 minutes.

5 Preheat the broiler. Put the zucchini in a flameproof dish and brown lightly under the heat for about 3 minutes, turning once.

6 Check that the lamb is cooked through and the sauce is thick, then add the zucchini and serve garnished with the fresh cilantro.

Spiced Lamb with Tomatoes and Peppers

Select lean tender lamb from the leg for this lightly spiced curry with bell peppers and wedges of onion. Serve warm nan bread to mop up the tomato-rich juices.

INGREDIENTS

Serves 6

1-inch piece fresh ginger root
3¼ pounds lean boneless lamb, cubed
1 cup plain yogurt
2 tablespoons sunflower oil
3 onions
2 red bell peppers, seeded and cut
    into chunks
3 garlic cloves, finely chopped
1 fresh red chile, seeded
    and chopped
2 tablespoons mild curry paste
2 x 14-ounce cans chopped tomatoes
large pinch of saffron threads
1¾ pounds plum tomatoes, halved,
    seeded, and cut into chunks
salt and black pepper
chopped fresh cilantro,
    to garnish

1 Thinly peel the ginger, using a sharp knife or a vegetable peeler, then grate the peeled root finely. Set the grated ginger aside.

VARIATION

Although pork would be unlikely to be used in India, it would work well for this dish. You can use pork tenderloin to replace the lamb.

2 Mix the lamb with the yogurt in a bowl. Cover and chill for about 1 hour.

3 Heat the oil in a large pan. Drain the lamb and reserve the yogurt, then cook the lamb in batches until it is golden on all sides—this will take about 15 minutes in total. Remove the lamb from the pan using a slotted spoon and set aside.

4 Cut two of the onions into wedges (six from each onion) and add to the oil remaining in the pan. Fry the onions over a medium heat for 10 minutes, or until they are beginning to color.

5 Add the bell peppers and cook for 5 minutes. Use a slotted spoon to remove the vegetables from the pan and set aside.

6 Meanwhile, chop the remaining onion. Add it to the rest of the oil in the pan with the chopped garlic, chile, and grated ginger, and cook for 4–5 minutes, stirring frequently, until the onion has softened.

7 Stir in the curry paste and canned tomatoes with the reserved yogurt. Return the lamb to the pan, season, and stir well. Bring to a boil, then reduce the heat and simmer for 30 minutes.

8 Pound the saffron to a powder in a mortar, then stir in a little boiling water to dissolve the saffron. Add this liquid to the curry and stir well.

9 Return the onion and pepper mixture to the pan, then stir in the fresh tomatoes. Bring the curry back to simmering point and cook for 15 minutes. Garnish with chopped fresh cilantro to serve.

NUTRITIONAL NOTES	
Per Portion	
Energy	594cal
Fat	32.8g
Saturated Fat	13.8g
Carbohydrate	19.7g
Fiber	4.3g

Khara Masala Lamb

This is a dish which involves a technique called bhooning—stirring with a semicircular motion. Whole spices are used, so warn the diners of their presence in advance! This curry is delicious served with freshly baked nan bread or plain rice.

INGREDIENTS

Serves 4

3 small onions, chopped
1 tablespoon oil
1 teaspoon shredded fresh ginger root
1 teaspoon sliced garlic
6 dried red chiles
3 cardamom pods
2 cinnamon sticks
6 black peppercorns
3 cloves
½ teaspoon salt
1 pound boned lean leg of lamb, cubed
2½ cups water
2 fresh green chiles, sliced
2 tablespoons chopped fresh cilantro

VARIATION

For a tasty alternative, instead of the boned leg of lamb used here, use the equivalent weight of either lean skinned chicken or beef cut into cubes.

1 Using a sharp knife, chop the onions finely. Heat the oil in a large pan.

2 Add the onions to the oil. Lower the heat and fry the onions until they are lightly browned, stirring occasionally.

3 Add half the ginger and half the garlic and stir well.

4 Drop in half the red chiles, the cardamom pods, cinnamon, peppercorns, cloves, and salt.

5 Add the lamb and fry over a medium heat. Stir continuously with a semicircular movement, using a wooden spoon to scrape the bottom of the pan and prevent the meat from burning. Cook for about 5 minutes.

6 Stir in the water, cover with a lid, and cook slowly over a medium-low heat for 35–40 minutes, or until the water has evaporated and the meat is tender, stirring from time to time to prevent the mixture from burning on the bottom of the pan.

7 Add the rest of the shredded ginger and sliced garlic and the remaining dried red chiles, along with the sliced fresh green chiles and the chopped cilantro.

8 Continue to stir the mixture over the heat until some free oil is visible on the sides of the pan. Remove the pan from the heat. Transfer the curry to a serving dish and serve immediately.

NUTRITIONAL NOTES	
Per Portion	
Energy	242cal
Fat	13.20g
Saturated Fat	5.19g
Carbohydrate	6.70g
Fiber	0.90g

Spiced Lamb with Chiles

This is a fairly hot stir-fry dish, although you can, of course, make it less so by either discarding the seeds from the chiles, or using just one chile of each color.

INGREDIENTS

Serves 4

8 ounces lean lamb tenderloin
½ cup plain low-fat yogurt
¼ teaspoon ground cardamom
1 teaspoon grated fresh ginger root
1 teaspoon crushed garlic
1 teaspoon chili powder
1 teaspoon garam masala
1 teaspoon salt
1 tablespoon oil
2 medium onions, chopped
1 bay leaf
1¼ cups water
2 fresh green chiles, sliced
    lengthwise
2 fresh red chiles, sliced
    lengthwise
2 tablespoons fresh cilantro leaves

NUTRITIONAL NOTES
Per Portion

Energy	169cal
Fat	8.13g
Saturated Fat	2.71g
Carbohydrate	10.01g
Fiber	1.32g

_____ COOK'S TIP _____

Letting the strips of lamb marinate for an hour in the spicy yogurt mixture allows the flavor to penetrate all the way through the meat and also makes it beautifully tender, so it cooks quickly.

1 Using a sharp knife, remove any excess fat from the lamb and cut the meat into even-size strips.

2 In a bowl, mix the yogurt, cardamom, ginger, garlic, chili powder, and garam masala. Stir in the salt. Add the lamb and let stand for about 1 hour to marinate.

3 Heat the oil in a karahi, wok, or heavy pan and fry the onions for 3-5 minutes, until golden.

4 Add the bay leaf, then add the lamb with the yogurt and spice mixture. Stir-fry for 2–3 minutes.

5 Pour over the water, cover, and cook for 15–20 minutes over a low heat, checking occasionally. Once the water has evaporated, stir-fry the mixture for 1 minute more.

6 Stir in the red and green chiles and the fresh cilantro. Spoon into a serving dish and serve hot.

Spicy Lamb and Potato Stew

Indian spices transform a simple lamb and potato stew into a dish fit for princes.

INGREDIENTS

Serves 6

1½ pounds lean lamb tenderloin
1 tablespoon oil
1 onion, finely chopped
2 bay leaves
1 fresh green chile, seeded and
  finely chopped
2 garlic cloves, finely chopped
2 teaspoons ground coriander
1 teaspoon ground cumin
½ teaspoon ground turmeric
½ teaspoon chili powder
½ teaspoon salt
2 tomatoes, peeled and chopped
2½ cups chicken stock
2 large potatoes, cut in large chunks
chopped fresh cilantro,
  to garnish

NUTRITIONAL NOTES	
Per Portion	
Energy	283cal
Fat	12.40g
Saturated Fat	5.02g
Carbohydrate	17.20g
Fiber	1.70g

1 Remove any visible fat from the lamb and cut the meat into neat 1-inch cubes.

2 Heat the oil in a large heavy pan and fry the onion, bay leaves, chile, and garlic for 5 minutes.

3 Add the meat and cook for about 6–8 minutes, until lightly browned.

4 Add the ground coriander, ground cumin, ground turmeric, chili powder, and salt and cook the spices for 3–4 minutes, stirring all the time to prevent the spices from sticking to the bottom of the pan.

5 Add the tomatoes and stock and simmer for 5 minutes. Bring to a boil, cover, and simmer for 1 hour.

6 Add the bitesize chunks of potato to the simmering mixture, stir in, and cook for another 30–40 minutes, or until the meat is tender and much of the excess juices have been absorbed, leaving a thick but minimal sauce. Garnish with chopped fresh cilantro and serve piping hot.

_____ COOK'S TIP _____

This stew is absolutely delicious served with warm, freshly made chapatis and a cucumber raita.

Lamb Dhansak

About 13 centuries ago, a small group of Persians fled their country to avoid religious persecution and landed in the state of Gujarat. They became known as Parsis. This is one of their traditional dishes. It is time-consuming to make, but the excellent flavor is just reward.

INGREDIENTS

Serves 4–6

6 tablespoons vegetable oil
5 fresh green chiles, chopped
1-inch piece fresh ginger root, grated
3 garlic cloves, crushed, plus 1 garlic clove, sliced
2 bay leaves
2-inch piece cinnamon stick
2 pounds lean lamb, cut into large pieces
2½ cups water
¾ cup whole red lentils, washed and drained
¼ cup each chana dhal or yellow split peas, husked moong dhal and split red lentils, washed and drained
2 potatoes, diced, soaked in water
1 eggplant, chopped, soaked in water
4 onions, finely sliced, deep-fried and drained
2 ounces fresh spinach, trimmed, washed and chopped
1 ounce fresh or dried fenugreek leaves
2 carrots, sliced
4 ounces fresh cilantro, chopped
2 ounces fresh mint, chopped
2 tablespoons dhansak masala
2 tablespoons sambhar masala
1 teaspoon salt
2 teaspoons soft brown sugar
4 tablespoons tamarind juice

1 Heat 3 tablespoons of the oil in a wok, karahi or large pan, and gently fry the fresh chiles, ginger, crushed garlic, bay leaves and cinnamon for 2 minutes. Add the lamb and the water. Bring to the boil, then simmer, covered, until the lamb is half cooked.

2 Drain the meat stock into another pan and put the lamb aside. Add the whole red lentils, chana dhal or split peas, moong dhal and split red lentils to the stock and cook gently for 25–30 minutes at a low temperature until they are tender. Mash the lentils with the back of a spoon.

3 Drain the potatoes and eggplant and add to the lentils. Reserve a little of the deep-fried onions and stir the remainder into the pan, along with the spinach, fenugreek and carrot.

4 Add some hot water to the pan if the mixture seems too thick. Cook until the vegetables are tender, then mash again with a spoon, keeping the vegetables a little coarse.

5 Heat 1 tablespoon of the remaining oil in a large frying pan. Reserve a few cilantro and mint leaves to use as a garnish, and gently fry the remaining leaves with the dhansak and sambhar masala, salt and sugar. Add the lamb pieces and fry gently for 5 minutes.

6 Add the lamb and spices to the lentil mixture and stir. Cover, reduce the heat to low and cook until the lamb is tender. The lentils will absorb liquid, so add more water if needed. Mix in the tamarind juice.

7 Heat the remaining vegetable oil in a small pan and fry the sliced garlic until golden brown.

8 Sprinkle the fried garlic slices over the dhansak. Garnish with the remaining deep-fried onion and the reserved fresh cilantro and mint leaves. Serve the dish hot, with caramelized basmati rice if desired.

NUTRITIONAL NOTES	
Per Portion	
Energy	720cal
Fat	34.8g
Saturated Fat	10g
Carbohydrate	58.6g
Fiber	7.6g

Lahore-style Lamb Curry

Named after Lahore, a former Indian city which has been in Pakistan since the Independence, this hearty dish has a wonderfully aromatic flavor imparted by the winter spices such as cloves, black peppercorns and cinnamon.

INGREDIENTS

Serves 4

4 tablespoons vegetable oil
1 bay leaf
2 cloves
4 black peppercorns
1 onion, sliced
1 pound lean boneless lamb, cubed
¼ teaspoon ground turmeric
1½ teaspoons chili powder
1 teaspoon crushed coriander seeds
1-inch piece cinnamon stick
1 teaspoon crushed garlic
1½ teaspoons salt
6 cups water
⅓ cup chana dhal (yellow split peas)
2 tomatoes, quartered
2 fresh green chiles, chopped
1 tablespoon chopped fresh
   cilantro

1 Heat the oil in a karahi, wok or large pan. Lower the heat slightly and add the bay leaf, cloves, peppercorns and onion. Fry for about 5 minutes, or until the onion is golden brown.

2 Add the cubed lamb, turmeric, chili powder, coriander seeds, cinnamon stick, garlic and most of the salt, and stir-fry for about 5 minutes over a medium heat.

3 Pour in 3¾ cups of the water and cover the pan with a lid or aluminum foil, making sure the foil does not come into contact with the food. Simmer for 35–40 minutes or until the lamb is tender.

4 Put the chana dhal into a large pan with the remaining measured water and a good pinch of salt and boil for 12–15 minutes, or until the water has almost evaporated and the dhal is soft enough to be mashed. If the mixture is too thick, add up to ⅔ cup water.

5 When the lamb is tender, remove the lid or foil and stir-fry the mixture using a wooden spoon, until some free oil begins to appear on the sides of the pan.

6 Add the cooked lentils to the lamb and mix together well. Stir in the tomatoes, chiles and chopped fresh cilantro and serve.

NUTRITIONAL NOTES	
Per Portion	
Energy	362cal
Fat	24g
Saturated Fat	7.3g
Carbohydrate	11.5g
Fiber	1.6g

Hot and Sour Lamb and Lentil Curry

This dish has a hot, sweet-and-sour flavor, through which should rise the slightly bitter flavor of fenugreek.

INGREDIENTS

Serves 4–6
6 tablespoons vegetable oil
2 fresh red chiles, chopped
2 fresh green chiles, chopped
1-inch piece fresh ginger root, crushed
3 garlic cloves crushed
2 bay leaves
2-inch piece cinnamon stick
2 pounds lean lamb, cubed
2½ cups water
2 cups mixed lentils
   (see Cook's Tip)
2 potatoes, cubed
1 eggplant, cubed
2 zucchini, cubed
4 onions, thinly sliced,
   deep-fried and drained
4 ounces frozen spinach,
   thawed and drained
1 ounce fenugreek leaves,
   fresh or dried
4 ounces pumpkin, cubed
4 cups fresh cilantro, chopped
2 cups fresh mint, chopped, or
   1 tablespoon mint sauce
3 tablespoons garam masala
salt, to taste
2 teaspoons brown sugar
lemon juice, to taste
1 garlic clove, sliced

1 Heat 3 tablespoons of the oil in a pan, wok, or karahi and fry the chiles, ginger, and garlic for 2 minutes. Add the bay leaves, cinnamon, lamb, and water. Bring to a boil, then reduce the heat and simmer until the lamb is half cooked.

2 Drain the water into another pan and put the lamb aside. Add the lentils to the water and cook until they are tender. Mash the lentils with the back of a spoon.

3 Add the cubes of potatoes and eggplant and stir into the mashed lentils, then add the zucchini cubes and deep-fried onions. Stir in the spinach, fenugreek, and pumpkin. Add some hot water if the mixture is too thick. Cook until the vegetables are tender, then mash again with a spoon, keeping the vegetables a little coarse.

<hr />

COOK'S TIP

India has dozens of different lentils and it is worth visiting an Indian market or grocer to familiarize yourself with some of the most popular. For this recipe, you might like to include bengal gram (a type of chickpea), moong dhal (small split yellow lentils), and masoor dhal (red split lentils). Cooking times will depend on the types chosen.

4 Heat 1 tablespoon of the oil in a skillet, and gently fry the fresh cilantro and mint (saving a little to garnish) with the masala, salt, and sugar. Add the reserved lamb and fry gently for about 5 minutes.

5 Return the lamb and spices to the lentil and vegetable mixture and stir well. If the mixture seems dry, add more water. Heat gently until the lamb is fully cooked.

6 Add the lemon juice and mix well. Heat the remaining oil and fry the sliced clove of garlic until golden brown. Pour over the curry. Garnish with the remaining deep-fried onion slices and the reserved cilantro and mint. Serve hot.

NUTRITIONAL NOTES	
Per Portion	
Energy	1,040cal
Fat	53.5g
Saturated Fat	14.9g
Carbohydrate	73.5g
Fiber	9.8g

Fragrant Lamb Curry with Cardamom-spiced Rice

Wonderfully aromatic, this Indian-style lamb biryani, with the meat and rice cooked together in a clay pot, is a delicious meal in itself.

INGREDIENTS

Serves 4

1 large onion, quartered
2 garlic cloves
1 fresh green chile, halved and seeded
2-inch piece fresh ginger root
1 tablespoon ghee
1 tablespoon vegetable oil
1½ pounds boned shoulder or leg
  of lamb, cut into chunks
1 tablespoon ground coriander
2 teaspoons ground cumin
1 cinnamon stick, broken
  into 3 pieces
⅔ cup thick plain yogurt
⅔ cup water
⅓ cup plumped dried apricots,
  cut into chunks
salt and black pepper

For the rice

1¼ cups basmati rice
6 cardamom pods, split open
2 tablespoons butter, cut into small
  pieces
3 tablespoons toasted cashew nuts
  or sliced almonds

For the garnish

1 onion, sliced and fried until golden
a few sprigs of fresh cilantro

1 Soak a large clay pot or chicken brick in cold water for 20 minutes, then drain. Place the onion, garlic, chile, and ginger in a food processor or blender and process with 1 tablespoon water to a smooth paste.

<hr>
COOK'S TIP
<hr>
Serve a cooling yogurt raita and a fresh fruit chutney or relish as an accompaniment.

2 Heat the ghee and vegetable oil in a heavy skillet. Fry the lamb chunks in batches over a high heat until golden brown. Remove from the pan using a slotted spoon and set aside.

3 Scrape the onion paste into the remaining oil left in the skillet, stir in the ground coriander and cumin, add the cinnamon stick pieces, and fry for 1–2 minutes, stirring constantly with a wooden spoon.

4 Return the meat to the skillet, then gradually add the yogurt, a spoonful at a time, stirring well between each addition with a wooden spoon. Season the meat well with plenty of salt and pepper and stir in the water.

5 Transfer the contents of the skillet to the prepared clay pot, cover with the lid, and place in an unheated oven. Set the oven to 350°F and cook for 45 minutes.

6 Meanwhile, prepare the basmati rice. Place it in a bowl, cover with cold water, and let soak for 20 minutes. Drain the rice and place it in a large pan of boiling salted water, bring back to a boil, and cook for 10 minutes. Drain and stir in the split cardamom pods.

7 Remove the clay pot from the oven and stir in the chopped, plumped dried apricots. Pile the cooked rice on top of the lamb and dot with the butter. Drizzle over 4 tablespoons water, then sprinkle the cashew nuts or sliced almonds on top. Cover the pot, reduce the oven temperature to 300°F, and cook the meat and rice for 30 minutes.

8 Remove the lid from the pot and fluff up the rice with a fork. Spoon into warmed individual bowls, then sprinkle over the fried onion slices and garnish with the sprigs of fresh cilantro.

NUTRITIONAL NOTES	
Per Portion	
Energy	427cal
Fat	25.3g
Saturated Fat	11.3g
Carbohydrate	14.4g
Fiber	2g

Creamy Lamb Korma

A heritage of the talented cooks who served the Mogul emperors, this is a rich and luxurious dish. Mild in flavor, it is ideal for serving when you are unsure about how hot your guests like their curries to be.

INGREDIENTS

Serves 4–6

1 tablespoon white sesame seeds
1 tablespoon white poppy seeds
½ cup blanched almonds
2 fresh green chiles, seeded
6 garlic cloves, sliced
2-inch piece fresh ginger root, sliced
1 onion, finely chopped
3 tablespoons ghee or vegetable oil
6 green cardamom pods
2-inch piece cinnamon stick
4 cloves
2 pounds lean lamb,
   boned and cubed
1 teaspoon ground cumin
1 teaspoon ground coriander
1¼ cups heavy cream mixed
   with ½ teaspoon cornstarch
salt
roasted sesame seeds,
   to garnish

NUTRITIONAL NOTES	
Per Portion	
Energy	939cal
Fat	80.8g
Saturated Fat	38.3g
Carbohydrate	5.1g
Fiber	1.5g

_____ COOK'S TIP _____

If white poppy seeds are not available, use sunflower seeds instead.

1 Preheat a karahi, wok, or large pan over a medium heat without any fat, and add the first seven ingredients. Stir until they begin to change color. They should go just a shade darker.

2 Let the mixture cool, then grind to a fine paste using a mortar and pestle or in a food processor. Heat the ghee or oil in the pan over a low heat.

3 Fry the cardamoms, cinnamon, and cloves until the cloves swell. Add the lamb, ground cumin and coriander, and the prepared paste, and season with salt to taste. Increase the heat to medium and stir well. Reduce the heat to low, then cover the pan and cook until the lamb is almost done.

4 Remove from the heat, let cool a little and gradually fold in the cream, reserving 1 teaspoon to garnish.

5 When ready to serve, gently reheat the lamb, uncovered. Spoon into a warmed dish and garnish with the sesame seeds and the reserved cream. This korma is very good served with pilau rice.

Rogan Josh

This is one of the most popular lamb dishes that has originated in Kashmir. Traditionally, fatty meat on the bone is slow cooked until most of the fat is separated from the meat. The fat that escapes from the meat in this way is known as rogan and josh refers to the rich red color.

INGREDIENTS

Serves 4–6

3 tablespoons lemon juice
1 cup plain yogurt
1 teaspoon salt
2 garlic cloves, crushed
1-inch piece fresh ginger root, finely grated
2 pounds lean lamb tenderloin, cubed
4 tablespoons vegetable oil
½ teaspoon cumin seeds
2 bay leaves
4 green cardamom pods
1 onion, finely chopped
2 teaspoons ground coriander
2 teaspoons ground cumin
1 teaspoon chili powder
14-ounce can chopped tomatoes
2 tablespoons tomato paste
⅔ cup water
toasted cumin seeds and bay leaves, to garnish
plain boiled rice, to serve

1 In a large bowl, mix together the lemon juice, yogurt, salt, half the crushed garlic, and the ginger. Add the lamb, cover, and marinate in the refrigerator overnight.

2 Heat the oil in a karahi, wok, or large pan and fry the cumin seeds for 2 minutes. Add the bay leaves and cardamom pods and fry for 2 minutes.

3 Add the onion and remaining garlic and fry for 5 minutes. Add the coriander, cumin, and chili powder. Fry for 2 minutes.

4 Add the marinated lamb to the pan and cook for another 5 minutes, stirring occasionally to prevent the mixture from sticking to the bottom of the pan and starting to burn.

5 Stir in the tomatoes, tomato paste, and water. Cover and simmer for 1–1½ hours. Garnish with toasted cumin seeds and bay leaves, and serve with the rice.

NUTRITIONAL NOTES	
Per Portion	
Energy	566cal
Fat	37g
Saturated Fat	13.3g
Carbohydrate	10.7g
Fiber	1.2g

Rezala

Essentially a Muslim dish, this delectable recipe comes from Bengal, where there is a tradition of Muslim cooking. This is a legacy from the Muslim rulers of the Mogul era.

INGREDIENTS

Serves 4

1 large onion, roughly chopped
2 teaspoons grated fresh ginger root
2 teaspoons crushed garlic
4–5 cloves
½ teaspoon black peppercorns
6 green cardamom pods
2-inch piece cinnamon stick, halved
8 lamb rib chops
4 tablespoons vegetable oil
1 large onion, finely sliced
¾ cup plain yogurt
¼ cup butter
1 teaspoon salt
½ teaspoon ground cumin
½ teaspoon hot chili powder
nutmeg
½ teaspoon sugar
1 tablespoon lime juice
pinch of saffron, steeped in 1 tablespoon hot water for 10–15 minutes
1 tablespoon rose water
rose petals, to garnish

1 Process the onion in a blender or food processor. Add a little water if necessary to form a paste.

2 Put the paste in a glass bowl and add the grated ginger, crushed garlic, cloves, peppercorns, cardamom pods, and cinnamon. Mix well.

3 Put the lamb chops in a large shallow glass dish and add the spice mixture. Mix thoroughly, cover the bowl, and let the lamb marinate for 3–4 hours, or overnight in the refrigerator. Bring back to room temperature before cooking.

4 In a karahi, wok, or large pan, heat the oil over a medium-high heat and fry the sliced onion for 6–7 minutes, until golden brown. Remove the onion slices with a slotted spoon, squeezing out as much oil as possible on the side of the pan. Drain the onions on paper towels.

5 In the remaining oil, fry the marinated lamb chops for 4–5 minutes, stirring frequently. Reduce the heat to low, cover, and cook for 5–7 minutes.

6 Meanwhile, mix the yogurt and butter together in a small pan and place over a low heat. Cook for 5–6 minutes, stirring constantly, then stir into the lamb chops along with salt. Add the cumin and chili powder and cover the pan. Cook for 45–50 minutes, until the chops are tender.

7 Using a nutmeg grater, or the finest cutting surface on a large, stainless steel grater, grate about ½ teaspoon nutmeg.

8 Add the nutmeg and sugar to the pan containing the lamb, cook for 1–2 minutes, and add the lime juice, saffron, and rose water. Stir and mix well, simmer for 2–3 minutes, and remove from the heat. Spoon into a dish and garnish with the fried onion and rose petals. Serve with nan bread or boiled basmati rice, if desired.

COOK'S TIP

If you don't have whole nutmegs in your pantry, use ground nutmeg. The flavor will not be as strong, so you may need to use a little more than if using fresh.

NUTRITIONAL NOTES
Per Portion

Energy	637cal
Fat	57.4g
Saturated Fat	25.7g
Carbohydrate	12.8g
Fiber	1.7g

Lamb with Peas and Mint

A simple dish for a family meal, this is easy to prepare and very versatile. It is equally delicious whether served with plain boiled rice or chapatis. Another excellent use for the lamb mixture is as a filling for samosas, or even in meat pies or turnovers.

INGREDIENTS

Serves 4

1 tablespoon oil
1 medium onion, chopped
½ teaspoon crushed garlic
½ teaspoon grated fresh ginger root
½ teaspoon chili powder
¼ teaspoon ground turmeric
1 teaspoon ground coriander
1 teaspoon salt
2 medium tomatoes, sliced
10 ounces lean leg of lamb, ground
1 large carrot, sliced or
  cut into batons
½ cup baby peas
1 tablespoon chopped fresh mint
1 tablespoon chopped fresh cilantro
1 fresh green chile, chopped
fresh cilantro, to garnish

NUTRITIONAL NOTES
Per Portion

Energy	178cal
Fat	9.40g
Saturated Fat	3.32g
Carbohydrate	7.20g
Fiber	2.10g

COOK'S TIP

To cut the carrot into batons, or thin sticks, first cut it into 2-inch lengths and square the sides. Slice the carrot lengthwise, then cut the pieces again at the identical width to make strips.

1 In a deep heavy skillet, heat the oil and fry the chopped onion over a medium heat for 5 minutes, until golden.

2 Meanwhile, in a small mixing bowl, mix the garlic, ginger, chili powder, turmeric, ground coriander, and salt. Stir well.

3 Add the sliced tomatoes and the spice mixture to the onions in the skillet and fry for 2–3 minutes, stirring continuously.

4 Add the ground lamb to the mixture and stir-fry for about 7–10 minutes to seal.

5 Break up any lumps of meat that form in the pan, using a potato masher if necessary.

6 Finally add the carrot, baby peas, chopped fresh mint and cilantro, and the chopped green chile and mix together well.

7 Cook, stirring for 2–3 minutes, until the carrot slices or batons and the baby peas are cooked, then serve immediately, garnished with fresh cilantro sprigs.

Ground Lamb with Curry Leaves and Chile

The whole chiles pack a real punch, but they can be removed from the dish before serving.

INGREDIENTS

Serves 4

2 teaspoons oil
2 medium onions, chopped
10 curry leaves
6 fresh green chiles
12 ounces lean ground lamb
1 teaspoon crushed garlic
1 teaspoon grated fresh ginger root
1 teaspoon chili powder
¼ teaspoon ground turmeric
1 teaspoon salt
2 tomatoes, peeled and quartered
1 tablespoon chopped fresh cilantro

1 Heat the oil in a karahi, wok, or heavy pan and fry the onions with the curry leaves and three of the whole green chiles.

_____ COOK'S TIP _____

This curry also makes a terrific brunch if served with fried eggs.

2 Put the lamb into a bowl. Mix with the garlic, ginger, and spices.

3 Add the lamb and salt to the onions and stir-fry for 7–10 minutes.

4 Add the tomatoes, cilantro, and remaining chiles and stir-fry for 2 minutes. Serve hot.

NUTRITIONAL NOTES	
Per Portion	
Energy	197cal
Fat	9.37g
Saturated Fat	3.59g
Carbohydrate	8.57g
Fiber	1.63g

Lamb with Apricots

Lamb is combined with apricots and traditional Indian spices to produce a rich, spicy curry with a hint of sweetness.

INGREDIENTS

Serves 6

2 pounds lean stewing lamb
1 tablespoon oil
1-inch cinnamon stick
4 green cardamom pods
1 onion, chopped
1 tablespoon curry paste
1 teaspoon ground cumin
1 teaspoon ground coriander
¼ teaspoon salt
⅔ cup plumped dried apricots
1½ cups lamb stock
fresh cilantro, to garnish
yellow rice and mango chutney, to serve

1 Remove all the fat from the lamb and cut into 1-inch cubes.

NUTRITIONAL NOTES	
Per Portion	
Energy	327cal
Fat	16.00g
Saturated Fat	6.59g
Carbohydrate	13.30g
Fiber	2.70g

2 Heat the oil in a large heavy pan and fry the cinnamon stick and cardamoms for 2 minutes. Add the onion and gently fry for about 6–8 minutes, stirring occasionally.

3 Add the curry paste and fry for 2 minutes. Stir in the cumin, coriander, and salt and stir-fry for another 2–3 minutes.

4 Add the meat, apricots, and the stock. Cover and cook for 1–1½ hours. Serve, garnished with fresh cilantro, on yellow rice, with the chutney in a separate bowl.

Spicy Spring Lamb Roast

Coating a leg of lamb with a spicy, fruity rub gives it a wonderful flavor. During the initial cooking process, the flavors permeate the meat, which remains moist inside its aluminum foil parcel. Later, the foil is removed to allow the roast to turn a wonderful brown color.

INGREDIENTS

Serves 6
3–3½ pounds lean leg
  of spring lamb
1 teaspoon chili powder
1 teaspoon crushed garlic
1 teaspoon ground coriander
1 teaspoon ground cumin
1 teaspoon salt
1 tablespoon dried bread crumbs
3 tablespoons plain low-fat yogurt
2 tablespoons lemon juice
2 tablespoons golden raisins
1 tablespoon oil

For the garnish
mixed salad greens
fresh cilantro
2 tomatoes, quartered
1 large carrot, shredded
lemon wedges

NUTRITIONAL NOTES	
Per Portion	
Energy	265cal
Fat	13.40g
Saturated Fat	5.59g
Carbohydrate	8.90g
Fiber	0.70g

1 Preheat the oven to 350°F. Trim any excess fat from the lamb. Rinse the joint, pat it dry, and set aside on a sheet of aluminum foil large enough to enclose it completely.

2 In a medium bowl, mix together the chili powder, garlic, ground coriander, ground cumin, and salt.

3 Mix together in a food processor the bread crumbs, yogurt, lemon juice, and golden raisins.

4 Add the contents of the food processor to the spice mixture together with the oil and mix together well. Pour this onto the leg of lamb and rub all over the meat.

5 Enclose the meat in the foil and place in an ovenproof dish. Cook in the oven for about 1½ hours.

6 Remove the lamb from the oven, open the foil, and, using the back of a spoon, spread the mixture evenly over the meat. Return the lamb, uncovered, to the oven for another 45 minutes, or until it is cooked all the way through and is tender.

7 Slice the meat and serve with the mixed salad greens, fresh cilantro, tomatoes, carrot, and lemon wedges.

COOK'S TIP

Make sure that the spice mixture is rubbed all over the leg of lamb so that its flavor penetrates all parts of the joint.

Mughlai-style Leg of Lamb

In India, there are different names for this style of cooking a leg of lamb, two of which are shahi raan and peshawari raan. Legend has it that roasting a whole leg of lamb was first popularized by the Mongolian warrior Genghis Khan.

INGREDIENTS

Serves 4–6
4 large onions, chopped
4 garlic cloves
2-inch piece fresh ginger root, chopped
3 tablespoons ground almonds
2 teaspoons ground cumin
2 teaspoons ground coriander
2 teaspoons ground turmeric
2 teaspoons garam masala
4–6 fresh green chiles
juice of 1 lemon
1¼ cups plain yogurt, beaten
4-pound leg of lamb
8–10 cloves
salt
1 tablespoon sliced almonds, to garnish
4 firm tomatoes, halved and broiled, to serve

1 Preheat the oven to 375°F. Place the onions, garlic, ginger, ground almonds, all the dry spices, chiles, and lemon juice in a food processor or blender. Add salt to taste, and process to a smooth paste. Gradually add the yogurt and blend briefly to mix. Grease a large, deep roasting pan.

NUTRITIONAL NOTES	
Per Portion	
Energy	852cal
Fat	51.2g
Saturated Fat	17g
Carbohydrate	25.4g
Fiber	3.5g

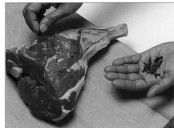

2 Remove most of the fat and skin from the lamb. Using a sharp knife, make deep pockets above the bone at each side of the thick end. Make deep diagonal gashes on both sides of the lamb.

3 Push the cloves firmly into the meat, spaced evenly on all sides.

4 Push some of the spice mixture into the pockets and gashes. Spread the remainder evenly all over the meat. Place the meat on the roasting pan and loosely cover the whole pan with aluminum foil. Roast for 2–2½ hours, or until the meat is cooked, removing the foil for the last 10 minutes of cooking time.

5 Remove from the oven and let rest for about 10 minutes before carving. Garnish the roast with the almonds and serve with the tomatoes.

_____ COOK'S TIP _____

If time permits, let the lamb stand at room temperature for a couple of hours before putting it in the oven.

Madras Beef Curry

Although Madras is renowned for the best vegetarian food in India, meat-based recipes such as this one are also extremely popular.

INGREDIENTS

Serves 4–6
4 tablespoons vegetable oil
1 large onion, finely sliced
3–4 cloves
4 green cardamoms
2 whole star anise
4 fresh green chiles, chopped
2 fresh or dried red chiles, chopped
3 tablespoons Madras masala paste
1 teaspoon ground turmeric
1 pound lean beef, cubed
4 tablespoons tamarind juice
sugar, to taste
salt
a few fresh cilantro leaves,
  chopped, to garnish

1 Heat the oil in a karahi, wok or large pan over a medium heat and fry the onion slices for about 8 minutes until they turn golden brown. Lower the heat, add all the spice ingredients, and fry for another 2–3 minutes.

2 Add the beef and mix well. Cover and cook over a low heat until the beef is tender and fully cooked. Cook uncovered on a higher heat for the last few minutes to reduce any excess liquid.

NUTRITIONAL NOTES	
Per Portion	
Energy	317cal
Fat	21.6g
Saturated Fat	5.6g
Carbohydrate	4.8g
Fiber	0.9g

3 Fold in the tamarind juice, sugar and salt. Reheat the dish and garnish with the chopped cilantro leaves. Pilau rice and a tomato and onion salad would make excellent accompaniments for this dish.

_____ COOK'S TIP _____

To tenderize the meat, add 4 tablespoons white wine vinegar in step 2, along with the meat, and omit the tamarind juice.

Spicy Meat Loaf

This mixture is baked in the oven and provides a hearty meal on cold winter days.

INGREDIENTS

Serves 4-6

5 eggs
1 pound lean ground beef
2 tablespoons grated fresh ginger root
2 tablespoons crushed garlic
6 fresh green chiles, chopped
2 small onions, finely chopped
½ teaspoon ground turmeric
2 cups fresh cilantro, chopped
6 ounces potato, grated
salt, to taste
salad greens, to serve
lemon twist, to garnish

1 Preheat the oven to 350°F. Beat 2 eggs until fluffy and pour into a greased 9 × 5 × 3-inch loaf pan.

2 Knead together the meat, ginger, and garlic, 4 green chiles, 1 chopped onion, 1 beaten egg, the turmeric, fresh cilantro, potato, and salt. Pack into the loaf pan and smooth the surface. Cook in the preheated oven for 45 minutes.

3 Meanwhile, beat the remaining eggs and fold in with the remaining green chiles and onion. Remove the loaf pan from the oven and pour the mixture all over the meat.

4 Return to the oven and cook until the eggs have set. Serve hot on a bed of salad greens, garnished with a twist of lemon.

NUTRITIONAL NOTES	
Per Portion	
Energy	394cal
Fat	25.4g
Saturated Fat	9.8g
Carbohydrate	10.1g
Fiber	1g

Beef Koftas

Serve these tasty treats piping hot with nan bread, raita, and a light salad. Leftover koftas can be chopped coarsely and packed into pita bread.

INGREDIENTS

Makes 20–25

1 pound lean ground beef
2 tablespoons grated fresh ginger root
2 tablespoons crushed garlic
4 fresh green chiles,
    finely chopped
1 small onion, finely chopped
1 egg
½ teaspoon ground turmeric
1 teaspoon garam masala
2 cups fresh cilantro, chopped
4–6 fresh mint leaves, chopped
6 ounces potato
salt, to taste
vegetable oil, for deep-frying

1 Mix the meat, ginger, garlic, chiles, onion, egg, spices, and herbs in a large bowl. Grate the potato into the bowl, and season with salt. Knead together to blend well and form a soft dough.

2 Shape the mixture into portions the size of golf balls. Place on a plate, cover, and let the koftas rest for about 25 minutes.

3 In a karahi, wok, or frying pan, heat the oil to medium-hot and fry the koftas in small batches, until they are golden brown in color. Drain well and serve hot.

NUTRITIONAL NOTES	
Per Portion	
Energy	63cal
Fat	4g
Saturated Fat	1.7g
Carbohydrate	1.8g
Fiber	0.2g

_____ VARIATION _____

Use lamb instead of the beef, if you prefer.

Beef Vindaloo

A fiery dish originally from Goa, a "vindaloo" curry is made using a unique blend of hot aromatic spices and vinegar to give it a distinctive flavor.

INGREDIENTS

Serves 6

1 tablespoon cumin seeds
4 dried red chiles
1 teaspoon black peppercorns
seeds from 5 green cardamom pods
1 teaspoon fenugreek seeds
1 teaspoon black mustard seeds
½ teaspoon salt
½ teaspoon raw sugar
4 tablespoons white wine vinegar
2 tablespoons oil
1 large onion, finely chopped
2 pounds lean stewing beef, cut
    into 1-inch cubes
1-inch piece fresh ginger root,
    finely chopped
1 garlic clove, crushed
2 teaspoons ground coriander
½ teaspoon ground turmeric
plain and yellow rice, see Cook's Tip,
    to serve

1 Put the cumin seeds, chiles, peppercorns, cardamom seeds, fenugreek seeds, and mustard seeds into a spice grinder (or a mortar and pestle) and grind to a fine powder.

2 Spoon into a bowl, add the salt, sugar, and white wine vinegar and mix to a thin paste. Heat 1 tablespoon of the oil in a large heavy pan and fry the onion for 10 minutes.

3 Put the onions and the spice mixture into a food processor or blender and process to a coarse paste.

4 Heat the remaining oil in the large pan and fry the meat cubes for about 10 minutes, until lightly browned. Remove with a slotted spoon.

5 Add the ginger and garlic to the oil remaining in the pan and fry for 2 minutes. Stir in the ground coriander and turmeric and fry for another 2 minutes.

6 Add the spice and onion paste and fry for about 5 minutes.

7 Return the beef cubes to the pan with 1¼ cups water. Cover and simmer for about 1–1½ hours, or until the meat is tender. Serve with plain and yellow rice.

NUTRITIONAL NOTES	
Per Portion	
Energy	269cal
Fat	11.6g
Saturated Fat	3.3g
Carbohydrate	7.3g
Fiber	0.6g

——————— COOK'S TIP ———————

To make plain and yellow rice, soak a pinch of saffron strands or dissolve a little ground turmeric in 1 tablespoon hot water. Stir into half the cooked rice until uniformly yellow. Mix the yellow rice into the plain rice.

Beef with Green Beans

Green beans cooked with beef is a variation on the traditional recipe using lamb. The sliced red bell pepper provides a contrast to the color of the beans and chiles, and adds extra flavor.

INGREDIENTS

Serves 4

10 ounces fine green beans,
    cut into 1-inch pieces
1 tablespoon oil
1 medium onion, sliced
1 teaspoon grated fresh ginger root
1 teaspoon crushed garlic
1 teaspoon chili powder
1¼ teaspoons salt
¼ teaspoon ground turmeric
2 tomatoes, chopped
1 pound lean beef, cubed
2 cups water
1 red bell pepper, seeded and sliced
1 tablespoon chopped fresh
    cilantro
2 fresh green chiles, chopped
warm chapatis, to serve (optional)

NUTRITIONAL NOTES	
Per Portion	
Energy	242cal
Fat	11.60g
Saturated Fat	2.91g
Carbohydrate	9.30g
Fiber	3.00g

--- COOK'S TIP ---

Blanching the beans in boiling water helps to preserve their bright green color. Rinsing them under cold water arrests the cooking process. Drain them well.

1 Blanch the beans in boiling water for 3–4 minutes, then rinse under cold running water, drain, and set aside.

2 Heat the oil in a large heavy pan and gently fry the onion slices until golden brown.

3 In a bowl, mix the ginger pulp, garlic, chili powder, salt, turmeric, and chopped tomatoes. Spoon the ginger and garlic mixture into the pan and stir-fry with the onion for 5–7 minutes.

4 Add the beef and stir-fry for another 3 minutes. Pour in the water, bring to a boil, and lower the heat. Half cover the pan and cook for 1–1¼ hours, until most of the water has evaporated and the meat is tender.

5 Add the green beans and mix everything together well.

6 Finally, add the red bell pepper, fresh cilantro, and green chiles. Cook the mixture, stirring, for another 7–10 minutes, or until the beans are tender.

7 Spoon into a large bowl or individual plates. Serve the beef hot, with warm chapatis if you like.

Citrus Beef Curry

This superbly aromatic curry is not exceptionally hot, but it is full of flavor.

INGREDIENTS

Serves 4

1 pound round steak
2 tablespoons vegetable oil
2 tablespoons medium curry paste
2 bay leaves
1⅔ cups coconut milk
1¼ cups beef stock
2 tablespoons lemon juice
grated rind and juice of ½ orange
1 tablespoon sugar
4 ounces pearl onions, peeled
   but left whole
8 ounces new potatoes, halved
1 cup unsalted roasted peanuts,
   roughly chopped
4 ounces fine green beans, halved
1 red bell pepper, seeded and
   thinly sliced
unsalted roasted peanuts, to
   garnish (optional)

4 Stir in the bay leaves, coconut milk, stock, lemon juice, orange rind and juice, and sugar, and bring to a boil, stirring frequently.

5 Add the onions and potatoes, then bring back to a boil, reduce the heat, and simmer, uncovered, for 5 minutes.

6 Stir in the peanuts, beans, and pepper and simmer for another 10 minutes, or until the beef and potatoes are tender. Serve in shallow bowls, with a spoon and fork, to enjoy all the rich and creamy juices. Sprinkle with extra unsalted roasted peanuts, if desired.

1 Trim any fat from the beef and cut the meat into 2-inch strips.

2 Heat the vegetable oil in a large, heavy pan, add the curry paste, and cook over a medium heat for 30 seconds, stirring constantly.

3 Add the beef and cook, stirring, for 2 minutes, until it is beginning to brown and is thoroughly coated with the spices.

NUTRITIONAL NOTES	
Per Portion	
Energy	444cal
Fat	24.2g
Saturated Fat	5.4g
Carbohydrate	23.5g
Fiber	4.2g

Steak and Kidney with Spinach

When this dish is cooked in India, the spinach is often pulverized. Here, it is coarsely chopped and added in at the last stages of cooking, which retains the nutritional value of the spinach and gives the dish a wonderful appearance.

INGREDIENTS

Serves 4–6
2-inch piece fresh ginger root
2 tablespoons vegetable oil
1 large onion, finely chopped
4 garlic cloves, crushed
4 tablespoons mild curry paste,
 or 4 tablespoons mild curry powder
¼ teaspoon ground turmeric
salt, to taste
2 pounds steak and kidney, cubed
1 pound fresh spinach, trimmed,
 washed and chopped or 1 pound
 frozen spinach, thawed and drained
4 tablespoons tomato paste
2 large tomatoes, finely chopped

1 Using a sharp knife or vegetable peeler, remove the skin from the ginger. Grate it on the fine side of a metal cheese grater.

COOK'S TIP

Fresh ginger freezes very easily and is actually much easier to grate when frozen. There's no need to defrost the ginger before adding it to the spicy onion mixture—it will thaw instantly upon contact with heat.

2 Heat the oil in a skillet, wok, or karahi and fry the onion, ginger, and garlic until the onion is soft and the ginger and garlic turn golden brown.

3 Lower the heat and add the curry paste or powder, turmeric, and salt. Add the steak and kidney to the pan and mix well. Cover and cook, stirring frequently, to prevent the mixture from sticking to the pan, for 20–30 minutes over a medium heat, until the meat is just tender.

4 Add the spinach and tomato paste and mix well. Cook, uncovered, until the spinach has softened and most of the liquid has evaporated.

5 Fold in the chopped tomatoes. Increase the heat (the tomatoes will have a cooling effect on the other ingredients) and cook the mixture for another 5 minutes, until they are soft.

6 Dish into shallow bowls and serve piping hot with a simple accompaniment to offset the rich, gamey flavor of the dish, such as plain boiled basmati rice. Go easy on any side portions, however, because this is a very rich and filling dish.

NUTRITIONAL NOTES	
Per Portion	
Energy	362cal
Fat	13.5g
Saturated Fat	3.5g
Carbohydrate	11.7g
Fiber	4.4g

Beef Biryani

This biryani, which uses beef, is a speciality of the Muslim community. The recipe may seem long, but biryani is one of the easiest and most relaxing ways of cooking, especially when you are entertaining. Once the dish is assembled and placed in the oven, it looks after itself and you can spend more time with your guests.

INGREDIENTS

Serves 4

2 large onions
2 garlic cloves, chopped
1-inch piece fresh ginger root, peeled and roughly chopped
½–1 fresh green chile, seeded and chopped
small bunch of fresh cilantro
4 tablespoons sliced almonds
2–3 tablespoons water
1 tablespoon ghee or butter, plus 2 tablespoons butter for the rice
3 tablespoons vegetable oil
2 tablespoons golden raisins
1¼ pounds braising or stewing steak, cubed
1 teaspoon ground coriander
1 tablespoon ground cumin
½ teaspoon ground turmeric
½ teaspoon ground fenugreek
good pinch of ground cinnamon
¾ cup plain yogurt, whisked
1½ cups basmati rice
about 5 cups hot chicken stock or water
salt and black pepper
2 hard-boiled eggs, quartered, to garnish
chapatis, to serve

> ___ COOK'S TIP ___
>
> Place a piece of buttered waxed paper on the rice. This will help to keep the top layer moist in the oven.

1 Roughly chop one onion and place it in a food processor or blender. Add the garlic, ginger, chile, fresh cilantro, and half the sliced almonds. Pour in the water and process to a smooth paste. Transfer the paste to a small bowl and set aside.

2 Finely slice the remaining onion into rings or half rings. Heat half the ghee or butter with half the oil in a heavy flameproof casserole and fry the onion rings for 10–15 minutes, until they are a deep golden brown. Transfer to a plate with a slotted spoon.

3 Fry the remaining sliced almonds briefly until golden and set aside with the onion rings, then quickly fry the golden raisins until they swell. Transfer to the plate.

4 Heat the remaining ghee or butter in the casserole with another 1 tablespoon of the oil. Fry the cubed meat, in batches, until evenly browned on all sides. Transfer the meat to a plate and set aside.

5 Wipe the casserole clean with paper towels, heat the remaining oil, and pour in the onion, spice, and coriander paste made earlier. Cook over a medium heat for 2–3 minutes, stirring all the time, until the mixture begins to brown lightly. Stir in all the additional spices, season with salt and ground black pepper, and cook for 1 minute more.

6 Lower the heat, then stir in the yogurt, a little at a time. When all of it has been incorporated into the spice mixture, return the meat to the casserole. Stir to coat, cover tightly, and simmer over a gentle heat for 40–45 minutes, until the meat is tender. Meanwhile, soak the rice in a bowl of cold water for 15–20 minutes.

7 Preheat the oven to 325°F. Drain the rice, place in a pan, and add the hot chicken stock or water, together with a little salt. Bring back to a boil, cover, and cook for 5 minutes.

8 Drain the rice and pile it in a mound on top of the meat in the casserole. Using the handle of a spoon, make a hole through the rice and meat mixture to the bottom of the pan. Place the fried onions, almonds, and raisins over the top and dot with butter. Cover the casserole tightly with a double layer of aluminum foil and secure with a lid.

9 Cook the biryani in the preheated oven for 30–40 minutes. To serve, spoon the mixture onto a warmed serving platter and garnish with the quartered hard-boiled eggs. Serve with chapatis.

NUTRITIONAL NOTES	
Per Portion	
Energy	741cal
Fat	29.3g
Saturated Fat	10.9g
Carbohydrate	79.1g
Fiber	3.1g

Chile Beef with Basil

This is a dish for chile lovers! It is very easy to prepare—all you need is a karahi or a wok.

INGREDIENTS

Serves 2
about 6 tablespoons vegetable oil
16–20 large fresh basil leaves
10 ounces round steak
2 tablespoons Worcestershire sauce
1 teaspoon brown sugar
1–2 fresh red chiles, sliced into rings
3 garlic cloves, chopped
1 teaspoon chopped fresh ginger root
1 shallot, thinly sliced
2 tablespoons finely chopped fresh basil
   leaves, plus extra to garnish
squeeze of lemon juice
salt and black pepper
rice, to serve

1 Heat the oil in a karahi or wok. Add the whole basil leaves and fry for about 1 minute, until crisp and golden. Drain on paper towels. Remove the pan from the heat and pour off all but 2 tablespoons of the oil.

_____ COOK'S TIP _____

Although Worcestershire sauce is often thought of as archetypally English, it is actually based on an Indian recipe. Ingredients include molasses, anchovies, and tamarind extract.

2 Cut the steak across the grain into thin strips. Mix the Worcestershire sauce and sugar in a bowl. Add the beef, mix well, then cover and let marinate for about 30 minutes.

3 Reheat the oil until hot, add the chile, garlic, ginger, and shallot and stir-fry for 30 seconds. Add the beef and chopped basil, then stir-fry for about 3 minutes. Flavor with lemon juice and salt and pepper to taste.

4 Transfer the chile beef to a warmed serving plate, sprinkle on the basil leaves to garnish, and serve immediately with rice.

NUTRITIONAL NOTES	
Per Portion	
Energy	469cal
Fat	38.6g
Saturated Fat	9g
Carbohydrate	0g
Fiber	0g

Portuguese Pork

This dish displays the influence of Portuguese cooking on Indian cuisine.

INGREDIENTS

Serves 4–6

4 ounces deep-fried onions, crushed
4 fresh red chiles
4 tablespoons vindaloo curry paste
6 tablespoons white wine vinegar
6 tablespoons tomato paste
½ teaspoon fenugreek seeds
1 teaspoon ground turmeric
1 teaspoon crushed mustard seeds, or ½ teaspoon mustard powder
salt, to taste
1½ teaspoons sugar
2 pounds boneless pork spareribs, cubed
1 cup water
plain boiled rice, to serve

1 Place the crushed onions, chiles, curry paste, vinegar, tomato paste, fenugreek seeds, turmeric, and mustard seeds or powder in a bowl, with the salt and sugar.

2 Add the pork cubes and mix well. Cover and marinate for 2 hours, then put into a large, heavy pan.

3 Stir in the water. Bring to a boil and simmer gently for 2 hours. Serve hot with the rice.

NUTRITIONAL NOTES	
Per Portion	
Energy	322cal
Fat	12.2g
Saturated Fat	3.6g
Carbohydrate	4.1g
Fiber	0.9g

Chili Pork with Curry Leaves

Curry leaves and chiles are two of the hallmark ingredients used in the southern states of India. This recipe is from the state of Andhra Pradesh, where the hottest chiles, known as guntur after the region where they are produced, are grown in abundance.

INGREDIENTS

Serves 4–6

2 tablespoons vegetable oil
1 large onion, finely sliced
2-inch piece fresh ginger root, grated
4 garlic cloves, crushed
12 curry leaves
3 tablespoons extra hot curry paste, or
    4 tablespoons hot curry powder
1 tablespoon chili powder
1 teaspoon five-spice powder
1 teaspoon ground turmeric
2 pounds lean lamb, beef, or pork,
    cubed
¾ cup thick coconut milk
salt
red onion, finely sliced, to garnish
Indian bread and fruit raita,
    to serve

1 Heat the oil in a karahi, wok, or large pan, and fry the onion, ginger, garlic, and curry leaves until the onion is soft. Add the curry paste or powder, chili and five-spice powder, turmeric, and salt. Stir well.

2 Add the meat and stir well over a medium heat to seal and evenly brown the meat pieces. Keep stirring until the oil separates. Cover the pan and cook for about 20 minutes.

NUTRITIONAL NOTES	
Per Portion	
Energy	484cal
Fat	31g
Saturated Fat	12.5g
Carbohydrate	6.9g
Fiber	0.9g

3 Stir in the coconut milk and simmer, covered, until the meat is cooked. Toward the end of cooking, uncover the pan to reduce the excess liquid. Garnish with onions and serve with any Indian bread, and with fruit raita, for a cooling effect.

_____ COOK'S TIP _____

For extra flavor, reserve half the curry leaves and add in step 3, along with the coconut milk.

Pork Balchao

Pork and beef dishes are not very common in India, but Goa, on the west coast of the country, has several of both. This spicy stew is flavored with vinegar and sugar, a combination that immediately identifies it as Goan.

INGREDIENTS

Serves 4

4 tablespoons vegetable oil
1 tablespoon grated fresh ginger root
1 tablespoon crushed garlic
1-inch piece cinnamon stick, broken up
2–4 dried red chiles, chopped or torn
4 cloves
2 teaspoons cumin seeds
10 black peppercorns
1½ pounds cubed leg of pork, crackling and visible fat removed
1 teaspoon ground turmeric
scant 1 cup warm water
1½ tablespoons tomato paste
½ teaspoon chili powder (optional)
1 large onion, finely sliced
1 teaspoon salt
1 teaspoon sugar
2 tablespoons cider vinegar
fresh chiles, to garnish

1 Heat 2 tablespoons of the oil in a karahi, wok, or large pan, and add the ginger and garlic. Fry for 30 seconds.

2 Grind the cinnamon stick, dried chiles, cloves, cumin seeds, and peppercorns to a fine powder, using a spice mill or coffee grinder reserved for spices.

3 Add the spice mix to the pan and fry for another 30 seconds, stirring.

4 Add the pork and turmeric and increase the heat slightly. Fry for 5–6 minutes, or until the meat starts to release its juices, stirring regularly.

5 Add the water, tomato paste, and chili powder, if using, and bring to a boil. Cover the pan and simmer gently for 35–40 minutes.

6 Heat the remaining oil and fry the onion for 8–9 minutes, until browned, stirring regularly.

7 Add the fried onion to the pork along with the salt, sugar, and vinegar. Stir, cover, and simmer for 30–35 minutes, or until the pork is tender. Remove from the heat and spoon into a serving dish. Garnish with chiles and serve.

NUTRITIONAL NOTES	
Per Portion	
Energy	326cal
Fat	17.9g
Saturated Fat	3.7g
Carbohydrate	4.8g
Fiber	0.9g

Lentils with Venison and Tomatoes

Venison curries well and tastes good in this simple dish. Serve it with pilau rice, nan, or bhaturas. Spinach with mushrooms and bell peppers would make a colorful accompaniment.

INGREDIENTS

Serves 4

4 tablespoons corn oil
1 bay leaf
2 cloves
4 black peppercorns
1 medium onion, sliced
1 pound diced venison
½ teaspoon ground turmeric
1½ teaspoons chili powder
1 teaspoon garam masala
1 teaspoon crushed coriander seeds
1-inch cinnamon stick
1 teaspoon crushed garlic
1 teaspoon grated fresh ginger root
1½ teaspoons salt
6 cups water
⅓ cup split red lentils
2 medium tomatoes, quartered
2 fresh green chiles, chopped
1 tablespoon chopped fresh cilantro

1 Heat the oil in a karahi, wok, or deep pan. Lower the heat slightly and add the bay leaf, cloves, peppercorns, and onion slices. Fry for about 5 minutes, or until the onions are golden brown, stirring occasionally.

2 Add the diced venison, turmeric, chili powder, garam masala, coriander seeds, cinnamon stick, garlic, ginger, and most of the salt, and stir-fry for about 5 minutes over a medium heat.

3 Pour in 3¾ cups of the measured water and cover the pan with a lid. Let simmer over a low heat for 35–40 minutes, or until the water has evaporated and the meat is tender.

4 Put the lentils into a pan with 2½ cups water and boil for 12–15 minutes, or until the water has almost evaporated and the lentils are soft enough to mash. If the lentils are too thick, add up to ⅔ cup water to loosen the mixture.

5 When the meat is tender, stir-fry the mixture, using a wooden spoon, until some free oil begins to appear on the sides of the pan.

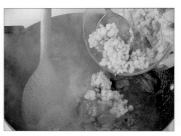

6 Add the cooked lentils to the venison and mix together well.

7 Add the tomatoes, chiles, and fresh cilantro and serve.

COOK'S TIP

If venison isn't available, you can use cubed boneless chicken as a substitute. In step 3, reduce the amount of water to 1¼ cups and cook uncovered, stirring occasionally, for 10–15 minutes, or until the water has evaporated and the chicken is cooked all the way through.

NUTRITIONAL NOTES
Per Portion

Energy	277cal
Fat	13.9g
Saturated Fat	2.6g
Carbohydrate	11.6g
Fiber	1.6g

Balti Dishes

THERE IS some confusion about the origins of balti, but there is certainly no doubt of its popularity. This style of cooking may well have originated in Kashmir, but it was perfected, developed, and adapted for Western tastes in the British city of Birmingham.

The balti style of cooking draws heavily on the traditional recipes and cooking methods from the north of the Indian subcontinent, but it easily adopts ingredients from elsewhere. What distinguishes balti dishes is their autonomy. Whereas many traditional Indian dishes are small players, sharing the limelight with numerous other dishes at the table, the balti meal is a solo star.

Everything is cooked and served in a single pan, and many balti dishes need only be served with a simple accompaniment, such as nan bread. They are easy to cook, even for the novice, are subtly spiced, and work equally well with either meat, poultry, fish, shellfish, or fresh vegetables as their base.

Chunky Fish Balti with Peppers

Try to find bell peppers in
different colors to make this
dish as colorful as possible.

INGREDIENTS

Serves 2-4
1 pound cod, or any other firm, white
  fish, such as haddock
1½ teaspoons ground cumin
2 teaspoons dried mango powder
  (amchur)
1 teaspoon ground coriander
½ teaspoon chili powder
1 teaspoon salt
1 teaspoon grated fresh ginger root
3 tablespoons cornstarch
⅔ cup corn oil
1 each green, orange and red bell
  peppers, seeded and chopped
8–10 cherry tomatoes

1 Skin the fish and cut into small
cubes. Put the cubes into a large
mixing bowl and add the ground
cumin, mango powder, ground
coriander, chili powder, salt, ginger,
and cornstarch. Mix together
thoroughly until the fish is
well coated.

2 Heat the oil in a karahi, wok, or
large, deep pan. Lower the heat
slightly and add the fish pieces, three or
four at a time. Fry for about 3 minutes,
turning constantly.

3 Drain the fish pieces on paper
towels and transfer to a serving
dish. Keep hot while you fry the
remaining fish pieces.

4 Fry the chopped bell peppers in
the oil remaining in the pan for
about 2 minutes. They should still be
slightly crisp. Drain on paper towels.

5 Add the cooked bell peppers to
the fish and garnish with the cherry
tomatoes. Serve.

NUTRITIONAL NOTES	
Per Portion	
Energy	495cal
Fat	30g
Saturated Fat	3.8g
Carbohydrate	13.3g
Fiber	3.4g

Balti Fish Fillets in Spicy Coconut Sauce

Although coconut milk is a familiar ingredient in Indian fish dishes, it is unusual to find shredded coconut in a starring role. It makes for a delicious and unusual dish.

INGREDIENTS

Serves 4

2 tablespoons corn oil
1 teaspoon onion seeds
4 dried red chiles
3 garlic cloves, sliced
1 medium onion, sliced
2 medium tomatoes, sliced
2 tablespoons dry unsweetened
  shredded coconut
1 teaspoon salt
1 teaspoon ground coriander
4 flatfish fillets, such as sole or
  flounder, each about 3 ounces
²/₃ cup water
1 tablespoon lime juice
1 tablespoon chopped fresh
  cilantro

1 Heat the oil in a karahi, wok, or deep pan. Lower the heat slightly and add the onion seeds, dried red chiles, garlic slices, and onion. Cook for 3–4 minutes, stirring once or twice.

___ COOK'S TIP ___

Use fresh fish fillets to make this dish if you can, because the flavor and texture will probably be superior. If you must use frozen fillets, make sure that they are completely thawed before cooking.

2 Add the tomatoes, coconut, salt, and coriander and stir thoroughly.

NUTRITIONAL NOTES	
Per Portion	
Energy	175cal
Fat	11.4g
Saturated Fat	5g
Carbohydrate	4.9g
Fiber	2g

3 Cut each fish fillet into three pieces. Drop the fish pieces into the mixture and turn them over gently until they are well coated.

4 Cook for 5–7 minutes, lowering the heat if necessary. Add the water, lime juice, and fresh cilantro and cook for another 3–5 minutes, until most of the water has evaporated. Serve immediately, with rice, if you like.

Seafood Balti with Vegetables

In this dish, the spicy seafood is cooked separately and combined with the vegetables at the last minute to give a truly delicious combination of flavors.

INGREDIENTS

Serves 4

½ pound cod, or any other firm,
   white fish
½ pound cooked shrimp
6 seafood sticks, halved lengthwise,
   or 4 ounces white crabmeat
1 tablespoon lemon juice
1 teaspoon ground coriander
1 teaspoon chili powder
1 teaspoon salt
1 teaspoon ground cumin
4 tablespoons cornstarch
⅔ cup corn oil

For the vegetables

⅔ cup corn oil
2 medium onions, chopped
5ml/1 teaspoon onion seeds
½ medium cauliflower,
   cut into florets
4 ounces green beans,
   cut into 1-inch lengths
1 cup corn kernels
1 teaspoon shredded fresh ginger root
1 teaspoon chili powder
1 teaspoon salt
4 fresh green chiles, sliced
2 tablespoons chopped fresh cilantro
lime slices

1 Skin the fish and cut into small cubes. Put into a medium mixing bowl with the shrimp and seafood sticks or crabmeat.

COOK'S TIP

Cover the seafood snugly when leaving it to stand in the refrigerator, or the spicy flavor will permeate the other foods stored there.

2 In a separate bowl, mix together the lemon juice, ground coriander, chili powder, salt, and ground cumin. Pour this over the seafood and mix together thoroughly, using your hands.

3 Sprinkle on the cornstarch and mix again until the seafood is well coated. Place in the refrigerator for about 1 hour to allow the flavors to develop.

4 To make the vegetable mixture, heat the oil in a karahi, wok, or deep pan. Add the onions and the onion seeds, and stir-fry until lightly browned.

5 Add the cauliflower, green beans, corn kernels, ginger, chili powder, salt, green chiles, and fresh cilantro. Stir-fry for about 7–10 minutes over a medium heat, making sure that the pieces of cauliflower retain their shape.

6 Spoon the fried vegetables around the edge of a shallow dish, leaving a space in the middle for the seafood, and keep hot.

7 Wash and dry the pan, then heat the oil to fry the seafood pieces. Fry the seafood pieces in 2–3 batches, until they turn a golden brown. Remove with a slotted spoon and drain on paper towels.

8 Arrange the seafood in the middle of the dish of vegetables and keep hot while you fry the remaining seafood. Garnish with lime slices and serve. Plain boiled rice and raita make ideal accompaniments.

NUTRITIONAL NOTES	
Per Portion	
Energy	279cal
Fat	11g
Saturated Fat	1.6g
Carbohydrate	18.5g
Fiber	4g

Sizzling Balti Shrimp in Hot Sauce

This sizzling shrimp dish is cooked in a fiery hot and spicy sauce. This sauce not only contains chili powder, but is further enhanced by the addition of ground green chiles mixed with other spices. If the heat seems extreme, serve with raita to moderate the piquant flavor.

INGREDIENTS

Serves 4

2 medium onions, roughly chopped
2 tablespoons tomato paste
1 teaspoon ground coriander
¼ teaspoon ground turmeric
1 teaspoon chili powder
2 fresh green chiles
3 tablespoons chopped fresh
   cilantro
2 tablespoons lemon juice
1 teaspoon salt
3 tablespoons corn oil
16 cooked jumbo shrimp
sliced green chile, to garnish, optional

1 Put the onions, tomato paste, ground coriander, turmeric, chili powder, 2 whole green chiles, 2 tablespoons of the fresh cilantro, the lemon juice, and salt into the bowl of a food processor. Process for about 1 minute. If the mixture seems too thick, add a little water to loosen it.

2 Heat the oil in a karahi, wok, or deep pan. Lower the heat slightly and add the spice mixture. Fry the mixture for 3–5 minutes, or until the sauce has thickened slightly.

--- COOK'S TIP ---

Make sure you don't overcook the shrimp or they will become tough.

3 Add the shrimp and stir-fry briefly over a medium heat.

4 As soon as the shrimp are heated through, transfer them to a serving dish, Garnish with the rest of the fresh cilantro and the chopped green chile, if using. Serve immediately.

NUTRITIONAL NOTES	
Per Portion	
Energy	139cal
Fat	8.7g
Saturated Fat	1.3g
Carbohydrate	5.9g
Fiber	1.1g

Karahi Shrimp and Fenugreek

The black-eyed peas, shrimp, and paneer in this recipe ensure that it is rich in protein. The combination of both ground and fresh fenugreek makes this a fragrant and delicious dish. When preparing fresh fenugreek, use the leaves whole, but discard the stalks, which would add a bitter flavor to the dish.

INGREDIENTS

Serves 4-6

4 tablespoons corn oil
2 medium onions, sliced
2 medium tomatoes, sliced
1½ teaspoons crushed garlic
1 teaspoon chili powder
1 teaspoon grated fresh ginger root
1 teaspoon ground cumin
1 teaspoon ground coriander
1 teaspoon salt
5 ounces paneer, cubed
1 teaspoon ground fenugreek
1 bunch fresh fenugreek leaves
4 ounces cooked shrimp
2 fresh red chiles, sliced
2 tablespoons chopped fresh
  cilantro
⅓ cup canned black-eyed peas,
  drained
1 tablespoon lemon juice

1 Heat the oil in a karahi, wok, or deep pan. Lower the heat slightly and add the onions and tomatoes. Fry for about 3 minutes.

2 Add the garlic, chili powder, ginger, ground cumin, ground coriander, salt, paneer, and the ground and fresh fenugreek. Lower the heat and stir-fry for about 2 minutes.

NUTRITIONAL NOTES	
Per Portion	
Energy	206cal
Fat	13g
Saturated Fat	2.6g
Carbohydrate	10.7g
Fiber	2.3g

3 Add the shrimp, red chiles, fresh cilantro, and the black-eyed peas and mix well. Toss over the heat for another 3–5 minutes, or until the shrimp are heated through. Sprinkle on the lemon juice and serve.

_____ COOK'S TIP _____

If you cannot locate paneer, tofu will make a good substitute.

Shrimp and Vegetable Balti

This makes a delicious light lunch or supper, and is ideal for those vegetarians who eat shellfish.

INGREDIENTS

Serves 4

6 ounces frozen cooked
   shelled shrimp
2 tablespoons oil
¼ teaspoon onion seeds
4–6 curry leaves
1 cup frozen peas
⅔ cup frozen corn kernels
1 large zucchini, sliced
1 medium red bell pepper,
   seeded and roughly diced
1 teaspoon crushed coriander seeds
1 teaspoon crushed dried red chiles
½ teaspoon salt
1 tablespoon lemon juice
1 tablespoon fresh cilantro leaves,
   to garnish

NUTRITIONAL NOTES	
Per Portion	
Energy	171cal
Fat	7.70g
Saturated Fat	1.05g
Carbohydrate	11.8g
Fiber	2.80g

--- COOK'S TIP ---

The best way to crush whole seeds is to use an electric spice grinder or a small marble mortar and pestle.

1 Thaw the shrimp and drain them of any excess liquid.

2 Heat the oil with the onion seeds and curry leaves in a karahi, wok, or heavy skillet.

3 Add the shrimp to the spicy mixture in the wok and stir-fry until the liquid has evaporated.

4 Next, add the peas, corn kernels, zucchini and red bell pepper. Continue to stir for 3–5 minutes.

5 Finally, add the crushed coriander seeds and chiles, salt to taste, and the lemon juice.

6 Serve immediately, garnished with fresh cilantro leaves.

Paneer Balti with Shrimp

Paneer is a protein food and makes an excellent substitute for red meat. Here, it is combined with jumbo shrimp to make a dish with unforgettable flavor.

INGREDIENTS

Serves 4

12 cooked jumbo shrimp
6 ounces paneer
2 tablespoons tomato paste
4 tablespoons strained plain yogurt
1½ teaspoons garam masala
1 teaspoon chili powder
1 teaspoon crushed garlic
1 teaspoon salt
2 teaspoons dried mango
    powder (amchur)
1 teaspoon ground coriander
½ cup butter
1 tablespoon vegetable oil
3 fresh green chiles, chopped
3 tablespoons chopped
    fresh cilantro
⅔ cup light cream

1 Shell the jumbo shrimp and cube the paneer.

2 Put the tomato paste, yogurt, garam masala, chili powder, garlic, salt, mango powder, and ground coriander in a mixing bowl. Mix to a paste and set aside.

3 Melt the butter with the oil in a karahi, wok, or deep pan. Lower the heat slightly and quickly fry the paneer and shrimp for about 2 minutes. Remove with a slotted spoon and drain on paper towels.

4 Pour the spice paste into the fat left in the pan and cook for about 1 minute, stirring constantly.

5 Add the paneer and shrimp, and cook for 7–10 minutes, stirring occasionally, until the shrimp are heated through.

6 Add the fresh chiles and most of the cilantro, and pour in the cream. Heat through for about 2 minutes, garnish with the remaining cilantro, and serve.

VARIATIONS

• For a less expensive dish, you can substitute regular shelled shrimp). You will need about 8 ounces.
• If you prefer not to use paneer, you can use tofu instead. It is very nutritious and absorbs the flavor of the spices extremely well. You can make it at home by bringing 4 cups soya milk to a boil over a low heat, then adding 2 tablespoons lemon juice and stirring continuously until the milk thickens and begins to curdle. Strain the curdled milk through a strainer lined with cheesecloth, and set aside under a heavy weight for 1½–2 hours to press the curd to a flat shape about ½-inch thick. This homemade tofu will keep in the refrigerator for about one week.

NUTRITIONAL NOTES
Per Portion

Energy	416cal
Fat	36g
Saturated Fat	21.2g
Carbohydrate	5.4g
Fiber	0g

Basic Balti Chicken

This recipe has a wonderfully delicate flavor, and it is probably the most popular of all balti dishes. Choose a young chicken because it will have more flavor.

INGREDIENTS

Serves 4-6

2½–3 pounds chicken
3 tablespoons corn oil
3 medium onions, sliced
3 medium tomatoes, halved and sliced
1-inch cinnamon stick
2 large black cardamom pods
4 black peppercorns
  teaspoon black cumin seeds
1 teaspoon grated fresh ginger root
1 teaspoon crushed garlic
1 teaspoon garam masala
1 teaspoon chili powder
1 teaspoon salt
2 tablespoons plain yogurt
4 tablespoons lemon juice
2 tablespoons chopped
  fresh cilantro
2 fresh green chiles, chopped

1 Skin the chicken, then use a sharp knife or cleaver to cut it into eight pieces. Wash and trim the chicken pieces, and set to one side.

2 Heat the oil in a large karahi, wok, or deep pan. Add the onions and fry until they are golden brown. Add the tomatoes and stir well.

3 Add the piece of cinnamon stick, cardamoms, peppercorns, black cumin seeds, ginger, garlic, garam masala, chili powder, and salt. Lower the heat and stir-fry for 3–5 minutes.

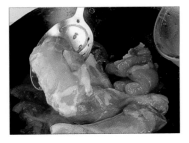

4 Add the chicken pieces, two at a time, and stir-fry for at least 7 minutes, or until the spice mixture has completely penetrated the chicken and they are beginning to brown.

5 Add the yogurt to the chicken and mix well.

6 Lower the heat and cover the pan with a piece of aluminum foil, making sure that it does not touch the food. Cook gently for about 15 minutes, checking once to make sure the food is not catching on the bottom of the pan.

7 Finally, add the lemon juice, fresh cilantro, and green chiles. Serve immediately, from the cooking pan.

NUTRITIONAL NOTES
Per Portion

Energy	569cal
Fat	38.2g
Saturated Fat	9.5g
Carbohydrate	13.2g
Fiber	2.3g

COOK'S TIP

Chicken cooked on the bone is both tender and full of flavor. However, you can substitute the whole chicken with 1½ pounds boned and cubed chicken, if desired. Chicken that has been taken off the bone will cook quickly, so check it frequently and be careful that you don't overcook it. The cooking time can be reduced at step 6, too.

Sweet and Sour Balti Chicken

This dish combines a sweet-and-sour flavor with a creamy texture. It is delicious served with pilau rice or nan bread.

INGREDIENTS

Serves 4

3 tablespoons tomato paste
2 tablespoons strained plain yogurt
1½ teaspoons garam masala
1 teaspoon chili powder
1 teaspoon crushed garlic
2 tablespoons mango chutney
1 teaspoon salt
½ teaspoon sugar
4 tablespoons corn oil
1½ pounds skinless, boneless
  chicken, cubed
⅔ cup water
2 fresh green chiles, chopped
2 tablespoons chopped fresh
  cilantro
2 tablespoons light cream

1 Mix the tomato paste, yogurt, garam masala, chili powder, garlic, mango chutney, salt, and sugar in a medium mixing bowl. Stir well.

NUTRITIONAL NOTES	
Per Portion	
Energy	227cal
Fat	4.2g
Saturated Fat	1.7g
Carbohydrate	6.7g
Fiber	0.3g

2 Heat the oil in a karahi, wok, or deep pan. Lower the heat slightly and pour in the spice mixture. Bring to a boil and cook for about 2 minutes, stirring occasionally.

3 Add the chicken pieces and stir until they are well coated.

4 Stir in the water to thin the sauce slightly. Continue cooking for 5–7 minutes, or until the chicken is fully cooked and tender.

5 Finally, add the fresh chiles, cilantro, and cream, cook for another 2 minutes over a low heat, then serve.

Balti Chicken Pasanda

Yogurt and cream give this tasty dish its characteristic richness. Serve it with Peshwari nan to complement the almonds.

INGREDIENTS

Serves 4

4 tablespoons strained plain yogurt
½ teaspoon black cumin seeds
4 cardamom pods
6 whole black peppercorns
2 teaspoons garam masala
1-inch cinnamon stick
1 tablespoon ground almonds
1 teaspoon crushed garlic
1 teaspoon grated fresh ginger root
1 teaspoon chili powder
1 teaspoon salt
1½ pounds skinless, boneless chicken, cubed
5 tablespoons corn oil
2 medium onions, diced
3 fresh green chiles, chopped
2 tablespoons chopped fresh cilantro
½ cup light cream

3 Tip in the chicken mixture and stir until it is well blended with the onions.

4 Cook for 12–15 minutes over a medium heat, until the sauce has thickened and the chicken is cooked through.

5 Add the green chiles and fresh cilantro, and pour in the cream. Bring to a boil, stirring constantly, and serve garnished with more cilantro, if desired.

NUTRITIONAL NOTES	
Per Portion	
Energy	453cal
Fat	26.8g
Saturated Fat	8.7g
Carbohydrate	10.9g
Fiber	1.1g

1 Mix the yogurt, cumin seeds, cardamoms, peppercorns, garam masala, cinnamon stick, ground almonds, garlic, ginger, chili powder, and salt in a medium mixing bowl. Add the chicken pieces, stir to coat, and let marinate for 2 hours.

2 Heat the oil in a large karahi, wok, or deep pan. Add the onions and fry for 2–3 minutes.

Khara Masala Balti Chicken

Whole spices (khara) are used in this recipe, giving it a wonderful, rich flavor. This is a dry dish, so it is best served with plenty of creamy raita.

INGREDIENTS

Serves 4

3 curry leaves
¼ teaspoon mustard seeds
¼ teaspoon fennel seeds
¼ teaspoon onion seeds
½ teaspoon crushed dried red chiles
½ teaspoon white cumin seeds
¼ teaspoon fenugreek seeds
½ teaspoon crushed pomegranate seeds
1 teaspoon salt
1 teaspoon shredded fresh ginger root
3 garlic cloves, sliced
4 tablespoons corn oil
4 fresh green chiles, slit
1 large onion, sliced
1 medium tomato, sliced
1½ pounds skinless, boneless chicken, cubed
1 tablespoon chopped fresh cilantro

1 Mix together the curry leaves, mustard seeds, fennel seeds, onion seeds, crushed red chiles, cumin seeds, fenugreek seeds, crushed pomegranate seeds, and salt in a large bowl.

2 Add the shredded ginger and garlic cloves.

3 Heat the oil in a medium karahi, wok, or deep pan. Add the spice mixture, then put in the green chiles.

4 Spoon the sliced onion into the pan and fry over a medium heat for 5–7 minutes, stirring constantly to flavor the onion with the spices.

5 Finally, add the tomato and chicken pieces, and cook over a medium heat for about 7 minutes. The chicken should be cooked through and the sauce reduced.

6 Stir everything together over the heat for another 3–5 minutes. Serve from the pan, garnished with chopped fresh cilantro.

NUTRITIONAL NOTES	
Per Portion	
Energy	313cal
Fat	13.7g
Saturated Fat	2.3g
Carbohydrate	8.1g
Fiber	2.3g

Chicken and Tomato Balti

If you like tomatoes, you will love this chicken recipe. It makes a semidry balti and is good served with a lentil dish and plain boiled rice.

INGREDIENTS

Serves 4

4 tablespoons corn oil
6 curry leaves
½ teaspoon mixed onion and mustard seeds
8 medium tomatoes, sliced
1 teaspoon ground coriander
1 teaspoon chili powder
1 teaspoon salt
1 teaspoon ground cumin
1 teaspoon crushed garlic
1½ pounds skinless, boneless chicken, cubed
⅔ cup water
1 tablespoon sesame seeds, roasted
1 tablespoon chopped fresh cilantro

1 Heat the oil in a karahi, wok, or deep, round-bottom large pan. Add the curry leaves and mixed onion and mustard seeds and toss over the heat for 1–2 minutes, so that they become fragrant. Do not let the seeds burn.

2 Lower the heat slightly and add the tomatoes.

3 While the tomatoes are gently cooking, mix together the ground coriander, chili powder, salt, ground cumin, and garlic in a bowl. Put the spices onto the tomatoes.

4 Add the chicken pieces and stir well. Stir-fry for about 5 minutes more.

5 Stir in the water and continue cooking, stirring occasionally, until the sauce thickens and the chicken is fully cooked.

6 Sprinkle the sesame seeds and fresh cilantro over the balti. Serve immediately, from the pan.

COOK'S TIP

Sesame seeds are available from Asian and health food stores. There are two types—unroasted seeds, which are white, and roasted ones, which are lightly browned. To roast sesame seeds at home, simply put a quantity into a skillet and place the pan over a high heat for about 1 minute. Shake the pan constantly to prevent the seeds from burning. Use immediately or cool, then store in a screw-topped jar.

NUTRITIONAL NOTES
Per Portion

Energy	360cal
Fat	18.3g
Saturated Fat	3g
Carbohydrate	8.6g
Fiber	2.3g

Balti Chicken Pieces with Cumin and Coriander

The potatoes are tossed in spices and cooked separately in the oven before being added to the chicken.

INGREDIENTS

Serves 4

⅔ cup plain low-fat yogurt
¼ cup ground almonds
1½ teaspoons ground coriander
½ teaspoon chili powder
1 teaspoon garam masala
1 tablespoon coconut milk
1 teaspoon crushed garlic
1 teaspoon grated fresh ginger root
2 tablespoons chopped fresh cilantro
1 fresh red chile, seeded
  and chopped
8 ounces skinless, boneless chicken
  breast fillets, cubed
1 tablespoon oil
2 medium onions, sliced
3 green cardamom pods
1-inch cinnamon stick
2 cloves

For the potatoes
1 tablespoon oil
8 baby potatoes, thickly sliced
¼ teaspoon cumin seeds
1 tablespoon finely chopped
  fresh cilantro

NUTRITIONAL NOTES	
Per Portion	
Energy	2,783cal
Fat	10.76g
Saturated Fat	1.58g
Carbohydrate	27.43g
Fiber	2.78g

_____ COOK'S TIP _____

Any variety of fresh mint may also be added to the potatoes. The flavor goes well with the spices.

1 In a large bowl, mix together the yogurt, ground almonds, ground coriander, chili powder, garam masala, coconut milk, garlic, ginger, half the fresh cilantro, and half the red chile.

2 Place the chicken pieces in the mixture, mix well, then cover and let stand to marinate for about 2 hours.

3 Meanwhile, start to prepare the spicy potatoes. Heat the oil in a karahi, wok, or heavy pan. Add the sliced potatoes, cumin seeds, and fresh cilantro and quickly stir-fry for 2–3 minutes.

4 Preheat the oven to 350°F. Spoon the potatoes into a baking dish, cover, and bake for about 30 minutes, or until they are cooked through.

5 Halfway through the potatoes' cooking time, heat the oil and fry the onions, cardamoms, cinnamon, and cloves for 1½ minutes.

6 Add the chicken mixture to the onions and stir-fry for 5–7 minutes. Lower the heat, cover, and cook for 5–7 minutes. Top with the potatoes and garnish with cilantro and red chile.

Balti Chicken in a Spicy Lentil Sauce

Traditionally, this dish is made with lamb, but it is equally delicious made with chicken. The lentils are flavored with a traditional tarka, which is poured over the dish just before serving.

INGREDIENTS

Serves 4

2 tablespoons chana dhal
   or yellow split peas
¼ cup masoor dhal or
   red split peas
1 tablespoon oil
2 medium onions, chopped
1 teaspoon crushed garlic
1 teaspoon grated fresh ginger root
½ teaspoon ground turmeric
1½ teaspoons chili powder
1 teaspoon garam masala
½ teaspoon ground coriander
1½ teaspoons salt
6 ounces skinless chicken breast
   fillets, cubed
3 tablespoons fresh cilantro leaves
1–2 fresh green chiles, seeded
   and chopped
2–3 tablespoons lemon juice
1¼ cups water
2 tomatoes, peeled and halved

For the tarka

1 teaspoon oil
½ teaspoon cumin seeds
2 garlic cloves
2 dried red chiles
4 curry leaves

NUTRITIONAL NOTES	
Per Portion	
Energy	207cal
Fat	7.07g
Saturated Fat	1.03g
Carbohydrate	20.37g
Fiber	2.84g

1 Put both the peas in a pan with water and bring to a boil. Cook for 30–45 minutes, until soft and mushy. Drain and set aside.

2 Heat the oil in a karahi, wok, or heavy skillet and fry the onions until soft and golden brown. Stir in the garlic, ginger, turmeric, chili powder, garam masala, ground coriander, and salt.

3 Next, add the chicken pieces and fry for 5–7 minutes, stirring constantly over a medium heat to seal in the juices and lightly brown the meat.

4 Add half the fresh cilantro, the green chiles, lemon juice, and water and cook for another 3–5 minutes. Stir in the cooked peas, then add the tomatoes.

5 Sprinkle over the remaining cilantro leaves. Take the pan off the heat and set aside.

6 To make the tarka, heat the oil and add the cumin seeds, whole garlic cloves, dried chiles, and curry leaves. Heat for about 30 seconds, then pour over the top of the dhal. Serve immediately.

Balti Chicken with Paneer and Peas

This is an unusual combination, but it really works well. Serve with plain boiled rice.

INGREDIENTS

Serves 4

1 small chicken, about 1½ pounds
2 tablespoons tomato paste
3 tablespoons plain low-fat
 yogurt
1½ teaspoons garam masala
1 teaspoon crushed garlic
1 teaspoon grated fresh ginger root
pinch of ground cardamom
1 tablespoon chili powder
¼ teaspoon ground turmeric
1 teaspoon salt
1 teaspoon sugar
2 teaspoons oil
1-inch cinnamon stick
2 black peppercorns
1¼ cups water
4 ounces paneer
2 fresh green chiles, seeded
 and chopped
2 tablespoons fresh cilantro leaves
2 ounces low-fat ricotta cheese
¾ cup frozen peas, thawed

2 Mix the tomato paste, yogurt, garam masala, garlic, ginger, cardamom, chili powder, turmeric, salt, and sugar in a bowl.

3 Heat the oil with the whole spices in a karahi, wok, or heavy pan, then pour the yogurt mixture into the oil. Lower the heat and cook gently for about 3 minutes, then pour in the water and bring to a simmer.

4 Cut the paneer into cubes. Chop the chiles, discarding the seeds if you like.

5 Add the chicken pieces to the pan. Stir-fry for 2 minutes, then cover the pan and cook over a medium heat for about 10 minutes.

6 Add the paneer cubes to the pan, followed by half the coriander and half the green chiles. Mix well and cook for another 5–7 minutes.

7 Stir in the ricotta cheese and peas, heat through, and serve with the reserved cilantro and chiles.

1 Skin the chicken and cut it into 6–8 equal pieces.

COOK'S TIP

Paneer is an Indian whole-milk cheese and provides a good source of protein.

NUTRITIONAL NOTES	
Per Portion	
Energy	233cal
Fat	10.28g
Saturated Fat	4.64g
Carbohydrate	8.14g
Fiber	1.49g

Balti Chicken with Green and Red Chiles

Ground chicken is seldom cooked in Indian homes. However, it works very well in this recipe.

INGREDIENTS

Serves 4

10 ounces skinless chicken breast
    fillet, cubed
2 plump fresh red chiles
3 plump fresh green chiles
2 tablespoons oil
6 curry leaves
3 medium onions, sliced
1½ teaspoons crushed garlic
1½ teaspoons ground coriander
1½ teaspoons grated fresh ginger root
1 teaspoon chili powder
1 teaspoon salt
1 tablespoon lemon juice
2 tablespoons chopped fresh cilantro
chapatis and lemon wedges,
    to serve

1 Cook the chicken in a pan of water for about 10 minutes, until soft and cooked through. Remove with a slotted spoon and place in the bowl of a food processor with a metal blade attached.

COOK'S TIP

Taste this dish during cooking because it is mild, especially if you seed the chiles, and you may find that it needs some additional spices to suit your palate.

2 Process the cooked chicken, or grind it roughly.

3 Cut the chiles in half lengthwise and remove the seeds, if you like. Cut the flesh into strips and set aside.

4 Heat the oil in a karahi, wok, or heavy pan and fry the curry leaves and onions until the onions are a soft golden brown. Lower the heat and stir in the garlic, ground coriander, ginger, chili powder, and salt.

5 Add the ground chicken and stir-fry for 3–5 minutes.

6 Add the lemon juice, the prepared chile strips, and most of the fresh cilantro. Stir-fry for another 3–5 minutes, then serve, garnished with the remaining fresh cilantro and accompanied by warm chapatis and lemon wedges.

NUTRITIONAL NOTES	
Per Portion	
Energy	184cal
Fat	8.40g
Saturated Fat	1.57g
Carbohydrate	10.10g
Fiber	1.30g

Balti Chicken with Leeks

This dish has an unusual combination of flavors. Mango powder gives it a deliciously tangy flavor.

INGREDIENTS

Serves 4–6

2 medium leeks
½ cup chana dhal or yellow
    split peas
4 tablespoons corn oil
6 large dried red chiles
4 curry leaves
1 teaspoon mustard seeds
2 teaspoons mango powder (amchur)
2 medium tomatoes, chopped
½ teaspoon chili powder
1 teaspoon ground coriander
1 teaspoon salt
1 pound skinless, boneless
    chicken, cubed
1 tablespoon chopped fresh
    cilantro

1 Using a sharp knife, slice the leeks thinly into circles. Separate the slices, rinse them in a colander under cold water to wash away any grit, then drain well.

2 Wash the chana dhal or split peas carefully and remove any stones.

3 Put the dhal or peas into a pan with enough water to cover, and boil for about 10 minutes, until they are soft but not mushy. Drain and set to one side in a bowl.

4 Heat the oil in a karahi, wok, or deep pan. Lower the heat slightly and add the leeks, dried red chiles, curry leaves, and mustard seeds. Stir-fry gently for a few minutes.

5 Add the mango powder, tomatoes, chili powder, ground coriander, salt, and chicken, and stir-fry for 7–10 minutes.

6 Mix in the cooked chana dhal or split peas and fry for another 2 minutes, or until you are sure that the chicken is cooked right through.

7 Garnish with fresh cilantro and serve immediately, from the pan.

— COOK'S TIPS —

• Chana dhal, a split yellow lentil, is available from Asian stores. However, yellow split peas are a good substitute.
• Dried mango powder is made from sun-dried green mangoes and has a sour taste. You may find it under the name amchur.

NUTRITIONAL NOTES
Per Portion

Energy	309cal
Fat	13.4g
Saturated Fat	2.2g
Carbohydrate	16.1g
Fiber	2.8g

Balti Butter Chicken

Butter Chicken is one of the most popular balti chicken dishes, especially in the West. Cooked in butter, with aromatic spices, cream, and almonds, this mild dish will be enjoyed by everyone. Serve with pilau rice.

INGREDIENTS

Serves 4

⅔ cup plain yogurt
½ cup ground almonds
1½ teaspoons chili powder
¼ teaspoon crushed bay leaves
¼ teaspoon ground cloves
¼ teaspoon ground cinnamon
1 teaspoon garam masala
4 green cardamom pods
1 teaspoon grated fresh ginger root
1 teaspoon crushed garlic
2 cups canned tomatoes
1¼ teaspoons salt
2¼ pounds skinless, boneless
    chicken, cubed
6 tablespoons butter
1 tablespoon corn oil
2 medium onions, sliced
2 tablespoons chopped
    fresh cilantro
4 tablespoons light cream
cilantro sprigs, to garnish

1 Put the yogurt into a bowl and add the ground almonds, chili powder, crushed bay leaves, ground cloves, cinnamon, garam masala, cardamoms, ginger, and garlic.

2 Chop the tomatoes and add them to the bowl with the salt. Mix thoroughly.

3 Put the chicken into a large mixing bowl and pour over the yogurt mixture. Set aside.

4 Melt together the butter and oil in a karahi, wok, or deep pan. Add the onions and fry for about 3 minutes.

5 Add the chicken mixture and stir-fry for 7–10 minutes.

COOK'S TIP

For a creamier flavor, strain the yogurt overnight in a strainer lined with cheese-cloth; cover with plastic wrap and refrigerate.

6 Sprinkle over about half of the cilantro and mix well.

7 Pour over the cream and stir in well. Heat through and serve, garnished with the remaining chopped cilantro and cilantro sprigs.

NUTRITIONAL NOTES	
Per Portion	
Energy	592cal
Fat	32.2g
Saturated Fat	13.7g
Carbohydrate	12.1g
Fiber	1.6g

Balti Chicken in Hara Masala Sauce

This chicken dish can be served as an accompaniment to any of the rice dishes in this book.

INGREDIENTS

Serves 4

1 crisp green apple, peeled, cored, and
  cut into small cubes
4 tablespoons fresh cilantro leaves
2 tablespoons fresh mint leaves
½ cup plain low-fat yogurt
3 tablespoons low-fat ricotta cheese
2 fresh green chiles, seeded
  and chopped
1 bunch scallions, chopped
1 teaspoon salt
1 teaspoon sugar
1 teaspoon crushed garlic
1 teaspoon grated fresh ginger root
1 tablespoon oil
8 ounces skinless chicken breast
  fillets, cubed
3 tablespoons golden raisins

1 Place the apple, 3 tablespoons of the cilantro, the mint, yogurt, ricotta cheese, chiles, scallions, salt, sugar, garlic, and ginger in a food processor and blend for about 1 minute.

2 Heat the oil in a karahi, wok, or heavy pan, pour in the yogurt mixture, and cook over a low heat for about 2 minutes.

NUTRITIONAL NOTES	
Per Portion	
Energy	158cal
Fat	4.37g
Saturated Fat	1.69g
Carbohydrate	14.54g
Fiber	1.08g

3 Next, add the chicken pieces and blend everything together. Cook over a medium-low heat for 12–15 minutes, or until the chicken is fully cooked.

4 Stir in the golden raisins and the remaining 1 tablespoon of fresh cilantro leaves and serve.

COOK'S TIP
This dish makes an attractive centerpiece for a dinner party.

Balti Chicken in Thick Creamy Coconut Sauce

If you enjoy the flavor of coconut, you will really love this aromatic curry.

INGREDIENTS

Serves 4

1 tablespoon ground almonds
1 tablespoon dry unsweetened
  shredded coconut
⅓ cup coconut milk
⅔ cup low-fat ricotta cheese
1½ teaspoons ground coriander
1 teaspoon chili powder
1 teaspoon crushed garlic
1½ teaspoons grated fresh ginger root
1 teaspoon salt
1 tablespoon oil
8 ounces skinless, boneless
  chicken, cubed
3 green cardamom pods
1 bay leaf
1 dried red chile, crushed
2 tablespoons chopped fresh
  cilantro

1 Using a heavy pan, dry-roast the ground almonds and shredded coconut, stirring frequently, until they turn just a shade darker. Transfer the nut mixture to a mixing bowl.

NUTRITIONAL NOTES	
Per Portion	
Energy	166cal
Fat	8.30g
Saturated Fat	2.84g
Carbohydrate	6.38g
Fiber	0.95g

2 Add the coconut milk, ricotta cheese, ground coriander, chili powder, garlic, ginger, and salt to the mixing bowl.

3 Heat the oil in a karahi, wok, or heavy pan and add the chicken cubes, cardamoms, and bay leaf. Stir-fry for about 2 minutes to seal the chicken but not cook it.

4 Pour in the coconut milk mixture and blend everything together. Lower the heat, add the chile and fresh cilantro, cover, and cook for 10–12 minutes, stirring occasionally. Uncover, then stir and cook for another 2 minutes before serving, making sure the chicken is cooked.

Balti Chicken in Saffron Sauce

This is a wonderfully aromatic chicken dish that is partly cooked in the oven. It contains saffron, the most expensive spice in the world, and is sure to impress your guests.

INGREDIENTS

Serves 4

4 tablespoons butter
2 tablespoons corn oil
2½–3 pounds chicken, skinned
 and cut into 8 pieces
1 medium onion, chopped
1 teaspoon crushed garlic
½ teaspoon crushed black
 peppercorns
½ teaspoon crushed cardamom pods
¼ teaspoon ground cinnamon
1½ teaspoons chili powder
⅔ cup plain yogurt
½ cup ground almonds
1 tablespoon lemon juice
1 teaspoon salt
1 teaspoon saffron strands
⅔ cup water
⅔ cup light cream
2 tablespoons chopped fresh
 cilantro

1 Preheat the oven to 350°F. Melt the butter with the oil in a karahi, wok, or deep pan. Add the chicken pieces and fry until lightly browned. This will take about 5 minutes. Remove the chicken using a slotted spoon, leaving behind as much of the fat as possible.

2 Add the onion to the same pan and fry over a medium heat. Meanwhile, mix together the garlic, black peppercorns, cardamom, cinnamon, chili powder, yogurt, ground almonds, lemon juice, salt, and saffron strands in a mixing bowl.

3 When the onions are lightly browned, pour the spice mixture into the pan and stir-fry for about 1 minute.

4 Add the chicken pieces, and continue to fry for another 2 minutes, stirring constantly. Pour in the water and bring to a simmer.

5 Transfer the contents of the pan to a casserole and cover with a lid, or, if using a karahi with heatproof handles, cover with aluminum foil. Transfer to the oven and cook for 30–35 minutes.

6 Once you are sure that the chicken is cooked all the way through, remove it from the oven. Transfer the mixture to a skillet or place the karahi on the stovetop and stir in the cream.

7 Reheat gently for about 2 minutes. Garnish with fresh cilantro and serve with a fruity pilau or plain boiled rice.

COOK'S TIP

There is no substitute for saffron, so don't be tempted to use turmeric instead. It is well worth buying just a small amount of saffron—either strands or in powdered form—to create this dish for a treat.

NUTRITIONAL NOTES	
Per Portion	
Energy	525cal
Fat	33g
Saturated Fat	13.3g
Carbohydrate	11g
Fiber	1.5g

Balti Chicken with Vegetables

This is an excellent recipe for making a small amount of chicken go a long way. The vegetables add color and boost the nutritional value.

INGREDIENTS

Serves 4-6

4 tablespoons corn oil
2 medium onions, sliced
4 garlic cloves, thickly sliced
1 pound skinless chicken breast fillets,
    cut into strips
1 teaspoon salt
2 tablespoons lime juice
3 fresh green chiles, chopped
2 medium carrots, cut into batons
2 medium potatoes, peeled and
    cut into ½-inch strips
1 medium zucchini,
    cut into batons
4 lime slices
1 tablespoon chopped fresh
    cilantro
2 fresh green chiles, cut into
    strips (optional)

1 Heat the oil in a large karahi, wok, or deep pan. Lower the heat slightly and add the onions. Fry until the onions are lightly browned.

2 Add half the garlic slices and fry for a few seconds before adding the chicken and salt. Cook everything together, stirring, until all the moisture has evaporated and the chicken is lightly browned.

3 Add the lime juice, green chiles, and all the vegetables to the pan. Increase the heat and add the rest of the garlic. Stir-fry for 7–10 minutes, or until the chicken is cooked through and the vegetables are just tender.

4 Transfer to a serving dish and garnish with the lime slices, fresh cilantro, and green chile strips, if wished. Serve immediately.

NUTRITIONAL NOTES	
Per Portion	
Energy	308cal
Fat	13.1g
Saturated Fat	2.1g
Carbohydrate	20.1g
Fiber	2.8g

Balti Chile Chicken

Hot and spicy would be the best way of describing this mouth-watering balti dish. The smell of the fresh chiles cooking is irresistible.

INGREDIENTS

Serves 4-6

5 tablespoons corn oil
8 large fresh green chiles, slit
½ teaspoon mixed onion seeds
    and cumin seeds
4 curry leaves
1 teaspoon grated fresh ginger root
1 teaspoon chili powder
1 teaspoon ground coriander
1 teaspoon crushed garlic
1 teaspoon salt
2 medium onions, chopped
1½ pounds skinless, boneless
    chicken, cubed
1 tablespoon lemon juice
1 tablespoon roughly chopped
    fresh mint
1 tablespoon roughly chopped
    fresh cilantro
8–10 cherry tomatoes

1 Heat the oil in a karahi, wok, or deep pan. Lower the heat slightly and add the slit green chiles. Fry until the skin starts to change color.

2 Add the onion seeds and cumin seeds, curry leaves, ginger, chili powder, ground coriander, garlic, salt, and onions, and fry for a few seconds, stirring continuously.

3 Add the chicken pieces to the pan. Stir-fry over a medium heat for 7–10 minutes, or until the chicken is cooked right through. Do not overcook the chicken or it will become tough in texture.

NUTRITIONAL NOTES	
Per Portion	
Energy	346cal
Fat	16.5g
Saturated Fat	2.7g
Carbohydrate	9.9g
Fiber	1.3g

4 Sprinkle on the lemon juice and add the roughly chopped fresh mint and cilantro.

5 Dot with the cherry tomatoes and serve from the pan.

Balti Baby Chicken in Tamarind Sauce

The tamarind in this recipe gives the dish a sweet-and-sour flavor; this is also a hot balti.

INGREDIENTS

Serves 4–6

4 tablespoons ketchup
1 tablespoon tamarind paste
4 tablespoons water
1½ teaspoons chili powder
1½ teaspoons salt
1 tablespoon sugar
1½ teaspoons grated fresh ginger root`
1½ teaspoons crushed garlic
2 tablespoons dry unsweetened
  shredded coconut
2 tablespoons sesame seeds
1 teaspoon poppy seeds
1 teaspoon ground cumin
1½ teaspoons ground coriander
2 × 1 pound baby chickens, skinned
  and cut into 6–8 pieces each
5 tablespoons corn oil
8 tablespoons curry leaves
½ teaspoon onion seeds
3 large dried red chiles
½ teaspoon fenugreek seeds
10–12 cherry tomatoes
3 tablespoons chopped fresh
  cilantro
2 fresh green chiles, chopped

1 Put the ketchup, tamarind paste, and water into a large mixing bowl and use a fork to blend everything together.

2 Add the chili powder, salt, sugar, ginger, garlic, coconut, sesame and poppy seeds, cumin, and coriander to the mixture. Stir to combine.

3 Add the chicken pieces and stir until they are well coated with the spice mixture. Set aside.

4 Heat the oil in a karahi, wok, or deep pan. Add the curry leaves, onion seeds, dried red chiles, and fenugreek seeds and fry for about 1 minute.

5 Lower the heat to medium and add 2 or 3 chicken pieces at a time, with their sauce, mixing as you go. When all the pieces have been added to the pan, stir well, using a slotted spoon.

6 Simmer gently for 12–15 minutes, or until the chicken is cooked all the way through.

7 Finally, add the tomatoes, fresh cilantro, and green chiles, and serve from the pan.

NUTRITIONAL NOTES	
Per Portion	
Energy	348cal
Fat	19.9g
Saturated Fat	6.4g
Carbohydrate	11.9g
Fiber	1.5g

Balti Chicken Madras

This is a fairly hot chicken curry
that is good served with either
plain boiled rice, pilau rice, or
nan bread.

INGREDIENTS

Serves 4

10 ounces skinless chicken
    breast fillets
3 tablespoons tomato paste
large pinch of ground fenugreek
¼ teaspoon ground fennel seeds
1 teaspoon grated fresh ginger root
1½ teaspoons ground coriander
1 teaspoon crushed garlic
1 teaspoon chili powder
¼ teaspoon ground turmeric
2 tablespoons lemon juice
1 teaspoon salt
1¼ cups water
1 tablespoon oil
2 medium onions, diced
2–4 curry leaves
2 fresh green chiles, seeded
    and chopped
1 tablespoon fresh cilantro leaves

NUTRITIONAL NOTES	
Per Portion	
Energy	141cal
Fat	4.11g
Saturated Fat	0.60g
Carbohydrate	8.60g
Fiber	1.53g

_____ COOK'S TIP _____

Always be careful not to be too generous
when you are using ground fenugreek
because it can be very bitter.

1 Remove any visible fat from the
chicken breasts and cut the meat
into bitesize cubes.

2 Mix the tomato paste in a bowl
with the fenugreek, fennel seeds,
ginger, coriander, garlic, chili powder,
turmeric, lemon juice, salt, and water.

3 Heat the oil in a karahi, wok,
or heavy pan and fry the onions
together with the curry leaves until
the onions are golden brown.

4 Add the chicken pieces to the
onions and stir over the heat for
about 1 minute to seal the meat.

5 Next, pour in the prepared spice
mixture and continue to stir the
chicken for about 2 minutes.

6 Lower the heat and cook for
8–10 minutes, stirring frequently
to prevent the mixture from catching
on the bottom of the pan. Add the
chiles and fresh cilantro and serve
immediately.

Balti Chicken Vindaloo

This version of a popular dish from Goa is not as fiery as some, but will still suit those who like their curry to have a definite impact.

INGREDIENTS

Serves 4

1 large potato
²/₃ cup malt vinegar
1½ teaspoons crushed coriander seeds
1 teaspoon crushed cumin seeds
1½ teaspoons chili powder
¼ teaspoon ground turmeric
1 teaspoon crushed garlic
1 teaspoon grated fresh ginger root
1 teaspoon salt
1½ teaspoons paprika
1 tablespoon tomato paste
large pinch of ground fenugreek
1¼ cups water
8 ounces skinless chicken breast fillets, cubed
1 tablespoon oil
2 medium onions, sliced
4 curry leaves
2 fresh green chiles, chopped

1 Peel the potato, cut it into large, irregular shapes, place these in a bowl of water, and set aside.

COOK'S TIP

The best thing to drink with a hot curry is either iced water or a yogurt-base lassi.

2 In a bowl, mix the vinegar, coriander, cumin, chili powder, turmeric, garlic, ginger, salt, paprika, tomato paste, fenugreek, and water.

3 Pour this spice mixture over the chicken, stir, and set aside.

4 Heat the oil in a karahi, wok, or heavy pan and quickly fry the onions with the curry leaves for 3–4 minutes without burning.

5 Lower the heat and add the chicken mixture to the pan with the spices. Continue to stir-fry for another 2 minutes.

6 Drain the potato pieces and add to the pan. Cover with a lid and cook over a medium to low heat for 5–7 minutes, or until the sauce has thickened slightly and the chicken and potatoes are cooked through.

7 Stir in the chopped green chiles and serve.

NUTRITIONAL NOTES	
Per Portion	
Energy	168cal
Fat	4.20g
Saturated Fat	0.60g
Carbohydrate	17.65g
Fiber	2.04g

Balti Lamb Tikka

This is a traditional tikka recipe, in which the lamb is marinated in yogurt and spices. The lamb is usually cut into cubes, but the cooking time can be halved by cutting it into strips instead.

INGREDIENTS

Serves 4

1 pound lean boneless lamb, cut
   into strips
³/₄ cup plain yogurt
1 teaspoon ground cumin
1 teaspoon ground coriander
1 teaspoon chili powder
1 teaspoon crushed garlic
1 teaspoon salt
1 teaspoon garam masala
2 tablespoons chopped fresh
   cilantro
2 tablespoons lemon juice
2 tablespoons corn oil
1 tablespoon tomato paste
1 large green bell pepper, seeded
   and sliced
3 large fresh red chiles

1 Put the lamb strips, yogurt, ground cumin, ground coriander, chili powder, garlic, salt, garam masala, fresh cilantro, and lemon juice into a large mixing bowl and stir thoroughly. Cover and marinate at cool room temperature for 1 hour.

2 Heat the oil in a karahi, wok, or deep pan. Lower the heat slightly and stir in the tomato paste.

NUTRITIONAL NOTES	
Per Portion	
Energy	289cal
Fat	18.7g
Saturated Fat	6.9g
Carbohydrate	6.1g
Fiber	0.7g

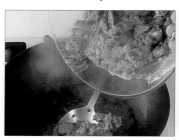

3 Add the lamb strips to the pan, a few at a time, leaving any excess marinade behind in the bowl.

4 Cook the lamb, stirring frequently, for 7–10 minutes, or until it is well browned.

5 Finally, add the green bell pepper slices and the whole red chiles. Heat through, checking that the lamb is fully cooked, spoon into a serving dish, and serve hot.

Balti Lamb with Potatoes and Fenugreek

The combination of lamb with fresh fenugreek works well in this dish, which is delicious accompanied by plain boiled rice and mango pickle. Only use the fenugreek leaves, because the stalks can be bitter. This dish is traditionally served with rice.

INGREDIENTS

Serves 4

1 pound lean ground lamb
1 teaspoon grated fresh ginger root
1 teaspoon crushed garlic
1½ teaspoons chili powder
1 teaspoon salt
¼ teaspoon turmeric
3 tablespoons corn oil
2 medium onions, sliced
2 medium potatoes, peeled, parboiled, and roughly diced
1 bunch fresh fenugreek, chopped
2 tomatoes, chopped
½ cup frozen peas
2 tablespoons chopped fresh cilantro
3 fresh red chiles, seeded and sliced

3 Add the ground lamb and fry over a medium heat for 5–7 minutes, stirring.

4 Stir in the potatoes, chopped fenugreek, tomatoes, and peas and cook for another 5–7 minutes, stirring continuously.

5 Just before serving, stir in the fresh cilantro. Spoon into a large dish or on to individual plates and serve hot. Garnish with fresh red chiles.

NUTRITIONAL NOTES	
Per Portion	
Energy	386cal
Fat	23.7g
Saturated Fat	8.2g
Carbohydrate	20.3g
Fiber	2.5g

1 Put the ground lamb, grated ginger, garlic, chili powder, salt, and turmeric into a large bowl, and blend together thoroughly. Set aside.

2 Heat the oil in a karahi, wok, or deep pan. Add the onion slices and fry for about 5 minutes, until golden brown.

Balti Lamb Koftas with Vegetables

These koftas look attractive served on their bed of vegetables, especially if you make them into small balls.

INGREDIENTS

Serves 4

1 pound lean ground lamb
1 teaspoon garam masala
1 teaspoon ground cumin
1 teaspoon ground coriander
1 teaspoon crushed garlic
1 teaspoon chili powder
1 teaspoon salt
1 tablespoon chopped fresh
  cilantro
1 small onion, finely diced
⅔ cup corn oil

For the vegetables

3 tablespoons corn oil
1 bunch scallions,
  roughly chopped
½ large red bell pepper,
  seeded and chopped
½ large green bell pepper,
  seeded and chopped
1 cup corn kernels
1½ cups canned lima beans
½ small cauliflower, cut into florets
4 fresh green chiles, chopped

To garnish

1 teaspoon chopped fresh mint
1 tablespoon chopped fresh
  cilantro
1 tablespoon shredded fresh
  ginger root
lime slices
1 tablespoon lemon juice

NUTRITIONAL NOTES	
Per Portion	
Energy	515cal
Fat	35g
Saturated Fat	9.9g
Carbohydrate	22g
Fiber	5.7g

1 Put the ground lamb into a food processor or blender and process for about 1 minute.

2 Transfer the lamb to a medium bowl. Add the dry spices, garlic, chili powder, salt, fresh cilantro, and onion, and use your fingers to blend the kofta mixture thoroughly. Cover and set aside in the refrigerator.

3 Heat the oil for the vegetables in a karahi, wok, or deep pan. Add the scallions and stir-fry for 2 minutes.

4 Add the bell peppers, corn, lima beans, cauliflower and green chiles, and stir-fry over a high heat for about 2 minutes. Set to one side.

5 Using your hands, roll small pieces of the kofta mixture into golf-ball size portions. You should have between 12 and 16 koftas.

6 Heat the oil for the koftas in a skillet. Lower the heat slightly and add the koftas, a few at a time. Shallow-fry each batch, turning the koftas, until they are evenly browned. Remove from the oil with a slotted spoon, and drain on paper towels.

7 Put the vegetable mixture back over a medium heat, and add the cooked koftas. Stir the mixture gently for about 5 minutes, or until everything is heated through.

8 Garnish with the mint, cilantro, shredded ginger, and lime slices. Just before serving, sprinkle over the lemon juice.

Balti Mini Lamb Kebabs with Pearl Onions

This is an unusual balti dish because the meat patties are cooked on skewers before being added to the karahi to be mixed with the vegetables.

Ingredients

Serves 6

1 pound lean ground lamb
1 medium onion, finely chopped
1 teaspoon garam masala
1 teaspoon crushed garlic
2 medium fresh green chiles, finely chopped
2 tablespoons chopped fresh cilantro
1 teaspoon salt
1 tablespoon all-purpose flour
4 tablespoons corn oil
12 pearl onions
4 fresh green chiles, sliced
12 cherry tomatoes
2 tablespoons chopped fresh cilantro

1 Mix the lamb, onion, garam masala, garlic, green chiles, fresh cilantro, salt, and flour in a medium bowl. Use your hands to make sure that all the ingredients are thoroughly mixed together.

2 Transfer the mixture to a food processor and process for about 1 minute to make the mixture even finer in texture.

3 Put the mixture back into the bowl. Break off small pieces, about the size of a lime, and wrap them around skewers to form small sausage shapes. Put about two of these shapes on each skewer.

4 Continue making the sausage shapes until you have used all of the mixture. Preheat the broiler to its maximum setting. Baste the meat with 1 tablespoon of the oil and broil the kebabs for 12–15 minutes, turning and basting occasionally, until the meat is evenly browned.

5 Heat the remaining 3 tablespoons of the oil in a karahi, wok, or deep pan. Lower the heat slightly and add the whole pearl onions. As soon as they start to darken, add the fresh chiles and tomatoes.

6 Slide the lamb patties from their skewers and add them to the onion and tomato mixture. Stir gently for about 3 minutes to heat them through.

7 Transfer to a serving dish and garnish with fresh cilantro.

Nutritional Notes	
Per Portion	
Energy	252cal
Fat	17.6g
Saturated Fat	5.7g
Carbohydrate	8.5g
Fiber	1.2g

Cook's Tip

In India, these shaped meat patties are called kababs. They are sometimes cooked and served on skewers, like the kebabs from which they are derived, but are often served simply as circles or sausage shapes.

Balti Lamb with Cauliflower

Cauliflower and lamb go well together. This tasty curry is given a final tarka, a dressing of oil, cumin seeds, and curry leaves to enhance the flavor.

INGREDIENTS

Serves 4

2 teaspoons oil
2 medium onions, sliced
1½ teaspoons grated fresh ginger root
1 teaspoon chili powder
1 teaspoon crushed garlic
¼ teaspoon ground turmeric
½ teaspoon ground coriander
2 tablespoons fresh fenugreek leaves
10 ounces boneless lean spring lamb, cut into strips
1 small cauliflower, cut into small florets
1¼ cups water
2 tablespoons fresh cilantro leaves
½ red bell pepper, seeded and sliced
1 tablespoon lemon juice

For the tarka

2 teaspoons oil
½ teaspoon cumin seeds
4–6 curry leaves

1 Heat the oil in a karahi, wok, or heavy pan and gently fry the onions until they are golden brown. Lower the heat and then add the ginger, chili powder, garlic, turmeric and ground coriander. Stir well to combine all the ingredients, then add the fresh fenugreek leaves and mix well.

2 Add the lamb strips to the wok and stir-fry until the lamb is completely coated with the spices. Add half the cauliflower florets and stir the mixture well.

3 Pour in the water, cover the wok, lower the heat, and cook for 5–7 minutes, until the cauliflower and lamb are almost cooked through.

4 Add the remaining cauliflower, half the fresh cilantro, the red bell pepper, and lemon juice and stir-fry for about 5 minutes, ensuring the sauce does not catch on the bottom of the pan.

5 Check that the lamb is completely cooked, then remove the pan from the heat and set it aside.

6 To make the tarka, heat the oil and fry the seeds and curry leaves for about 30 seconds. While it is still hot, pour the seasoned oil over the cauliflower and lamb and serve garnished with the remaining fresh cilantro leaves.

NUTRITIONAL NOTES	
Per Portion	
Energy	202cal
Fat	9.88g
Saturated Fat	3.24g
Carbohydrate	10.86g
Fiber	2.88g

COOK'S TIP

Peanut oil is ideal for curries because it doesn't burn so easily at high temperatures.

Balti Bhoona Lamb

Bhooning is a traditional way of stir-frying, which simply involves semicircular movements, scraping the bottom of the pan each time in the center. Serve this dish with freshly made chapatis.

INGREDIENTS

Serves 4

8–10 ounces boneless lean spring lamb
3 medium onions
1 tablespoon oil
1 tablespoon tomato paste
1 teaspoon crushed garlic
1½ teaspoons finely grated fresh
    ginger root
1 teaspoon salt
¼ teaspoon ground turmeric
2½ cups water
1 tablespoon lemon juice
1 tablespoon shredded fresh ginger root
1 tablespoon chopped fresh cilantro
1 tablespoon chopped fresh mint
1 fresh red chile, chopped

1 Using a sharp knife remove any excess fat from the lamb and cut the meat into small cubes.

_____ COOK'S TIP _____

Bhooning ensures that the meat becomes well-coated and combines with the spice mixture before the cooking liquid is added. The action of stirring the mixture can be satisfying, like cooking a risotto.

2 Dice the onions finely. Heat the oil in a karahi, wok, or heavy pan and fry the onions until soft.

3 Meanwhile, mix together the tomato paste, garlic, and ginger, salt, and turmeric. Pour the spice mixture onto the onions in the pan and stir-fry for a few seconds.

4 Add the lamb and continue to stir-fry for about 2–3 minutes. Stir in the water, lower the heat, cover the pan, and cook for 15–20 minutes, stirring occasionally.

5 When the water has almost evaporated, start bhooning over a medium heat (see the introduction, above left), making sure that the sauce does not catch on the bottom of the pan. Continue for 5–7 minutes.

6 Pour in the lemon juice, followed by the shredded ginger, cilantro, mint, and red chile. Stir to mix, then serve from the pan.

NUTRITIONAL NOTES	
Per Portion	
Energy	198cal
Fat	10.37g
Saturated Fat	3.24g
Carbohydrate	11.05g
Fiber	1.84g

Balti Lamb with Peas and Potatoes

Fresh mint leaves are used in this dish, but if they are unobtainable, use frozen peas with mint already added to bring an added freshness. Serve with plain rice.

INGREDIENTS

Serves 4

8 ounces boneless lean spring lamb
½ cup plain low-fat yogurt
1 cinnamon stick
2 green cardamom pods
3 black peppercorns
1 teaspoon crushed garlic
1 teaspoon grated fresh ginger root
1 teaspoon chili powder
1 teaspoon garam masala
1 teaspoon salt
2 tablespoons roughly chopped
    fresh mint
1 tablespoon oil
2 medium onions, sliced
1¼ cups water
1 large potato, diced
1 cup frozen peas
1 firm tomato, peeled, seeded,
    and diced

1 Using a sharp knife, trim any excess fat from the lamb and cut the meat into strips. Place it in a bowl.

2 Add the yogurt, cinnamon, cardamoms, peppercorns, garlic, ginger, chili powder, garam masala, salt, and half the mint. Stir well, cover the bowl, and let stand in a cool place to marinate for about 2 hours.

3 Heat the oil in a karahi, wok, or heavy pan and fry the onions until golden brown. Stir in the lamb and the marinade and stir-fry for about 3 minutes.

NUTRITIONAL NOTES	
Per Portion	
Energy	231cal
Fat	8.47g
Saturated Fat	2.79g
Carbohydrate	22.72g
Fiber	3.73g

4 Pour in the water, lower the heat, and cook for about 15 minutes, until the meat is cooked through. Meanwhile, cook the potato in boiling water until just soft, but not mushy.

5 Add the peas and potato to the lamb and stir gently to mix.

6 Finally, add the remaining mint and the tomato and cook for another 5 minutes before serving.

COOK'S TIP
This dish will improve in flavor if cooked a day ahead and kept in the refrigerator.

Balti Lamb in Yogurt and Garam Masala Sauce

The lamb is first marinated, then cooked slowly in a hot yogurt sauce, and it is served with dried apricots, which have been lightly sautéed in ghee with cinnamon and cardamom.

INGREDIENTS

Serves 4

1 tablespoon tomato paste
¾ cup plain low-fat yogurt
1 teaspoon garam masala
¼ teaspoon cumin seeds
1 teaspoon salt
1 teaspoon crushed garlic
1 teaspoon grated fresh ginger root
1 teaspoon chili powder
8 ounces boneless lean spring lamb,
   cut into strips
1 tablespoon oil
2 medium onions, finely sliced
2 tablespoons ghee or
   unsalted butter
1-inch cinnamon stick
2 green cardamom pods
5 dried apricots, quartered
1 tablespoon fresh cilantro leaves,
   to garnish

1 In a bowl, blend together the tomato paste, yogurt, garam masala, cumin seeds, salt, garlic, ginger, and chili powder.

2 Add the lamb to the sauce and mix well. Cover and let marinate in a cool place for about 1 hour.

3 Heat 2 teaspoons of the oil in a wok or heavy skillet and fry the onions over a medium heat until they are crisp and golden brown.

4 Remove the onions using a slotted spoon, let cool, and then grind down by processing briefly in a food processor or with a mortar and pestle. Reheat the oil remaining in the pan and return the onions to the wok.

NUTRITIONAL NOTES	
Per Portion	
Energy	221cal
Fat	11.20g
Saturated Fat	3.64g
Carbohydrate	14.60g
Fiber	1.80g

___ COOK'S TIP ___

If you want this curry to be slightly hotter, increase the quantity of garam masala and chili powder to 1½ teaspoons each.

5 Add the lamb and stir-fry for about 2 minutes. Cover with a lid, lower the heat, and cook, stirring occasionally, for about 15 minutes, or until the meat is cooked through. If required, add about ⅔ cup water during the cooking. Remove from the heat and set aside.

6 Heat the ghee or butter with the remaining 1 teaspoon of oil and drop in the cinnamon stick and cardamoms. Add the dried apricots and stir over a low heat for about 2 minutes. Pour this over the lamb.

7 Serve garnished with the fresh cilantro leaves.

Balti Lamb with Stuffed Vegetables

Eggplants and bell peppers make an excellent combination. Here, they are stuffed with an aromatic lamb filling and served on a bed of sautéed onions. The presentation is very attractive.

INGREDIENTS

Serves 4-6
3 small eggplants
1 each red, green, and yellow
  bell peppers

Stuffing

3 tablespoons corn oil
3 medium onions, sliced
1 teaspoon chili powder
¼ teaspoon ground turmeric
1 teaspoon ground coriander
1 teaspoon ground cumin
1 teaspoon grated fresh ginger root
1 teaspoon crushed garlic
1 teaspoon salt
1 pound lean ground lamb
3 fresh green chiles, chopped
2 tablespoons chopped fresh
  cilantro

For the sautéed onions

3 tablespoons corn oil
1 teaspoon mixed onion,
  mustard, fenugreek and
  white cumin seeds
4 dried red chiles
3 medium onions, roughly chopped
1 teaspoon salt
1 teaspoon chili powder
2 medium tomatoes, sliced
2 fresh green chiles, chopped
2 tablespoons chopped fresh cilantro

NUTRITIONAL NOTES	
Per Portion	
Energy	606cal
Fat	40.8g
Saturated Fat	10.6g
Carbohydrate	35g
Fiber	7.4g

1 Prepare the vegetables. Slit the eggplants lengthwise to the stalks; keep the stalks intact. Cut the tops off the bell peppers and remove the seeds.

2 Make the stuffing. Heat the oil in a medium pan. Add the onions and fry for about 3 minutes. Lower the heat and add the chili powder, turmeric, ground coriander, ground cumin, ginger, garlic, and salt, and stir-fry for about 1 minute. Add the lamb to the pan and increase the heat.

3 Stir-fry for 7–10 minutes, or until the lamb is cooked, using a wooden spoon to scrape the bottom of the pan. Add the green chiles and fresh cilantro toward the end. Remove from the heat, cover, and set to one side.

4 Make the sautéed onions. Heat the oil in a karahi, wok, or deep pan and add the mixed onion, mustard, fenugreek, and white cumin seeds. Stir in the dried red chiles and fry for about 1 minute. Add the onions and fry for about 2 minutes, or until soft.

5 Add the salt, chili powder, tomatoes, green chiles, and fresh cilantro. Cook for another minute. Remove from the heat and set to one side.

6 The ground lamb should by now be cool enough to stuff the prepared eggplants and bell peppers. Fill the vegetables loosely with the meat mixture.

7 As you stuff the vegetables, place them on top of the sautéed onions in the karahi. Cover with aluminum foil, making sure the foil doesn't touch the food, and cook over a low heat for about 15 minutes.

8 The dish is ready as soon as the eggplants and bell peppers are tender. Serve with a dish of plain boiled rice or colorful pilau rice.

--- COOK'S TIP ---

You can retain the bell pepper tops and use them as "lids" after the vegetables have been stuffed, if you like.

Balti Lamb Chops with Potatoes

These chops are marinated before being cooked in a deliciously spicy sauce. They are ideal for a family meal, served with a simple mixed salad.

INGREDIENTS

Serves 6–8

8 lamb chops (about 2–3 ounces each)
2 tablespoons olive oil
⅔ cup lemon juice
1 teaspoon salt
1 tablespoon chopped fresh mint
  and cilantro
⅔ cup corn oil
fresh mint sprigs
lime slices

For the sauce

3 tablespoons corn oil
8 medium tomatoes,
  roughly chopped
1 bay leaf
1 teaspoon garam masala
2 tablespoons plain yogurt
1 teaspoon crushed garlic
1 teaspoon chili powder
1 teaspoon salt
½ teaspoon black cumin seeds
3 black peppercorns
2 medium potatoes, peeled, roughly
  chopped, and boiled

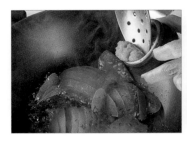

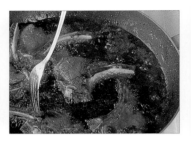

1 Put the chops into a large bowl. Mix together the olive oil, lemon juice, salt, and fresh mint and cilantro.

2 Pour the oil mixture over the chops and rub it in well with your fingers. Cover and let marinate for at least 3 hours in the refrigerator.

3 To make the sauce, heat the corn oil in a karahi, wok, or deep pan. Lower the heat and add the chopped tomatoes. Stir-fry for about 2 minutes.

4 Add the bay leaf, garam masala, yogurt, garlic, chili powder, salt, black cumin seeds, and black peppercorns, and stir-fry for another 2–3 minutes.

5 Lower the heat again and add the cooked potatoes, mixing everything together well. Remove from the heat and set to one side.

6 Heat ⅔ cup corn oil in a separate skillet. Lower the heat slightly and fry the marinated chops until they are cooked through. This will take 10–12 minutes. Remove with a slotted spoon and drain the cooked chops on paper towels.

7 Heat the sauce in the karahi, bringing it to a boil. Add the chops and lower the heat. Simmer for 5–7 minutes.

8 Transfer to a warmed serving dish and garnish with the mint sprigs and lime slices.

NUTRITIONAL NOTES	
Per Portion	
Energy	327cal
Fat	18.7g
Saturated Fat	6.3g
Carbohydrate	14.8g
Fiber	2g

Balti Beef

There's no marinating involved with this simple recipe, which can be prepared and cooked in under an hour.

INGREDIENTS

Serves 4

1 red bell pepper
1 green bell pepper
1 tablespoon oil
1 teaspoon cumin seeds
½ teaspoon fennel seeds
1 onion, cut into thick wedges
1 garlic clove, crushed
1-inch piece fresh ginger root,
   finely chopped
1 fresh red chile, finely chopped
1 tablespoon curry paste
½ teaspoon salt
1½ pounds lean round steak or beef
   tenderloin, cut into thick strips
nan bread, to serve

1 Cut the red and green bell peppers into 1-inch chunks.

2 Heat the oil in a karahi, wok, or skillet and fry the cumin and fennel seeds for 2 minutes, or until they begin to splutter. Add the onion, garlic, ginger, and chile and fry for another 5 minutes.

3 Stir in the curry paste and salt and fry for another 3–4 minutes.

NUTRITIONAL NOTES	
Per Portion	
Energy	278cal
Fat	11.60g
Saturated Fat	3.52g
Carbohydrate	7.70g
Fiber	2.50g

4 Add the bell peppers and toss over the heat for about 5 minutes. Stir in the beef strips and continue to fry for 10–12 minutes, or until the meat is tender. Serve from the pan, with warm nan bread.

Balti Potatoes with Eggplant

Using new potatoes adds to the attractiveness of this dish. Choose the smaller variety of eggplant, too, because they are tastier than the large ones, which contain a lot of water and little flavor. Small eggplants are readily available from speciality grocers.

INGREDIENTS

Serves 4

10–12 new potatoes
6 small eggplants
1 medium red bell pepper
1 tablespoon oil
2 medium onions, sliced
4–6 curry leaves
½ teaspoon onion seeds
1 teaspoon crushed coriander seeds
½ teaspoon cumin seeds
1 teaspoon grated fresh ginger root
1 teaspoon crushed garlic
1 teaspoon crushed dried red chiles
1 tablespoon chopped fresh
    fenugreek leaves
1 teaspoon chopped fresh
    cilantro
1 tablespoon plain low-fat yogurt
fresh cilantro leaves,
    to garnish

1 Cook the unpeeled potatoes in a pan of boiling water until they are just soft, but still whole.

2 Cut the eggplants into quarters, or eighths if using large eggplants.

3 Cut the bell pepper in half, remove the seeds and ribs, then slice the flesh into thin even-size strips.

4 Heat the oil in a karahi, wok, or heavy pan and fry the sliced onions, curry leaves, onion seeds, crushed coriander seeds, and cumin seeds until the onion slices are a soft golden brown, stirring constantly.

5 Add the ginger, garlic, crushed chiles, and fenugreek, followed by the eggplants and potatoes. Stir everything together and cover the pan with a lid. Lower the heat and cook the vegetables for 5–7 minutes.

6 Remove the lid, add the fresh cilantro followed by the yogurt, and stir well. Serve garnished with cilantro leaves.

NUTRITIONAL NOTES	
Per Portion	
Energy	183cal
Fat	4.42g
Saturated Fat	0.70g
Carbohydrate	33.02g
Fiber	5.43g

COOK'S TIP
Remember to whisk yogurt before adding it to a hot dish to prevent it from curdling.

Balti Stir-fried Vegetables with Cashew Nuts

This quick and versatile stir-fry will accommodate most other combinations of vegetables—you do not have to use the selection suggested here.

INGREDIENTS

Serves 4

2 medium carrots
1 medium red bell pepper, seeded
1 medium green bell pepper, seeded
2 zucchini
4 ounces green beans
1 medium bunch scallions
1 tablespoon oil
4–6 curry leaves
½ teaspoon cumin seeds
4 dried red chiles
10–12 cashew nuts
1 teaspoon salt
2 tablespoons lemon juice
fresh mint leaves, to garnish

1 Prepare the vegetables: cut the carrots, bell peppers, and zucchini into matchsticks, halve the beans, and chop the scallions. Set aside.

NUTRITIONAL NOTES	
Per Portion	
Energy	98cal
Fat	5.28g
Saturated Fat	0.88g
Carbohydrate	10.36g
Fiber	3.94g

2 Heat the oil in a karahi, wok, or heavy pan and fry the curry leaves, cumin seeds, and dried chiles for about 1 minute.

3 Add the vegetables and nuts and stir them around gently. Add the salt and lemon juice. Continue to stir and cook for about 3–5 minutes.

4 Transfer the vegetables to a serving dish, garnish with fresh mint leaves, and serve immediately.

Karahi Potatoes with Whole Spices

The potato is transformed into something exotic when it is cooked like this with a delicious mixture of spices.

INGREDIENTS

Serves 4

1 tablespoon oil
1 teaspoon cumin seeds
3 curry leaves
1 teaspoon crushed dried red chiles
½ teaspoon mixed onion, mustard, and fenugreek seeds
½ teaspoon fennel seeds
3 garlic cloves, sliced
1-inch piece fresh ginger root, grated
2 onions, sliced
6 new potatoes, thinly sliced
1 tablespoon chopped fresh cilantro
1 fresh red chile, seeded and sliced
1 fresh green chile, seeded and sliced

COOK'S TIP

Choose a waxy variety of new potato for this fairly hot vegetable dish; if you use a soft potato, you won't be able to cut it into thin slices without it breaking up. The varieties used as "salad potatoes" are those suitable for this recipe. Leave the skin on for a tastier, and more nutritious, result.

NUTRITIONAL NOTES
Per Portion

Energy	110cal
Fat	3.60g
Saturated Fat	0.39g
Carbohydrate	17.1g
Fiber	1.60g

1 Heat the oil in a karahi, wok, or heavy pan. Lower the heat slightly and add the cumin seeds, curry leaves, dried red chiles, mixed onion, mustard and fenugreek seeds, fennel seeds, garlic slices, and ginger. Fry for 1 minute.

2 Add the onions and fry for another 5 minutes, or until the onions are golden brown.

3 Add the potatoes, fresh cilantro, and fresh red and green chiles and mix well. Cover the pan tightly with a lid or aluminum foil; if using foil, make sure that it does not touch the food. Cook over a low heat for 7 minutes, or until the potatoes are tender.

4 Remove the pan from the heat, and take off the lid or foil cover. Serve hot straight from the pan.

Balti Mushrooms in a Creamy Garlic Sauce

This is a simple and delicious balti recipe, which could be accompanied by one of the rice side dishes from this book.

INGREDIENTS

Serves 4

4½ cups white mushrooms
1 tablespoon oil
1 bay leaf
3 garlic cloves, roughly chopped
2 green chiles, seeded
   and chopped
1 cup low-fat ricotta cheese
1 tablespoon chopped fresh mint
1 tablespoon chopped
   fresh cilantro
1 teaspoon salt
fresh mint and cilantro leaves,
   to garnish

1 Cut the mushrooms in half, or in quarters if large, and set aside.

NUTRITIONAL NOTES	
Per Portion	
Energy	76cal
Fat	3.40g
Saturated Fat	0.55g
Carbohydrate	5.20g
Fiber	1.10g

2 Heat the oil in a karahi, wok, or heavy pan, then add the bay leaf, garlic, and chiles, and quickly stir-fry for about 1 minute.

3 Add the mushrooms. Stir-fry for another 2 minutes.

4 Remove from the heat and stir in the ricotta cheese, followed by the mint, cilantro, and salt. Return to the heat and stir-fry for 2–3 minutes, then transfer to a warmed serving dish and garnish with mint and cilantro leaves.

Balti Corn with Cauliflower

This quick and tasty vegetable side dish can be made with frozen corn kernels, so it is an excellent standby. If you do not have any cauliflower, you can substitute broccoli or another vegetable.

INGREDIENTS

Serves 4

3 small onions
1 fresh red chile
1 tablespoon oil
4 curry leaves
¼ teaspoon onion seeds
1 cup frozen corn kernels
½ small cauliflower, separated
   into florets
3–7 mint leaves

NUTRITIONAL NOTES	
Per Portion	
Energy	124cal
Fat	3.89g
Saturated Fat	0.58g
Carbohydrate	19.31g
Fiber	2.56g

COOK'S TIP

It is best to cook this dish immediately before serving and eating, because the flavor tends to spoil if it is kept warm.

2 Heat the oil in a karahi, wok, or heavy pan and stir-fry the curry leaves and the onion seeds for about 30 seconds.

4 Add the chile, frozen corn kernels, and cauliflower florets and stir-fry for 5–8 minutes.

1 Using a sharp knife, dice the onions finely. Slit the chile, scrape out the seeds, and then slice the chile thinly.

3 Add the onions and fry them for 5–8 minutes, until golden brown.

5 Toss with the mint leaves and serve immediately.

Balti Dhal with Scallions and Tomatoes

This rich-tasting dish is made using toor dhal, a shiny, yellow split lentil that resembles chana dhal. Fresh fenugreek leaves impart a stunning aroma.

INGREDIENTS

Serves 4

½ cup toor dhal or yellow split peas
2 tablespoons oil
¼ teaspoon onion seeds
1 medium bunch scallions,
  roughly chopped
1 teaspoon crushed garlic
¼ teaspoon ground turmeric
1½ teaspoons grated fresh ginger root
1 teaspoon chili powder
2 tablespoons fresh fenugreek leaves
1 teaspoon salt
⅔ cup water
6-8 cherry tomatoes
2 tablespoons fresh cilantro leaves
½ green bell pepper, seeded
  and sliced
1 tablespoon lemon juice
shredded scallion tops and
  fresh cilantro leaves,
  to garnish

COOK'S TIP

Fresh fenugreek leaves are too bitter to use as a vegetable on their own, but they are excellent mixed with peas and lentils. If you cannot get fresh fenugreek leaves, use dried leaves, which are available in Indian stores.

NUTRITIONAL NOTES
Per Portion

Energy	152cal
Fat	6.1g
Saturated Fat	0.9g
Carbohydrate	17.8g
Fiber	2.1g

1 Cook the dhal in a pan of boiling water for 40–45 minutes, until soft and mushy. Drain and set aside.

2 Heat the oil with the onion seeds in a karahi, wok, or heavy pan for a few seconds until hot.

3 Add the drained dhal to the wok or pan and stir-fry with the onion seeds for about 3 minutes.

4 Add the scallions followed by the garlic, turmeric, ginger, chili powder, fenugreek leaves, and salt and continue to stir-fry for 5–7 minutes.

5 Pour in just enough of the water to loosen the mixture.

6 Add the whole cherry tomatoes, cilantro leaves, green bell pepper, and lemon juice. Stir well and serve garnished with shredded scallion tops and some extra cilantro leaves.

Balti Baby Vegetables

There is a wide and wonderful selection of baby vegetables available in supermarkets these days, and this simple recipe does full justice to their delicate flavor and attractive appearance. Serve as part of a main meal or even as a light appetizer.

INGREDIENTS

Serves 4-6

10 new potatoes, halved
12–14 baby carrots
12–14 baby zucchini
2 tablespoons corn oil
15 pearl onions
2 tablespoons chili sauce
1 teaspoon crushed garlic
1 teaspoon grated fresh ginger root
1 teaspoon salt
2 cups drained canned chickpeas
10 cherry tomatoes
1 teaspoon crushed dried
   red chiles
2 tablespoons sesame seeds

1 Bring a medium pan of salted water to a boil and add the potatoes and carrots. Cook for 12–15 minutes, then add the zucchini and boil for another 5 minutes, or until all the vegetables are just tender. Be careful to avoid overcooking the vegetables, because they will be given a brief additional cooking time later.

2 Drain the vegetables well and put them in a bowl. Set aside.

3 Heat the oil in a karahi, wok, or deep pan and add the pearl onions. Fry until the onions turn golden brown. Lower the heat and add the chili sauce, garlic, ginger, and salt, being careful not to burn the mixture.

4 Stir in the chickpeas and stir-fry over a medium heat until the moisture has been absorbed.

5 Add the cooked vegetables and cherry tomatoes and stir over the heat with a slotted spoon for about 2 minutes.

6 Sprinkle the crushed red chiles and sesame seeds evenly over the vegetable mixture as a garnish and serve.

VARIATION

By varying the vegetables chosen and experimenting with different combinations, this recipe can be used to form the basis for a wide variety of vegetable accompaniments. For example, try experimenting with baby corn cobs, green beans, snow peas, cauliflower florets, and okra.

NUTRITIONAL NOTES
Per Portion

Energy	311cal
Fat	8.5g
Saturated Fat	1.3g
Carbohydrate	48.7g
Fiber	8.4g

Vegetarian
Main Dishes

THE COMPLAINT that there's nothing suitable on the menu for vegetarian diners never applies in India, where many sections of the population eat neither meat or fish nor dairy products as a matter of religious principle. The following dishes prove just how versatile vegetables can be, whether stuffed with spices, layered with rice, or roasted on skewers. Some dishes are light and easy to digest; others are bulked with lentils or chickpeas to make a substantial lunch or supper.

Careful spicing transforms the most ordinary ingredients into tasty treats. Spinach and potatoes, for instance, take on tremendous flavor when cooked with mustard seeds, ginger, and chili. Corn and Pea Curry is another winning combination, as is Okra with Green Mango and Lentils. Most of the dishes in this chapter are quick and easy to prepare, making them ideal for those occasions when a son or daughter announces that they have just become vegetarian.

Stuffed Eggplant in Seasoned Tamarind Juice

The traditional way of cooking with tamarind is in a terra-cotta dish, which brings out the full fruity tartness of the tamarind. This spicy eggplant dish will add a refreshing tang to any meal.

INGREDIENTS

Serves 4

12 baby eggplants
2 tablespoons vegetable oil
1 small onion, chopped
2 teaspoons grated fresh ginger root
2 teaspoons crushed garlic
1 teaspoon coriander seeds
1 teaspoon cumin seeds
2 teaspoons white poppy seeds
2 teaspoons sesame seeds
2 teaspoons dry unsweetened
   shredded coconut
1 tablespoon dry-roasted
   skinned peanuts
½–1 teaspoon chili powder
1 teaspoon salt
6–8 curry leaves
1–2 dried red chiles, chopped
½ teaspoon concentrated tamarind paste
7 tablespoons hot water

1 Make three deep slits lengthwise on each eggplant, without cutting through, then soak in salted water for 20 minutes.

2 Heat half the oil in a pan and sauté the onion for 3–4 minutes. Add the ginger and garlic and cook for 30 seconds.

3 Add the coriander and cumin seeds and sauté for 30 seconds, then add the poppy seeds, sesame seeds, and coconut. Sauté for 1 minute, stirring constantly. Let cool slightly, then grind the spices in a food processor, adding 7 tablespoons warm water. The mixture should resemble a thick, slightly coarse paste.

4 Mix the peanuts, chili powder, and salt into the spice paste. Drain the eggplants and dry on paper towels. Stuff each of the slits with the spice paste and reserve any remaining paste.

5 Heat the remaining oil in a wok, karahi, or large pan over a medium heat and add the curry leaves and chiles. Let the chiles blacken, then add the eggplants and the tamarind blended with 7 tablespoons hot water. Add any remaining spice paste and stir to mix.

6 Cover the pan and simmer gently for 15–20 minutes, or until the eggplants are tender. Serve with chapatis and a meat or poultry dish, if you like.

NUTRITIONAL NOTES	
Per Portion	
Energy	141cal
Fat	12g
Saturated Fat	1.7g
Carbohydrate	5.1g
Fiber	3.3g

Potatoes Stuffed with Spicy Cottage Cheese

For this recipe, it is important to choose a variety of potato recommended for baking, because the texture of the potato should not be too dry. This makes an excellent low-fat snack at any time of the day.

INGREDIENTS

Serves 4
4 medium baking potatoes
1 cup low-fat cottage cheese
2 teaspoons tomato paste
½ teaspoon ground cumin
½ teaspoon ground coriander
½ teaspoon chili powder
½ teaspoon salt
1 tablespoon oil
½ teaspoon mixed onion and
   mustard seeds
3 curry leaves
2 tablespoons water

For the garnish
mixed salad greens
fresh cilantro sprigs
lemon wedges
2 tomatoes, quartered

1 Preheat the oven to 350°F. Wash each potato and pat dry. Make a slit in the middle of each one and prick a few times with a fork or skewer, then wrap individually in aluminum foil. Bake in the oven directly on the shelf for about 1 hour, or until soft.

2 Put the cottage cheese into a heatproof dish and set aside.

3 In a separate bowl, mix the tomato paste, ground cumin, ground coriander, chili powder, and salt.

4 Heat the oil in a small pan for about 1 minute. Add the mixed onion and mustard seeds and the curry leaves and tilt the pan so the oil covers all the seeds and leaves.

_____ COOK'S TIP _____

This recipe can also be used as a basis for a tangy vegetable accompaniment to a main meal. Instead of using baked potatoes, boil some small new potatoes in their skins, then cut each one in half. Add the cooked potatoes to the spicy cottage cheese mixture, mix together well, and serve.

5 When the curry leaves turn a shade darker and you can smell their beautiful aroma, pour the tomato paste mixture into the pan and turn the heat immediately to low. Add the water and mix well. Cook for another minute, then pour the spicy tomato mixture on to the cottage cheese and stir together well.

6 Check that the baked potatoes are cooked right through by inserting a knife or skewer into the middle of the flesh. If it is soft, unwrap the potatoes from the foil and divide the cottage cheese equally between them.

7 Garnish the filled potatoes with mixed salad greens, fresh cilantro sprigs, lemon wedges, and tomato quarters and serve hot.

NUTRITIONAL NOTES	
Per Portion	
Energy	175cal
Fat	4.30g
Saturated Fat	0.43g
Carbohydrate	24.40g
Fiber	1.90g

Stuffed Baby Vegetables

The combination of potatoes and eggplants is popular in Indian cooking. This recipe uses small vegetables, which are stuffed with a dry, spicy masala paste.

INGREDIENTS

Serves 4
12 small potatoes, peeled
8 baby eggplants

For the stuffing
1 tablespoon sesame seeds
2 tablespoons ground coriander
2 tablespoons ground cumin
½ teaspoon salt
¼ teaspoon chili powder
½ teaspoon ground turmeric
2 teaspoons sugar
¼ teaspoon garam masala
1 tablespoon besan flour
2 garlic cloves, crushed
1 tablespoon lemon juice
2 tablespoons chopped fresh
  cilantro

For the sauce
1 tablespoon oil
½ teaspoon black mustard seeds
14-ounce can chopped tomatoes
2 tablespoons chopped fresh
  cilantro
⅔ cup water

1 Preheat the oven to 400°F. Make slits in the potatoes and eggplants, ensuring that you do not cut right through them.

2 Mix all the ingredients for the stuffing together on a plate.

3 Carefully spoon the spicy stuffing mixture into each of the slits in the potatoes and eggplants.

4 Arrange the stuffed potatoes and eggplants in a greased ovenproof dish, filling-side up.

COOK'S TIP

Make sure that the potatoes are all about the same size and the baby eggplants are a similar size, so that they all cook evenly. Baby eggplants are often on sale in supermarkets; however, if you find it difficult to obtain them in your supermarket, try an Asian market or Indian grocer.

5 For the sauce, heat the oil in a heavy pan and fry the mustard seeds for 2 minutes, until they begin to splutter, then add the canned tomatoes, chopped cilantro, and any leftover stuffing. Stir in the water. Bring to a boil and simmer for 5 minutes, until the sauce thickens.

6 Pour the sauce over the potatoes and eggplants. Cover and bake in the oven for 25–30 minutes, until the potatoes and eggplants are soft.

NUTRITIONAL NOTES	
Per Portion	
Energy	259cal
Fat	7.60g
Saturated Fat	0.73g
Carbohydrate	41.30g
Fiber	4g

Mushroom and Okra Curry with Mango Relish

The sliced okra not only flavors this unusual curry, but thickens it, too. Mushrooms are an excellent addition, but it is the mango relish that really pulls this dish together, adding an inspired touch of spicy sweetness.

INGREDIENTS

Serves 4
4 garlic cloves, roughly chopped
1-inch piece fresh ginger root,
   peeled and roughly chopped
1–2 fresh red chiles, seeded
   and chopped
¾ cup cold water
1 tablespoon sunflower oil
1 teaspoon coriander seeds
1 teaspoon cumin seeds
1 teaspoon ground cumin
seeds from 2 green cardamom
   pods, ground
pinch of ground turmeric
14-ounce can chopped tomatoes
6 cups mushrooms, quartered if large
8 ounces okra, trimmed and sliced
2 tablespoons chopped fresh
   cilantro
basmati rice, to serve

For the mango relish
1 large ripe mango, about 1¼ pounds
1 small garlic clove, crushed
1 small onion, finely chopped
2 teaspoons grated fresh ginger root
1 fresh red chile, seeded and
   finely chopped
pinch each of salt and sugar

1 Make the mango relish. Peel the mango, cut the flesh off the pit, and chop it finely. Put it in a bowl.

2 Mash the mango with a fork and mix in the garlic, onion, ginger, chile, salt, and sugar. Set aside.

3 Put the garlic, ginger, chiles, and 3 tablespoons of the water in a blender or food processor and blend to a smooth paste.

4 Heat the oil in a large pan. Add the whole coriander and cumin seeds and let them sizzle for a few seconds. Add the ground cumin, ground cardamom, and turmeric and cook for 1 minute more, until aromatic.

5 Scrape in the garlic paste, then add the tomatoes, mushrooms, and okra. Pour in the remaining water. Stir to mix well, and bring to a boil. Reduce the heat, cover, and simmer the curry for 5 minutes.

6 Remove the lid, increase the heat slightly, and cook for 5–10 minutes more, until the okra is tender. Stir in the fresh cilantro and serve with the rice and the mango relish.

COOK'S TIP

Stir the mango relish just before serving it.

NUTRITIONAL NOTES
Per Portion

Energy	152cal
Fat	4.4g
Saturated Fat	0.7g
Carbohydrate	24.2g
Fiber	8g

Cumin-scented Vegetable Curry with Toasted Almonds

Cabbage is widely enjoyed in India. Baby corn cobs and snow peas are less well known, except in the larger cities. This is, therefore, an example of a modern fusion curry, applying traditional cooking methods to what, for some, are exotic ingredients.

INGREDIENTS

Serves 4

1 tablespoon vegetable oil
4 tablespoons butter
½ teaspoon crushed coriander seeds
½ teaspoon white cumin seeds
6 dried red chiles
1 small savoy cabbage, shredded
12 snow peas
3 fresh red chiles, seeded and sliced
12 baby corn cobs, halved
salt
¼ cup sliced almonds, toasted and
   1 tablespoon chopped fresh cilantro,
   to garnish

1 Heat the oil and butter in a wok, karahi, or large pan and add the crushed coriander seeds, white cumin seeds, and dried red chiles.

_____ COOK'S TIP _____

Julienne strips of other vegetables will make this dish visually more appealing, and they will add superb taste at the same time. Try julienne carrots and leeks instead of snow peas and baby corn. Add the cabbage and carrots together, and add the leeks in step 3.

2 Add the shredded cabbage and snow peas to the spices in the pan and stir-fry briskly for about 5 minutes, until the cabbage starts to turn crisp.

3 Add the fresh red chiles and baby corn cobs to the pan and season with salt to taste. Stir-fry for 3 minutes more.

4 Garnish with the toasted almonds and fresh cilantro, and serve hot. This dish would go well with any meat curry and with a classic pilau.

NUTRITIONAL NOTES	
Per Portion	
Energy	133cal
Fat	12.2g
Saturated Fat	6.1g
Carbohydrate	3.6g
Fiber	2.1g

Spicy Potato and Tomato Curry

Diced potatoes are cooked gently in a fresh tomato sauce, which is flavored with curry leaves and green chiles.

INGREDIENTS

Serves 4

2 medium potatoes
1 tablespoon oil
2 medium onions, finely chopped
4 curry leaves
¼ teaspoon onion seeds
1 fresh green chile, seeded and chopped
4 tomatoes, sliced
1 teaspoon grated fresh ginger root
1 teaspoon crushed garlic
1 teaspoon chili powder
1 teaspoon ground coriander
¼ teaspoon salt
1 teaspoon lemon juice
1 tablespoon chopped fresh cilantro
3 hard-boiled eggs, to garnish

1 Peel the potatoes and cut them into small cubes.

NUTRITIONAL NOTES	
Per Portion	
Energy	188cal
Fat	7.62g
Saturated Fat	1.66g
Carbohydrate	23.41g
Fiber	3.10g

2 Heat the oil in a karahi, wok, or heavy pan and stir-fry the onions, curry leaves, onion seeds, and green chile for about 40 seconds.

3 Add the tomatoes and cook for about 2 minutes over a low heat.

4 Add the ginger and garlic, chili powder, ground coriander, and salt to taste. Continue to stir-fry for 1–2 minutes, then add the potatoes and cook over a low heat for 5–7 minutes, until the potatoes are tender.

5 Add the lemon juice and fresh cilantro and stir to mix together.

6 Shell the hard-boiled eggs, cut into quarters, and add as a garnish to the finished dish.

COOK'S TIPS
• Drain the hard-boiled eggs and cool them under cold running water, then tap the shells and let the eggs stand until cold. This prevents a discolored rim from forming around the outside of the yolk and enables the shell to be removed easily.
• Discoloration can also be a problem if the potatoes are cubed and left to stand before being cooked. Prepare them just before frying the onion mixture.

Spinach and Potato Curry

Spinach, potatoes, and traditional Indian spices are the main ingredients in this simple but authentic curry.

INGREDIENTS

Serves 4

1 pound spinach
1 tablespoon oil
1 teaspoon black mustard seeds
1 onion, thinly sliced
2 garlic cloves, crushed
1-inch piece fresh ginger root, finely chopped
1½ pounds potatoes, cut into 1-inch chunks
1 teaspoon chili powder
1 teaspoon salt
½ cup water

NUTRITIONAL NOTES	
Per Portion	
Energy	203cal
Fat	4.60g
Saturated Fat	0.65g
Carbohydrate	34.40g
Fiber	5.10g

_____ COOK'S TIPS _____

• To make certain that the spinach is completely dry, put it in a clean dish towel, roll up tightly, and squeeze gently to remove any excess liquid.

• Use a waxy variety of potato for this dish so that the pieces do not break up during cooking.

• When frying the mustard seeds, put a lid on the pan so that, when they splutter, they do not escape.

1 Wash and trim the spinach, then blanch it in a pan of boiling water for about 3–4 minutes.

2 Drain the spinach thoroughly and set aside. When it is cool enough to handle, use your hands to squeeze out any remaining liquid (see Cook's Tip) and set aside.

3 Heat the oil in a large heavy pan and fry the mustard seeds for 2 minutes, or until they splutter.

4 Add the sliced onion, garlic cloves, and chopped ginger to the mustard seeds and fry for 5 minutes, stirring.

5 Add the potato chunks, chili powder, salt, and water and stir-fry for another 8 minutes.

6 Add the drained spinach. Cover the pan with a lid and simmer for 10–15 minutes, or until the potatoes are tender. Serve hot.

Okra with Green Mango and Lentils

If you like okra, you'll love this spicy tangy dish.

INGREDIENTS

Serves 4

½ cup toor dhal or yellow split peas
1 pound okra
1 tablespoon oil
½ teaspoon onion seeds
2 onions, sliced
½ teaspoon ground fenugreek
¼ teaspoon ground turmeric
1 teaspoon ground coriander
1½ teaspoons chili powder
1 teaspoon grated fresh ginger root
1 teaspoon crushed garlic
1 green mango, peeled and sliced
1½ teaspoons salt
2 red chiles, seeded and sliced
2 tablespoons chopped
   fresh cilantro
1 tomato, sliced

1 Wash the toor dhal thoroughly to remove any grit and place in a large pan with enough cold water to cover. Bring to a boil and cook for 30–45 minutes, until soft but not mushy.

2 Trim the okra and cut the pods into ½-inch pieces.

3 Heat the oil in a karahi, wok, or heavy pan and fry the onion seeds until they begin to pop. Add the onions and fry until golden brown. Lower the heat and stir in the ground fenugreek, turmeric, and coriander, and the chili powder, ginger, and garlic.

4 Add the mango slices and the okra pieces. Stir well and then add the salt, red chiles, and fresh cilantro. Stir-fry for 3–4 minutes, or until the okra is well cooked and tender.

5 Finally, add the cooked dhal and sliced tomato and cook for another 3 minutes. Serve hot.

COOK'S TIP

When buying okra, always choose small, bright green ones with no brown patches. If cooking whole, trim off the conical cap, being careful not to pierce through to the seedpod, where there are tiny edible seeds and a sticky juice.

NUTRITIONAL NOTES
Per Portion

Energy	229cal
Fat	5.00g
Saturated Fat	0.55g
Carbohydrate	36.00g
Fiber	8.10g

Fava Bean and Cauliflower Curry

This is a hot and spicy vegetable curry, tasty when served with cooked rice (especially a brown basmati variety), a few small poppadums, and cucumber raita.

INGREDIENTS

Serves 4
2 garlic cloves, chopped
1-inch piece fresh ginger root
1 fresh green chile, seeded
    and chopped
2 tablespoons oil
1 onion, sliced
1 large potato, chopped
1 tablespoon curry powder, mild or hot
1 cauliflower, cut into small florets
2½ cups vegetable stock
salt and black pepper
10-ounce can fava beans
juice of ½ lemon, optional
fresh cilantro sprig,
    to garnish
plain rice, to serve

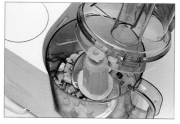

1 Blend the garlic, ginger, chile, and 1 tablespoon of the oil in a food processor or blender until the mixture forms a smooth paste.

2 In a large heavy pan, fry the onion and potato in the remaining oil for 5 minutes, then stir in the spice paste and curry powder. Cook for another minute.

3 Add the cauliflower florets to the onion and potato and stir well until they are thoroughly combined with the spicy mixture, then pour in the stock and bring to a boil over a medium to high heat.

4 Season well, cover, and simmer for 10 minutes. Add the beans with the liquid from the can and cook, uncovered, for another 10 minutes.

5 Check the seasoning and adjust if necessary. Add a good squeeze of lemon juice, if liked, and serve hot, garnished with cilantro and accompanied by plain boiled rice.

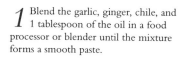

COOK'S TIP

Other root vegetables, such as parsnips and carrots, can be used in this recipe.

NUTRITIONAL NOTES	
Per Portion	
Energy	216cal
Fat	7.70g
Saturated Fat	0.75g
Carbohydrate	25.80g
Fiber	7.90g

Lentils Seasoned with Fried Spices

A simple supper dish for family or friends.

INGREDIENTS

Serves 4-6

½ cup red gram or pigeon peas
¼ cup Bengal gram (black chickpeas)
4 fresh green chiles
1 teaspoon ground turmeric
1 large onion, sliced
salt, to taste
14-ounce can chopped tomatoes
4 tablespoons vegetable oil
½ teaspoon mustard seeds
½ teaspoon cumin seeds
1 garlic clove, crushed
6 curry leaves
2 dried red chiles
deep-fried onions and fresh cilantro,
    to garnish

1 Place the red gram or pigeon peas and Bengal gram in a heavy pan and pour in 1½ cups water. Add the chiles, turmeric, and onion slices and bring to a boil. Simmer, covered, until the lentils are soft and the water has evaporated.

2 Mash the lentils with the back of a spoon. When nearly smooth, add the salt and tomatoes and mix well. If necessary, thin with hot water.

3 Heat the oil in a skillet. Fry the remaining ingredients until the garlic browns. Pour the oil and spices over the lentils and cover. After 5 minutes, mix well, garnish, and serve.

NUTRITIONAL NOTES	
Per Portion	
Energy	268cal
Fat	11.8g
Saturated Fat	1.4g
Carbohydrate	31g
Fiber	3.6g

South Indian Lentils and Vegetables

Lentils are perfect for easy, inexpensive meals.

INGREDIENTS

Serves 4-6

4 tablespoons vegetable oil
½ teaspoon mustard seeds
½ teaspoon cumin seeds
2 dried red chiles
¼ teaspoon asafetida
6–8 curry leaves
2 garlic cloves, crushed
2 tablespoons dry unsweetened
    shredded coconut
1 cup masoor dhal or
    red split lentils
2 teaspoons sambhar masala or
    garam masala
½ teaspoon ground turmeric
1 pound mixed vegetables
4 tablespoons tamarind juice
4 firm tomatoes, quartered
4 tablespoons vegetable oil
2 garlic cloves, finely sliced
handful fresh cilantro, chopped

1 Heat the oil in a heavy pan. Fry the next seven ingredients until the coconut browns. Mix in the lentils, sambhar masala, and turmeric. Stir in scant 2 cups water.

2 Simmer until the lentils are mushy. Add the vegetables, tamarind juice, and tomatoes. Cook so the vegetables are crunchy.

3 In the oil, fry the garlic slices and fresh cilantro. Pour over the lentils and vegetables. Mix at the table before serving.

NUTRITIONAL NOTES	
Per Portion	
Energy	459cal
Fat	28.1g
Saturated Fat	7g
Carbohydrate	37.3g
Fiber	5.8g

Lentil Dhal with Roasted Garlic and Whole Spices

This spicy lentil dhal makes a sustaining and comforting meal when served with rice or Indian breads and any dry-spiced dish, particularly a cauliflower or potato dish. The spicy garnish offers a contrast in texture and flavor.

INGREDIENTS

Serves 4–6

3 tablespoons butter or ghee
1 onion, chopped
2 fresh green chiles, seeded and chopped
1 tablespoon chopped fresh ginger root
1 cup yellow or red lentils
3¾ cups water
3 tablespoons roasted garlic paste
1 teaspoon ground cumin
1 teaspoon ground coriander
7 ounces tomatoes, peeled and diced
a little lemon juice
salt and black pepper
2–3 tablespoons cilantro sprigs, to garnish

For the spicy garnish

2 tablespoons peanut oil
4–5 shallots, sliced
2 garlic cloves, thinly sliced
1 tablespoon butter or ghee
1 teaspoon cumin seeds
1 teaspoon mustard seeds
3–4 small dried red chiles
8–10 fresh curry leaves

1 First begin the spicy garnish. Heat the oil in a large, heavy pan. Add the shallots and fry them over a medium heat, stirring occasionally, until they are crisp and browned. Add the garlic and cook, stirring frequently, for a moment or two, until the garlic colors slightly. Use a slotted spoon to remove the mixture from the pan and set it aside in a bowl.

2 Melt the butter or ghee in the pan and cook the onion, chiles, and ginger for 10 minutes, until golden.

3 Stir in the lentils and water, then bring to a boil, reduce the heat, and partly cover the pan. Simmer, stirring occasionally, for 50–60 minutes, until similar to a very thick soup.

4 Stir in the roasted garlic paste, cumin, and ground coriander, then season with salt and pepper to taste. Cook for another 10–15 minutes, uncovered, stirring frequently.

5 Stir in the tomatoes and then adjust the seasoning, adding a little lemon juice to taste if necessary.

6 Finish the spicy garnish. Melt the butter or ghee in a skillet. Add the cumin and mustard seeds and fry until the mustard seeds pop. Stir in the chiles, curry leaves, and the shallot mixture, then immediately swirl the mixture into the cooked dhal. Garnish with cilantro and serve.

NUTRITIONAL NOTES
Per Portion

Energy	340cal
Fat	16.3g
Saturated Fat	7.5g
Carbohydrate	36.3g
Fiber	3.8g

COOK'S TIP

Ghee is a type of clarified butter that has had all the milk solids removed by heating—it was originally made to extend the keeping qualities of butter in India. It is the main cooking fat used in Indian cooking. Because the milk solids have been removed, ghee has a high smoking point and can, therefore, be cooked at higher temperatures than ordinary butter. Look for it in Indian and Asian stores.

Black-eyed Peas and Potato Curry

A nutritious supper dish for a chilly evening.

INGREDIENTS

Serves 4-6

1⅓ cups black-eyed peas soaked
   overnight and drained
¼ teaspoon baking soda
1 teaspoon five-spice powder
¼ teaspoon asafetida
2 onions, finely chopped
1-inch piece fresh ginger root, crushed
few fresh mint leaves
scant 2 cups water
4 tablespoons vegetable oil
½ teaspoon each, turmeric,
   ground cumin, ground
   coriander, and chili powder
4 fresh green chiles, chopped
5 tablespoons tamarind juice
2 potatoes, cubed and boiled
4 cups fresh cilantro, chopped
2 firm tomatoes, chopped
salt, to taste

1 Place the black-eyed peas with the first seven ingredients in a heavy pan. Simmer until the beans are soft. Remove any excess water and reserve.

2 Heat the oil in a skillet. Gently fry the spices, chiles, and tamarind juice, until they are well blended. Pour over the black-eyed peas and mix.

3 Add the potatoes, fresh cilantro, tomatoes, and salt. Mix well, and, if necessary, thin with a little reserved water. Reheat and serve.

NUTRITIONAL NOTES	
Per Portion	
Energy	362cal
Fat	12.4g
Saturated Fat	1.6g
Carbohydrate	49.6g
Fiber	6.6g

Bengal Gram and Bottle Gourd Curry

Tamarind gives this vegetable dish a lemony flavor.

INGREDIENTS

Serves 4-6

⅔ cup Bengal gram (black chickpeas)
4 tablespoons vegetable oil
2 fresh green chiles, chopped
1 onion, chopped
2 garlic cloves, crushed
2-inch piece fresh ginger root, crushed
6–8 curry leaves
1 teaspoon chili powder
1 teaspoon ground turmeric
salt, to taste
1 pound bottle gourd or zucchini,
   peeled, pithed, and sliced
4 tablespoons tamarind juice
2 tomatoes, chopped
chopped fresh cilantro

1 Put the Bengal gram in a pan with scant 2 cups water, and cook the lentils in the water until the grains are tender but not mushy. Put aside without draining away any excess water.

2 Heat the oil and fry the chiles, onion, garlic, and spices. Add the gourd and cook until soft.

3 Add the gram and any water remaining in the pan. Bring to a boil. Stir in the tamarind juice, tomatoes, and fresh cilantro. Simmer gently until the gourd is cooked. Serve hot with a dry meat curry.

NUTRITIONAL NOTES	
Per Portion	
Energy	280cal
Fat	12.2g
Saturated Fat	1.6g
Carbohydrate	31.1g
Fiber	4.2g

Eggplant Curry

A simple and delicious way of cooking eggplant, which retains its full flavor.

INGREDIENTS

Serves 4

2 large eggplants
1½ cups white mushrooms
1 tablespoon oil
½ teaspoon black mustard seeds
1 bunch scallions,
  finely chopped
2 garlic cloves, crushed
1 fresh red chile,
  finely chopped
½ teaspoon chili powder
1 teaspoon ground cumin
1 teaspoon ground coriander
¼ teaspoon ground turmeric
1 teaspoon salt
14-ounce can chopped tomatoes
1 tablespoon chopped fresh cilantro,
  plus a sprig to garnish

1 Preheat the oven to 400°F. Wrap each eggplant in aluminum foil and bake for 1 hour, or until soft. Unwrap and let cool.

2 Cut the mushrooms in half, or in quarters, if large, and set aside.

3 While the eggplants are baking, heat the oil in a heavy pan and fry the mustard seeds for 2 minutes, until they begin to splutter. Add the scallions, mushrooms, garlic, and chile and fry for 5 minutes. Stir in the chili powder, cumin, ground coriander, turmeric, and salt and fry for 3–4 minutes. Add the tomatoes and simmer for 5 minutes.

4 Cut each of the eggplants in half lengthwise and scoop out the soft flesh into a mixing bowl. Mash the flesh roughly with a fork.

5 Add the mashed eggplants and chopped fresh cilantro to the pan. Bring to a boil and simmer for 5 minutes, or until the sauce thickens. Serve immediately, garnished with a fresh cilantro sprig.

NUTRITIONAL NOTES	
Per Portion	
Energy	99cal
Fat	4.60g
Saturated Fat	0.45g
Carbohydrate	10.40g
Fiber	6g

COOK'S TIP

This curry can be served as a vegetarian main course or as an accompaniment to a lamb or chicken dish. If preferred, you can use four large zucchini in place of the eggplants used here.

Mushroom Curry

This is a delicious way of cooking mushrooms. It goes well with meat dishes, but it is also great served on its own.

INGREDIENTS

Serves 4

2 tablespoons oil
½ teaspoon cumin seeds
¼ teaspoon black peppercorns
4 green cardamom pods
¼ teaspoon ground turmeric
1 onion, finely chopped
1 teaspoon ground cumin
1 teaspoon ground coriander
½ teaspoon garam masala
1 fresh green chile,
    finely chopped
2 garlic cloves, crushed
1-inch piece fresh ginger root,
    grated
14-ounce can chopped tomatoes
¼ teaspoon salt
6 cups white mushrooms, halved
chopped fresh cilantro,
    to garnish

NUTRITIONAL NOTES	
Per Portion	
Energy	113cal
Fat	6.90g
Saturated Fat	0.88g
Carbohydrate	8.80g
Fiber	2.50g

___ COOK'S TIP ___

The distinctive flavor of mushrooms goes well with this mixture of spices. If you don't want to use white mushrooms, you can substitute any other mushrooms. Dried mushrooms can be added, if you like. Their intense flavor holds its own against the taste of the curry spices. Soak dried mushrooms before using, and add them to the recipe with the tomatoes.

1 Heat the oil in a large heavy pan and fry the cumin seeds, peppercorns, cardamom pods, and turmeric for 2–3 minutes.

2 Add the onion and fry for about 5 minutes, until golden. Stir in the cumin, ground coriander, and garam masala and fry for another 2 minutes.

3 Add the chile, garlic, and ginger and fry for 2–3 minutes, stirring all the time to prevent the spices from sticking to the pan. Add the tomatoes and salt. Bring to a boil and simmer for 5 minutes.

4 Add the mushrooms. Cover and simmer over a low heat for 10 minutes. Garnish with chopped fresh cilantro before serving.

Corn Cob Curry

Corn cobs are rubbed with lemon juice, salt, and chili powder and then roasted over charcoal in India. In season, the aroma of these treats tempts everyone to buy.

INGREDIENTS

Serves 4-6
4 whole corn cobs,
    fresh or frozen
vegetable oil, for frying
1 large onion, finely chopped
2 garlic cloves, crushed
2-inch piece fresh ginger root,
    crushed
½ teaspoon ground turmeric
½ teaspoon onion seeds
½ teaspoon cumin seeds
½ teaspoon five-spice powder
chili powder, to taste
6–8 curry leaves
½ teaspoon sugar
scant 1 cup plain yogurt

2 Heat the oil in a large skillet and fry the corn pieces until golden brown on all sides. Remove the corn cobs and set aside.

3 Remove any excess oil, leaving about 2 tablespoons in the skillet. Grind the onion, garlic, and ginger to a paste using a mortar and pestle or food processor. Remove and mix in all the spices, curry leaves, and sugar.

4 Reheat the oil gently and fry the onion mixture until all the spices have blended well and the oil separates from the paste.

5 Cool the mixture and gradually fold in the yogurt. Mix well until you have a smooth sauce. Add the corn to the mixture and mix well so all the pieces are evenly covered with the sauce. Gently reheat for about 10 minutes or until the corn is tender. Serve hot.

1 Cut each corn cob in half, using a sharp, heavy knife or cleaver to make clean cuts and limit damage to the kernels.

NUTRITIONAL NOTES	
Per Portion	
Energy	214cal
Fat	15.1g
Saturated Fat	2g
Carbohydrate	15.9g
Fiber	1.5g

Curried Stuffed Peppers

Hot, spicy, and delicious, these bell peppers are often prepared for weddings in Hyderabad.

INGREDIENTS

Serves 4–6

1 tablespoon sesame seeds
1 tablespoon white poppy seeds
1 teaspoon coriander seeds
4 tablespoons dry unsweetened shredded coconut
½ onion, sliced
1-inch piece fresh ginger root, sliced
4 garlic cloves, sliced
handful of fresh cilantro
6 fresh green chiles
4 tablespoons vegetable oil
2 potatoes, boiled and coarsely mashed
salt, to taste
2 each, green, red, and yellow bell peppers
2 tablespoons sesame oil
1 teaspoon cumin seeds
4 tablespoons tamarind juice

1 In a skillet, dry-fry the sesame, poppy, and coriander seeds, then add the coconut and continue to roast until the coconut turns golden brown.

2 Add the onion, ginger, garlic, cilantro, and two of the chiles and roast for another 5 minutes. Let cool, then grind to a paste, using a mortar and pestle or food processor. Put aside.

3 Heat 2 tablespoons of the oil in a skillet and fry the ground paste for 4–5 minutes. Add the potatoes and salt and stir well until the spices have blended evenly into the potatoes.

4 Trim the bottoms of the bell peppers so they stand, then slice off the tops and reserve. Remove the seeds and any white pith. Fill the bell peppers with equal amounts of the potato mixture and replace the tops.

5 Slit the remaining chiles and remove the seeds, if you like. Heat the sesame oil and remaining vegetable oil in a skillet and fry the cumin seeds and the slit green chiles.

6 When the chiles turn white, add the tamarind juice and bring to a boil. Place the peppers over the mixture, cover the skillet, and cook until they are just tender. Serve immediately.

NUTRITIONAL NOTES	
Per Portion	
Energy	390cal
Fat	27.3g
Saturated Fat	10.4g
Carbohydrate	31.1g
Fiber	7.8g

Corn and Pea Curry

Tender corn cooked in a spicy tomato sauce makes a curry full of flavor.

Ingredients

Serves 4

6 frozen corn cobs, thawed
1 tablespoon oil
½ teaspoon cumin seeds
1 onion, finely chopped
2 garlic cloves, crushed
1 fresh green chile,
   finely chopped
1 tablespoon curry paste
1 teaspoon ground coriander
1 teaspoon ground cumin
¼ teaspoon ground turmeric
½ teaspoon salt
½ teaspoon sugar
14-ounce can chopped tomatoes
1 tablespoon tomato paste
⅔ cup water
1 cup frozen peas, thawed
2 tablespoons chopped fresh cilantro
chapatis, to serve (optional)

Nutritional Notes	
Per Portion	
Energy	159cal
Fat	5.20g
Saturated Fat	0.48g
Carbohydrate	23.00g
Fiber	4.60g

2 Bring a large pan of water to a boil and cook the corn cob pieces for 10–12 minutes. Drain well.

3 Heat the oil in a large heavy pan and fry the cumin seeds for 2 minutes, or until they begin to splutter. Add the onion, garlic, and chile and fry for about 5–6 minutes, until the onion is golden.

4 Add the curry paste and fry for 2 minutes. Stir in the remaining spices, salt, and sugar and fry for another 2–3 minutes, adding some water if the mixture is too dry.

5 Add the chopped tomatoes and tomato paste together with the water and simmer for 5 minutes, or until the sauce thickens. Add the peas and cook for another 5 minutes.

6 Stir in the pieces of corn and the fresh cilantro and cook for 6–8 minutes more, until the corn and peas are tender. Serve with chapatis, for mopping up the rich sauce, if desired.

Variation
If you don't like peas, you can replace them with the same quantity of thawed frozen fava beans.

1 Using a sharp knife, cut each piece of corn in half crosswise to make 12 equal pieces in total.

Zucchini Curry

Thickly sliced zucchini are combined with authentic Indian spices for a tasty vegetable curry.

INGREDIENTS

Serves 4

1½ pounds zucchini
2 tablespoons oil
½ teaspoon cumin seeds
½ teaspoon mustard seeds
1 onion, thinly sliced
2 garlic cloves, crushed
¼ teaspoon ground turmeric
¼ teaspoon chili powder
1 teaspoon ground coriander
1 teaspoon ground cumin
½ teaspoon salt
1 tablespoon tomato paste
14-ounce can chopped tomatoes
⅔ cup water
1 tablespoon chopped fresh
    cilantro
1 teaspoon garam masala

1 Trim the ends from the zucchini and then cut them evenly into ½-inch thick slices.

COOK'S TIP

You can use medium zucchini or the slightly larger ones for this dish; the very large ones have less flavor. Whichever size you choose, look out for smooth, shiny zucchini without blemishes.

2 Heat the oil in a large heavy pan and fry the cumin and the mustard seeds for 2 minutes, until they begin to splutter.

3 Add the onion and garlic and fry for about 5–6 minutes.

4 Add the turmeric, chili powder, ground coriander, cumin, and salt and fry for 2–3 minutes.

5 Add the sliced zucchini all at once, and cook for 5 minutes, stirring so they do not burn.

6 Mix together the tomato paste and chopped tomatoes and add to the pan with the water. Cover and simmer for 10 minutes, until the sauce thickens.

7 Stir in the fresh cilantro and garam masala, then cook for 5 minutes, or until the zucchini are tender.

NUTRITIONAL NOTES	
Per Portion	
Energy	133cal
Fat	7.20g
Saturated Fat	0.91g
Carbohydrate	11.60g
Fiber	2.80g

Mixed Vegetable Curry

This is a good all-around vegetable curry that goes well with most Indian meat dishes. You can use any combination of vegetables that are in season for this basic recipe.

Ingredients

Serves 4

1 tablespoon oil
½ teaspoon black mustard seeds
½ teaspoon cumin seeds
1 onion, thinly sliced
2 curry leaves
1 fresh green chile, finely chopped
1-inch piece fresh ginger root, finely chopped
2 tablespoons curry paste
1 small cauliflower, broken into florets
1 large carrot, thickly sliced
4 ounces green beans, cut into 1-inch lengths
¼ teaspoon ground turmeric
¼ teaspoon chili powder
½ teaspoon salt
2 tomatoes, finely chopped
½ cup frozen peas, thawed
⅔ cup vegetable stock
fresh curry leaves, to garnish

Nutritional Notes	
Per Portion	
Energy	130cal
Fat	6.20g
Saturated Fat	0.61g
Carbohydrate	12.30g
Fiber	6.20g

Variation

To turn this dish into a nonvegetarian main course, add some shrimp or cubes of cooked chicken with the stock.

1 Heat the oil in a large heavy pan and fry the mustard seeds and cumin seeds for 2 minutes, until they begin to splutter. If they are very lively, put a lid on the pan.

2 Add the onion and the curry leaves and fry for 5 minutes.

3 Add the chopped chile and fresh ginger and fry for 2 minutes. Stir in the curry paste, mix well, and fry for 3–4 minutes.

4 Add the cauliflower florets, sliced carrot, and beans and cook for 4–5 minutes. Add the turmeric, chili powder, salt, and tomatoes and cook for 2–3 minutes.

5 Put in the thawed peas and cook for another 2–3 minutes.

6 Add the stock. Cover and simmer over a low heat for 10–15 minutes, until all the vegetables are tender. Serve garnished with curry leaves.

Vegetable Korma

Careful blending of spices is an ancient art in India. Here the aim is to produce a subtle, aromatic curry instead of an assault on the senses.

INGREDIENTS

Serves 4

4 tablespoons butter
2 onions, sliced
2 garlic cloves, crushed
1-inch piece fresh ginger root, grated
1 teaspoon ground cumin
1 tablespoon ground coriander
6 cardamom pods
2-inch piece of cinnamon stick
1 teaspoon ground turmeric
1 fresh red chile, seeded and
    finely chopped
1 potato, peeled and cut into
    1-inch cubes
1 small eggplant, chopped
1½ cups mushrooms,
    thickly sliced
¾ cup water
1 cup green beans, cut into
    1-inch lengths
4 tablespoons plain yogurt
⅔ cup heavy cream
1 teaspoon garam masala
salt and black pepper
fresh cilantro sprigs,
    to garnish
boiled rice and poppadums,
    to serve

--- COOK'S TIP ---

Try using canned chickpeas or lima beans to really bulk out this curry.

NUTRITIONAL NOTES
Per Portion

Energy	361cal
Fat	31.3g
Saturated Fat	19.3g
Carbohydrate	16.7g
Fiber	3.2g

1 Melt the butter in a heavy pan. Add the onions and cook for 5 minutes, until soft. Add the garlic and ginger and cook for 2 minutes, then stir in the cumin, coriander, cardamom pods, cinnamon stick, turmeric, and finely chopped chile. Cook, stirring constantly, for 30 seconds.

2 Add the potato cubes, eggplant, and mushrooms and the water. Cover the pan, bring to a boil, then lower the heat and simmer for 15 minutes.

3 Add the beans and cook, uncovered, for 5 minutes. With a slotted spoon, remove the vegetables to a warmed serving dish and keep hot.

4 Let the cooking liquid bubble until it has reduced a little. Season with salt and pepper, then stir in the yogurt, cream, and garam masala. Pour the sauce over the vegetables and garnish with fresh cilantro. Serve with boiled rice and poppadums.

Sweet and Sour Vegetables with Paneer

The cheese used in this recipe is Indian paneer, which can be bought at some Asian stores; tofu can be used in its place.

INGREDIENTS

Serves 4

1 green bell pepper, seeded
   and cut into squares
1 yellow bell pepper, seeded
   and cut into squares
8 cherry tomatoes
8 cauliflower florets
8 pineapple chunks
8 cubes paneer
plain, boiled rice, to serve

For the seasoned oil

1 tablespoon oil
2 tablespoons lemon juice
1 teaspoon salt
1 teaspoon crushed black peppercorns
1 tablespoon honey
2 tablespoons chili sauce

NUTRITIONAL NOTES	
Per Portion	
Energy	75cal
Fat	3.30g
Saturated Fat	0.38g
Carbohydrate	9.90g
Fiber	2.10g

1 Preheat the broiler to hot. Thread the bell pepper squares, cherry tomatoes, cauliflower florets, pineapple chunks, and paneer cubes onto four skewers, alternating the ingredients. Place the skewers on a flameproof dish or in a broiler pan.

2 In a small bowl, combine all the ingredients for the seasoned oil. If too thick, add 1 tablespoon water.

--- COOK'S TIP ---

Metal skewers are ideal for this recipe. Some of the traditional Indian ones are very pretty and will enhance the color of the dish. Wooden or bamboo skewers can be used instead, but remember to soak them in water for at least 30 minutes before threading them with the vegetables and paneer, or the exposed tips may burn under the heat.

3 Brush the vegetables with the seasoned oil. Broil for about 10 minutes, until the vegetables begin to darken slightly, turning the skewers regularly to cook evenly. Serve on a bed of plain boiled rice.

Spiced Vegetable Curry with Yogurt

This is a delicately spiced vegetable dish that makes an appetizing snack when served with plain yogurt. It is also a good accompaniment to a main meal of heavily spiced curries.

INGREDIENTS

Serves 4–6

12 ounces mixed vegetables, such as beans, peas, potatoes, cauliflower, carrots, cabbage, baby eggplants, snow peas, and mushrooms
2 tablespoons vegetable oil
1 teaspoon cumin seeds, freshly roasted
½ teaspoon mustard seeds
½ teaspoon onion seeds
1 teaspoon ground turmeric
2 garlic cloves, crushed
6–8 curry leaves
1 dried red chile
salt, to taste
1 teaspoon sugar
⅔ cup plain yogurt mixed with 1 teaspoon cornstarch

1 Prepare all the vegetables you have chosen: string the beans; thaw the peas, if frozen; cube the potatoes; cut the cauliflower into florets; dice the carrots; shred the cabbage; trim the snow peas; and wash the mushrooms and eggplants and leave whole.

NUTRITIONAL NOTES	
Per Portion	
Energy	99cal
Fat	6.1g
Saturated Fat	0.9g
Carbohydrate	6.5g
Fiber	2g

2 Heat a large pan with enough water to cook all the vegetables and bring to a boil. First add the potatoes and carrots and cook until nearly tender, then add all the other vegetables and cook until crisp-tender. All the vegetables should be crunchy except the potatoes. Drain.

3 Heat the oil in a frying pan and fry the cumin, mustard, and onion seeds, the turmeric, garlic, curry leaves, and dried chile gently until the garlic is golden brown and the chile nearly burnt. Reduce the heat.

4 Fold in the drained vegetables, add the sugar and salt, and gradually add the yogurt and cornstarch mixture. When hot, serve immediately.

Spicy Omelet

Another popular contribution by the Parsis, this irresistible omelet is known to them as poro. Parsi cuisine offers some unique flavors, which appeal to both Eastern and Western palates.

INGREDIENTS

Serves 4–6
2 tablespoons vegetable oil
1 onion, finely chopped
½ teaspoon ground cumin
1 garlic clove, crushed
1 or 2 fresh green chiles, finely chopped
a few cilantro sprigs, chopped,
    plus extra, to garnish
1 firm tomato, chopped
1 small potato, cubed and boiled
¼ cup cooked peas
¼ cup cooked corn,
    or drained canned corn
2 eggs, beaten
¼ cup grated cheddar cheese or
    Monterey Jack
salt and black pepper

1 Heat the oil in a karahi, wok, or omelet pan, and add the onion, cumin, garlic, chiles, cilantro, tomato, potato, peas, and corn. Mix well.

NUTRITIONAL NOTES	
Per Portion	
Energy	167cal
Fat	11.3g
Saturated Fat	3g
Carbohydrate	9.7g
Fiber	1.5g

2 Cook over a medium heat, stirring, for 5 minutes, until the potato and tomato are almost tender. Season well.

3 Preheat the broiler to high. Increase the heat under the pan and pour in the beaten eggs. Reduce the heat, cover, and cook until the bottom layer is brown. Turn the omelet over and sprinkle with the grated cheese. Place under the hot broiler and cook until the egg sets and the cheese has melted.

4 Garnish the omelet with sprigs of cilantro and serve with salad for a light lunch. If desired, serve it for breakfast, in the typical Parsi style.

_____ VARIATION _____

You can use any vegetable with the potatoes. Try thickly sliced white mushrooms, which can be added in step 1.

Eggs on Potato Sticks

This is an unusual and delicious way of combining eggs with potato sticks, and is known as sali pur eeda in the Parsi language. The potato sticks are cooked with chiles and spices. Eggs are then placed on top of the potato mixture and gently cooked.

INGREDIENTS

Serves 4–6

8 ounces salted potato sticks
2 fresh green chiles,
   finely chopped
a few cilantro sprigs, chopped
¼ teaspoon ground turmeric
4 tablespoons vegetable oil
5 tablespoons water
6 eggs
3 scallions, finely chopped
salt and black pepper

1 In a large bowl, mix the salted potato sticks with the chopped chiles, cilantro, and turmeric. Heat 2 tablespoons of the oil in a heavy skillet. Add the potato-stick mixture and water. Cook until the potato sticks turn soft, and then crisp.

2 Place a dinner plate over the skillet, and hold in place as you turn the pan over and carefully transfer the potato-stick "pancake" onto the plate. Heat the remaining oil in the skillet and slide the "pancake" back into it to brown the other side. Do this very gently, so no potato sticks break off.

3 Gently break the eggs over the top, cover the skillet, and let the eggs set over a low heat. Season well and sprinkle with scallions. Cook until the bottom is crisp. Serve hot for breakfast in the Parsi style, or with chapatis and a salad for lunch or supper.

_____ COOK'S TIP _____

As the potato sticks cook, the starch they contain will cause them to stick together. To encourage this, use a spoon to press them down.

NUTRITIONAL NOTES	
Per Portion	
Energy	482cal
Fat	33.3g
Saturated Fat	6.8g
Carbohydrate	36.6g
Fiber	1.6g

Cauliflower and Coconut Milk Curry

Here is a delicious vegetable stew that combines coconut milk with spices and is perfect as a vegetarian main course or as part of a buffet.

INGREDIENTS

Serves 4
1 cauliflower
2 medium tomatoes
1 onion, chopped
2 garlic cloves, crushed
1 fresh green chile, seeded
½ teaspoon ground turmeric
2 tablespoons sunflower oil
1¾ cups coconut milk
1 cup water
1 teaspoon sugar
1 teaspoon tamarind pulp, soaked in
   3 tablespoons warm water
salt

1 Trim the stalk from the cauliflower and divide into tiny florets. Peel the tomatoes if you like, then chop them into ½–1-inch pieces.

2 Grind the chopped onion, garlic, green chile, and ground turmeric to a paste in a food processor.

3 Heat the oil in a karahi, wok, or large skillet and fry the spice paste to bring out the aromatic flavors, without letting it brown.

4 Add the cauliflower florets and toss well to coat in the spices. Stir in the coconut milk, water, sugar, and salt to taste. Simmer for 5 minutes. Strain the tamarind and reserve the juice.

5 Add the tamarind juice and chopped tomatoes to the pan, then cook for only 2–3 minutes. Taste and check the seasoning and serve.

NUTRITIONAL NOTES	
Per Portion	
Energy	119cal
Fat	6.7g
Saturated Fat	1.1g
Carbohydrate	11.5g
Fiber	2.3g

Scrambled Eggs with Chile

This is a lovely way to liven up scrambled eggs. Prepare all the ingredients ahead so that the vegetables can be cooked quickly and retain crunch and color.

INGREDIENTS

Serves 4
2 tablespoons sunflower oil
1 onion, finely sliced
8 ounces Chinese cabbage,
   finely sliced or cut in diamonds
7-ounce can corn kernels
1 small fresh red chile, seeded and
   finely sliced
2 tablespoons water
2 eggs, beaten
salt and black pepper
deep-fried onions, to garnish

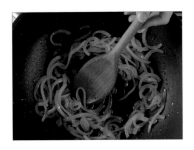

1 Heat a karahi, wok, or deep pan. Add the oil and, when it is hot, fry the onion, until soft but not browned.

2 Add the Chinese cabbage and toss over the heat until well mixed.

3 Add the corn, chile, and water. Cover with a lid and cook for 2 minutes.

4 Remove the lid and stir in the beaten eggs and seasoning. Stir constantly until the eggs are creamy and just set. Serve on warmed plates, sprinkled with crisp deep-fried onions.

NUTRITIONAL NOTES	
Per Portion	
Energy	171cal
Fat	10.3g
Saturated Fat	1.8g
Carbohydrate	13.7g
Fiber	2.1g

Masala Chana

Chickpeas are used and cooked in a variety of ways all over the Indian subcontinent. Tamarind adds a sharp, tangy flavor.

INGREDIENTS

Serves 4

1¼ cups dried chickpeas
2 ounces tamarind stick
½ cup boiling water
2 tablespoons oil
½ teaspoon cumin seeds
1 onion, finely chopped
1-inch piece fresh ginger root, grated
1 fresh green chile,
    finely chopped
1 teaspoon ground cumin
1 teaspoon ground coriander
¼ teaspoon ground turmeric
½ teaspoon salt
8 ounces tomatoes, peeled and
    finely chopped
½ teaspoon garam masala
chopped fresh chiles and chopped
    onion, to garnish

1 Put the chickpeas in a large bowl and cover with plenty of cold water. Let soak overnight.

2 Drain the chickpeas and place in a large pan with double the volume of cold water. Bring to a boil and boil vigorously for 10 minutes.

3 Skim off any scum that has risen to the surface of the liquid, using a slotted spoon. Lower the heat, cover the pan, and simmer for 1½–2 hours, or until the chickpeas are soft.

4 Meanwhile, break up the tamarind and soak in the boiling water for about 15 minutes. Rub the tamarind through a strainer into a bowl, discarding any pits and fiber left behind in the strainer.

5 Heat the oil in a large heavy pan and fry the cumin seeds for 2 minutes, until they splutter. Add the onion, garlic, ginger, and chile and fry for 5 minutes.

6 Stir in the cumin and coriander, with the turmeric and salt, and fry for 3–4 minutes. Add the chopped tomatoes. Bring to a boil and simmer for 5 minutes.

7 Drain the chickpeas and add to the tomato mixture together with the garam masala and tamarind pulp. Cover and simmer gently for about 15 minutes. Garnish with the chopped chiles and onion before serving.

COOK'S TIP

Tamarind is usually sold as compressed blocks of pulp and seeds. To use, break off a small piece and soak it in a few spoonfuls of hot water for 15 minutes. Strain off the water, pressing some of the pulp through the strainer. Discard the rest of the pulp.

NUTRITIONAL NOTES
Per Portion

Energy	313cal
Fat	9.40g
Saturated Fat	0.77g
Carbohydrate	44.60g
Fiber	1.50g

Vegetable Kashmiri

This is a wonderful vegetable curry, in which fresh mixed vegetables are cooked in a spicy aromatic yogurt sauce. The spicing is gentle, so it will appeal to most palates.

INGREDIENTS

Serves 4

2 teaspoons cumin seeds
8 black peppercorns
seeds from 2 green cardamom pods
2-inch piece of cinnamon stick
½ teaspoon grated nutmeg
2 tablespoons oil
1 fresh green chile, chopped
1-inch piece fresh ginger root,
    grated
1 teaspoon chili powder
½ teaspoon salt
2 large potatoes, cut into
    1-inch chunks
8 ounces cauliflower,
    broken into florets
8 ounces okra, trimmed
    and thickly sliced
⅔ cup plain low-fat yogurt
⅔ cup vegetable stock
toasted sliced almonds
    and fresh cilantro sprigs,
    to garnish

1 Grind the cumin seeds and peppercorns, cardamom seeds, cinnamon stick, and nutmeg to a fine powder, using a spice blender or a mortar and pestle.

2 Heat the oil in a large heavy pan and fry the chile and ginger for 2 minutes, stirring all the time.

3 Add the chili powder, salt, and ground spice mixture and fry for about 2–3 minutes, stirring all the time to prevent the spices from sticking to the bottom of the pan.

NUTRITIONAL NOTES	
Per Portion	
Energy	220cal
Fat	8.20g
Saturated Fat	1.02g
Carbohydrate	29.10g
Fiber	4.70g

—————— COOK'S TIP ——————

Instead of the vegetable mixture used here, try cooking other ones of your choice in this lovely yogurt sauce.

4 Stir in the potatoes, cover, and cook for 10 minutes over a low heat, stirring from time to time.

5 Add the cauliflower and okra and cook for 5 minutes.

6 Add the yogurt and stock. Bring to a boil, then reduce the heat. Cover and simmer for 20 minutes, or until all the vegetables are tender. Garnish with the toasted almonds and the cilantro sprigs.

Basmati Rice and Peas with Curry Leaves

This is a very simple rice dish, but it is full of flavor.

INGREDIENTS

Serves 4

1½ cups basmati rice
1 tablespoon oil
6–8 curry leaves
¼ teaspoon mustard seeds
¼ teaspoon onion seeds
2 tablespoons fresh fenugreek leaves
1 teaspoon crushed garlic
1 teaspoon grated fresh ginger root
1 teaspoon salt
1 cup frozen peas
2 cups water

_____ COOK'S TIP _____

Curry leaves freeze very well, so it is worth keeping a stock in the freezer.

1 Wash the rice well and let it soak in water for 30 minutes.

NUTRITIONAL NOTES	
Per Portion	
Energy	336cal
Fat	5.96g
Saturated Fat	1.09g
Carbohydrate	67.67g
Fiber	1.83g

2 Heat the oil in a heavy pan and add the curry leaves, mustard seeds, onion seeds, fenugreek leaves, garlic, ginger, and salt and stir-fry for 2–3 minutes.

3 Drain the rice, add it to the pan, and stir gently.

4 Add the frozen peas and water and bring to a boil. Lower the heat, cover with a lid, and cook for 15–20 minutes. Remove from the heat and let stand, still covered, for 10 minutes.

5 When ready to serve, fluff up the rice with a fork. Spoon the mixture onto serving plates.

Tomato Biryani

Although generally served as an accompaniment to meat, poultry, or fish dishes, this tasty rice dish can also be eaten as a complete meal on its own.

INGREDIENTS

Serves 4

2 cups basmati rice
1 tablespoon oil
½ teaspoon onion seeds
1 medium onion, sliced
2 medium tomatoes, sliced
1 orange or yellow bell pepper, seeded and sliced
1 teaspoon grated fresh ginger root
1 teaspoon crushed garlic
1 teaspoon chili powder
2 tablespoons chopped fresh cilantro
1 medium potato, diced
1½ teaspoon salt
½ cup frozen peas
3 cups water

1 Wash the rice well and let it soak in water for 30 minutes. Heat the oil in a heavy pan and fry the onion seeds for about 30 seconds. Add the sliced onion and fry for 5 minutes, stirring occasionally to prevent the slices from sticking to the pan.

_____ COOK'S TIP _____

Plain rice can look dull, but you can enhance it by adding colorful ingredients, such as tomatoes, bell peppers, and peas.

2 Add the sliced tomatoes and peppers, ginger, garlic, and chili powder. Stir-fry for 2 minutes.

3 Add the fresh cilantro, potato, salt, and peas and stir-fry over a medium heat for another 5 minutes.

4 Put the rice into a colander and drain it thoroughly. Add it to the spiced tomato and potato mixture and stir-fry for 1–2 minutes.

5 Pour in the water and bring to a boil, then lower the heat to medium. Cover and cook the rice for 12–15 minutes. Let stand for 5 minutes and then serve.

NUTRITIONAL NOTES	
Per Portion	
Energy	409cal
Fat	3.70g
Saturated Fat	0.44g
Carbohydrate	89.70g
Fiber	2.40g

Vegetable Biryani

This is a good-tempered dish made from everyday ingredients, and, thus, indispensable for the cook catering for an unexpected vegetarian guest. It is extremely low in fat, but packed full of exciting flavors.

Ingredients

Serves 4–6

scant 1 cup long-grain rice
2 whole cloves
seeds from 2 cardamom pods
scant 2 cups vegetable stock
2 garlic cloves
1 small onion, roughly chopped
1 teaspoon cumin seeds
1 teaspoon ground coriander
½ teaspoon ground turmeric
½ teaspoon chili powder
salt and black pepper
1 large potato, cut into
    1-inch cubes
2 carrots, sliced
½ cauliflower, broken
    into florets
2 ounces green beans,
    cut into 1-inch lengths
2 tablespoons chopped fresh cilantro,
    plus extra to garnish
2 tablespoons lime juice

Nutritional Notes	
Per Portion (6)	
Energy	260cal
Fat	1.90g
Saturated Fat	0.07g
Carbohydrate	55.80g
Fiber	3.20g

Variations

Substitute other vegetables for the ones chosen here, if you like. Zucchini, broccoli, parsnip, and sweet potatoes would all be excellent choices. Or add some toasted almond slices.

1 Wash the rice and put it with the cloves and cardamom seeds into a large heavy pan. Pour over the stock and bring to a boil.

2 Reduce the heat, cover the pan, and simmer for 20 minutes, or until all the stock has been absorbed.

3 Meanwhile, put the garlic cloves, onion, cumin seeds, ground coriander, turmeric, chili powder, and seasoning into a blender or food processor together with 2 tablespoons water. Blend to a smooth paste. Scrape the paste into a flameproof casserole that is large enough to hold all the vegetables.

4 Preheat the oven to 350°F. Cook the spicy paste in the casserole over a low heat for 2 minutes, stirring occasionally.

5 Add the potato, carrots, cauliflower, beans, and 6 tablespoons water. Cover and cook over a low heat for 12 minutes, stirring occasionally. Add the chopped fresh cilantro.

6 Remove the cloves from the rice. Spoon the rice over the vegetables. Sprinkle with the lime juice. Cover and cook in the oven for 25 minutes, or until the vegetables are tender. Fluff up the rice with a fork before serving and garnish with more cilantro.

Pea and Mushroom Pilau

Tiny white mushrooms and baby peas look great in this delectable rice dish.

INGREDIENTS

Serves 6

2¼ cups basmati rice
1 tablespoon oil
½ teaspoon cumin seeds
2 black cardamom pods
2 cinnamon sticks
3 garlic cloves, sliced
1 teaspoon salt
1 medium tomato, sliced
⅔ cup white mushrooms
¾ cup baby peas
3 cups water

1 Wash the rice well and let it soak in water for 30 minutes.

2 In a medium heavy pan, heat the oil and add the spices, garlic, and salt.

3 Add the tomato and mushrooms and stir-fry for 2–3 minutes.

4 Put the rice into a colander and drain it thoroughly. Add it to the pan with the peas. Stir gently, making sure that you do not break up the grains of rice.

5 Add the water and bring to a boil. Lower the heat, cover, and continue to cook for 15–20 minutes. Just before serving, remove the lid from the pan and fluff up the rice with a fork. Spoon into a dish and serve immediately.

NUTRITIONAL NOTES	
Per Portion	
Energy	423cal
Fat	3.80g
Saturated Fat	0.39g
Carbohydrate	92.90g
Fiber	1.30g

_____ COOK'S TIP _____

Baby peas, sometimes called petits pois, are small green peas, picked when very young. The tender, sweet peas inside the immature pods are ideal for this delicately flavored rice dish. However, if you can't find baby peas, regular peas can be used instead.

Nut Pilau

Versions of this rice dish are cooked throughout Asia, always with the best-quality long grain rice. In India, basmati rice is the natural choice. In this particular interpretation of the recipe, walnuts and cashews are added. Serve the pilau with a raita or a bowl of yogurt.

INGREDIENTS

Serves 4

1–2 tablespoons vegetable oil
1 onion, chopped
1 garlic clove, crushed
1 large carrot,
    coarsely grated
generous 1 cup basmati rice,
    soaked for 20–30 minutes
1 teaspoon cumin seeds
2 teaspoons ground coriander
2 teaspoons black mustard seeds
4 green cardamom pods
scant 2 cups vegetable stock
1 bay leaf
¾ cup unsalted walnuts
    and cashew nuts
salt and black pepper
fresh cilantro sprigs,
    to garnish

1 Heat the oil in a karahi, wok, or large pan. Fry the onion, garlic and carrot for 3–4 minutes. Drain the rice and add with the spices. Cook for 2 minutes, stirring to coat the grains in oil.

2 Pour in the vegetable stock, stirring. Add the bay leaf and season well.

3 Bring to a boil, lower the heat, cover, and simmer very gently for 10–12 minutes, without stirring.

4 Remove the pan from the heat without lifting the lid. Let stand for 5 minutes, then check the rice. If it is cooked, there will be small steam holes on the surface of the rice. Discard the bay leaf and the cardamom pods.

5 Stir in the walnuts and cashew nuts and check the seasoning. Spoon on to a warmed platter, garnish with the fresh cilantro, and serve.

NUTRITIONAL NOTES	
Per Portion	
Energy	376cal
Fat	16g
Saturated Fat	1.4g
Carbohydrate	50g
Fiber	1.6g

Lentils and Rice

Lentils are cooked with whole and ground spices, potato, rice, and onion to produce a tasty and nutritious meal.

INGREDIENTS

Serves 4

¾ cup tuvar dhal
   or red split lentils
½ cup basmati rice
1 large potato
1 large onion
2 tablespoons oil
4 whole cloves
¼ teaspoon cumin seeds
¼ teaspoon ground turmeric
2 teaspoons salt
1¼ cups water

1 Wash the tuvar dhal or red split lentils and rice in several changes of cold water. Put in a bowl and cover with water. Let soak for 15 minutes, then put in a strainer and drain well.

NUTRITIONAL NOTES
Per Portion

Energy	332cal
Fat	6.70g
Saturated Fat	0.76g
Carbohydrate	58.60g
Fiber	3.40g

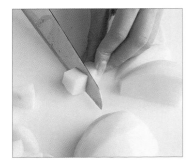

2 Peel the potato, then cut it into 1-inch chunks.

3 Using a sharp knife, thinly slice the onion and set aside for later.

4 Heat the oil in a large heavy pan and fry the cloves and cumin seeds for 2 minutes, until the seeds are beginning to splutter.

5 Add the onion and potato chunks and fry for 5 minutes. Add the lentils, rice, turmeric, and salt and fry for another 3 minutes.

6 Add the water. Bring to a boil, cover, and simmer gently for 15–20 minutes, until all the water has been absorbed and the potato chunks are tender. Let stand, covered, for about 10 minutes before serving.

COOK'S TIP

Red split lentils are widely available in most supermarkets. Before cooking they are salmon-colored, and they turn a pale, dull yellow during cooking. They have a mild, pleasant, nutty flavor. Soaking them in water speeds up the cooking process but isn't strictly necessary.

Rice Layered with Bengal Gram

Bhori Muslims in India have their own special style of cooking and have adapted many of the traditional dishes from other Indian communities. This rice and lentil dish is served with a gourd curry, or palida, which is prominently flavored with fenugreek and soured with dried mangosteen (kokum). Lemon juice will provide the same effect.

INGREDIENTS

Serves 4–6
²⁄₃ cup Bengal gram (black chickpeas) or lentils of own choice
2¹⁄₂ cups water
¹⁄₂ teaspoon ground turmeric
2 ounces deep-fried onions, crushed
3 tablespoons green masala paste
few fresh mint and cilantro leaves, chopped
salt, to taste
1³⁄₄ cups basmati rice, cooked
2 tablespoons ghee

For the curry
4 tablespoons vegetable oil
¹⁄₄ teaspoon fenugreek seeds
¹⁄₂ ounce dried fenugreek leaves
2 garlic cloves, crushed
1 teaspoon ground coriander
1 teaspoon cumin seeds
1 teaspoon chili powder
4 tablespoons besan flour mixed with 4 tablespoons water
1 pound bottle gourd, peeled, pith and seeds removed, and cut into bitesize pieces, or firm zucchini prepared in the same way
³⁄₄ cup tomato juice
6 dried mangosteen (kokum), or juice of 3 lemons
salt, to taste

1 For the rice, boil the Bengal gram in the water with the turmeric until the grains are soft but not mushy. Drain and reserve the water for the curry.

2 Toss the Bengal gram gently with the deep-fried onions, green masala paste, chopped mint, and cilantro. Stir in salt to taste.

3 Grease a heavy pan and place a layer of rice in the bottom. Add the Bengal gram mixture and another layer of the remaining rice. Place small pats of ghee on top, sprinkle with a little water, and heat gently until steam rises from the mixture.

4 To make the curry, heat the oil in a pan and fry the fenugreek seeds and leaves and garlic until the garlic turns golden brown.

5 Mix the ground coriander, cumin, and chili powder to a paste with a little water. Add to the pan and simmer until all the water has evaporated.

6 Add the besan flour paste, with the gourd or alternative vegetable. Pour in the tomato juice and add the mangosteen and salt. Cook until the gourd is soft and transparent. Serve hot with the rice.

NUTRITIONAL NOTES	
Per Portion	
Energy	536cal
Fat	14g
Saturated Fat	1.8g
Carbohydrate	82.3g
Fiber	4.9g

Root Vegetable Gratin with Indian Spices

Subtly spiced with curry powder, turmeric, coriander, and mild chili powder, this rich gratin is substantial enough to serve on its own for lunch or supper. It also makes a good accompaniment to a vegetable or bean curry.

INGREDIENTS

Serves 4

2 large potatoes, total weight about 1 pound
2 sweet potatoes, total weight about 10 ounces
6 ounces celeriac
1 tablespoon unsalted butter
1 teaspoon curry powder
1 teaspoon ground turmeric
½ teaspoon ground coriander
1 teaspoon mild chili powder
3 shallots, chopped
⅔ cup light cream
⅔ cup milk
salt and black pepper
chopped fresh flat-leaf parsley, to garnish

1 Peel the potatoes, sweet potatoes, and celeriac and cut into thin, even slices, using a sharp knife or the slicing attachment on a food processor. Immediately place the vegetables in a bowl of cold water to prevent them from discoloring.

2 Preheat the oven to 350°F. Heat half the butter in a heavy pan, add the curry powder, ground turmeric and coriander, and half the chili powder. Cook for 2 minutes, then let cool slightly. Drain the vegetables, then pat them dry with paper towels. Place in a bowl, add the spice mixture and the shallots, and mix well.

3 Arrange the vegetables in a shallow baking dish, seasoning well with salt and pepper between the layers. Mix together the cream and milk, pour the mixture over the vegetables, then sprinkle the remaining chili powder on top.

4 Cover the dish with parchment paper and bake for 45 minutes. Remove the parchment paper, dot the vegetables with the remaining butter, and bake for another 50 minutes, or until the top is golden brown. Serve the gratin garnished with chopped parsley.

NUTRITIONAL NOTES	
Per Portion	
Energy	205cal
Fat	5.1g
Saturated Fat	2.9g
Carbohydrate	36.9g
Fiber	4.7g

Rice and Vegetable
Side Dishes
and Light Salads

ALTHOUGH DEFINED as side dishes, the recipes in this chapter play an important role in Indian cuisine, and their size makes them especially versatile. They can be served alongside curries, as simple snacks, or enjoyed as main courses. Tomato and Spinach Pilau, for instance, makes a satisfying supper, whether served solo or in the company of another curry, such as Masala Okra or Bombay Potatoes.

Some dishes simply refuse to be sidelined. Stuffed Bananas, for instance, is a real showstopper. A popular Indian treat, they taste as intriguing as they look, and will make an excellent centerpiece for a special occasion meal.

Also included in this chapter are several light and tasty salads. While not all are authentically Indian, they have been selected for their cooling qualities, and are the perfect partners for spicy dishes. Vegetables, fruits, and nuts all feature, and there's even a recipe for Coronation Chicken.

Saffron Rice

The saffron crocus is a perennial bulb that only flowers for two weeks of the year, and each stigma has to be removed by hand and dried with care. Consequently, saffron is said to be worth its weight in gold. Kashmir, in the northern region of India, is a major producer, so it isn't surprising that the subcontinent has some wonderful recipes for the spice.

INGREDIENTS

Serves 6
2⅓ cups basmati rice
3 cups water
3 green cardamom pods
2 cloves
1 teaspoon salt
3 tablespoons low-fat milk
½ teaspoon saffron threads, crushed

NUTRITIONAL NOTES	
Per Portion	
Energy	273cal
Fat	0.5g
Saturated Fat	0.1g
Carbohydrate	60.2g
Fiber	0g

1 Wash the rice, put it in a bowl, and pour over water to cover. Let soak for 20 minutes.

2 Drain the basmati rice and put it in a large pan with the measured water. Add the cardamoms, cloves, and salt. Stir, then bring to a boil. Lower the heat and cover tightly, and simmer for 5 minutes.

3 Meanwhile, place the milk in a small pan. Add the saffron threads and heat through gently.

4 Pour the saffron milk over the rice and stir. Cover again and continue cooking over a low heat for 5–6 minutes.

5 Remove the pan from the heat without lifting the lid. Let the rice stand for about 5 minutes, then fork through just before serving.

_____ COOK'S TIP _____

Washing and soaking the rice before cooking makes it fluffier.

Caramelized Basmati Rice

This dish is the traditional accompaniment to a dhansak curry. Sugar is caramelized in hot oil before the rice is added, along with a few whole spices.

INGREDIENTS

Serves 4

generous 1 cup basmati rice
3 tablespoons vegetable oil
4 teaspoons sugar
4–5 green cardamom pods, bruised
1-inch piece cinnamon stick
4 cloves
1 bay leaf, crumpled
½ teaspoon salt
2 cups hot water

1 Wash the rice, put it in a bowl, and pour over water to cover. Let soak for 20 minutes.

2 Drain the rice in a colander, shaking it a little as you do so. Run the washed grains through your fingers to check that there is no excess water trapped between them. Set aside.

3 In a large pan, heat the vegetable oil over a medium heat. When the oil is hot, sprinkle the sugar over the surface and wait until it has caramelized. Do not stir.

4 Reduce the heat to low and add the spices and bay leaf. Let sizzle for about 15–20 seconds, then add the rice and salt. Fry gently, stirring, for 2–3 minutes.

5 Pour in the water and bring to a boil. Let it boil steadily for 2 minutes, then reduce the heat to very low. Cover the pan and cook for 8 minutes.

6 Remove the rice from the heat and let it stand for 6–8 minutes. Gently fluff up the rice with a fork and transfer to a warmed dish to serve.

NUTRITIONAL NOTES	
Per Portion	
Energy	276cal
Fat	8.5g
Saturated Fat	1g
Carbohydrate	44.9g
Fiber	0g

Golden Raisin and Cashew Pilau

The secret of a perfect pilau is to wash the rice thoroughly, then soak it briefly. This softens and moistens the grains, enabling the rice to absorb moisture during cooking, which results in fluffier rice.

INGREDIENTS

Serves 4

2½ cups hot chicken or
   vegetable stock
generous pinch of saffron threads
4 tablespoons butter
1 onion, chopped
1 garlic clove, crushed
1-inch piece cinnamon stick
6 green cardamom pods
1 bay leaf
1⅓ cups basmati rice, soaked in
   water for 20–30 minutes
⅓ cup golden raisins
1 tablespoon vegetable oil
½ cup cashew nuts
nan bread and tomato and
   onion salad, to serve

1 Pour the hot chicken stock into a pitcher. Stir in the saffron threads and set aside.

2 Heat the butter in a pan and fry the onion and garlic for 5 minutes. Stir in the cinnamon stick, cardamoms, and bay leaf and cook for 2 minutes.

3 Drain the rice and add to the pan, then cook, stirring, for 2 minutes more. Pour in the saffron stock and add the golden raisins. Bring to a boil, stir, then lower the heat, cover, and cook gently for 10 minutes, or until the rice is tender and all the liquid is absorbed.

4 Meanwhile, heat the oil in a wok, karahi, or large pan and fry the cashew nuts until browned. Drain on paper towels, then sprinkle the cashew nuts over the rice. Serve with nan bread and tomato and onion salad.

COOK'S TIP

Saffron powder can be used instead of saffron threads, if you prefer. Dissolve it in the hot stock.

NUTRITIONAL NOTES
Per Portion

Energy	462cal
Fat	19.5g
Saturated Fat	8g
Carbohydrate	63.9g
Fiber	1.2g

Tomato and Spinach Pilau

A tasty and nourishing dish for
vegetarians and meat eaters alike.
Serve it with another vegetable
curry, or with tandoori chicken,
marinated fried fish, or shammi
kabab. Add a cooling fruit raita
for a completely balanced meal.

INGREDIENTS

Serves 4

2 tablespoons vegetable oil
1 tablespoon ghee or
    unsalted butter
1 onion, chopped
2 garlic cloves, crushed
3 tomatoes, peeled and
    chopped
generous 1 cup brown basmati rice
2 teaspoons dhana jeera powder
    or 1 teaspoon ground coriander
    and 1 teaspoon ground cumin
2 carrots, coarsely grated
3¾ cups vegetable stock
10 ounces young spinach leaves
½ cup unsalted cashew nuts
salt and black pepper
nan bread, to serve

1 Wash the basmati rice. Place it in a
bowl, cover with cold water, and
let soak for 20 minutes.

2 Drain the rice and place it in a
large pan of boiling salted water,
bring back to a boil, and cook for
10 minutes.

3 Heat the oil and ghee or butter in
a karahi, wok, or large pan, and fry
the onion and garlic for 4–5 minutes
until soft. Add the tomatoes and cook
for 3–4 minutes, stirring, until the
mixture thickens.

4 Drain the rice, add it to the pan,
and cook for another 1–2 minutes,
stirring, until the grains of rice
are coated.

5 Stir in the dhana jeera powder or
coriander and cumin, then add the
carrots. Season with salt and pepper.
Pour in the stock and stir well to mix.

6 Bring to a boil, then cover tightly
and simmer over a very gentle
heat for 20–25 minutes, until the rice
is tender.

7 Lay the spinach on the surface of
the rice, cover again, and cook
for another 2–3 minutes, until the
spinach has wilted. Fold the spinach
into the rest of the rice.

8 Fry the cashew nuts until lightly
browned and sprinkle over the
rice mixture. Serve with nan bread.

NUTRITIONAL NOTES	
Per Portion	
Energy	402cal
Fat	17.1g
Saturated Fat	4.4g
Carbohydrate	56.4g
Fiber	4.8g

Basmati Rice with Vegetables

Serve this delectable dish with roast chicken, lamb cutlets, or pan-fried fish. Add the vegetables near the end of cooking so that they remain crisp.

INGREDIENTS

Serves 4

1¾ cups basmati rice
3 tablespoons vegetable oil
1 onion, chopped
2 garlic cloves, crushed
3 cups water or vegetable stock
⅔ cup fresh or drained canned
   corn kernels
1 red or green bell pepper,
   seeded and chopped
1 large carrot, grated
fresh chervil sprigs,
   to garnish

1 Wash the rice in a strainer, soak in cold water for 20 minutes, then drain very thoroughly.

2 Heat the oil in a large pan and fry the onion for a few minutes over a medium heat until it starts to soften.

3 Add the rice to the pan and fry for about 10 minutes, stirring constantly to prevent the rice from sticking to the bottom of the pan. Stir in the crushed garlic.

4 Pour in the water or stock and stir well. Bring to a boil, then lower the heat. Cover and simmer for 10 minutes.

5 Sprinkle the corn over the rice, spread the chopped bell pepper on top, and sprinkle over the grated carrot. Cover tightly and steam over a low heat until the rice is tender, then mix with a fork. Pile onto a serving plate and garnish with chervil.

NUTRITIONAL NOTES	
Per Portion	
Energy	454cal
Fat	9.7g
Saturated Fat	1.2g
Carbohydrate	82.7g
Fiber	2.3g

Basmati Rice with Potato

Rice is eaten at all meals in
Indian and Pakistani homes.
There are several ways of cooking
rice and mostly whole spices
are used. Always choose a good-
quality basmati rice.

INGREDIENTS

Serves 4

1½ cups basmati rice
1 tablespoon oil
1 small cinnamon stick
1 bay leaf
¼ teaspoon black cumin seeds
3 green cardamom pods
1 medium onion, sliced
1 teaspoon grated fresh ginger root
1 teaspoon crushed garlic
¼ teaspoon ground turmeric
1½ teaspoons salt
1 large potato, roughly diced
2 cups water
1 tablespoon chopped fresh
  cilantro

1 Wash the rice well and let it soak
in water for 20 minutes. Heat
the oil in a heavy pan, add the
cinnamon, bay leaf, black cumin
seeds, cardamoms, and onion and
cook for about 2 minutes.

COOK'S TIP

It is important to observe the standing time
of this dish before serving. Use a slotted
spoon to serve the rice and potato mixture
and handle it gently to avoid breaking the
delicate grains of rice.

2 Add the ginger, garlic, turmeric, salt,
and potato and cook for 1 minute.

3 Drain the rice very well. Add it to
the potato and spices in the pan.

4 Stir to mix, then pour in the
water followed by the cilantro.
Cover the pan with a lid and cook
for 15–20 minutes. Remove from the
heat and let stand, still covered, for
5–10 minutes before serving.

NUTRITIONAL NOTES	
Per Portion	
Energy	371cal
Fat	5.72g
Saturated Fat	1.03g
Carbohydrate	77.36g
Fiber	1.62g

Tricolor Pilau

Most Indian restaurants in the West serve this popular vegetable pilau, which has three different vegetables. The effect is easily achieved with canned or frozen vegetables, but for entertaining or a special occasion dinner, you may prefer to use fresh produce.

INGREDIENTS

Serves 4–6

1 cup basmati rice
2 tablespoons vegetable oil
½ teaspoon cumin seeds
2 dried bay leaves
4 green cardamom pods
4 cloves
1 onion, finely chopped
1 carrot, finely diced
½ cup frozen peas, thawed
⅓ cup frozen corn kernels, thawed
¼ cup cashew nuts, lightly fried
2 cups water
¼ teaspoon ground cumin
salt

1 Wash the rice, then soak it in cold water for 20 minutes.

2 Heat the oil in a karahi, wok, or large pan over a medium heat, and fry the cumin seeds for 2 minutes. Add the bay leaves, cardamoms, and cloves, and fry gently for 2 minutes more, stirring the spices from time to time.

3 Add the onion and fry until lightly browned. Stir in the diced carrot and cook, stirring, for 3–4 minutes.

4 Drain the soaked basmati rice and add to the contents in the pan. Stir well to mix. Add the peas, corn, and fried cashew nuts.

5 Add the measured water and the ground cumin, and stir in salt to taste. Bring to a boil, cover, and simmer over a low heat for 15 minutes, until all the water is absorbed.

6 Let stand, covered, for 10 minutes. Fluff up the rice with a fork, transfer to a warmed dish, and serve.

NUTRITIONAL NOTES	
Per Portion	
Energy	331cal
Fat	9.4g
Saturated Fat	1.4g
Carbohydrate	54.1g
Fiber	2g

Green Lentils and Rice

Also known as continental lentils, green lentils retain their shape and color when cooked.

INGREDIENTS

Serves 4-6

1¾ cups patna rice
⅔ cup green split lentils
¼ cup ghee
1 onion, finely chopped
2 garlic cloves, crushed
1-inch piece fresh ginger root, shredded
4 fresh green chiles, chopped
4 cloves
1-inch piece cinnamon stick
4 green cardamom pods
1 teaspoon ground turmeric
salt, to taste
2½ cups water

1 Wash the rice and lentils, then soak them in a bowl of cold water for 20 minutes.

2 Gently heat the ghee in a large heavy pan with a tight-fitting cover and fry the onion, garlic, ginger, chiles, cloves, cinnamon, cardamoms, turmeric, and salt until the onion is soft and translucent.

3 Drain the rice and lentils, add to the spices; sauté for 2–3 minutes. Add the water and bring to a boil. Reduce the heat, cover, and cook for about 20–25 minutes, or until all the water has been absorbed.

4 Take the pan off the heat and let rest with the lid on for 5 minutes. Just before serving gently toss the mixture with a flat spatula.

NUTRITIONAL NOTES	
Per Portion	
Energy	669cal
Fat	23.5g
Saturated Fat	15g
Carbohydrate	97.4g
Fiber	2.7g

Zucchini with Split Lentils

This recipe also works well with split red lentils.

INGREDIENTS

Serves 4-6

8 ounces zucchini,
  cut into wedges
⅔ cup mung dhal
  or yellow split peas
½ teaspoon ground turmeric
4 tablespoons vegetable oil
1 large onion, finely sliced
2 garlic cloves, crushed
2 fresh green chiles, chopped
½ teaspoon mustard seeds
½ teaspoon cumin seeds
¼ teaspoon asafetida
few fresh cilantro and mint leaves,
  chopped
6–8 curry leaves
salt, to taste
½ teaspoon sugar
7-ounce can chopped tomatoes
4 tablespoons lemon juice

1 In a pan, simmer the lentils and turmeric in 1¼ cups water, until cooked but not mushy.

NUTRITIONAL NOTES	
Per Portion	
Energy	278cal
Fat	12g
Saturated Fat	1.5g
Carbohydrate	31.9g
Fiber	3.9g

2 Heat the oil in a skillet and fry the remaining ingredients except the lemon juice. Cover and cook until the zucchini are nearly tender but still crunchy.

3 Fold in the drained lentils and the lemon juice. If the dish is too dry, add some of the cooking water. Reheat and serve.

Creamy Black Lentils

Black lentils or urad dhal are available whole, split, and skinned and split. Generally, the split and the skinned and split versions are used in west and south Indian cooking, whereas whole black lentils are a typical ingredient in the north.

INGREDIENTS

Serves 4–6

¾ cup black lentils, soaked
¼ cup red split lentils
½ cup heavy cream
½ cup plain yogurt
1 teaspoon cornstarch
3 tablespoons ghee or
   vegetable oil
1 onion, finely chopped
2-inch piece fresh ginger
   root, crushed
4 fresh green chiles, chopped
1 tomato, chopped
½ teaspoon chili powder
½ teaspoon ground turmeric
½ teaspoon ground cumin
2 garlic cloves, sliced
salt
cilantro sprigs and sliced
   fresh red chile, to garnish

NUTRITIONAL NOTES	
Per Portion	
Energy	431cal
Fat	26.5g
Saturated Fat	16.2g
Carbohydrate	35g
Fiber	2.9g

1 Drain the black lentils and place in a large pan with the red lentils. Cover with water and bring to a boil. Reduce the heat, cover the pan, and simmer until tender. Mash with a spoon and let cool.

2 In a bowl, mix together the cream, yogurt, and cornstarch and stir into the lentils in the pan.

3 Heat 1 tablespoon of the ghee or oil in a karahi, wok, or large pan, and fry the onion, ginger, two green chiles, and the tomato until the onion is soft.

4 Add the ground spices and salt and fry for another 2 minutes. Stir into the lentil mixture and mix well. Reheat, transfer to a heatproof serving dish, and keep warm.

5 Heat the remaining ghee or oil in a skillet over a low heat and fry the garlic slices and remaining chiles until the garlic slices are golden brown.

6 Pour over the lentils and fold in the garlic and chile just before serving. Place extra cream on the table so that diners can add more as they eat, if they want.

Lentils Seasoned with Garlic-infused Oil

This dish is popular in southern India, where there are numerous variations. A single vegetable can be added to the lentils, or a combination of two or more. It is traditionally served with steamed rice dumplings or stuffed rice pancakes. The garlic-flavored lentils are also extremely satisfying with plain boiled rice.

INGREDIENTS

Serves 4–6
½ cup vegetable oil
½ teaspoon mustard seeds
½ teaspoon cumin seeds
2 dried red chiles
¼ teaspoon asafetida
6–8 curry leaves
2 garlic cloves, crushed, plus 2 garlic
  cloves, sliced
2 tablespoons dry unsweetened
  shredded coconut
1 cup red lentils, washed
  and drained
2 teaspoons sambhar masala or other
  curry powder
½ teaspoon ground turmeric
scant 2 cups water
1 pound mixed vegetables, such
  as okra, zucchini, eggplant
  cauliflower, shallots, and
  bell peppers
4 tablespoons tamarind juice
4 firm tomatoes, quartered
a few cilantro leaves, chopped

NUTRITIONAL NOTES *Per Portion*	
Energy	477cal
Fat	28.7g
Saturated Fat	7.1g
Carbohydrate	38.6g
Fiber	6.8g

1 Heat half the oil in a karahi, wok, or large pan, and stir-fry the next seven ingredients until the coconut begins to brown.

2 Stir in the prepared red lentils with the masala and turmeric. Stir-fry for 2–3 minutes and add the water. Bring it to a boil and reduce the heat to low.

3 Cover the pan and let simmer for 25–30 minutes, until the lentils are mushy. Add the mixed vegetables, tamarind juice, and tomato quarters. Cook until the vegetables are just tender.

4 Heat the remaining oil in a small pan over a low heat, and fry the garlic slices until golden. Stir in the cilantro leaves, then pour over the lentils and vegetables. Mix at the table before serving.

Spinach Dhal

Many different types of dhal are eaten in India and each region has its own specialty. This is a delicious, lightly spiced dish with a mild nutty flavor from the yellow lentils, which combine well with the spinach.

INGREDIENTS

Serves 4

1 cup chana dhal or yellow split peas
¾ cup water
1 tablespoon oil
¼ teaspoon black mustard seeds
1 onion, thinly sliced
2 garlic cloves, crushed
1-inch piece fresh ginger root, grated
1 fresh red chile, finely chopped
10 ounces frozen spinach, thawed
¼ teaspoon chili powder
½ teaspoon ground coriander
½ teaspoon garam masala
½ teaspoon salt

1 Wash the chana dhal or split peas in several changes of cold water. Put into a bowl and cover with plenty of water. Let soak for 30 minutes.

NUTRITIONAL NOTES	
Per Portion	
Energy	183cal
Fat	2.00g
Saturated Fat	0.44g
Carbohydrate	30.30g
Fiber	4.90g

2 Drain the dhal and peas and put them in a large pan with the water. Bring to a boil, cover, and simmer for 20–25 minutes until soft.

3 Meanwhile, heat the oil in a large heavy pan and fry the mustard seeds for 2 minutes, until they begin to splutter. Add the onion, garlic, ginger, and chile and fry for 5–6 minutes. Add the spinach and cook for 10 minutes, or until the spinach is dry and the liquid has been absorbed. Stir in the remaining spices and salt and cook for 2–3 minutes.

4 Drain the split peas, add to the spinach, and cook for about 5 minutes. Serve immediately.

Tarka Dhal

Tarka Dhal is probably the most popular Indian lentil dish and is found today in most Indian and Pakistani restaurants.

INGREDIENTS

Serves 4

½ cup masoor dhal (red split lentils)
¼ cup mung dhal or yellow split peas
2½ cups water
1 teaspoon grated fresh ginger root
1 teaspoon crushed garlic
¼ teaspoon ground turmeric
2 fresh green chiles, chopped
1½ teaspoons salt

For the tarka

2 tablespoons oil
1 onion, sliced
¼ teaspoon mixed mustard and
  onion seeds
4 dried red chiles
1 tomato, sliced

For the garnish

1 tablespoon chopped fresh
  cilantro
1–2 fresh green chiles,
  seeded and sliced
1 tablespoon chopped fresh mint

1 Boil all the dhal, lentils or peas in the water with the ginger and garlic, turmeric, and chopped green chiles for 15–20 minutes, until soft.

2 Pound the mixture with a rolling pin or mash with a fork until it has the consistency of a creamy chicken soup.

3 If the lentil mixture looks too dry, add a little more water. Season with the salt. To prepare the tarka, heat the oil in a heavy pan and fry the onion with the mustard and onion seeds, dried red chiles, and tomato for 2 minutes.

4 Spoon the mashed lentils into a serving dish and pour the tarka over. Garnish with fresh cilantro, green chiles, and mint. Serve immediately.

NUTRITIONAL NOTES	
Per Portion	
Energy	162cal
Fat	6.60g
Saturated Fat	0.74g
Carbohydrate	18.70g
Fiber	3.20g

—————— COOK'S TIP ——————

Dried red chiles are available in many different sizes. If the ones you have are large, or if you want a less spicy flavor, reduce the quantity specified to 1 or 2.

Vegetables with Almonds

Yogurt gives this dish a tangy flavor and also makes it creamy.

INGREDIENTS

Serves 4
2 tablespoons oil
2 medium onions, sliced
2-inch piece fresh ginger root, shredded
1 teaspoon crushed black peppercorns
1 bay leaf
¼ teaspoon ground turmeric
1 teaspoon ground coriander
1 teaspoon salt
½ teaspoon garam masala
2½ cups mushrooms, thickly sliced
1 medium zucchini, thickly sliced
2 ounces green beans, cut into 1-inch lengths
1 tablespoon roughly chopped fresh mint
⅔ cup water
2 tablespoons plain low-fat yogurt
¼ cup sliced almonds

1 Heat the oil in a heavy pan, and fry the onions, ginger, peppercorns, and bay leaf for 3–5 minutes.

NUTRITIONAL NOTES	
Per Portion	
Energy	140cal
Fat	9.80g
Saturated Fat	1.13g
Carbohydrate	9.00g
Fiber	2.20g

2 Lower the heat and stir in the turmeric, coriander, salt, and garam masala. Gradually add the sliced mushrooms, zucchini, green beans, and mint. Stir gently to coat the vegetables, being careful not to break them up.

3 Pour in the water and bring to a simmer, then lower the heat and cook until the water has been totally absorbed by the vegetables.

4 Beat the yogurt lightly with a fork, then pour it onto the vegetables in the pan and mix together well until the vegetables are coated.

5 Cook the vegetables for another 2–3 minutes, stirring occasionally. Spoon into a large serving dish or onto individual plates. Serve immediately, garnished with the sliced almonds.

Vegetables and Beans with Curry Leaves

Bright, shiny green curry leaves look like small bay leaves, but they are not as tough. A popular seasoning ingredient in Indian cooking, curry leaves add a spicy flavor to dishes, such as this dry vegetable and bean curry.

INGREDIENTS

Serves 4

3 fresh green chiles
1 tablespoon oil
6 curry leaves
3 garlic cloves, sliced
3 dried red chiles
¼ teaspoon onion seeds
¼ teaspoon fenugreek seeds
½ cup drained canned red kidney beans
1 medium carrot, cut into strips
2 ounces green beans,
    sliced diagonally
1 medium red bell pepper,
    seeded and cut into strips
1 teaspoon salt
2 tablespoons lemon juice

NUTRITIONAL NOTES	
Per Portion	
Energy	79cal
Fat	3.30g
Saturated Fat	0.37g
Carbohydrate	9.70g
Fiber	2.60g

1 Cut the chiles in half lengthwise. Remove the membranes and seeds and chop the flesh.

2 Heat the oil in a karahi, wok, or deep heavy pan. Add the curry leaves, garlic cloves, dried chiles, and onion and fenugreek seeds.

3 When these ingredients turn a shade darker, add the chiles, kidney beans, carrot strips, green beans and bell pepper strips, stirring constantly.

4 Stir in the salt and the lemon juice. Lower the heat, cover, and cook for about 5 minutes.

5 Transfer the hot curry to a serving dish and serve immediately.

Spiced Coconut Mushrooms

Here is a simple and delicious way to cook mushrooms. They can be served with almost any Indian meal, as well as with traditional western broiled or roasted meats and poultry.

INGREDIENTS

Serves 4

2 tablespoons peanut oil
2 garlic cloves, finely chopped
2 fresh red chiles, seeded and
  sliced into rings
3 shallots, finely chopped
3 cups cremini mushrooms,
  thickly sliced
²/₃ cup coconut milk
2 tablespoons chopped fresh
  cilantro
salt and black pepper

1 Heat a karahi, wok, or shallow pan until hot, add the oil, and swirl it around. Add the garlic and chiles, then stir-fry for a few seconds.

2 Add the shallots and stir-fry them for 2–3 minutes, until softened. Add the mushrooms and stir-fry for 3 minutes.

COOK'S TIP

Use snipped fresh chives instead of chopped fresh cilantro, if you want.

3 Pour in the coconut milk and bring to a boil. Boil rapidly over a high heat until the liquid has reduced by about half and coats the mushrooms. Season to taste with salt and pepper.

4 Sprinkle over the chopped cilantro and toss the mushrooms gently to mix. Serve immediately.

NUTRITIONAL NOTES	
Per Portion	
Energy	67cal
Fat	5.9g
Saturated Fat	1.2g
Carbohydrate	2.4g
Fiber	0.8g

Zucchini with Mushrooms in a Yogurt Sauce

Yogurt makes a creamy sauce which is delicious with cooked mushrooms and zucchini.

INGREDIENTS

Serves 4
1 tablespoon oil
1 medium onion, roughly chopped
1 teaspoon ground coriander
1 teaspoon ground cumin
1 teaspoon salt
½ teaspoon chili powder
3 cups mushrooms, sliced
2 zucchini, sliced
3 tablespoons plain low-fat yogurt
1 tablespoon chopped
   fresh cilantro

1 Heat the oil in a heavy pan and fry the onion until golden brown. Lower the heat to medium, add the ground coriander, cumin, salt, and chili powder and stir together well.

2 Once the onion and the spices are well blended, add the mushrooms and zucchini and stir-fry gently for about 5 minutes, until soft. If the mixture is too dry, add just a little water to loosen.

3 Finally add the yogurt and mix it well into the vegetables.

4 Sprinkle with chopped fresh cilantro and serve immediately.

NUTRITIONAL NOTES	
Per Portion	
Energy	64cal
Fat	3.70g
Saturated Fat	0.58g
Carbohydrate	4.80g
Fiber	1.40g

――――――― COOK'S TIP ―――――――

Yogurt has a great affinity with stir-fried vegetables and this lovely combination of sliced zucchini and mushrooms would make a tasty accompaniment to serve with poultry or lamb dishes. If preferred, you can use eggplant to replace the zucchini, or use only mushrooms instead.

Mung Beans with Potatoes

Mung beans are one of the quicker-cooking beans. They do not require soaking and are very easy and convenient to use. In this recipe, they are cooked with potatoes and Indian spices to give a tasty nutritious dish.

INGREDIENTS

Serves 4

1 cup mung beans
3 cups water
8 ounces potatoes, cut into
   ¾-inch chunks
2 tablespoons oil
½ teaspoon cumin seeds
1 fresh green chile, finely chopped
1 garlic clove, crushed
1-inch piece fresh ginger root,
   finely chopped
¼ teaspoon ground turmeric
½ teaspoon chili powder
1 teaspoon salt
1 teaspoon sugar
4 curry leaves
5 tomatoes, peeled and finely chopped
1 tablespoon tomato paste
curry leaves, to garnish
plain rice, to serve

1 Wash the beans. Pour the water into a pan, add the beans, and bring to a boil. Boil rapidly for 15 minutes, then reduce the heat, cover the pan, and simmer until soft, about 30 minutes cooking time. Drain.

2 In a separate pan, parboil the potatoes in boiling water for 10 minutes, then drain well.

3 Heat the oil in a heavy pan and fry the cumin seeds until they splutter. Add the chile, garlic, and ginger and fry for 3–4 minutes.

4 Add the turmeric, chili powder, salt, and sugar and cook for 2 minutes, stirring to prevent the mixture from sticking to the pan.

5 Add the 4 curry leaves, chopped tomatoes, and tomato paste and simmer for about 5 minutes, until the sauce thickens. Mix the tomato sauce and the potatoes with the mung beans and heat through. Garnish with the extra curry leaves and serve with plain boiled rice.

NUTRITIONAL NOTES	
Per Portion	
Energy	254cal
Fat	6.80g
Saturated Fat	0.89g
Carbohydrate	36.90g
Fiber	6.30g

Madras Sambal

There are many variations of this popular dish but it is regularly cooked in one form or another in almost every South Indian home. You can use any combination of vegetables that are in season.

INGREDIENTS

Serves 4

1 cup tuvar dhal or red split lentils
2½ cups water
½ teaspoon ground turmeric
2 large potatoes, cut into
　1-inch chunks
2 tablespoons oil
½ teaspoon black mustard seeds
¼ teaspoon fenugreek seeds
4 curry leaves
1 onion, thinly sliced
4 ounces green beans,
　cut into 1-inch lengths
1 teaspoon salt
½ teaspoon chili powder
1 tablespoon lemon juice
toasted coconut, to garnish
coriander chutney, to serve

1 Wash the tuvar dhal or lentils in several changes of water. Place in a heavy pan with the measured water and the turmeric. Bring to a boil, then reduce the heat, cover the pan, and simmer for 30–35 minutes, until the lentils are soft.

2 Parboil the potatoes in a large pan of boiling water for 10 minutes. Drain well and set aside.

NUTRITIONAL NOTES	
Per Portion	
Energy	335cal
Fat	6.10g
Saturated Fat	1.98g
Carbohydrate	55.70g
Fiber	5.60g

3 Heat the oil in a large skillet and fry the mustard and fenugreek seeds and curry leaves for 2–3 minutes, until the seeds begin to splutter. Add the sliced onion and the green beans and stir-fry for 7–8 minutes. Add the parboiled potatoes and cook for another 2 minutes.

4 Drain the lentils. Stir them into the potato mixture with the salt, chili powder, and lemon juice. Simmer for 2 minutes, or until heated through. Garnish with toasted coconut and serve with freshly made coriander chutney.

Okra in Yogurt

This tangy vegetable dish can be served as an accompaniment, but it also makes an excellent vegetarian meal if served with Tarka Dhal and warm, freshly made chapatis.

INGREDIENTS

Serves 4

1 pound okra
1 tablespoon oil
½ teaspoon onion seeds
3 medium fresh green chiles, chopped
1 medium onion, sliced
¼ teaspoon ground turmeric
½ teaspoon salt
1 tablespoon plain low-fat yogurt
2 medium tomatoes, sliced
1 tablespoon chopped fresh cilantro
chapatis, to serve

NUTRITIONAL NOTES	
Per Portion	
Energy	82cal
Fat	4.20g
Saturated Fat	0.41g
Carbohydrate	7.60g
Fiber	5.30g

1 Wash, trim the ends off the okra, cut into ½-inch pieces, and place in a bowl. Set aside.

2 Heat the oil in a medium heavy pan, add the onion seeds, green chiles, and onion and fry for about 5 minutes, until the onion has turned golden brown.

3 Reduce the heat. Add the ground turmeric and salt to the onions and fry for about 1 minute.

4 Next, add the prepared okra, turn the heat to medium-high and quickly stir-fry the okra for a few minutes, until they are lightly golden.

5 Stir in the yogurt, tomatoes and, finally, the cilantro. Cook for another 2 minutes.

6 Transfer the okra to a serving dish and serve immediately with freshly made chapatis.

COOK'S TIP

Be careful when preparing the chiles. Many people forget that they can be a strong irritant, due to the capsaicin they contain. If you rub your eyes after handling, and especially after chopping, chiles, or touch another sensitive part of your anatomy, the burning sensation will be very unpleasant. It is wise to take simple precautionary measures, such as wearing gloves when cutting up chiles, if possible, or wash your hands several times and very thoroughly in soapy water afterward. In particular, if you wear contact lenses, make sure your fingers have been thoroughly cleansed before attempting to remove the lenses from your eyes.

Masala Okra

Okra, or "ladies' fingers," are a very popular Indian vegetable. Here the pods are stir-fried with a dry masala mixture to make a tasty side dish.

INGREDIENTS

Serves 4

1 pound okra
½ teaspoon ground turmeric
1 teaspoon chili powder
1 tablespoon ground cumin
1 tablespoon ground coriander
¼ teaspoon salt
¼ teaspoon sugar
1 tablespoon lemon juice
2 tablespoons chopped fresh cilantro
1 tablespoon oil
½ teaspoon cumin seeds
½ teaspoon black mustard seeds
chopped fresh tomatoes, to garnish
poppadums, to serve

1 Wash, dry, and trim the okra and set aside. In a bowl, mix together the turmeric, chili powder, cumin, ground coriander, salt, sugar, lemon juice, and fresh cilantro.

COOK'S TIP

When buying okra, choose firm, brightly coloured pods that are less than 4 inches long; larger ones can be stringy.

2 Heat the oil in a large heavy pan. Add the cumin seeds and mustard seeds and fry for about 2 minutes, or until they start to splutter.

3 Scrape in the spice mixture and continue to fry for 2 minutes.

4 Add the okra, cover, and cook over a low heat for 10 minutes, or until tender. Garnish with chopped fresh tomatoes and serve with poppadums.

NUTRITIONAL NOTES	
Per Portion	
Energy	102cal
Fat	5.4g
Saturated Fat	0.4g
Carbohydrate	8.6g
Fiber	4.7g

Spicy Bitter Gourds

Bitter gourds are widely used in Indian cooking, often combined with other vegetables in a curry.

INGREDIENTS

Serves 4

1½ pounds bitter gourds
1 tablespoon oil
½ teaspoon cumin seeds
6 scallions, finely chopped
5 tomatoes, finely chopped
1-inch piece fresh ginger root,
   finely chopped
2 garlic cloves, crushed
2 fresh green chiles,
   finely chopped
½ teaspoon salt
½ teaspoon chili powder
1 teaspoon ground coriander
1 teaspoon ground cumin
3 tablespoons molasses sugar
1 tablespoon besan flour
fresh cilantro sprigs,
   to garnish

1 Bring a large pan of lightly salted water to a boil. Peel the bitter gourds and halve them. Discard the seeds. Cut into ¾-inch pieces, then cook in a boiling water for 10–15 minutes, or until just tender. Drain well.

2 Heat the oil in a large heavy pan and fry the cumin seeds for 2 minutes, until they begin to splutter. Add the scallions and fry for 3–4 minutes. Add the tomatoes, ginger, garlic, and chiles.

3 Cook the mixture, stirring occasionally, for 5 minutes. Add the salt, remaining spices, and sugar to the pan and cook for another 2–3 minutes. Add the bitter gourds to the pan and mix well.

4 Sprinkle over the besan flour. Cover and simmer over a low heat for 5–8 minutes, or until all of the besan flour has been absorbed into the sauce. Stir well, then serve garnished with fresh cilantro sprigs.

NUTRITIONAL NOTES	
Per Portion	
Energy	120cal
Fat	3.50g
Saturated Fat	0.41g
Carbohydrate	9.20g
Fiber	0.40g

_____ COOK'S TIP _____

Bitter gourds, which are also known as karelas, resemble small cucumbers with a warty skin. True to their name, they are extremely bitter. The medium ones (about 4 inches long) are usually slightly less bitter than the tiny ones.

Corn on the Cob in Rich Onion Sauce

Corn is grown extensively in the Punjab region, where it is used in many delicacies. Corn bread, makki ki roti, along with spiced mustard greens, sarson ka saag, is a combination that is hard to beat, and it is what the Punjabis thrive on. Here, corn is cooked in a thick rich onion sauce, in another classic Punjabi dish. It is excellent served with nan bread.

INGREDIENTS

Serves 4–6
4 corn cobs, thawed if frozen
vegetable oil, for frying
1 large onion, finely chopped
2 garlic cloves, crushed
2-inch piece fresh ginger root, crushed
½ teaspoon ground turmeric
½ teaspoon onion seeds
½ teaspoon cumin seeds
½ teaspoon chili powder
6–8 curry leaves
½ teaspoon sugar
scant 1 cup plain yogurt
chili powder, to taste

1 Cut each corn cob in half, using a heavy knife or cleaver to make clean cuts. Heat the oil in a karahi, wok, or large pan and fry the corn until golden brown. Remove the corn and set aside. Remove any excess oil, leaving 2 tablespoons in the wok.

2 Grind the onion, garlic, and ginger to a paste, using a mortar and pestle or in a food processor. Transfer the paste to a bowl and mix in the spices, curry leaves, and sugar.

3 Heat the oil and fry the onion paste mixture over a low heat for 8–10 minutes, until all the spices have blended well and the oil separates from the sauce.

4 Cool the mixture and fold in the yogurt. Mix to a smooth sauce. Add the corn and mix well, so that all the pieces are covered with the sauce. Reheat gently for about 10 minutes. Serve hot.

NUTRITIONAL NOTES	
Per Portion	
Energy	214cal
Fat	15.1g
Saturated Fat	2g
Carbohydrate	15.9g
Fiber	1.5g

Stir-fried Indian Cheese with Mushrooms and Peas

Indian cheese, known as paneer, is a very versatile ingredient. It is used in both sweet and savory dishes. Indian housewives generally make this cheese at home, although in recent years it has become available commercially. It is a useful source of protein for those people in the north of the subcontinent who are vegetarian.

INGREDIENTS

Serves 4–6

6 tablespoons ghee or vegetable oil
8 ounces paneer, cubed
1 onion, finely chopped
a few fresh mint leaves, chopped,
    plus extra sprigs to garnish
2 ounces chopped fresh cilantro
3 fresh green chiles, chopped
3 garlic cloves
1-inch piece fresh ginger root, sliced
1 teaspoon ground turmeric
1 teaspoon chili powder,
    optional
1 teaspoon garam masala
3 cups tiny white mushrooms,
    washed
2 cups frozen peas, thawed
¾ cup plain yogurt, mixed
    with 1 teaspoon cornstarch
salt

1 Heat the ghee or oil in a karahi, wok, or large pan, and fry the paneer cubes until they are golden brown on all sides. Remove and drain on paper towels.

2 Grind the onion, mint, cilantro, chiles, garlic, and ginger with a mortar and pestle or in a food processor to a fairly smooth paste. Remove and mix in the turmeric, chili powder, if using, and garam masala, with salt to taste.

3 Remove excess ghee or oil from the pan, leaving about 1 tablespoon. Heat and fry the paste over a medium heat for 8–10 minutes, or until the raw onion smell disappears and the oil separates.

4 Add the mushrooms, thawed peas, and paneer and mix well. Cool the mixture slightly and gradually fold in the yogurt.

5 Simmer for about 10 minutes, until the vegetables are tender and the flavors are well mixed. Remove to a serving dish, garnish with sprigs of fresh mint, and serve immediately.

COOK'S TIP

If paneer is not available, you can use tofu or substitute broiled goat's cheese, adding it just before the garnish.

NUTRITIONAL NOTES
Per Portion

Energy	280cal
Fat	19.9g
Saturated Fat	3.7g
Carbohydrate	11.7g
Fiber	3.7g

Spinach and Potatoes and Red Chiles

India is blessed with more than 18 varieties of spinach. If you have access to an Indian or Chinese grocer, look out for some of the unusual varieties.

INGREDIENTS

Serves 4-6

4 tablespoons vegetable oil
8 ounces potatoes
1-inch piece fresh ginger root, crushed
4 garlic cloves, crushed
1 onion, chopped
2 fresh green chiles, chopped
2 dried red chiles, chopped
1 teaspoon cumin seeds
salt, to taste
8 ounces fresh spinach, trimmed, washed, and chopped or
   8 ounces frozen spinach, thawed and drained
2 firm tomatoes, roughly chopped, to garnish

1 Wash the potatoes and cut into quarters. If using small new potatoes, leave them whole. Heat the oil in a skillet and fry the potatoes until brown on all sides. Remove and put aside.

2 Remove the excess oil, leaving about 1 tablespoon in the pan. Fry the ginger, garlic, onion, green chiles, dried chiles, and cumin seeds until the onion is golden brown.

3 Add the potatoes and salt and stir well. Cover the pan and cook over a medium heat, stirring occasionally, until the potatoes are tender when pierced with a sharp knife.

4 Add the spinach and stir well. Using two wooden spoons or spatulas, toss the mixture over the heat until the spinach is tender and all the excess fluid has evaporated.

5 Spoon into a heated serving dish or onto individual plates and garnish with the chopped tomatoes. Serve hot.

VARIATION

This also tastes very good if you substitute sweet potatoes for ordinary potatoes. Make sure you slice them just before cooking, or they may discolor.

NUTRITIONAL NOTES
Per Portion

Energy	177cal
Fat	11.8g
Saturated Fat	1.4g
Carbohydrate	15g
Fiber	2.9g

Spinach with Mushrooms

A tasty vegetable that is often overlooked, spinach is highly nutritious. Cooked in this way it tastes wonderful. Serve with chapatis.

INGREDIENTS

Serves 4

1 pound fresh or frozen spinach,
   thawed
2 tablespoons oil
2 medium onions, diced
6–8 curry leaves
¼ teaspoon onion seeds
1 teaspoon crushed garlic
1 teaspoon grated fresh ginger root
1 teaspoon chili powder
1 teaspoon salt
1½ teaspoons ground coriander
1 large red bell pepper, seeded
   and sliced
1½ cups mushrooms,
   roughly chopped
1 cup low-fat ricotta cheese
2 tablespoons fresh cilantro leaves

1 If using fresh spinach, blanch it briefly in boiling water and drain thoroughly. If using frozen spinach, drain well. Set aside.

2 Heat the oil in a karahi, wok, or heavy pan and fry the onions with the curry leaves and the onion seeds for 1–2 minutes. Add the garlic, ginger, chili powder, salt, and ground coriander. Stir-fry for another 2–3 minutes.

4 Add the spinach and stir-fry for 4–6 minutes, then add the ricotta cheese and half the fresh cilantro, followed by the remaining red bell pepper slices. Stir-fry for another 2–3 minutes before serving, garnished with the remaining cilantro.

3 Add half the red bell pepper slices and all the mushrooms and continue to stir-fry for 2–3 minutes.

NUTRITIONAL NOTES	
Per Portion	
Energy	188cal
Fat	11.57g
Saturated Fat	5.99g
Carbohydrate	14.71g
Fiber	4.68g

COOK'S TIP

Whether you use fresh or frozen spinach, make sure it is well drained, otherwise the stir-fried mixture will be too wet when you add the ricotta cheese. It is a good idea to put the spinach into a colander, and press it against the sides of the colander with a wooden spoon to extract as much liquid as possible.

Carrot and Cauliflower Stir-fry

Slicing the carrots thinly into thin batons helps them cook quickly. This dish has a crunchy texture and only a few whole spices.

INGREDIENTS

Serves 4

2 large carrots
1 small cauliflower
1 tablespoon oil
1 bay leaf
2 cloves
1 small cinnamon stick
2 cardamom pods
3 black peppercorns
1 teaspoon salt
½ cup frozen peas, thawed
2 teaspoons lemon juice
1 tablespoon chopped fresh
  cilantro, plus fresh leaves,
  to garnish

1 Cut the carrots into thin batons about 1-inch long. Separate the cauliflower into small florets.

NUTRITIONAL NOTES	
Per Portion	
Energy	84cal
Fat	3.75g
Saturated Fat	0.60g
Carbohydrate	9.05g
Fiber	3.67g

2 Heat the oil in a karahi, wok, or heavy pan and add the bay leaf, cloves, cinnamon stick, cardamom pods, and peppercorns. Quickly stir-fry over a medium heat for 30–35 seconds, then add the salt.

3 Next add the carrot batons and cauliflower florets and continue to stir-fry for 3–5 minutes.

4 Add the peas, lemon juice, and chopped cilantro and cook for another 4–5 minutes. Serve garnished with the whole cilantro leaves.

___ COOK'S TIP ___

Both carrots and cauliflower can be eaten raw, and they need only minimal cooking or they will lose their crunchy texture.

Cauliflower and Potato Curry

Cauliflower and potatoes are encrusted with Indian spices in this delicious recipe.

INGREDIENTS

Serves 4

1 pound potatoes, cut into
   1-inch chunks
2 tablespoons oil
1 teaspoon cumin seeds
1 fresh green chile, finely chopped
1 pound cauliflower, broken into florets
1 teaspoon ground coriander
1 teaspoon ground cumin
¼ teaspoon chili powder
½ teaspoon ground turmeric
½ teaspoons salt
chopped fresh cilantro,
   to garnish
tomato and onion salad and pickle,
   to serve

1 Parboil the potatoes in a large pan of boiling water for about 10 minutes. Drain well and set aside.

2 Heat the oil in a large heavy pan. Add the cumin seeds and fry them for 2 minutes, until they begin to splutter. Add the chile and fry for another 1 minute.

3 Add the cauliflower florets and fry, stirring, for 5 minutes.

4 Add the potatoes and the ground spices and salt and cook for another 7–10 minutes, or until both the vegetables are tender. Garnish with fresh cilantro and serve with tomato and onion salad and pickle.

NUTRITIONAL NOTES	
Per Portion	
Energy	189cal
Fat	7.40g
Saturated Fat	0.77g
Carbohydrate	24.60g
Fiber	3.50g

———— COOK'S TIP ————

Use sweet potatoes instead of ordinary potatoes for a curry with a sweeter flavor.

Masala Beans with Fenugreek

The term masala refers to the blending of several spices to achieve a distinctive taste, with different spice combinations being used to complement specific ingredients. Households will traditionally create their own blends, and many are unique.

INGREDIENTS

Serves 4

1 onion
1 teaspoon ground cumin
1 teaspoon ground coriander
1 teaspoon sesame seeds
1 teaspoon chili powder
½ teaspoon crushed garlic
¼ teaspoon ground turmeric
1 teaspoon salt
2 tablespoons vegetable oil
1 tomato, quartered
1½ cups green beans, blanched
1 bunch fresh fenugreek leaves,
  stems discarded
4 tablespoons chopped fresh
  cilantro
1 tablespoon lemon juice

1 Roughly chop the onion. Mix together the cumin and coriander, sesame seeds, chili powder, garlic, turmeric, and salt.

2 Put the chopped onion and spice mixture into a food processor or blender, and process for 30–45 seconds until you have a rough paste.

3 In a karahi, wok, or large pan, heat the oil over a medium heat and fry the spice paste for about 5 minutes, stirring the mixture occasionally.

4 Add the tomato quarters, blanched green beans, fresh fenugreek, and chopped cilantro.

5 Stir-fry the contents of the pan for about 5 minutes, then sprinkle in the lemon juice and serve.

VARIATION

Instead of fresh fenugreek, you can also use 1 tablespoon dried fenugreek for this recipe. Dried fenugreek is readily available from Indian stores and markets.

NUTRITIONAL NOTES
Per Portion

Energy	80cal
Fat	5.9g
Saturated Fat	0.8g
Carbohydrate	5.4g
Fiber	2g

Green Beans with Corn

Frozen green beans are useful for this dish, because they are quick to cook. It makes an excellent vegetable accompaniment.

INGREDIENTS

Serves 4

1 teaspoon oil
¼ teaspoon mustard seeds
1 medium red onion, diced
⅓ cup frozen corn kernels
¼ cup canned red kidney
   beans, drained
6 ounces frozen green beans
1 fresh red chile, seeded and diced
1 garlic clove, chopped
1-inch piece fresh ginger root, finely
   chopped
1 tablespoon chopped fresh
   cilantro
1 teaspoon salt
1 medium tomato, seeded and diced,
   to garnish

1 Heat the oil in a karahi, wok, or heavy pan for about 30 seconds, then add the mustard seeds and onion. Stir-fry for 2–3 minutes.

NUTRITIONAL NOTES	
Per Portion	
Energy	84cal
Fat	3.44g
Saturated Fat	0.50g
Carbohydrate	11.13g
Fiber	2.70g

2 Add the corn, red kidney beans, and green beans. Stir-fry for 3–5 minutes.

3 Add the red chile, chopped garlic and ginger, cilantro, and salt and stir-fry for 2–3 minutes.

4 Remove the pan from the heat. Transfer the vegetables to a serving dish and garnish with the diced tomato.

_____ COOK'S TIP _____

This is a good standby dish because it uses frozen and canned ingredients. You can make sure you always have a chile available for making this dish, or others like it, by freezing whole fresh chiles, washed but not blanched.

Fiery Spiced Potatoes

The quantity of red chiles used here may be too fiery for some palates. For a milder version, seed the chiles, use fewer, or substitute them with a roughly chopped red bell pepper.

INGREDIENTS

Serves 4
12-14 new potatoes, peeled and halved
½ teaspoon salt
1 tablespoon oil
½ teaspoon crushed dried red chiles
½ teaspoon cumin seeds
½ teaspoon fennel seeds
½ teaspoon crushed coriander seeds
1 medium onion, sliced
3–4 fresh red chiles, chopped
1 tablespoon chopped fresh cilantro

1 Boil the potatoes in a pan of salted water until just cooked but still firm. Remove from the heat and drain off the water.

NUTRITIONAL NOTES	
Per Portion	
Energy	122cal
Fat	3.50g
Saturated Fat	0.37g
Carbohydrate	21.20g
Fiber	1.50g

2 In a karahi, wok, or deep pan, heat the oil quickly over a high heat, then turn down the heat to medium. Add the crushed chiles, cumin, fennel and coriander seeds, and a little salt and quickly stir-fry for about 30–40 seconds.

3 Add the onion and fry gently until golden brown. Then add the new potatoes, fresh red chiles, and fresh cilantro.

4 Cover and cook for 5–7 minutes over a very low heat. Serve hot.

Potatoes with Roasted Poppy Seeds

Poppy seeds are used in Indian cooking as thickening agents, and to lend a nutty taste to sauces. It is the creamy white variety of poppy seed that is used here, instead of the ones with a blue-gray hue that are used for baking.

INGREDIENTS

Serves 4

3 tablespoons white poppy seeds
3–4 tablespoons vegetable oil
1½ pounds potatoes, peeled and
 cut into ½-inch cubes
½ teaspoon black mustard seeds
½ teaspoon onion seeds
½ teaspoon cumin seeds
½ teaspoon fennel seeds
1–2 dried red chiles, chopped or
 broken into small pieces
½ teaspoon ground turmeric
½ teaspoon salt
⅔ cup warm water
fresh cilantro sprigs,
 to garnish
pooris and plain yogurt,
 to serve

1 Peel the potatoes and cut into small cubes.

2 Preheat a karahi, wok, or large pan over a medium setting. When the pan is hot, reduce the heat slightly and add the poppy seeds. Stir them around in the pan until they are just a shade darker. Remove from the pan and let cool.

3 In the pan, heat the vegetable oil over a medium heat and fry the cubes of potato until they are light brown. Remove them with a slotted spoon and drain on paper towels.

4 To the same oil, add the mustard seeds. As soon as they begin to pop, add the onion, cumin and fennel seeds, and the chiles. Let the chiles blacken, but remove them from the pan before they burn.

5 Stir in the turmeric and follow quickly with the fried potatoes and salt. Stir well and add the warm water. Cover the pan with the lid and reduce the heat to low. Cook for 8–10 minutes, or until the potatoes are tender.

6 Grind the cooled poppy seeds in a mortar and pestle or coffee grinder. Stir the ground seeds into the potatoes. It should form a thick paste that should cling to the potatoes. If there is too much liquid, continue to stir over a medium heat until you have the right consistency. Transfer to a serving dish. Garnish with cilantro and serve with pooris and plain yogurt.

NUTRITIONAL NOTES	
Per Portion	
Energy	201cal
Fat	13.5g
Saturated Fat	1.6g
Carbohydrate	29g
Fiber	2.2g

Potatoes in Chile Tamarind Sauce

In this favorite potato dish from the state of Karnataka, the combination of chile and tamarind awakens the taste buds immediately. This version adapts the traditional recipe slightly to reduce the customary pungency and enhance the fiery appearance of this delicious combination.

INGREDIENTS

Serves 4–6

1 pound small new potatoes, washed and dried
1 ounce whole dried red chiles, preferably Kashmiri
1½ teaspoons cumin seeds
4 garlic cloves, chopped
6 tablespoons vegetable oil
4 tablespoons thick tamarind juice
2 tablespoons tomato paste
4 curry leaves
1 teaspoon sugar
¼ teaspoon asafetida
salt
cilantro sprigs and lemon wedges, to garnish

NUTRITIONAL NOTES	
Per Portion	
Energy	227cal
Fat	16.8g
Saturated Fat	2.1g
Carbohydrate	18.1g
Fiber	1.1g

___ VARIATION ___

Chunks of large potatoes can be used as an alternative to new potatoes. Alternatively, try this with sweet potatoes. The spicy sweet and sour taste works very well in this variation.

1 Boil the potatoes until they are fully cooked, ensuring they do not break. To test, insert a thin sharp knife into the potatoes. It should come out clean when the potatoes are fully cooked. Drain and cool the potatoes in iced water to prevent further cooking.

2 Soak the chiles in warm water for 5 minutes. Drain and grind with the cumin seeds and garlic to a coarse paste, using either a mortar and pestle or in a food processor.

3 Heat the oil and fry the paste, tamarind juice, tomato paste, curry leaves, sugar, asafetida, and salt until the oil can be seen to have separated from the spice paste.

4 Add the potatoes and stir to coat. Reduce the heat, cover, and simmer for 5 minutes. Garnish and serve.

Golden Chunky Potatoes with Spinach and Mustard Seeds

The combination of spinach and potato is a common one in India and there are numerous versions using the same or similar ingredients. This recipe is from Bengal, where it is known as palong saaker ghonto.

INGREDIENTS

Serves 4–6

1 pound spinach
2 tablespoons vegetable oil
1 teaspoon black mustard seeds
1 onion, thinly sliced
2 garlic cloves, crushed
1-inch piece fresh ginger root, finely chopped
1½ pounds firm potatoes, cut into 1-inch chunks
1 teaspoon chili powder
1 teaspoon salt
½ cup water

1 Blanch the spinach in a pan of boiling water for 3–4 minutes, then drain in a colander and let cool. When it is cool enough to handle, squeeze out any remaining liquid using the back of a wooden spoon or with your hands.

2 Heat the oil in a large pan over a medium heat and fry the mustard seeds until they begin to splutter.

3 Add the sliced onion, crushed garlic, and chopped ginger and fry for about 5 minutes, stirring.

4 Stir in the potatoes, chili powder, and salt. Pour in the measure of water and cook for 8 minutes, stirring occasionally.

_____ VARIATION _____

For an excellent alternative to spinach, use 1 pound collard greens. Whether you use spinach or an alternative, choose young vegetables for the best result.

5 Add the spinach to the pan. Cover and simmer for 10–15 minutes, until the potatoes are tender. Serve.

NUTRITIONAL NOTES	
Per Portion	
Energy	209cal
Fat	7g
Saturated Fat	1g
Carbohydrate	31.9g
Fiber	4.6g

Potatoes in Yogurt Sauce

It is nice to use tiny new potatoes with the skins on for this recipe. The yogurt adds a tangy flavor to this fairly spicy dish, which is delicious served with plain or whole-wheat chapatis.

INGREDIENTS

Serves 4
small bunch fresh cilantro
12 new potatoes, halved
1¼ cups plain low-fat yogurt
1¼ cups water
¼ teaspoon ground turmeric
1 teaspoon chili powder
1 teaspoon ground coriander
½ teaspoon ground cumin
1 teaspoon soft brown sugar
¼ teaspoon salt
1 tablespoon oil
1 teaspoon cumin seeds
2 green chiles, sliced

COOK'S TIP

If new potatoes are unavailable, you can use 1 pound ordinary potatoes instead. Peel them and cut into large chunks, then cook as described above.

2 Boil the potatoes in salted water with their skins on until they are just tender, then drain and set aside.

3 Mix together the yogurt, water, turmeric, chili powder, ground coriander, ground cumin, sugar, and salt in a bowl. Set aside.

5 Reduce the heat, stir in the spicy yogurt mixture, and cook over a medium heat for about 3 minutes.

6 Add the chopped fresh cilantro, green chiles, and cooked potatoes. Blend everything together and cook for another 5–7 minutes, stirring from time to time. Serve hot.

NUTRITIONAL NOTES	
Per Portion	
Energy	169cal
Fat	4.30g
Saturated Fat	0.78g
Carbohydrate	27.60g
Fiber	1.20g

1 Cut off the roots and any thick stalks from the cilantro and chop the leaves finely. Set aside.

4 Heat the oil in a medium heavy pan and stir in the cumin seeds. Fry for 1 minute.

Masala Mashed Potatoes

This delightfully simple variation on the popular Western side dish can be used as an accompaniment to just about any main course dish, not just Indian food. There are easily attainable alternatives to mango powder if you cannot find it in the store (see Cook's Tip).

INGREDIENTS

Serves 4

3 medium potatoes
1 tablespoon chopped fresh mint and cilantro, mixed
1 teaspoon dried mango powder (amchur)
1 teaspoon salt
1 teaspoon crushed black peppercorns
1 fresh red chile, chopped
1 fresh green chile, chopped
4 tablespoons butter

1 Boil the potatoes until soft, then mash them.

2 Stir the remaining ingredients together in a small bowl.

3 Stir the spice mixture into the mashed potatoes. Mix together thoroughly with a fork and serve warm as an accompaniment.

_____ COOK'S TIP _____

Mango powder, also known as amchur, is the unripe green fruit of the mango tree ground to a powder. The sour mangoes are sliced and dried in the sun, turning a light brown, before they are ground. Mango powder adds a fruity sharpness, and a slightly resinous bouquet, to a dish. It is widely used with vegetables and is usually added toward the end of the cooking time. If mango powder is unavailable, the nearest substitute is lemon or lime juice, in double or treble quantity.

NUTRITIONAL NOTES
Per Portion

Energy	100cal
Fat	5.30g
Saturated Fat	1.25g
Carbohydrate	11.40g
Fiber	0.80g

Spicy Cabbage

Another spicy twist on a Western favorite. This nutritious side dish is a great way to jazz up the flavor of cabbage for those not usually keen on the vegetable. Note the colorful variations.

INGREDIENTS

Serves 4

4 tablespoons ghee or butter
½ teaspoon white cumin seeds
3-8 dried red chiles, to taste
1 small onion, sliced
2½ cups cabbage, shredded
2 medium carrots, grated
½ teaspoon salt
2 tablespoons lemon juice

1 Melt the ghee or butter in a medium pan and fry the cumin seeds and dried chiles for about 30 seconds.

2 Add the onion and fry for about 2 minutes. Add the cabbage and carrots and stir-fry for another 5 minutes, or until the cabbage is soft.

3 Finally, stir in the salt and lemon juice and serve immediately.

_____ VARIATION _____

Try this with red onion and red cabbage for a colorful alternative.

NUTRITIONAL NOTES
Per Portion

Energy	91cal
Fat	5.50g
Saturated Fat	1.27g
Carbohydrate	8.50g
Fiber	2.40g

Spiced Potatoes and Carrots Parisienne

Prepared "parisienne" vegetables have recently become available in many supermarkets. These are simply root vegetables that have been peeled and cut into spherical shapes. This dish looks extremely fresh and appetizing and is delicious.

INGREDIENTS

Serves 4

6 ounces carrots parisienne
6 ounces potatoes parisienne
4 ounces green beans, sliced
6 tablespoons butter
1 tablespoon vegetable oil
¼ teaspoon onion seeds
¼ teaspoon fenugreek seeds
4 dried red chiles
½ teaspoon mustard seeds
6 curry leaves
1 medium onion, sliced
1 teaspoon salt
4 garlic cloves, sliced
4 fresh red chiles
1 tablespoon chopped fresh
   cilantro
1 tablespoon chopped fresh mint, plus
   1 mint sprig to garnish

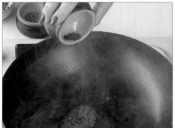

1 Drop the carrots, potatoes, and green beans into a pan of boiling water, and cook for about 7 minutes, or until they are just tender but not overcooked. Drain in a colander, then refresh under cold water to stop the cooking process. Drain again and set to one side.

2 Heat the butter and oil in a deep skillet or a large karahi and add the onion seeds, fenugreek seeds, dried red chiles, mustard seeds, and curry leaves. When these have sizzled for a few seconds, add the onion and fry for 3–5 minutes, stirring the mixture occasionally.

3 Add the salt, garlic, and fresh chiles, followed by the cooked vegetables, and stir gently over a medium heat for about 5 minutes.

4 Add the fresh cilantro and mint and serve hot, garnished with a sprig of mint.

NUTRITIONAL NOTES	
Per Portion	
Energy	232cal
Fat	18.6g
Saturated Fat	10.2g
Carbohydrate	15g
Fiber	2.7g

___ COOK'S TIP ___

If you can't locate "parisienne" vegetables, you can simply dice the potatoes and carrots yourself, or cut them into batons.

Karahi Shredded Cabbage with Cumin

This is one of the best ways to cook cabbage, stir-fried with butter and crushed spices. This mild side dish makes a wonderful accompaniment to many other meats or vegetables.

INGREDIENTS

Serves 4

1 tablespoon corn oil
4 tablespoons ghee or butter
½ teaspoon crushed coriander seeds
½ teaspoon white cumin seeds
6 dried red chiles
1 small savoy cabbage, shredded
12 snow peas
3 fresh red chiles, seeded and sliced
12 baby corn cobs
salt, to taste
¼ cup sliced almonds, toasted
1 tablespoon chopped fresh
   cilantro

1 Heat the oil and butter in a deep round-bottom pan or a karahi and add the crushed coriander seeds, white cumin seeds, and dried red chiles.

2 Add the shredded cabbage and snow peas and stir-fry for about 5 minutes.

3 Add the sliced fresh red chiles, baby corn cobs, and salt, and fry for another 3 minutes.

4 Garnish with the toasted almonds and fresh cilantro and serve hot.

NUTRITIONAL NOTES	
Per Portion	
Energy	184cal
Fat	16.9g
Saturated Fat	7.2g
Carbohydrate	4.3g
Fiber	3g

Potatoes in Red Sauce

This is a lightly spiced dish, perfect for children or those who like mild curries.

INGREDIENTS

Serves 4–6

1 pound small new potatoes
1½ teaspoons coriander seeds
1½ teaspoons cumin seeds
4 garlic cloves
6 tablespoons vegetable oil
3 tablespoons thick tamarind juice
4 tablespoons tomato paste
4 curry leaves
salt, to taste
1 teaspoon sugar
cilantro sprig, to garnish

1 Boil the potatoes until they are fully cooked but still retain their shape. To test, insert a thin sharp knife into the potatoes. It should come out clean when the potatoes are fully cooked. Drain well.

2 Grind the coriander seeds with the cumin seeds and garlic to a coarse paste using a mortar and pestle or food processor.

3 Heat the oil in a karahi, wok, or skillet. Fry the paste, tamarind juice, tomato paste, curry leaves, salt, and sugar until the oil separates.

4 Add the potatoes and stir to coat them in the spicy tomato mixture. Reduce the heat, cover, and simmer for about 5 minutes. Garnish and serve.

NUTRITIONAL NOTES	
Per Portion	
Energy	231cal
Fat	16.8g
Saturated Fat	2.1g
Carbohydrate	19.2g
Fiber	1.1g

Cucumber Curry

Served hot, this is good with fish dishes and can also be served cold with cooked meats.

INGREDIENTS

Serves 4–6

½ cup water
½ cup coconut cream
½ teaspoon ground turmeric
salt, to taste
1 teaspoon sugar
1 large cucumber, cut into small pieces
1 large red bell pepper, cut into
    small pieces
½ cup salted peanuts, crushed
4 tablespoons vegetable oil
2 dried red chiles
1 teaspoon cumin seeds
1 teaspoon mustard seeds
4–6 curry leaves
4 garlic cloves, crushed
a few whole salted peanuts,
    to garnish

1 Bring the water to a boil in a heavy pan and add the coconut cream, turmeric, salt, and sugar. Simmer until the coconut dissolves and the mixture becomes a smooth, thick sauce.

2 Add the cucumber, red bell pepper, and crushed peanuts and simmer for about 5 minutes. Transfer to a heat-proof serving dish and keep hot.

3 Heat the oil in a karahi, wok, or skillet. Fry the chiles and cumin with the mustard seeds until they start to pop.

4 Reduce the heat, add the curry leaves and garlic, and fry for 2 minutes. Pour over the cucumber mixture and stir well. Garnish with whole peanuts and serve hot.

NUTRITIONAL NOTES	
Per Portion	
Energy	385cal
Fat	37.6g
Saturated Fat	19.6g
Carbohydrate	6.4g
Fiber	1.7g

Potatoes in Tomato Sauce

This curry makes an excellent accompaniment to almost any other savory dish, but it goes particularly well with balti dishes. Served with rice, it makes a great vegetarian main course.

INGREDIENTS

Serves 4

2 teaspoons oil
¼ teaspoon onion seeds
4 curry leaves
2 medium onions, diced
14-ounce can tomatoes
1 teaspoon ground cumin
1½ teaspoons ground coriander
1 teaspoon chili powder
1 teaspoon grated fresh ginger root
1 teaspoon crushed garlic
¼ teaspoon ground turmeric
1 teaspoon salt
1 tablespoon lemon juice
1 tablespoon chopped fresh
  cilantro
2 medium potatoes, diced

1 Heat the oil in a karahi, wok, or heavy pan and fry the onion seeds, curry leaves, and onions over a medium heat for a few minutes, being careful not to burn the onions.

NUTRITIONAL NOTES	
Per Portion	
Energy	119cal
Fat	2.27g
Saturated Fat	0.24g
Carbohydrate	22.91g
Fiber	2.88g

2 Meanwhile, place the canned tomatoes in a bowl and add the cumin, ground coriander, chili powder, ginger, garlic, turmeric, salt, lemon juice, and fresh cilantro. Mix together until well blended.

— VARIATIONS —

This curry is also delicious if you add a few cauliflower or broccoli florets with the potatoes, or if you substitute diced parsnips for the potatoes. To emphasize the tomato flavor, you can stir in 1 tablespoon tomato paste.

3 Pour this mixture into the pan and stir for about 1 minute to mix thoroughly with the onions.

4 Finally, add the diced potatoes, cover the pan, and cook gently for 7–10 minutes over a low heat. Check that the potatoes are properly cooked through, then serve.

Kidney Bean Curry

This is a popular Punjabi-style dish using red kidney beans. You can substitute the same quantity of other beans, if you prefer.

INGREDIENTS

Serves 4

1 cup dried red kidney beans
2 tablespoons oil
½ teaspoon cumin seeds
1 onion, thinly sliced
1 fresh green chile, finely chopped
2 garlic cloves, crushed
1-inch piece fresh ginger root, grated
2 tablespoons curry paste
1 teaspoon ground cumin
1 teaspoon ground coriander
½ teaspoon chili powder
½ teaspoon salt
14-ounce can chopped tomatoes
2 tablespoons chopped fresh
  cilantro

1 Let the kidney beans soak overnight in a bowl of cold water.

3 Meanwhile, heat the oil in a large heavy skillet and fry the cumin seeds for 2 minutes, until they begin to splutter. Add the onion, chile, garlic, and ginger and fry for 5 minutes. Stir in the curry paste, cumin, ground coriander, chili powder, and salt and cook for 5 minutes.

4 Add the tomatoes and simmer for 5 minutes. Drain the kidney beans and stir them in with the fresh cilantro, reserving a little for the garnish. Cover and cook for 15 minutes, adding a little water if necessary. Serve garnished with the reserved fresh cilantro.

2 Drain the beans and put in a large pan with double the volume of water. Boil vigorously for 10 minutes. Skim off any scum. Cover and cook for 1–1½ hours, or until the beans are soft.

NUTRITIONAL NOTES	
Per Portion	
Energy	258cal
Fat	7.80g
Saturated Fat	0.86g
Carbohydrate	33.70g
Fiber	11.70g

COOK'S TIP

If you want to reduce the cooking time, cook the beans in a pressure cooker for 20–25 minutes after boiling them vigorously for 10 minutes. Alternatively, replace the dried beans with canned beans. Use a 14-ounce can and drain it well.

Bombay Potatoes

This authentic dish is a staple for the Gujarati, who are totally vegetarian and are the largest population group in Mumbai.

INGREDIENTS

Serves 4–6
1 pound new potatoes
salt, to taste
1 teaspoon turmeric
4 tablespoons vegetable oil
2 dried red chiles
6–8 curry leaves
2 onions, finely chopped
2 fresh green chiles, finely chopped
2 cups fresh cilantro,
    coarsely chopped
¼ teaspoon asafetida
½ teaspoon each, cumin, mustard,
    onion, fennel, and nigella seeds
lemon juice, to taste

1 Scrub the potatoes under cold running water and cut them into small pieces. Boil the potatoes in water with a little salt and ½ teaspoon of the turmeric for 10–15 minutes, or until tender. Drain the potatoes well then mash them and set aside.

2 Heat the oil in a skillet and fry the dried chiles and curry leaves until the chiles are nearly burned.

3 Add the onions, green chiles, fresh cilantro, remaining turmeric, asafetida, and spice seeds to the pan and cook until the onions are soft.

4 Fold in the potatoes and add a few drops of water. Cook over a low heat for about 10 minutes, stirring well to make sure the spices are mixed. Add lemon juice to taste, and serve.

NUTRITIONAL NOTES	
Per Portion	
Energy	207cal
Fat	11.6g
Saturated Fat	1.4g
Carbohydrate	24.3g
Fiber	2.2g

Curried Cauliflower

In this dish, the creamy coconut sauce complements the flavor of the spiced cauliflower.

INGREDIENTS

Serves 4–6
1 tablespoon besan flour
½ cup water
1 teaspoon chili powder
1 tablespoon ground coriander
1 teaspoon ground cumin
1 teaspoon mustard powder
1 teaspoon ground turmeric
salt, to taste
4 tablespoons vegetable oil
6–8 curry leaves
1 teaspoon cumin seeds
1 cauliflower, broken into florets
¾ cup thick coconut milk
juice of 2 lemons
lime wedges, to serve

1 Put the besan flour in a small bowl and stir in enough of the water to make a smooth paste. Add the chile, coriander, cumin, mustard, turmeric, and salt. Add the remaining water and keep mixing to blend all the ingredients well.

2 Heat the oil in a skillet and add the curry leaves and cumin seeds. Add the spice paste and simmer for about 5 minutes. If the sauce has become too thick, add a little hot water.

3 Add the cauliflower and coconut milk. Bring to a boil, reduce the heat, cover, and cook until the cauliflower is tender but crunchy. Cook longer if you prefer. Add the lemon juice, mix well and serve hot with the lime wedges.

NUTRITIONAL NOTES	
Per Portion	
Energy	160cal
Fat	12.1g
Saturated Fat	1.6g
Carbohydrate	9g
Fiber	2g

—— VARIATION ——

This sauce also goes well with broccoli. For a pretty presentation, you can use whole miniature vegetables.

Peppers Filled with Spiced Vegetables

Nigella, or kalonji as it is also known, is a tiny black seed. It is widely used in Indian cooking, especially sprinkled over breads or in potato dishes. It has a mild, slightly nutty flavor and is best toasted for a few seconds in a dry or lightly oiled skillet over a medium heat before being used in a recipe. This helps to bring out its flavor.

INGREDIENTS

Serves 6

6 large evenly shaped red
   or yellow bell peppers
1¼ pounds waxy potatoes
1 small onion, chopped
4–5 garlic cloves, chopped
2-inch piece fresh ginger root, chopped
1–2 fresh green chiles, seeded
   and chopped
7 tablespoons water
6–7 tablespoons vegetable oil
1 eggplant, diced
2 teaspoons cumin seeds
1 teaspoon nigella seeds
½ teaspoon ground turmeric
1 teaspoon ground coriander
1 teaspoon ground toasted
   cumin seeds
cayenne pepper
2 tablespoons lemon juice
sea salt and black pepper
2 tablespoons chopped fresh
   cilantro, to garnish

1 Cut the tops off the red or yellow bell peppers, then remove and discard the seeds. Cut a thin slice off the bottom of any wobbly peppers so that they stand upright.

___

COOK'S TIP

The hottest part of a chile is the white membrane that connects the seeds to the flesh. Removing the seeds and membrane before cooking gives a milder flavor.

___

2 Bring a large pan of lightly salted water to a boil. Add the bell peppers and cook for 5–6 minutes. Drain and let them stand upside down in a colander.

3 Cook the potatoes in lightly salted, boiling water for 10–12 minutes, until just tender. Drain, cool, and peel, then cut into ½-inch dice.

4 Put the onion, garlic, ginger, and green chiles in a food processor or blender with 4 tablespoons of the water and process to a paste.

5 Heat 3 tablespoons of the vegetable oil in a large, deep skillet and cook the diced eggplant, stirring occasionally, until it is evenly browned on all sides. Remove the eggplant from the skillet, using a slotted spoon and set aside.

6 Add another 2 tablespoons of the vegetable oil to the skillet, add the diced potatoes, and cook until lightly browned on all sides. Remove the potatoes from the skillet and set aside.

7 Add another 1 tablespoon sunflower oil to the skillet, if needed, then add the cumin and nigella seeds. Fry briefly until the seeds darken, then add the turmeric, coriander, and ground cumin. Cook for 15 seconds. Stir in the onion and garlic paste and fry, scraping the skillet with a spatula, until the onions begin to brown.

8 Return the potatoes and eggplant to the skillet, season with salt, pepper, and 1–2 pinches of cayenne. Add the remaining water and 1 tablespoon lemon juice and cook, stirring, until the liquid evaporates. Preheat the oven to 375°F.

9 Fill the bell peppers with the spiced vegetable mixture and place on a lightly greased baking sheet. Brush the peppers with a little oil and bake for 30–35 minutes, until they are cooked. Let cool a little, then sprinkle with a little more lemon juice. Garnish with the cilantro and serve.

NUTRITIONAL NOTES	
Per Portion	
Energy	221cal
Fat	12.1g
Saturated Fat	1.6g
Carbohydrate	26.1g
Fiber	4.4g

Stuffed Bananas

Bananas are cooked with spices in many different ways in southern India. Some recipes contain large quantities of chiles, but the taste is skillfully mellowed by adding coconut milk and tamarind juice. Green bananas are available from Indian stores, or you can use plantains or unripe eating bananas that are firm to the touch.

INGREDIENTS

Serves 4

1 bunch fresh cilantro
4 green bananas or plantains
2 tablespoons ground coriander
1 tablespoon ground cumin
1 teaspoon chili powder
½ teaspoon salt
¼ teaspoon ground turmeric
1 teaspoon sugar
1 tablespoon besan flour
6 tablespoons vegetable oil
¼ teaspoon cumin seeds
¼ teaspoon black mustard seeds

NUTRITIONAL NOTES	
Per Portion	
Energy	265cal
Fat	16.8g
Saturated Fat	2.1g
Carbohydrate	29.4g
Fiber	1.3g

COOK'S TIP

Baby zucchini would make a delicious alternative to bananas.

1 Set aside two or three cilantro sprigs for the garnish. If necessary, remove the roots and any thick stems from the remaining cilantro, then chop the leaves finely.

2 Trim the bananas or plantains and cut each crosswise into three equal pieces, leaving the skin on. Make a lengthwise slit along each piece of banana, without cutting all the way through the flesh.

3 On a plate mix together the ground coriander, cumin, chili powder, salt, turmeric, sugar, besan flour, chopped fresh cilantro, and 1 tablespoon of the oil. Use your fingers to combine well.

4 Carefully stuff each piece of banana with the spice mixture, being careful not to break the bananas in half.

5 Heat the remaining oil in a wok, karahi, or large pan, and fry the cumin and mustard seeds for 2 minutes, or until they begin to splutter. Add the bananas and toss gently in the oil.

6 Cover and simmer over a low heat for 15 minutes, stirring from time to time, until the bananas are soft but not mushy.

7 Garnish with the fresh cilantro sprigs, and serve with warm chapatis, if desired.

Chile and Mustard Flavored Pineapple

Pineapple is cooked with coconut milk and a blend of spices in this South Indian dish, which could be served with any meat, fish, or vegetable curry. The chile adds heat, and the mustard seeds lend a rich, nutty flavor that complements the sharpness of the pineapple, while the coconut milk provides a delectable creamy sweetness.

INGREDIENTS

Serves 4
1 pineapple
¼ cup water
⅔ cup coconut milk
½ teaspoon ground turmeric
½ teaspoon crushed dried chiles
1 teaspoon salt
2 teaspoons sugar
1 tablespoon peanut oil
½ teaspoon mustard seeds
½ teaspoon cumin seeds
1 small onion, finely chopped
1–2 dried red chiles, broken
6–8 fresh curry leaves

1 Using a sharp knife, halve the pineapple lengthwise, then cut each half into two, so that you end up with four boat-shaped wedges. Peel them and remove the eyes and the central core. Cut into bitesize pieces.

2 Put the pineapple in a karahi, wok, or large pan and add the measured water, with the coconut milk, turmeric, and crushed chiles. Bring to a slow simmer over a low heat, and cook, covered, for 10–12 minutes, or until the pineapple is soft, but not mushy.

3 Add the salt and sugar, and cook, uncovered, until the sauce thickens.

4 Heat the oil in a second pan and add the mustard seeds. As soon as they begin to pop, add the cumin seeds and the onion. Fry for 6–7 minutes, stirring regularly, until the onion is soft.

5 Add the chiles and curry leaves. Fry for 1–2 minutes more, then pour the entire contents over the pineapple. Stir well, then remove from the heat. Serve hot or cold, but not chilled.

COOK'S TIP

Use canned pineapple in natural juice to save time. You will need approximately 1¼ pounds drained pineapple.

NUTRITIONAL NOTES
Per Portion

Energy	60cal
Fat	3g
Saturated Fat	0.6g
Carbohydrate	8.3g
Fiber	0.8g

Yogurt Salad

If this salad looks and tastes familiar, it isn't surprising. It is very similar to coleslaw, except that yogurt is used instead of mayonnaise, and cashew nuts are added.

INGREDIENTS

Serves 4

1½ cups plain low-fat yogurt
2 teaspoons honey
2 medium carrots,
   thickly sliced
2 scallions, roughly chopped
4 ounces cabbage,
   finely shredded
⅓ cup golden raisins
½ cup cashew nuts, optional
16 white grapes, halved
½ teaspoon salt
1 teaspoon chopped fresh mint

1 Using a fork, beat the yogurt in a bowl with the honey.

2 In a separate bowl, which will be suitable for serving the salad, mix together the carrots, scallions, cabbage, golden raisins, cashew nuts (if you are using them), grapes, salt, and chopped mint.

3 Pour the sweetened yogurt mixture over the salad, mix well, and serve.

NUTRITIONAL NOTES	
Per Portion	
Energy	119cal
Fat	0.90g
Saturated Fat	0.49g
Carbohydrate	23.40g
Fiber	1.80g

Spicy Baby Vegetable Salad

This warm vegetable salad makes an excellent accompaniment.

INGREDIENTS

Serves 6

10 small new potatoes, halved
15 baby carrots
10 baby zucchini
1½ cups white mushrooms

For the dressing

3 tablespoons lemon juice
1½ tablespoons oil
1 tablespoon chopped fresh
   cilantro
1 teaspoon salt
2 fresh green chiles,
   finely sliced

1 Boil the potatoes, carrots, and zucchini in water until tender. Drain them and place in a serving dish with the mushrooms.

2 Make the dressing in a separate bowl. Mix together the lemon juice, oil, fresh cilantro, salt, and chiles.

3 Toss the vegetables in the dressing and serve immediately.

NUTRITIONAL NOTES	
Per Portion	
Energy	73cal
Fat	3.10g
Saturated Fat	0.39g
Carbohydrate	10.10g
Fiber	1.50g

COOK'S TIP

As well as looking extremely attractive, the tiny baby vegetables give this salad a lovely flavor. Other baby vegetables, such as leeks, miniature corn cobs or egg-size cauliflowers can be used just as well.

Spinach and Mushroom Salad

This salad is especially good served with glazed garlic shrimp or any other seafood curry.

INGREDIENTS

Serves 4
10 baby corn cobs
3 cups mushrooms
2 medium tomatoes
20 small spinach leaves
8–10 onion rings
salt and black pepper
fresh cilantro sprigs and lime slices, to garnish, optional

1 Halve the baby corn cobs and slice the mushrooms and tomatoes.

2 Arrange all the salad ingredients in a bowl. Season with salt and pepper and garnish with fresh cilantro and lime slices, if desired.

_____ COOK'S TIP _____

Baby corn can be eaten whole or sliced in half lengthwise. Don't overcook them or they will lose their sweetness and be tough. To use in salads, cook for about 3 minutes.

NUTRITIONAL NOTES	
Per Portion	
Energy	25cal
Fat	0.60g
Saturated Fat	0.09g
Carbohydrate	2.80g
Fiber	1.80g

Nutty Salad

The smooth creamy dressing is perfect with the crunchy nuts.

INGREDIENTS

Serves 4
5 ounce can red kidney beans, drained
1 medium onion, cut into 12 rings
1 medium zucchini, sliced
1 medium yellow squash, sliced
²⁄₃ cup pasta shells, cooked
½ cup cashew nuts
¼ cup peanuts
fresh cilantro and lime wedges, to garnish

For the dressing
4 ounces low-fat ricotta cheese
2 tablespoons plain low-fat yogurt
1 fresh green chile, chopped
1 tablespoon chopped fresh cilantro
salt and pepper
½ teaspoon crushed dried red chiles
1 tablespoon lemon juice

1 Drain the kidney beans. Arrange them with the onion rings, kidney beans, zucchini slices, and pasta in a salad dish and sprinkle the cashew nuts and peanuts over the top.

2 In a separate bowl, mix together the ricotta cheese, yogurt, green chile, fresh cilantro, and salt. Beat well using a fork until all the ingredients are thoroughly combined. You may find it easier to add the cilantro leaves a few at a time and mix in to let their flavor permeate the mixture and ensure the resulting dressing is smooth in texture.

3 Sprinkle the crushed peppercorns, red chiles, and lemon juice over the dressing. Garnish the salad with fresh cilantro and lime wedges and serve with the dressing.

NUTRITIONAL NOTES	
Per Portion	
Energy	199cal
Fat	11.60g
Saturated Fat	2.63g
Carbohydrate	15.20g
Fiber	2.90g

_____ COOK'S TIP _____

Make the dressing just before serving the salad, when the flavor of the cilantro will be at its most intense.

Sweet Potato and Carrot Salad

This warm salad has a piquant flavor. As a main course, it will serve two.

INGREDIENTS

Serves 4
1 medium sweet potato
2 carrots, cut into thick diagonal slices
3 medium tomatoes
8–10 iceberg lettuce leaves
½ cup drained canned chickpeas

For the dressing
1 tablespoon honey
6 tablespoons plain low-fat yogurt
½ teaspoon salt
1 teaspoon coarsely ground
   black pepper

For the garnish
1 tablespoon walnuts
1 tablespoon golden raisins
1 small onion, cut into rings

1 Peel and dice the sweet potato. Cook in boiling water until soft but not mushy, remove from the heat, cover the pan, and set aside.

NUTRITIONAL NOTES	
Per Portion	
Energy	127cal
Fat	3.70g
Saturated Fat	0.47g
Carbohydrate	20.60g
Fiber	3.10g

2 Cook the carrots in a pan of boiling water for just a few minutes, making sure that they remain crunchy. Add the carrots to the sweet potatoes.

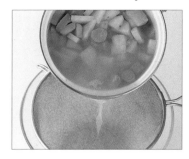

3 Drain the water from the sweet potatoes and carrots and mix them together in a bowl.

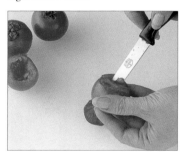

4 Slice the tops off the tomatoes, then scoop out and discard the seeds. Roughly chop the flesh.

COOK'S TIP
The skin of sweet potatoes may be pink or orangey yellow and the flesh can range from mealy to moist and from almost white to deep yellow in color. It is best to boil or bake sweet potatoes in their skins if possible, because some varieties turn a dullish color if boiled peeled.

5 Line a glass bowl with the lettuce. Add the carrots, chickpeas, and tomatoes to the potatoes and carrots. Mix lightly, then spoon the mixture into the lettuce-lined bowl.

6 Mix together all the dressing ingredients and beat, using a fork.

7 Garnish the salad with the walnuts, golden raisins, and onion rings. Pour the dressing over the salad or serve it in a separate bowl.

Carrot and Orange Salad

A fruit and a vegetable that could have been made for each other form the basis of this wonderful, fresh-tasting salad.

INGREDIENTS

Serves 4
1 pound carrots
2 large oranges
1 tablespoon olive oil
2 tablespoons lemon juice
pinch of sugar, optional
2 tablespoons chopped pistachio nuts
   or toasted pine nuts
salt and black pepper

1 Peel the carrots and grate them into a large bowl.

2 Peel the oranges with a sharp knife and cut into segments, catching the juice in a small bowl.

_____ COOK'S TIP _____

Squeeze the orange pulp after removing the segments to extract the maximum amount of juice.

3 Mix together the olive oil, lemon juice, and orange juice. Season with a little salt and pepper to taste, and sugar if you like.

NUTRITIONAL NOTES	
Per Portion	
Energy	148cal
Fat	7.4g
Saturated Fat	1.1g
Carbohydrate	18.4g
Fiber	5g

4 Toss the orange segments together with the carrots and pour the dressing over. Sprinkle the salad with the pistachio nuts or pine nuts before serving.

Fennel Coleslaw

Here is another variation on traditional coleslaw, in which the aniseed flavor of fennel plays a major role.

INGREDIENTS

Serves 4
6 ounces fennel
2 scallions
6 ounces white cabbage
4 ounces celery
6 ounces carrots
⅓ cup golden raisins
½ teaspoon caraway seeds
1 tablespoon chopped
   fresh parsley
3 tablespoons extra-virgin olive oil
1 teaspoon lemon juice
shreds of scallion, to garnish

1 Using a sharp knife, cut the fennel and scallions into thin slices.

2 Slice the cabbage and celery finely and cut the carrots into fine strips. Place in a bowl with the fennel and scallions. Add the golden raisins and caraway seeds and toss lightly to mix.

3 Stir in the chopped parsley, olive oil, and lemon juice and mix all the ingredients thoroughly. Cover and chill for 3 hours to let the flavors mingle. Serve garnished with shreds of scallion.

--- VARIATION ---

Use sour cream instead of olive oil for a creamier dressing.

NUTRITIONAL NOTES	
Per Portion	
Energy	146cal
Fat	8.7g
Saturated Fat	1.2g
Carbohydrate	15.9g
Fiber	3.8g

Spicy Potato Salad

This tasty salad is quick to prepare, and it makes a satisfying accompaniment to broiled or barbecued meat or fish.

INGREDIENTS

Serves 6
2 pounds potatoes
2 red bell peppers
2 celery stalks
1 shallot
2 or 3 scallions
1 fresh green chile
1 garlic clove, crushed
2 teaspoons finely chopped fresh chives
2 teaspoons finely chopped fresh basil
1 tablespoon finely chopped
  fresh parsley
2 tablespoons light cream
3 tablespoons mayonnaise
1 teaspoon prepared mild mustard
1½ teaspoons sugar
salt
chopped fresh chives, to garnish

3 Mix the cream, mayonnaise, mustard, and sugar in a small bowl, stirring until the mixture is well combined.

4 Pour the dressing over the salad and stir gently to coat evenly. Serve, garnished with the chopped chives.

NUTRITIONAL NOTES	
Per Portion	
Energy	185cal
Fat	6.7g
Saturated Fat	1.3g
Carbohydrate	29.3g
Fiber	2.6g

1 Peel the potatoes. Boil in salted water for 10–12 minutes, until tender. Drain and cool, then cut into cubes and place in a large mixing bowl.

2 Halve the bell peppers, cut away and discard the core and seeds, and cut the flesh into small pieces. Finely chop the celery, shallot, and scallions and slice the chile very thinly, discarding the seeds. Add the vegetables to the potatoes, together with the garlic and herbs.

Coronation Chicken

The connection between this recipe and traditional Indian cooking is tenuous, but coronation chicken is such a popular dish that it would have been churlish to leave it out.

INGREDIENTS

Serves 6
1 pound new potatoes
3 tablespoons French dressing
3 scallions, chopped
6 eggs, hard-boiled and halved
frilly lettuce
¼ cucumber, cut into thin strips
6 large radishes, sliced
salad cress, optional
salt and pepper

For the coronation dressing
2 tablespoons olive oil
1 small onion, chopped
1 tablespoon mild curry powder
   or korma spice mix
2 teaspoons tomato paste
2 tablespoons lemon juice
2 tablespoons sherry
1¼ cups mayonnaise
⅔ cup plain yogurt

1 Boil the potatoes in salted water until tender. Drain them, transfer to a large bowl, and toss in the French dressing while they are still warm.

2 Stir in the scallions and the salt and pepper, and let stand to cool thoroughly.

3 Meanwhile, make the coronation dressing. Heat the oil in a small pan. Fry the onion for 3 minutes, until soft. Stir in the curry powder or spice mix and fry for another 1 minute. Remove from the heat and mix in all the other dressing ingredients.

4 Stir the dressing into the potatoes, add the eggs, then chill.

5 Line a serving platter with the lettuce and pile the salad in the center. Sprinkle over the cucumber and radishes with the cress, if using.

NUTRITIONAL NOTES	
Per Portion	
Energy	597cal
Fat	53g
Saturated Fat	8.8g
Carbohydrate	15.2g
Fiber	1.2g

Peppery Bean Salad

This pretty salad uses canned beans for speed and convenience.

INGREDIENTS

Serves 4–6

15-ounce can red kidney beans
15-ounce can black-eyed peas
15 ounce can chickpeas
¼ red bell pepper
¼ green bell pepper
6 radishes
1 tablespoon chopped scallion

For the dressing

1 teaspoon ground cumin
1 tablespoon ketchup
2 tablespoons olive oil
1 tablespoon white wine vinegar
1 garlic clove, crushed
½ teaspoon hot pepper sauce

1 Drain the red kidney beans, black-eyed peas, and chickpeas and rinse under cold running water. Shake off the excess water and put them into a large bowl.

2 Core, seed, and chop the bell peppers. Trim the radishes and slice thinly. Add the bell peppers, radishes, and scallion to the bowl.

3 Make the dressing. Mix together the cumin, ketchup, oil, vinegar, and garlic in a small bowl. Add a little salt and hot pepper sauce to taste and stir again thoroughly.

4 Pour the dressing over the salad and mix. Cover the salad and chill for at least 1 hour before serving, garnished with the sliced scallion.

_____ COOK'S TIP _____

Look out for cans of mixed beans at the supermarket. These contain a colorful medley and would be perfect for this salad.

NUTRITIONAL NOTES	
Per Portion	
Energy	430cal
Fat	9.3g
Saturated Fat	1.3g
Carbohydrate	64.8g
Fiber	19.8g

Mango, Tomato, and Red Onion Salad

This salad makes a delicious appetizer. The under-ripe mango blends well with the tomato.

INGREDIENTS

Serves 4

1 firm under-ripe mango
2 large tomatoes or 1 beef
   tomato, sliced
½ red onion, sliced into rings
½ cucumber, peeled and thinly sliced
chopped chives, to garnish

For the dressing

2 tablespoons vegetable oil
1 tablespoon lemon juice
1 garlic clove, crushed
½ teaspoon hot pepper sauce
salt and black pepper

1 Have the mango lengthwise, cutting either side of the pit. Cut the flesh into slices and peel the skin away neatly.

2 Arrange the mango, tomatoes, onion, and cucumber on a large serving plate.

3 Make the dressing. Blend the oil, lemon juice, garlic, pepper sauce, and seasoning in a blender or food processor, or shake vigorously in a small screw-top jar.

NUTRITIONAL NOTES	
Per Portion	
Energy	89cal
Fat	5.8g
Saturated Fat	0.7g
Carbohydrate	8.6g
Fiber	1.9g

4 Spoon the dressing over the salad. Garnish with the chopped chives and serve.

Relishes and Chutneys

ONE OF the delights of dining out on Indian food is the dazzling selection of relishes and chutneys that always accompanies the meal. Unlike bottled chutneys, which are slow-cooked and tend to be jamlike in consistency, these are usually freshly made mixtures, where each of the component flavors can be easily discerned.

Relishes and chutneys have a variety of purposes at the table. Raita cools the palate, while Hot Lime Pickle has the opposite effect. Fresh Cilantro Relish is ideal for providing lovely color and fresh flavor, and works perfectly with spicy kebabs and samosas. Mango Chutney is an old favorite, often served as a sweet and fruity dip with poppadums, as well as in its more traditional role as a tangy accompaniment for curries. Finally, there's Bombay Duck Pickle, one of the curiosities of the culinary world. Made with salted fish rather than fowl, it's a special and unique contribution to Indian cuisine.

Spiced Yogurt

Yogurt is always a welcome accompaniment to hot curries. This is topped with a hot spice mixture to provide a contrast in both taste and temperature.

INGREDIENTS

Makes scant 2 cups
scant 2 cups plain yogurt
½ teaspoon freshly ground
    fennel seeds
salt, to taste
½ teaspoon sugar
4 tablespoons vegetable oil
1 dried red chile
¼ teaspoon mustard seeds
¼ teaspoon cumin seeds
4–6 curry leaves
pinch each of asafetida and
    ground turmeric

1 In a heatproof serving dish, mix together the yogurt, fennel seeds, salt, and sugar. Cover and chill until you are nearly ready to serve.

2 Heat the oil in a skillet and fry the dried chile, mustard and cumin seeds, curry leaves, asafetida, and turmeric. When the chile turns dark, pour the oil and spices over the yogurt. Fold the yogurt together with the spices at the table when serving.

NUTRITIONAL NOTES	
Per 2-tablespoon Portion	
Energy	36cal
Fat	2.6g
Saturated Fat	0.4g
Carbohydrate	1.8g
Fiber	0g

——————— COOK'S TIP ———————

Asafetida is bitter, but you can leave it out if you prefer.

Raita

Raitas are served to cool the effect of
hot curries. Cucumber and mint raita
is the best known combination. This
is a refreshing fruit and nut version,
which is particularly good with
beef curries.

INGREDIENTS

Serves 4

1½ cups plain yogurt
3 ounces seedless grapes
½ cup shelled walnuts
2 firm bananas
1 teaspoon sugar
salt, to taste
1 teaspoon freshly ground cumin seeds
¼ teaspoon freshly roasted cumin
  seeds, chili powder, or paprika,
  to garnish

1 Place the yogurt in a chilled bowl
and add the grapes and walnuts.
Slice the bananas directly into the bowl
and fold in gently before the bananas
turn brown.

2 Add the sugar, salt, and ground
cumin, and gently mix together.
Chill, and just before serving, sprinkle
on the cumin seeds, chili powder,
or paprika.

―――――― VARIATIONS ――――――

Instead of grapes, try kiwis, peaches, or
nectarines. Almonds or hazelnuts can be
used instead of, or as well as, the walnuts.

NUTRITIONAL NOTES	
Per Portion	
Energy	184cal
Fat	9.6g
Saturated Fat	1.2g
Carbohydrate	19.2g
Fiber	1g

Sweet and Sour Raita

This raita teams honey with mint sauce, chile, and fresh cilantro to make a soothing mixture with underlying warmth. It goes well with biryanis.

INGREDIENTS

Serves 4

2 cups plain low-fat yogurt
1 teaspoon salt
1 teaspoon sugar
2 tablespoons honey
1½ teaspoons mint sauce
2 tablespoons roughly chopped
　fresh cilantro
1 fresh green chile, seeded and
　finely chopped
1 medium onion, diced
¼ cup water

1 Pour the yogurt into a bowl and whisk it well. Add the salt, sugar, honey, and mint sauce.

2 Taste to check the sweetness and add more honey, if desired.

3 Reserve a little chopped cilantro for the garnish and add the rest to the yogurt mixture, with the chile, onion, and water.

4 Whisk once again and pour into a serving bowl. Garnish with the reserved cilantro and place in the refrigerator until ready to serve.

NUTRITIONAL NOTES	
Per Portion	
Energy	128cal
Fat	1.18g
Saturated Fat	0.64g
Carbohydrate	24.40g
Fiber	0.53g

COOK'S TIP

A 2–4-inch piece of peeled, seeded, and grated cucumber can also be added to raita. Drain the cucumber in a colander, pressing it against the sides to extract excess liquid, which would dilute the raita.

Fried Sesame Seed Chutney

This versatile chutney doubles as a dip, and also a sandwich filling with thin slices of cucumber.

INGREDIENTS

Serves 4

3/4 cup sesame seeds
1 teaspoon salt
1/2–2/3 cup water
2 fresh green chiles, seeded and diced
4 tablespoons chopped fresh cilantro
1 tablespoon chopped fresh mint
1 tablespoon tamarind paste
2 tablespoons sugar
1 teaspoon oil
1/4 teaspoon onion seeds
4 curry leaves
onion rings, sliced chiles, and fresh cilantro leaves, to garnish

1 Dry-roast the sesame seeds and let cool. Grind them in a coffee grinder to a grainy powder.

NUTRITIONAL NOTES	
Per Portion	
Energy	347cal
Fat	28.31g
Saturated Fat	4.03g
Carbohydrate	25.31g
Fiber	3.63g

2 Transfer the sesame powder to a bowl. Add the salt, water, diced chiles, cilantro, mint, tamarind paste, and sugar, and use a fork to mix everything together. Taste and adjust the seasoning if necessary; the mixture should have a sweet-and-sour flavor.

3 Heat the oil in a heavy pan and fry the onion seeds and curry leaves. Tip the sesame seed paste into the pan and stir-fry for about 45 seconds. Transfer the chutney to a serving dish and let cool.

4 Garnish with onion rings, sliced green and red chiles, and fresh cilantro leaves and serve with your chosen curry.

Fresh Tomato and Onion Chutney

Chutneys are served with most meat dishes in Indian cuisine.

INGREDIENTS

Serves 4

8 tomatoes
1 medium onion, chopped
3 tablespoons brown sugar
1 teaspoon garam masala
1 teaspoon ground ginger
³/₄ cup malt vinegar
1 teaspoon salt
1 tablespoon honey
plain yogurt, sliced green chile, and
    fresh mint leaves, to garnish

—————— COOK'S TIP ——————

This chutney will keep for about 2 weeks in a covered jar in the refrigerator.

1 Wash the tomatoes and cut them into quarters.

NUTRITIONAL NOTES	
Per Portion	
Energy	118cal
Fat	0.66g
Saturated Fat	0.18g
Carbohydrate	43.90g
Fiber	2.34g

2 Place them with the onion in a heavy pan.

3 Add the sugar, garam masala, ginger, vinegar, salt, and honey, half-cover the pan with a lid, and cook over a low heat for about 20 minutes.

4 Mash the tomatoes with a fork to break them up, then continue to cook on a slightly higher heat until the chutney thickens.

5 Spoon the chutney into a bowl and let cool, then cover and place in the refrigerator until needed. Serve chilled, garnished with yogurt, sliced chile, and mint leaves.

Sweet and Sour Tomato and Onion Relish

This delicious relish can be served with any savory meal.

INGREDIENTS

Serves 4
2 medium firm tomatoes
1 medium onion
1 fresh green chile
1 tablespoon fresh mint leaves
1 tablespoon fresh cilantro leaves
½ teaspoon Tabasco sauce
1 tablespoon honey
½ teaspoon salt
2 tablespoons lime juice
1 tablespoon plain low-fat yogurt

1 Place the tomatoes in hot water for a few seconds. Lift each tomato out in turn, using a slotted spoon. The skins should have split, making it easy to remove them. Peel off carefully. Cut the tomatoes in half, and squeeze out the seeds. Chop them roughly. Set aside.

2 Using a sharp knife, roughly chop the onion, green chile, mint, and fresh cilantro.

3 Place the herb mixture in a food processor with the Tabasco sauce, honey, salt, and lime juice. Add the tomatoes to this and grind everything together for a few seconds.

___ COOK'S TIP ___

This relish will keep for up to 1 week in the refrigerator: prepare up to the end of step 3 but do not add the yogurt until just before you want to serve it.

4 Pour into a small serving bowl. Stir in the yogurt just before you serve the relish.

NUTRITIONAL NOTES	
Per Portion	
Energy	43cal
Fat	0.29g
Saturated Fat	0.06g
Carbohydrate	9.43g
Fiber	0.96g

Spicy Tomato Chutney

This delicious relish is especially good with lentil dishes. If kept in a covered bowl in the refrigerator, it will keep for a week.

INGREDIENTS

Makes 2–2¼ cups
6 tablespoons vegetable oil
2-inch piece cinnamon stick
4 cloves
1 teaspoon freshly roasted cumin seeds
1 teaspoon nigella seeds
4 bay leaves
1 teaspoon mustard seeds, crushed
1¾ pounds canned, chopped tomatoes
4 garlic cloves, crushed
2-inch piece fresh ginger root, crushed
1 teaspoon chili powder
1 teaspoon ground turmeric
4 tablespoons brown sugar

1 Pour the oil into a skillet, karahi, or wok and place over a medium heat. When the oil is hot, fry the cinnamon, cloves, cumin and nigella seeds, bay leaves, and mustard seeds for about 5 minutes.

2 Crush the garlic cloves and add them to the spice mixture. Fry until golden. Meanwhile, drain the tomatoes, reserving the juices.

3 Add the ginger, chili powder, turmeric, sugar, and the reserved tomato juices. Simmer until reduced, add the tomatoes, and cook for 15–20 minutes. Cool and serve.

NUTRITIONAL NOTES	
Per 2-tablespoon Portion	
Energy	53cal
Fat	3.8g
Saturated Fat	0.5g
Carbohydrate	4.8g
Fiber	0.4g

Mango Chutney

Chutneys are usually served as an accompaniment to curry, but this one is particularly nice served in a cheese sandwich or as a dip with poppadums.

INGREDIENTS

Makes 2 cups
4 tablespoons vinegar
½ teaspoon crushed dried chiles
6 cloves
6 peppercorns
1 teaspoon roasted cumin seeds
½ teaspoon onion seeds
salt, to taste
¾ cup sugar
1 pound unripe mangoes,
    peeled and cubed
2-inch piece fresh ginger,
    thinly sliced
2 garlic cloves, crushed
thin peel of 1 orange or lemon,
    optional

1 Pour the vinegar into a pan, and add the chiles, cloves, peppercorns, cumin and onion seeds, salt, and sugar. Place over a low heat and simmer until the spices infuse the vinegar—about 15 minutes.

2 Add the mango, ginger, garlic, and peel, if using. Simmer until the mango is mushy and most of the vinegar has evaporated. When cool, pour into sterilized bottles. Cover and let stand for a few days before serving.

_____ COOK'S TIP _____

Ginger freezes very well, which can be handy if you find it difficult to get fresh ginger locally. It can be sliced or grated straight from the freezer and will thaw on contact with hot food.

NUTRITIONAL NOTES	
Per 2-tablespoon Portion	
Energy	52cal
Fat	0g
Saturated Fat	0g
Carbohydrate	13.7g
Fiber	0.7g

Tomato Relish

This is a simple relish served with most meals. It provides a contrast to hot curries, with its crunchy texture and refreshing ingredients.

INGREDIENTS

Serves 4–6

2 small fresh green chiles
2 limes
½ teaspoon sugar
2 onions, finely chopped
4 firm tomatoes, finely chopped
½ cucumber, finely chopped
few fresh cilantro
   leaves, chopped
salt and black pepper
few fresh mint leaves, to garnish

1 Using a sharp knife, cut both chiles in half. Scrape out the seeds, then chop the chiles finely and place them in a small bowl.

--- COOK'S TIP ---

For a milder flavor, use just one chile, or dispense with the chiles altogether and substitute with a green bell pepper.

2 Squeeze the limes. Pour the juice into a glass bowl and add the sugar, with salt and pepper to taste. Set the bowl aside until the sugar and salt have dissolved, stirring the mixture occasionally.

3 Add the chopped chiles to the bowl, with the chopped onions, tomatoes, cucumber, and fresh cilantro leaves. Mix well.

4 Cover the bowl with plastic wrap and place in the refrigerator for at least 3 hours, so that the flavors blend. Just before serving, taste the relish and add more salt, pepper, or sugar if needed. Garnish with mint and serve.

NUTRITIONAL NOTES	
Per Portion	
Energy	47cal
Fat	0.5g
Saturated Fat	0.1g
Carbohydrate	9.4g
Fiber	2.3g

Fresh Cilantro Relish

Delicious as an accompaniment
to kebabs, samosas, and bhajias,
this relish can also be used as
a spread for cucumber or
tomato sandwiches.

INGREDIENTS

Makes about 2 cups
2 tablespoons vegetable oil
1 dried red chile
¼ teaspoon each, cumin, fennel,
   and onion seeds
¼ teaspoon asafetida
4 curry leaves
1⅓ cups dry unsweetened
   shredded coconut
2 teaspoons sugar
salt, to taste
3 fresh green chiles, chopped
6–8 ounces fresh cilantro, chopped
4 tablespoons mint sauce
juice of 3 lemons

1 Heat the oil in a skillet and add
the dried chile, the cumin, fennel,
and onion seeds, the asafetida, curry
leaves, shredded coconut, sugar, and
salt. Fry, stirring often, until the
coconut turns golden brown. Pour
into a bowl and let cool.

2 Grind the spice mixture with
the green chiles, fresh cilantro,
and mint sauce. Moisten with lemon
juice. Scrape into a bowl and chill
before serving.

NUTRITIONAL NOTES	
Per 2-tablespoon Portion	
Energy	51cal
Fat	5.2g
Saturated Fat	3.5g
Carbohydrate	0.8g
Fiber	0.9g

_____ COOK'S TIP _____

This may seem like a lot of cilantro, but it
is compacted when ground with the spices.

Red Onion, Garlic, and Lemon Relish

This powerful relish is flavored with spices and punchy preserved lemons. It reached India by way of Spain, being introduced by Jewish refugees forced to leave that country in the 15th century.

INGREDIENTS

Serves 6
3 tablespoons olive oil
3 large red onions, sliced
2 heads of garlic, separated
    into cloves and peeled
2 teaspoons coriander seeds, crushed
    but not finely ground
2 teaspoons light brown sugar,
    plus a little extra
pinch of saffron threads
2-inch piece cinnamon stick
2–3 small whole dried red
    chiles, optional
2 fresh bay leaves
2–3 tablespoons sherry vinegar
juice of ½ small orange
2 tablespoons chopped preserved lemon
salt and black pepper

1 Heat the oil in a heavy pan. Add the onions and stir, then cover and reduce the heat to the lowest setting. Cook for 10–15 minutes, stirring occasionally, until the onions are soft and pale gold in color.

2 Add the whole peeled garlic cloves and the crushed coriander seeds. Cover and cook for 5–8 minutes, until the garlic is soft.

3 Add a pinch of salt, a lot of pepper, and the sugar. Stir, then cook, uncovered, for 5 minutes. Soak the saffron in about 3 tablespoons warm water for 5 minutes, then add to the onions, with the soaking water.

4 Add the cinnamon stick, dried chiles, if using, and bay leaves. Stir in 2 tablespoons of the sherry vinegar and the orange juice.

NUTRITIONAL NOTES	
Per Portion	
Energy	107cal
Fat	5.8g
Saturated Fat	0.8g
Carbohydrate	12g
Fiber	2.2g

5 Cook over a low heat, uncovered, until the onions are very soft and most of the liquid has evaporated. Stir in the preserved lemon and cook gently for another 5 minutes. Taste and adjust the seasoning, adding more salt, sugar, and/or vinegar to taste.

6 Serve warm or cold, but not hot or chilled. The relish tastes best if it is left to stand for 24 hours.

English Pickled Onions

The English love of pickled onions is famous, and at the time of the Raj the popular pickle was introduced into India. They should be stored for at least 6 weeks before being eaten.

INGREDIENTS

Makes 1 pound jar

2¼ pounds pearl onions
½ cup salt
3 cups malt vinegar
1 tablespoon sugar
2–3 dried red chiles
1 teaspoon brown mustard seeds
1 tablespoon coriander seeds
1 teaspoon allspice berries
1 teaspoon black peppercorns
2-inch piece fresh ginger root, sliced
2–3 blades of mace
2–3 fresh bay leaves

1 Trim off the root end of each onion, but leave the onion layers attached. Cut a thin slice off the top (neck) end of each onion. Place the onions in a bowl, then cover with boiling water. Let stand for about 4 minutes, then drain. Peel off the skin from each onion with a small, sharp knife.

2 Place the peeled onions in a bowl and cover with cold water, then drain the water off and pour it into a large pan. Add the salt and heat slightly to dissolve it, then cool before pouring the brine over the onions.

3 Cover the bowl with a plate and weigh it down slightly so that all the onions are submerged in the brine. Let the onions stand in the salted water for 24 hours.

4 Pour the vinegar into a large pan. Wrap all the remaining ingredients, except the bay leaves, in a piece of cheesecloth or sew them into a coffee filter paper and add to the vinegar with the bay leaves. Bring to a boil, simmer for 5 minutes, then remove from the heat. Set aside to cool and soak overnight.

5 Drain the onions, rinse, and pat dry. Pack them into sterilized jars. Add some or all of the spice from the vinegar, but not the ginger slices. The pickle will get hotter if you add the chiles. Pour the vinegar over the onions to cover and add the bay leaves. Cover the jars with nonmetallic lids and store in a cool dark place for at least 6 weeks before eating.

NUTRITIONAL NOTES	
Per Portion	
Energy	120cal
Fat	0.7g
Saturated Fat	0g
Carbohydrate	26.3g
Fiber	4.7g

_____ VARIATION _____

To make sweet pickled onions, follow the same method, but add 4 tablespoons light brown sugar to the vinegar. A couple of pieces of cinnamon stick and 1 teaspoon cloves are good additions to this version.

_____ COOK'S TIP _____

For sterilizing, stand clean, rinsed jars upside down on a rack on a baking sheet and place in the oven at 350°F for about 20 minutes.

Fresh Coconut Chutney with Onion and Chile

Serve a bowl of this tasty fresh chutney as an accompaniment for any Indian-style main course.

INGREDIENTS

Serves 4–6
7 ounces fresh coconut, grated
3–4 fresh green chiles, seeded
  and chopped
⅔ cup fresh cilantro, chopped,
  plus 2–3 sprigs to garnish
2 tablespoons chopped fresh mint
2–3 tablespoons lime juice
½ teaspoon salt
½ teaspoon sugar
1–2 tablespoons coconut milk, optional
2 tablespoons peanut oil
1 teaspoon nigella seeds
1 small onion, very finely chopped

1 Place the coconut, chiles, cilantro, and mint in a food processor. Add 2 tablespoons of the lime juice, then process until thoroughly chopped.

2 Scrape the mixture into a bowl and add more lime juice to taste. Add salt and sugar to taste. If the mixture is dry, stir in 1–2 tablespoons coconut milk.

3 Heat the oil in a small pan and fry the nigella seeds until they begin to pop, then reduce the heat and add the onion. Fry, stirring frequently, for 4–5 minutes, until the onion is soft.

4 Stir the onion mixture into the coconut mixture and let cool. Garnish with cilantro before serving.

NUTRITIONAL NOTES	
Per Portion	
Energy	168cal
Fat	17.2g
Saturated Fat	11.1g
Carbohydrate	2.4g
Fiber	2.8g

Onion, Mango, and Peanut Chaat

Chaats are spiced relishes of vegetables and nuts, delicious with many savory Indian dishes.

INGREDIENTS

Serves 4
scant 1 cup unsalted peanuts
1 tablespoon peanut oil
1 onion, chopped
½ cucumber, seeded and diced
1 mango, peeled, pitted, and diced
1 fresh green chile, seeded and chopped
2 tablespoons chopped fresh cilantro
1 tablespoon chopped fresh mint
1 tablespoon lime juice
pinch of light brown sugar

For the chaat masala
2 teaspoons ground toasted cumin seeds
½ teaspoon cayenne pepper
1 teaspoon dried mango powder
  (amchur)
½ teaspoon garam masala
pinch ground asafetida
salt and black pepper

1 To make the chaat masala, grind all the spices together, then season with ½ teaspoon each of salt and pepper.

2 Fry the peanuts in the oil until lightly browned, then drain on paper towels until cool.

3 Mix the onion, cucumber, mango, chile, fresh cilantro, and mint in a bowl. Sprinkle in 1 teaspoon of the chaat masala. Stir in the peanuts and then add lime juice and/or sugar to taste. Set the mixture aside for 20–30 minutes so the flavors mature.

4 Spoon the mixture into a serving bowl, sprinkle another 1 teaspoon of the chaat masala over, and serve.

_____ COOK'S TIP _____

Any remaining chaat masala will keep in a sealed jar for 4–6 weeks.

NUTRITIONAL NOTES	
Per Portion	
Energy	187cal
Fat	13.3g
Saturated Fat	2.5g
Carbohydrate	11.1g
Fiber	2.9g

Apricot Chutney

Chutneys can add zest to most meals, and in India you will usually find a selection of different kinds served in tiny bowls for people to choose from. Dried apricots are readily available from supermarkets or health food stores.

INGREDIENTS

Makes about 2 cups
3 cups dried apricots, finely diced
1 teaspoon garam masala
1¼ cups brown sugar
scant 2 cups malt vinegar
1 teaspoon grated fresh ginger root
1 teaspoon salt
½ cup golden raisins
scant 2 cups water

1 Put all the ingredients into a medium pan and mix thoroughly with a spoon.

NUTRITIONAL NOTES	
Per 2-tablespoon Portion	
Energy	118cal
Fat	0.2g
Saturated Fat	0g
Carbohydrate	29.7g
Fiber	2.0g

2 Bring to a boil, reduce the heat, and simmer for 30–35 minutes, stirring occasionally.

3 When the chutney has thickened to a stiff consistency, spoon it into 2–3 clean jam jars and let cool. This chutney should be stored in the refrigerator.

Tasty Toasts

These crunchy toasts make an ideal snack or part of a brunch. They are especially delicious served with broiled tomatoes and baked beans.

INGREDIENTS

Makes 4
4 eggs
1¼ cups milk
2 fresh green chiles, finely chopped
2 tablespoons chopped fresh cilantro
¾ cup cheddar or mozzarella cheese, grated
½ teaspoon salt
¼ teaspoon ground black pepper
4 slices bread
corn oil for frying

1 Break the eggs into a medium bowl and whisk together. Slowly add the milk and whisk again. Add the chiles, cilantro, cheese, salt, and pepper, and mix well.

2 Cut the bread slices in half diagonally, and soak them, one at a time, in the egg mixture.

NUTRITIONAL NOTES	
Per Portion	
Energy	267cal
Fat	14.5g
Saturated Fat	6.9g
Carbohydrate	17.8g
Fiber	0.9g

3 Heat the oil in a medium skillet and fry the bread slices over a medium heat, turning them once or twice, until they are golden brown.

4 Drain off any excess oil as you remove the toasts from the skillet and serve immediately.

Hot Lime Pickle

A good lime pickle is not only delicious served with any meal, but it increases the appetite and aids digestion.

INGREDIENTS

Makes 2 cups

25 limes
1 cup salt
1/2 cup fenugreek powder
1/2 cup mustard powder
2/3 cup chili powder
2 tablespoons ground turmeric
2 1/2 cups mustard oil
1 teaspoon asafetida
2 tablespoons yellow mustard
   seeds, crushed

1 Cut each lime into eight pieces and remove the seeds, if you like. Put the limes in a large sterilized jar or glass bowl. Add the salt and toss with the limes. Cover and let stand in a warm place for 1–2 weeks, until they become soft and dull brown in color.

2 Mix together the fenugreek, mustard powder, chili powder, and turmeric and add to the limes.

NUTRITIONAL NOTES	
Per 1/2-tablespoon Portion	
Energy	82cal
Fat	8.9g
Saturated Fat	1.1g
Carbohydrate	0g
Fiber	0g

3 Cover and let rest in a warm place for another 2 or 3 days.

4 Heat the mustard oil in a skillet and fry the asafetida and mustard seeds. When the oil reaches smoking point, pour it over the limes. Mix well, cover with a clean cloth and let stand in a warm place for about 1 week before serving.

Green Chile Pickle

Southern India is the source of some of the hottest curries and pickles. You might imagine that eating them would be a case of making yourself too hot, but they actually cool the body.

INGREDIENTS

Makes 2–2 1/2 cups

4 tablespoons yellow mustard
   seeds, crushed
4 tablespoons freshly ground
   cumin seeds
1/4 cup ground turmeric
2 ounces garlic cloves, crushed, plus
   20 small garlic cloves, peeled but
   left whole
2/3 cup white vinegar
1/3 cup sugar
2 teaspoons salt
2/3 cup mustard oil
1 pound small fresh green
   chiles, halved

1 Mix the mustard and cumin seeds, the turmeric, crushed garlic, vinegar, sugar, and salt together in a sterilized glass bowl. Cover with a cloth and let rest for 24 hours. This enables the spices to blend and the sugar and salt to melt.

2 Heat the mustard oil in a skillet and gently fry the spice mixture for about 5 minutes. (Keep a window open while cooking with mustard oil because it is pungent and the smoke may irritate the eyes.) Add the garlic cloves and fry for another 5 minutes.

NUTRITIONAL NOTES	
Per 2-tablespoon Portion	
Energy	54cal
Fat	5.7g
Saturated Fat	0.6g
Carbohydrate	0.1g
Fiber	0g

3 Add the chiles and cook gently until tender but still green in color. This will take about 30 minutes at a low heat.

4 Cool thoroughly, then pour into sterilized bottles, ensuring the oil is evenly distributed if you are using more than one bottle. Let rest for a week before serving.

Bombay Duck Pickle

Boil is the name of a fish that is found off the west coast of India during the monsoon season. It is salted and dried in the sun and is characterized by a strong smell and distinctive piquancy. How this fish acquired the name Bombay duck in the Western world is still unknown. Bombay duck can be served hot or cold, and is usually eaten with Indian breads as an accompaniment to vegetable dishes.

INGREDIENTS

Serves 4–6

6–8 pieces boil (Bombay duck), soaked
   in water for 5 minutes
4 tablespoons vegetable oil
2 fresh red chiles, chopped
1 tablespoon sugar
1 pound cherry tomatoes, halved
4 ounces deep-fried onions
red onion rings, to garnish (optional)

———————— COOK'S TIP ————————

As an alternative to boil, try using skinned mackerel fillets, but don't fry them. You will only need 2 tablespoons vegetable oil to make the sauce.

1 Pat the fish dry with paper towels. Heat the oil in a skillet and fry the fish pieces for about 30–45 seconds on both sides, until crisp. Be careful not to burn them or they will taste bitter. Drain well. When cool, break into small pieces.

2 Cook the remaining ingredients until the tomatoes become pulpy and the onions are blended into a sauce. Fold in the Bombay duck and mix well. Let cool, then garnish and serve, or ladle into a hot sterilized jar, cover and let stand to cool.

NUTRITIONAL NOTES	
Per Portion	
Energy	233cal
Fat	15.3g
Saturated Fat	1.8g
Carbohydrate	11.5g
Fiber	2g

Sweet-and-Sour Pineapple

This may sound like a Chinese recipe, but it is a traditional Bengali dish known as tok. The predominant flavor is ginger, and the pieces of golden pineapple, dotted with plump, juicy raisins, have plenty of visual appeal with taste to match. It is equally delicious if made with mangoes instead of the pineapple.

INGREDIENTS

Serves 4

1¾ pounds canned pineapple rings or chunks in natural juice
1 tablespoon vegetable oil
½ teaspoon black mustard seeds
½ teaspoon cumin seeds
½ teaspoon onion seeds
2 teaspoons grated fresh ginger root
1 teaspoon crushed dried chiles
⅓ cup seedless raisins
½ cup sugar
1½ teaspoons salt

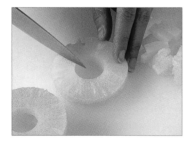

1 Drain the pineapple in a colander and reserve the juice. Chop the pineapple rings or chunks finely (you should have about 1¼ pounds).

NUTRITIONAL NOTES	
Per Portion	
Energy	264cal
Fat	3.2g
Saturated Fat	0.3g
Carbohydrate	61.5g
Fiber	2.7g

2 Heat the vegetable oil in a karahi, wok, or large pan over a medium heat and immediately add the mustard seeds. As soon as they pop, add the cumin seeds, then the onion seeds. Add the ginger and chiles and stir-fry the spices briskly for 30 seconds, until they release their flavors.

3 Add the pineapple, seedless raisins, sugar, and salt. Add 1¼ cups of the juice (made up with cold water if necessary) and stir into the pineapple mixture.

4 Bring the mixture to a boil, reduce the heat to medium, and cook, uncovered, for 20–25 minutes.

Indian Breads

NO INDIAN meal would be complete without some form of bread. Flat and crisp or soft and puffy, they seem to be the perfect complement to spicy food, and are ideal for mopping up the juices of a particularly sumptuous curry.

Most Indian breads are cooked on a griddle, which gives them their characteristically dimpled appearance. Nan is traditionally baked in the tandoor, the clay oven also employed for cooking meat and fish, but excellent results can be obtained using a combination of a conventional oven and a broiler. Whole-wheat flour is a popular choice for making the dough, although in southern India, lentils and rice are ground to make the popular pancakes known as dosas. Besan, or gram, flour is made from chickpeas and is used in the making of Missi Rotis. Although many Indian breads are now on sale in the supermarket, it is plenty of fun—and also impressive—to try making your own.

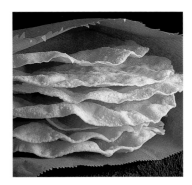

Chapatis

A chapati is an unleavened bread made from chapati flour, a ground whole-wheat flour known as atta, which is finer than the Western equivalent. An equal quantity of standard whole-wheat flour and all-purpose flour will also produce satisfactory results, although chapati flour is available from Indian markets. This is the everyday bread of the Indian home.

INGREDIENTS

Makes 8–10

2 cups chapati flour or ground
   whole-wheat flour
½ teaspoon salt
¾ cup water

1 Place the flour and salt in a mixing bowl. Make a well in the middle and gradually stir in the water, mixing well with your fingers. Form a supple dough and knead for 7–10 minutes. Ideally, cover with plastic wrap and let stand on one side for 15–20 minutes to rest.

2 Divide the dough into 8–10 equal portions. Roll out each piece to a circle on a well-floured surface.

3 Place a tava (chapati griddle) or heavy skillet over a high heat. When steam rises from it, lower the heat to medium and add the first chapati to the pan.

4 When the chapati begins to bubble, turn it over. Press down with a clean dish towel or a flat spoon and turn once again. Remove the cooked chapati from the pan and keep warm in a piece of aluminum foil lined with paper towels while you cook the other chapatis. Repeat the process until all the breads are cooked. Serve hot.

NUTRITIONAL NOTES	
Per Portion	
Energy	96cal
Fat	0.4g
Saturated Fat	0.1g
Carbohydrate	21.9g
Fiber	0.9g

Nan

This bread was introduced to India by the Moguls, who originally came from Persia via Afghanistan. In Persian, the word nan means bread. Traditionally, nan is not rolled, but patted and stretched until the teardrop shape is achieved. You can, of course, roll it out to a circle, then gently pull the lower end, which will give you the traditional shape.

INGREDIENTS

Makes about 3

2 cups unbleached white bread flour
½ teaspoon salt
½ ounce active dry yeast
4 tablespoons lukewarm milk
1 tablespoon vegetable oil
2 tablespoons plain yogurt
1 egg
2–3 tablespoons melted ghee or
   butter, for brushing

1 Sift the flour and salt together into a large bowl. In a smaller bowl, cream the yeast with the milk. Set aside for 15 minutes.

2 Add the yeast and milk mixture, vegetable oil, yogurt, and egg to the flour. Combine the mixture using your hands until it forms a soft dough. Add a little more of the lukewarm water if the dough is too dry.

3 Turn the dough out onto a lightly floured surface and knead for about 10 minutes, or until it feels smooth. Return the dough to the bowl, cover, and let stand in a warm place for about 1 hour, or until it has doubled in size. Preheat the oven to its highest setting—it should not be any lower than 450°F.

4 Turn out the dough back onto the floured surface and knead for another 2 minutes.

5 Divide into three equal pieces, shape into balls, and roll out into teardrop shapes 10 inches long, 5 inches wide, and ¼–⅓ inch thick.

6 Preheat the broiler to its highest setting. Meanwhile, place the nan on preheated baking sheets and bake for 3–4 minutes, or until puffed up.

7 Remove from the oven and place under the broiler for a few seconds, until the tops brown slightly. Brush with ghee or butter and serve warm.

NUTRITIONAL NOTES	
Per Portion	
Energy	197cal
Fat	8.2g
Saturated Fat	5g
Carbohydrate	29.2g
Fiber	1.2g

Garlic and Cilantro Nan

From the Caucasus through the Punjab region of northwest India and beyond, these leavened breads are served. Traditionally cooked in a very hot clay oven known as a tandoor, nan are usually eaten with dry meat or vegetable dishes.

INGREDIENTS

Makes 3 nan

2½ cups unbleached white bread flour
1 teaspoon salt
1 teaspoon active dry yeast
4 tablespoons plain yogurt
1 tablespoon melted butter or ghee
1 garlic clove, finely chopped
1 teaspoon black onion seeds
1 tablespoon fresh cilantro
2 teaspoons honey
2–3 tablespoons melted ghee or butter, for brushing

VARIATIONS

You can flavor nan in numerous ways:
• To make poppy seed nan, brush the rolled-out nan with a little ghee and sprinkle with poppy seeds.
• To make onion-flavored nan, add 1 small finely chopped or coarsely grated onion to the dough in step 2. You may need to reduce the amount of egg if the onion is very moist to prevent making the dough too soft.
• To make Peshwari nan, roll out each ball of dough and sprinkle with sliced almonds and golden raisins. Fold over and roll to the teardrop shape.

COOK'S TIP

To help the dough to puff up and brown, place the baking sheets in an oven pre-heated to the maximum temperature for at least 10 minutes before baking. Preheat the broiler while the nan are baking.

1 Sift the flour and salt together into a large bowl. In a smaller bowl, cream the yeast with the plain yogurt. Set aside for 15 minutes.

2 Add the yeast mixture to the flour with the melted butter or ghee, and add the chopped garlic, black onion seeds, and chopped cilantro, mixing to a soft dough.

3 Turn out the dough onto a lightly floured surface and knead for about 10 minutes, until smooth and elastic. Place in a lightly oiled bowl, cover with lightly oiled plastic wrap and let rise in a warm place for 45 minutes, or until the dough has doubled in bulk.

4 Preheat the oven to its highest setting, at least 450°F. Place three heavy baking sheets in the oven to heat.

5 Turn the dough out onto a lightly floured surface and punch down. Divide into three equal pieces and shape each into a ball.

6 Cover two of the balls of dough with oiled plastic wrap and roll out the third into a teardrop shape about 10 inches long, 5 inches wide, and ¼–⅓ inch thick.

7 Preheat the broiler to its highest setting. Meanwhile, place the nan on the hot baking sheets and bake for 3–4 minutes, or until puffy.

8 Remove the nan from the oven and place under the hot broiler for a few seconds, or until the top of each nan browns slightly. Wrap the cooked nan in a dish towel to keep hot while you roll out and cook the remaining nan. Brush with melted ghee or butter and serve warm.

NUTRITIONAL NOTES	
Per Portion	
Energy	326cal
Fat	6.8g
Saturated Fat	1.3g
Carbohydrate	59.7g
Fiber	2.3g

Spiced Nan

Another excellent recipe for nan bread, this time with fennel seeds, onion seeds, and cumin seeds.

INGREDIENTS

Makes 6

4 cups all-purpose flour
1 teaspoon baking powder
½ teaspoon salt
1 envelope rapid-rise yeast
1 teaspoon superfine sugar
1 teaspoon fennel seeds
2 teaspoons onion seeds
1 teaspoon cumin seeds
⅔ cup lukewarm milk
2 tablespoons oil, plus
  extra for brushing
⅔ cup plain yogurt
1 egg, beaten

3 Put a heavy baking sheet in the oven and preheat the oven to 475°F. Also preheat the broiler. Knead the dough again lightly and divide it into six pieces. Keep five pieces covered while working with the sixth. Quickly roll the piece of dough out to a teardrop shape, brush lightly with oil, and slap the nan onto the hot baking sheet. Repeat with the remaining dough.

NUTRITIONAL NOTES	
Per Portion	
Energy	294cal
Fat	2.6g
Saturated Fat	0.8g
Carbohydrate	61.3g
Fiber	2.3g

4 Bake the nan in the oven for 3 minutes, until puffed up, then place the baking sheet under the broiler for about 30 seconds, or until the nan are lightly browned. Serve hot or warm as an accompaniment to an Indian curry.

1 Sift the flour, baking powder, and salt into a mixing bowl. Stir in the yeast, sugar, fennel seeds, onion seeds, and cumin seeds. Make a well in the center. Stir the lukewarm milk into the flour mixture, then add the oil, yogurt, and beaten egg. Mix to form a ball of dough.

2 Turn the dough out onto a lightly floured surface and knead it for 10 minutes, until smooth. Return to the clean, lightly oiled bowl and roll the dough to coat it with oil. Cover the bowl with plastic wrap and set aside in a warm place until the dough has doubled in bulk.

Sugar Bread Rolls

These delicious sweet rolls make an unusual end to a meal.

INGREDIENTS

Makes 10

3 cups white bread flour
1 teaspoon salt
1 tablespoon superfine sugar
1 teaspoon active dry yeast
⅔ cup lukewarm water
3 egg yolks
4 tablespoons unsalted butter, softened, plus 2 tablespoons extra
¾ cup grated cheddar cheese or Monterey Jack
¼ cup sugar

1 Sift the flour, salt, and sugar into a food processor with a dough blade attached or the bowl of an electric mixer with a dough hook attached. Make a well in the center. Dissolve the yeast in the lukewarm water and pour into the well. Add the egg yolks and let stand for a few minutes until bubbles appear on the surface of the liquid.

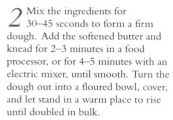

2 Mix the ingredients for 30–45 seconds to form a firm dough. Add the softened butter and knead for 2–3 minutes in a food processor, or for 4–5 minutes with an electric mixer, until smooth. Turn the dough out into a floured bowl, cover, and let stand in a warm place to rise until doubled in bulk.

3 Transfer the dough to a lightly floured surface and divide it into 10 pieces. Spread the grated cheese over the surface. Roll each of the dough pieces into 5-inch lengths, incorporating the cheese as you do so. Coil into snail shapes and place on a lightly greased 8 × 12 inch baking sheet with high sides.

4 Cover the sheet with a loose-fitting plastic bag and let stand in a warm place for 45 minutes, or until the dough has doubled in bulk.

5 Preheat the oven to 375°F and bake the rolls for 20–25 minutes. Melt the remaining butter, brush it over the rolls, sprinkle with the sugar, and let cool. Separate the rolls before serving.

NUTRITIONAL NOTES	
Per Portion	
Energy	235cal
Fat	9.5g
Saturated Fat	5.9g
Carbohydrate	33.7g
Fiber	1.1g

Red Lentil Pancakes

This is a type of dosa, which is essentially a pancake from southern India, but used in the similar fashion to north Indian bread. North Indian breads are made of whole-wheat or refined flour; in the south they are made of ground lentils and rice.

INGREDIENTS

Makes 6 pancakes
¾ cup long grain rice
¼ cup red lentils
1 cup warm water
1 teaspoon salt
½ teaspoon ground turmeric
½ teaspoon ground black pepper
2 tablespoons chopped fresh
  cilantro
oil, for frying and drizzling

1 Place the long grain rice and lentils in a large mixing bowl, cover with the warm water, cover, and soak for at least 8 hours, or overnight.

2 Drain off the water and reserve. Place the rice and lentils in a food processor and blend until smooth. Blend in the reserved water. Scrape into a bowl, cover with plastic wrap, and let stand in a warm place to ferment for about 24 hours.

VARIATION

Add 4 tablespoons grated coconut to the batter just before cooking.

3 Stir in the salt, turmeric, pepper, and cilantro. Heat a heavy skillet over a medium heat for a few minutes until hot. Smear with oil and add about 2–3 tablespoons batter.

4 Using the rounded bottom of a soup spoon, gently spread the batter out, using a circular motion, to make a pancake 6 inches in diameter.

5 Cook in the pan for 1½–2 minutes, or until set. Drizzle a little oil over the pancake and around the edges. Turn over and cook for about 1 minute, or until golden brown. Keep the cooked pancakes warm in a low oven or on a heatproof plate over simmering water while cooking the remaining pancakes. Serve warm.

NUTRITIONAL NOTES	
Per Portion	
Energy	190cal
Fat	8.5g
Saturated Fat	1.1g
Carbohydrate	26.1g
Fiber	0.5g

Parathas

Making a paratha is somewhat similar to the technique used when making flaky pastry. The difference lies in the handling of the dough; this can be handled freely, unlike that for a flaky pastry.

INGREDIENTS

Makes 12–15

3 cups chapati flour or
    whole-wheat flour, plus
    ½ cup for dusting
½ cup all-purpose flour
1 teaspoon salt
3 tablespoons ghee or unsalted butter,
    melted
water, to mix

1 Sift the flours and salt into a bowl. Make a well in the center and add 2 teaspoons of unmelted ghee. Fold it into the flour to make a crumbly texture. Gradually add water to make a soft, pliable dough. Knead until smooth. Cover and let rest for 30 minutes.

2 Uncover the dough, divide into 12–15 equal portions, and cover again. Take one portion at a time and roll out on a lightly floured surface to about 4 inches in diameter. Brush the dough with a little of the melted ghee or unsalted butter and sprinkle with chapati flour.

3 With a sharp knife, make a straight cut from the center to the edge of the dough, then lift a cut edge and roll the dough into a cone shape. Lift it and flatten it again into a ball. Roll the dough again on a lightly floured surface until it is 7 inches wide.

4 Heat a griddle and cook one paratha at a time, placing a little of the remaining ghee along the edges. Cook on each side until golden brown. Serve hot.

_____ COOK'S TIP _____

If you cannot find chapati flour, which is also known as atta, you can substitute an equal quantity of whole-wheat flour and all-purpose flour.

NUTRITIONAL NOTES	
Per Portion	
Energy	123cal
Fat	2.8g
Saturated Fat	1.4g
Carbohydrate	21.9g
Fiber	2.8g

Missi Rotis

These unleavened breads are a speciality from Punjab. Besan flour, also known as gram flour, is made from chickpeas and is combined here with the more traditional wheat flour. In Punjab, missi rotis are popular with a glass of lassi, a refreshing yogurt drink.

INGREDIENTS

Makes 4

1 cup besan flour
1 cup whole-wheat flour
1 fresh green chile, seeded and chopped
½ onion, finely chopped
1 tablespoon chopped fresh cilantro
½ teaspoon ground turmeric
½ teaspoon salt
1 tablespoon vegetable oil
½–⅔ cup lukewarm water
2–3 tablespoons melted unsalted butter or ghee

1 Mix the two types of flour, chile, onion, cilantro, turmeric, and salt together in a large bowl. Stir in the vegetable oil.

2 Mix in sufficient water to make a pliable soft dough. Turn out the dough onto a lightly floured surface and knead until smooth.

3 Place the dough in a lightly oiled bowl, cover with lightly oiled plastic wrap, and let rest for 30 minutes.

4 Place the dough onto a lightly floured surface. Divide into four equal pieces and shape into balls in the palms of your hands. Roll out each ball into a thick circle about 6–7 inches in diameter.

5 Heat a griddle or heavy skillet over a medium heat for a few minutes until hot.

6 Brush both sides of one roti with some melted butter or ghee. Add it to the griddle or skillet and cook for about 2 minutes, turning after 1 minute. Brush the cooked roti lightly with melted butter or ghee again, slide it onto a plate, and keep warm in a low oven while cooking the remaining rotis in the same way. Serve the rotis warm.

NUTRITIONAL NOTES	
Per Portion	
Energy	226cal
Fat	3.5g
Saturated Fat	0.5g
Carbohydrate	45.9g
Fiber	2g

Tandoori Rotis

Roti means bread and is the most common food eaten in central and northern India. Tandoori roti is traditionally baked in a tandoor, or clay oven, but it can also be made successfully in an electric or gas oven at the highest setting.

INGREDIENTS

Makes 6

3 cups chapati flour or ground
    whole-wheat flour
1 teaspoon salt
1 cup water
2–3 tablespoons melted ghee or
    unsalted butter, for brushing

1 Sift the flour and salt into a large mixing bowl. Add the water and mix to a soft, pliable dough.

2 Knead on a lightly floured surface for 3–4 minutes, until smooth. Place the dough in a lightly oiled bowl, cover with lightly oiled plastic wrap and let rest for about 1 hour.

NUTRITIONAL NOTES	
Per Portion	
Energy	181cal
Fat	1.3g
Saturated Fat	0.2g
Carbohydrate	37.3g
Fiber	5.3g

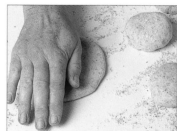

3 Turn out the dough onto a lightly floured surface. Divide the dough into six pieces and shape each into a ball. Press out into a larger circle with the palm of your hand, cover with lightly oiled plastic wrap and let rest for about 10 minutes.

4 Meanwhile, preheat the oven to 450°F. Place three baking sheets in the oven to heat. Roll the rotis into 6-inch circles, place two on each baking sheet, and bake for 8–10 minutes. Brush with melted ghee or butter and serve warm.

Pooris

These delicious little deep-fried breads, shaped into disks, make it temptingly easy to overindulge. In most areas, they are made of whole-wheat flour, but in the east and northeast of India, they are made from plain refined flour, and are known as loochis.

INGREDIENTS

Makes 12
1 cup unbleached all-purpose flour
1 cup whole-wheat flour
½ teaspoon salt
½ teaspoon chili powder
2 tablespoons vegetable oil
7–8 tablespoons water
oil, for frying

1 Sift the flours, salt, and chili powder, if using, into a large mixing bowl. Add the vegetable oil, then add sufficient water to mix to a dough.

2 Turn the dough out onto a lightly floured surface and knead for 8–10 minutes, until smooth.

3 Place in an oiled bowl and cover with oiled plastic wrap. Let stand for 30 minutes.

4 Place the dough on the floured surface. Divide into 12 equal pieces. Keeping the rest of the dough covered, roll one piece into a 5-inch circle. Repeat with the remaining dough. Stack the pooris, layered between plastic wrap to keep moist.

NUTRITIONAL NOTES	
Per Portion	
Energy	79cal
Fat	2.2g
Saturated Fat	0.3g
Carbohydrate	13.6g
Fiber	1.2g

5 Pour the oil for frying to a depth of 1 inch in a deep skillet and heat it to 350°F. Using a metal spatula, lift one poori and gently slide it into the oil; it will sink but will then return to the surface and begin to sizzle. Gently press the poori into the oil. It will puff up. Turn the poori over after a few seconds and let it cook for another 20–30 seconds.

6 Remove the poori from the skillet and pat dry with paper towels. Place the cooked poori on a large baking sheet and keep warm in a low oven while you cook the remaining pooris. Serve warm.

___ COOK'S TIP ___

For spinach-flavored pooris, thaw 2 ounces frozen spinach, put it into a strainer or colander, and press it against the sides to extract as much liquid as possible. Add the spinach to the dough, along with a little grated fresh ginger root and ½ teaspoon ground cumin for additional seasoning.

Bhaturas

These leavened and deep-fried breads are from Punjab, where the local people enjoy them with a bowl of spicy chickpea curry. The combination has become a classic over the years and is known as choley bhature. Bhaturas must be eaten hot and cannot be reheated.

INGREDIENTS

Makes 10 bhaturas
½ ounce active dry yeast
1 teaspoon sugar
½ cup lukewarm water
1¾ cups all-purpose flour
½ cup semolina
½ teaspoon salt
1 tablespoon ghee or butter
2 tablespoons plain yogurt
oil, for frying

1 Mix the yeast with the sugar and water in a pitcher. Sift the flour into a large bowl and stir in the semolina and salt. Rub in the butter or ghee.

2 Add the yeast mixture and yogurt and mix to a dough. Turn out onto a lightly floured surface and knead for 10 minutes, until smooth and elastic.

3 Place the dough in an oiled bowl, cover with oiled plastic wrap, and let stand to rise, in a warm place, for about 1 hour, or until doubled in bulk.

4 Turn out onto a lightly floured surface and punch down. Divide into ten equal pieces and shape each into a ball. Flatten into disks with the palm of your hand. Roll out on a lightly floured surface into 5-inch circles.

5 Heat oil to a depth of ½ inch in a deep skillet and slide one bhatura into the oil. Fry for about 1 minute, turning over after 30 seconds, then drain well on paper towels. Keep each bhatura warm in a low oven while frying the remaining bhaturas. Serve immediately, while hot.

NUTRITIONAL NOTES	
Per Portion	
Energy	144cal
Fat	6.6g
Saturated Fat	1.4g
Carbohydrate	19.7g
Fiber	0.7g

Desserts
and Drinks

ONE OF the finest ways to end an Indian meal is with a selection of fresh fruit, especially if slightly tart. Pineapple fits the bill perfectly, but mangoes are just as refreshing. Mango flesh can be used in a range of imaginative desserts: pulped for inclusion in a stunning sorbet or stir-fried with pieces of coconut.

Indeed, coconut is used very effectively in a number of Indian-style desserts. Sweetened, it makes a crunchy filling for pancakes, while the milk is the basis of a glorious custard. In fact, Indians love milk-based puddings. Another favorite is ground rice and rose water, while fine vermicelli is used for a milk pudding flavored with

nuts, dates, and golden raisins. Kulfi, India's famous ice cream, is easy to make and tastes superb. Finally, there are the gloriously sticky sweet treats, such as Toffee Apples and Sesame Fried Fruits. After such indulgence, a glass of Tea and Fruit Punch, or Pistachio Lassi, will cleanse the palate.

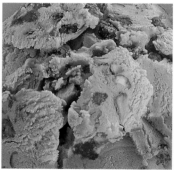

Ground Rice Pudding

This delicious and light ground rice pudding is the perfect end to a spicy meal. It can be served either hot or cold.

INGREDIENTS

Serves 4–6
½ cup coarsely ground rice
4 green cardamom pods, crushed
3¾ cups low-fat milk
6 tablespoons sugar
1 tablespoon rose water
1 tablespoon crushed pistachio nuts, to garnish

1 Place the ground rice in a pan with the cardamoms. Add 2½ cups of the milk and bring to a boil over a medium heat, stirring occasionally.

2 Add the remaining milk and stir over a medium heat for about 10 minutes, or until the rice mixture thickens to the consistency of a creamy chicken soup.

3 Stir in the sugar and rose water and continue to cook for another 2 minutes. Serve garnished with the pistachio nuts.

_____ COOK'S TIP _____

Rose water is a distillation of scented rose petals, which has the intense fragrance and flavor of roses. It is a popular flavoring in Indian cooking. Use it cautiously, adding just enough to suit your taste.

NUTRITIONAL NOTES
Per Portion

Energy	260cal
Fat	5.80g
Saturated Fat	2.53g
Carbohydrate	46.00g
Fiber	0.30g

Traditional Indian Vermicelli

Indian vermicelli, made from wheat, is much finer than Italian vermicelli and is readily available from Asian stores.

INGREDIENTS

Serves 4

1 cup vermicelli
5 cups water
½ teaspoon saffron threads
1 tablespoon sugar
4 tablespoons low-fat strained plain
  yogurt, to serve

To decorate

1 tablespoon shredded fresh or dry
  unsweetened shredded coconut
1 tablespoon sliced almonds
1 tablespoon chopped pistachio nuts
1 tablespoon sugar

2 Stir in the sugar and continue cooking until the water has evaporated. Strain through a strainer, if necessary, to remove any excess liquid.

3 Place the vermicelli in a serving dish and decorate with the coconut, almonds, pistachio nuts, and sugar. Serve with yogurt.

NUTRITIONAL NOTES	
Per Portion	
Energy	196cal
Fat	6.60g
Saturated Fat	2.27g
Carbohydrate	31.80g
Fiber	0.80g

1 Crush the vermicelli in your hands and place it in a pan. Pour in the water, add the saffron, and bring to a boil. Boil for about 5 minutes.

_____ COOK'S TIP _____

You can use a variety of fruits instead of nuts to garnish this dessert. Try a few berries, such as blackberries, raspberries, or strawberries, or add some chopped dried apricots or golden raisins.

Kheer

Both Muslim and Hindu communities prepare Kheer, which is traditionally served at mosques and temples.

INGREDIENTS

Serves 4-6
1 tablespoon ghee
2-inch piece cinnamon stick
³/₄ cup brown sugar
1 cup coarsely ground rice
5 cups whole milk
1 teaspoon ground cardamom
¹/₃ cup golden raisins
¹/₄ cup sliced almonds
¹/₂ teaspoon freshly ground nutmeg,
   to serve

1 In a heavy pan, melt the ghee and fry the cinnamon stick and sugar. Keep frying until the sugar begins to caramelize. Reduce the heat immediately when this happens.

2 Add the rice and half the milk. Bring to a boil, stirring constantly to avoid the milk boiling over. Reduce the heat and simmer until the rice is cooked, stirring regularly.

3 Stir in the remaining milk, with the cardamom, golden raisins, and almonds. Let simmer until the mixture thickens, stirring constantly to prevent the kheer from sticking to the bottom of the pan.

4 When the mixture is thick and creamy, spoon it into a serving dish or individual dishes. Serve hot or cold, sprinkled with the nutmeg.

NUTRITIONAL NOTES	
Per Portion	
Energy	588cal
Fat	20.6g
Saturated Fat	11.1g
Carbohydrate	90.6g
Fiber	0.7g

Fruit Vermicelli Pudding

This tasty sweet is prepared by Muslims early in the morning of Id-ul-Fitr, the feast after the 30 days of Ramadan.

INGREDIENTS

Serves 4-6
6 tablespoons ghee
1 cup vermicelli, coarsely broken
¹/₄ cup sliced almonds
¹/₄ cup pistachio nuts, slivered
¹/₄ cup cuddapah nuts or almonds
¹/₃ cup golden raisins
¹/₃ cup dates, pitted, and
   thinly sliced
5 cups whole milk
4 tablespoons brown sugar
1 envelope saffron powder

1 Heat 4 tablespoons of the ghee in a skillet and sauté the vermicelli until golden brown. (If you are using the Italian variety, sauté it for a little longer.) Remove and set aside.

2 Heat the remaining ghee in a separate pan and fry the nuts, golden raisins, and dates over a medium heat until the raisins swell. Add to the vermicelli and mix gently.

3 Heat the milk in a large heavy pan and add the sugar. Bring to a boil, add the vermicelli mixture, and let the liquid return to a boil, stirring constantly.

4 Reduce the heat and simmer until the vermicelli is soft and you have a thick pudding. Stir in the saffron powder and cook for 1 minute more. Serve hot or cold.

NUTRITIONAL NOTES	
Per Portion	
Energy	732cal
Fat	44.6g
Saturated Fat	23.6g
Carbohydrate	68.3g
Fiber	1.7g

Black Rice Pudding

This unusual rice pudding, flavored with fresh ginger, is delicious. When cooked, black rice still retains its husk and has a nutty texture. Serve in small bowls, with a little coconut cream poured over each helping.

INGREDIENTS

Serves 6
generous ½ cup black glutinous rice
2 cups water
½-inch fresh ginger root,
    peeled and bruised
⅓ cup molasses sugar
¼ cup sugar
1¼ cups coconut milk or cream,
    to serve

1 Put the rice in a strainer and rinse well under cold running water. Drain and put in a large pan, with the water. Bring to a boil and stir to prevent the rice from settling on the bottom of the pan. Cover and cook for about 30 minutes.

NUTRITIONAL NOTES	
Per Portion	
Energy	146cal
Fat	0.5g
Saturated Fat	0.1g
Carbohydrate	34.2g
Fiber	0g

2 Add the ginger and both the brown and white sugars. Cook for another 15 minutes, adding a little more water if necessary, until the rice is cooked and porridgelike. Remove the ginger and serve warm, in bowls, topped with coconut milk or cream.

Deep-fried Bananas

Fry these bananas at the last minute, so that the outer crust of batter is crisp in texture and the banana is soft and warm inside.

INGREDIENTS

Serves 8
1 cup self-rising flour
⅓ cup rice flour
½ teaspoon salt
scant 1 cup water
finely grated lime rind
8 small bananas
oil for deep-frying
sugar and 1 lime,
    cut in wedges, to serve

1 Sift the self-rising flour, the rice flour, and the salt together into a bowl. Add just enough of the water to make a smooth, coating batter. Mix well, then stir in the lime rind.

2 Heat the oil until it reaches 375°F, or until a cube of day-old bread dropped into the oil browns within 30 seconds.

NUTRITIONAL NOTES	
Per Portion	
Energy	201cal
Fat	10g
Saturated Fat	1.3g
Carbohydrate	27.1g
Fiber	1.2g

3 Peel the bananas and dip them into the batter two or three times. Deep-fry the battered bananas in the hot oil until crisp and golden. Drain and serve hot, dredged with sugar. Offer the lime wedges to squeeze over the bananas.

Tapioca Pudding

This pudding, made from large pearl tapioca and coconut milk and served warm, is much lighter than the Western-style version. You can adjust the sweetness to your taste. Serve with lychees or the smaller, similar-tasting logans.

INGREDIENTS

Serves 4
⅔ cup tapioca
2 cups water
¾ cup sugar
pinch of salt
1 cup coconut milk
9 ounces prepared tropical fruits
finely shredded rind of 1 lime,
    to decorate

1 Soak the tapioca in warm water for 1 hour so the grains swell. Drain.

2 Put the measured water in a pan and bring to a boil. Stir in the sugar and salt.

NUTRITIONAL NOTES	
Per Portion	
Energy	327cal
Fat	0.6g
Saturated Fat	0.2g
Carbohydrate	80.6g
Fiber	2.2g

3 Add the tapioca and coconut milk and simmer for 10 minutes, or until the tapioca turns transparent.

4 Serve warm with some tropical fruits and decorate with the finely shredded lime rind.

Sesame Fried Fruits

These delicious treats are a favorite among children and adults alike. Use any firm fruit in season. Bananas are a real favorite, but the batter also works well with pineapple and apple.

INGREDIENTS

Serves 4
1 cup all-purpose flour
½ teaspoon baking soda
2 tablespoons sugar
1 egg
6 tablespoons water
1 tablespoons sesame seeds or
    2 tablespoons dry unsweetened
    shredded coconut
4 firm bananas
oil for deep-frying
salt
2 tablespoons honey, to serve
mint sprigs and lychees, to decorate

1 Sift the flour, baking soda, and a pinch of salt into a bowl. Stir in the sugar.

2 Whisk in the egg and just enough water to make a thin batter. Then whisk in the sesame seeds or the shredded coconut.

3 Peel the bananas. Carefully cut each one in half lengthwise, then cut in half crosswise.

NUTRITIONAL NOTES	
Per Portion	
Energy	384cal
Fat	20.7g
Saturated Fat	6.3g
Carbohydrate	46g
Fiber	3g

4 Heat the oil in a preheated wok. Dip the bananas in the batter, then gently drop a few pieces at a time into the hot oil. Fry until golden brown.

5 Remove the bananas from the oil and drain on paper towels. Serve immediately with honey, and decorate with mint sprigs and lychees.

Indian Ice Cream

Kulfi-wallahs (ice cream vendors) have always made kulfi, and continue to this day, without using modern freezers. Kulfi is packed into metal cones sealed with dough and then churned in clay pots until set. Try this method—it works extremely well in an ordinary freezer.

Ingredients

Serves 4-6

3 × 14 fluid ounce cans unsweetened condensed milk
3 egg whites
3 cups confectioners' sugar
1 teaspoon ground cardamom
1 tablespoon rose water
1½ cups pistachio nuts, chopped
½ cup golden raisins
¾ cup sliced almonds
3 tablespoons candied cherries, halved

3 Gently fold in the remaining ingredients, cover the bowl with plastic wrap, and place in the freezer for 1 hour.

4 Remove the ice cream from the freezer and mix well with a fork. Transfer to a serving container and return to the freezer for a final setting. Remove from the freezer 10 minutes before serving.

Nutritional Notes	
Per Portion	
Energy	1,123cal
Fat	47.3g
Saturated Fat	10.3g
Carbohydrate	144.2g
Fiber	5.1g

_____ Cook's Tip _____

Don't leave the cans of condensed milk unattended. Add additional water if necessary; the water must never boil dry.

1 Remove the labels from the cans of unsweetened condensed milk and lay the cans down in a pan with a tight-fitting cover. Fill the pan with water to reach three-quarters up the cans. Bring to a boil, cover, and simmer for 20 minutes. When cool, remove the cans and chill in the refrigerator for 24 hours. Chill a large bowl, too.

2 Whisk the egg whites in a large bowl until peaks form. Open the cans and empty the milk into the chilled bowl. Whisk until doubled in quantity, then fold in the whisked egg whites and sugar.

Mango Sherbet with Sauce

After a heavy meal, this makes a very refreshing dessert. Mango is said to be one of the oldest fruit cultivated in India, having been brought by Lord Shiva for his beautiful wife, Parvathi.

INGREDIENTS

Serves 4-6
2 pounds mango pulp
½ teaspoon lemon juice
grated rind of 1 orange and
   1 lemon
4 egg whites
¼ cup sugar
½ cup heavy cream
½ cup confectioners' sugar

3 Remove from the freezer and beat again. Transfer to an ice cream container, and freeze until fully set.

4 In a bowl, whip the heavy cream with the confectioners' sugar and the remaining mango pulp. Cover and chill the sauce for 24 hours.

5 Remove the sherbet 10 minutes before serving. Scoop out individual servings and cover with a generous helping of mango sauce. Serve immediately.

NUTRITIONAL NOTES	
Per Portion	
Energy	387cal
Fat	16.6g
Saturated Fat	10.3g
Carbohydrate	58.4g
Fiber	5.9g

1 In a large, chilled bowl, mix half of the mango pulp with the lemon juice and the grated rind.

2 Whisk the egg whites until peaks form, then gently fold them into the mango mixture, with the sugar. Cover with plastic wrap and place in the freezer for at least 1 hour.

Pancakes Filled with Sweet Coconut

Traditionally, the pale green color in the pancake batter was obtained from the juice squeezed from fresh pandanus leaves. Green food coloring can be used instead.

INGREDIENTS

Makes 12–15 pancakes
1 cup molasses sugar
scant 2 cups water
1 pandanus leaf, stripped through with a fork and tied into a knot
2 cups dry unsweetened shredded coconut
oil, for frying
salt

For the pancake batter
2 cups all-purpose flour, sifted
2 eggs, beaten
2 drops of edible green food coloring
few drops of vanilla extract
scant 2 cups water
3 tablespoons peanut oil

1 Dissolve the sugar in the water with the pandanus leaf, in a pan over gentle heat, stirring all the time. Increase the heat and allow to boil gently for 3–4 minutes, until the mixture just becomes syrupy. Do not let it caramelize.

2 Put the coconut in a karahi or wok with a pinch of salt. Pour over the prepared sugar syrup and cook over a very gentle heat, stirring from time to time, until the mixture becomes almost dry; this will take 5–10 minutes. Set aside until required.

NUTRITIONAL NOTES	
Per Portion	
Energy	191cal
Fat	13.1g
Saturated Fat	8.5g
Carbohydrate	15.5g
Fiber	2.6g

3 To make the batter, blend together the flour, eggs, food coloring, vanilla extract, water, and oil, either by hand or in a food processor.

4 Brush a 7-inch skillet with oil and cook 12–15 pancakes. Keep the pancakes warm. Fill each pancake with a generous spoonful of the sweet coconut mixture, roll up, and serve immediately.

Steamed Coconut Custard

This popular dessert migrated to India from Southeast Asia. Coconut milk makes marvelous custard. Here it is cooked with cellophane noodles and chopped bananas, a combination that works very well.

INGREDIENTS

Serves 8

1 ounce cellophane noodles
3 eggs
14-fluid ounce can coconut milk
5 tablespoons water
2 tablespoons sugar
4 ripe bananas, peeled and cut in small pieces
salt
vanilla ice cream, to serve (optional)

1 Soak the cellophane noodles in a bowl of warm water for 5 minutes.

2 Beat the eggs in a bowl until pale. Whisk in the coconut milk, water, and sugar.

3 Strain into a 7½-cup heatproof soufflé dish.

NUTRITIONAL NOTES	
Per Portion	
Energy	115cal
Fat	2.8g
Saturated Fat	0.9g
Carbohydrate	19.9g
Fiber	0.6g

4 Drain the noodles well and cut them into small pieces with scissors. Stir the noodles into the coconut milk mixture, together with the chopped bananas. Add a pinch of salt and mix well.

5 Cover the dish with aluminum foil and place in a steamer for about 1 hour, or until set. A skewer inserted in the center should come out clean. Serve hot or cold, on its own or topped with vanilla ice cream.

Toffee Apples

A wickedly sweet way to end
a meal, this dessert evokes
memories of childhood.

INGREDIENTS

Serves 4

4 firm eating apples
1 cup all-purpose flour
½ cup water
1 egg, beaten
vegetable oil, for deep-frying, plus
  2 tablespoons for the toffee
½ cup sugar

1 Peel and core each apple and cut
into eight pieces. Dust each piece
of apple with a little of the flour.

2 Sift the remaining flour into a
mixing bowl, then slowly add the
cold water and stir well to make a
smooth batter. Add the beaten egg and
blend well.

VARIATION

Try this with bananas or pineapple pieces
for a delicious change.

NUTRITIONAL NOTES
Per Portion

Energy	410cal
Fat	18.5g
Saturated Fat	2.5g
Carbohydrate	60g
Fiber	2g

3 Heat the oil for deep-frying in a
karahi, wok, or deep pan. It will be
ready when a cube of day-old bread
browns in 45 seconds. Dip the apple
pieces in the batter and deep-fry for
about 3 minutes, or until golden.
Remove and drain on paper towels.
Drain off the oil from the pan.

4 Heat the remaining oil in the pan,
add the sugar, and stir constantly
until the sugar has caramelized.
Quickly add the apple pieces and
blend well so that each piece of apple
is thoroughly coated with the toffee.
Dip the apple pieces in cold water to
harden before serving.

Spiced Fruit Salad

Exotic fruits are becoming commonplace in supermarkets these days and it is fun to experiment with the different varieties. Look out in particular for cape gooseberry, carambola, papaya, and passion fruit.

INGREDIENTS

Serves 4–6
6 tablespoons granulated sugar
1¼ cups water
2 tablespoons syrup from a jar of
    stem ginger
2 pieces star anise
1-inch cinnamon stick
1 clove
juice of ½ lemon
2 fresh mint sprigs
1 mango
2 bananas, sliced
8 fresh or drained canned lychees
2 cups strawberries, hulled and halved
2 pieces stem ginger,
    cut into sticks
1 medium pineapple

1 Put the sugar, water, ginger syrup, star anise, cinnamon, clove, lemon juice, and mint into a pan. Bring to a boil, then simmer for 3 minutes. Strain into a bowl and set aside to cool.

2 Remove the top and bottom from the mango and cut off the outer skin. Stand the mango on one end and remove the flesh in two pieces either side of the flat pit. Slice evenly.

3 Add the mango slices to the syrup with the bananas, lychees, strawberries, and stem ginger. Mix in well, making sure the fruits are well coated in the sugary liquid.

4 Cut the pineapple in half by slicing down the center, using a very sharp knife. Loosen the flesh with a smaller, serrated knife, and remove the flesh by cutting around the rim and scooping it out. The pineapple halves will resemble two boat shapes. Do not discard the pineapple flesh, but cut into chunks and add to the fruity syrup.

5 Spoon some of the fruit salad into the pineapple halves and serve on a large dish. There will be sufficient fruit salad in the bowl to refill the pineapple halves at least once.

NUTRITIONAL NOTES	
Per Portion	
Energy	110cal
Fat	0.3g
Saturated Fat	0.1g
Carbohydrate	27.1g
Fiber	2.4g

Melon and Strawberry Salad

A beautiful and colorful fruit salad, this is suitable to serve as a refreshing appetizer or to round off a spicy meal. Don't be tempted to chill the salad; it tastes best at room temperature.

INGREDIENTS

Serves 4

1 Ogen melon
1 honeydew melon or other melon of own choice (see Cook's Tip)
½ watermelon
2 cups strawberries
1 tablespoon lemon juice
1 tablespoon honey
1 tablespoon chopped fresh mint

1 Prepare the melons by cutting them in half and discarding the seeds. Use a melon ball to scoop out the flesh into balls or a knife to cut it into cubes. Place these in a fruit bowl.

2 Rinse and remove the stems from the strawberries, cut the fruit in half, and add them to the bowl.

3 Mix together the lemon juice and honey and add 1 tablespoon water to make this easier to pour over the fruit. Mix into the fruit gently.

4 Sprinkle the chopped mint over the top of the fruit and serve.

NUTRITIONAL NOTES	
Per Portion	
Energy	114cal
Fat	0.70g
Saturated Fat	0.00g
Carbohydrate	26.50g
Fiber	1.60g

_____ COOK'S TIP _____

Use whichever melons are available: replace Ogen with cantaloupe or watermelon with charentais, for example. Try to choose three melons with a variation in color for an attractive effect.

Caramel Custard with Fresh Fruit

A creamy caramel dessert is a wonderful way to end a meal. It is light and delicious, and this recipe is very simple.

INGREDIENTS

Serves 6
For the caramel
2 tablespoons sugar
2 tablespoons water

For the custard
6 eggs
4 drops vanilla extract
½ cup sugar
3 cups low-fat milk
fresh fruit, such as strawberries, blueberries, orange and banana slices, and raspberries, to serve

1 To make the caramel, place the sugar and water in a heavy pan and heat until the sugar has dissolved and the mixture is bubbling and pale gold in color. Pour carefully into a 5-cup soufflé dish. Let stand to cool.

2 Preheat the oven to 350°F. To make the custard, break the eggs into a medium mixing bowl and whisk until frothy.

_____ COOK'S TIP _____

Use pure vanilla extract, not synthetic vanilla flavoring for this custard because the flavor is much better; remember, the extract is strong and you need only a few drops.

3 Stir in the vanilla extract and gradually add the sugar, then the milk, whisking constantly.

4 Pour the custard over the top of the caramel.

5 Cook the custard in the oven for 35–40 minutes. Remove from the oven and ley cool for 30 minutes, or until the mixture is set.

6 Loosen the custard from the sides of the dish with a knife. Place a serving dish upside down on top of the soufflé dish and invert, giving a gentle shake if necessary to turn out the custard onto the serving dish.

7 Arrange any fresh fruit of your choice around the custard on the serving dish and serve immediately.

NUTRITIONAL NOTES	
Per Portion	
Energy	194cal
Fat	4.70g
Saturated Fat	2.01g
Carbohydrate	32.90g
Fiber	0.00g

Kulfi with Cardamom

To make kulfi, you can use yogurt containers or dariole molds.

INGREDIENTS

Serves 6

8 cups whole milk
12 cardamoms
¾ cup superfine sugar
¼ cup blanched almonds,
  chopped
toasted sliced almonds
  and cardamoms,
  to decorate

1 Place the milk and cardamoms in a large heavy pan. Bring to a boil then simmer vigorously until reduced by one-third. Strain the milk into a bowl, discarding the cardamoms, then stir in the sugar and almonds until the sugar is dissolved. Cool.

2 Pour the mixture into a freezerproof container, cover, and freeze until almost firm, stirring every 30 minutes.

3 When almost solid, pack the ice cream into six clean yogurt containers. Return to the freezer until required, removing the containers about 10 minutes before serving and turning the individual ices out.

4 Decorate with toasted almonds and cardamoms before serving.

NUTRITIONAL NOTES	
Per Portion	
Energy	401cal
Fat	19.3g
Saturated Fat	11.2g
Carbohydrate	46.8g
Fiber	0.3g

COOK'S TIP

Use a large pan for reducing the milk because there needs to be plenty of room for it to foam up.

Pears in Spiced Wine

Familiar Indian spices, soaked in a red wine syrup, give pears a lovely warm flavor. The color is beautiful, too.

INGREDIENTS

Serves 4

1 bottle full-bodied red wine
1 cinnamon stick
4 cloves
½ teaspoon grated nutmeg
½ teaspoon ground ginger
8 peppercorns
¾ cup superfine sugar
thinly pared rind of ½ orange
thinly pared rind of ½ lemon
8 firm ripe pears

1 Pour the wine into a heavy pan into which the pears will fit snugly when standing upright. Stir the cinnamon stick, cloves, nutmeg, ginger, peppercorns, sugar, and citrus rinds into the wine.

2 Peel the pears, leaving the stalks intact, and stand them in the pan. The wine should only just cover the pears. Bring the liquid to a boil, lower the heat, cover, and simmer very gently for 30 minutes, or until the pears are tender. Using a slotted spoon, transfer the pears to a bowl.

3 Boil the poaching liquid until it has reduced by half and is syrupy. Strain the syrup over and around the pears and serve hot or cold.

COOK'S TIP

Serve the pears with a mascarpone cream, made by combining equal quantities of mascarpone cheese and heavy cream, and adding a little vanilla extract for flavor. They also taste good with plain yogurt or ice cream.

NUTRITIONAL NOTES	
Per Portion	
Energy	191cal
Fat	0.3g
Saturated Fat	0g
Carbohydrate	43.1g
Fiber	6.6g

Mango and Coconut Stir-Fry

Choose a ripe mango for this recipe. If you buy one that is a little under-ripe, let it stand in a warm place for a day or two before using.

INGREDIENTS

Serves 4
¼ coconut
1 large, ripe mango
finely grated rind and juice of
    2 limes
1 tablespoon sunflower oil
1 tablespoon butter
2 tablespoons honey
crème fraîche or ice cream, to serve

1 Prepare the coconut if necessary. Drain the milk and remove the flesh. Peel with a vegetable peeler so that it forms flakes.

VARIATION

Nectarine or peach slices can be used instead of the mango.

NUTRITIONAL NOTES
Per Portion

Energy	357cal
Fat	32.7g
Saturated Fat	24.1g
Carbohydrate	13.8g
Fiber	7g

2 Peel the mango. Cut the pit out of the middle of the fruit. Cut each half of the mango into slices.

3 Place the mango slices in a bowl and pour over the lime juice and rind. Set aside.

4 Meanwhile heat a karahi or wok, then add 2 teaspoons of the oil. When the oil is hot, add the butter. Once the butter has melted, stir in the coconut flakes and stir-fry for 1–2 minutes, until the coconut is golden brown. Remove and drain on paper towels. Wipe out the pan. Strain the mango slices, reserving the juice.

5 Heat the pan again and add the remaining oil. When the oil is hot, add the mango and stir-fry for 1–2 minutes, then add the juice, let bubble, and reduce for 1 minute.

6 Stir in the honey. When it has dissolved, spoon the mango and coconut dessert into one large serving bowl or individual dishes. Sprinkle on the coconut flakes and serve with crème fraîche or ice cream.

COOK'S TIP

You can sometimes buy "fresh" coconut that has already been cracked open and is sold in pieces ready for use from supermarkets, but buying the whole nut ensures greater freshness. Choose one that is heavy for its size and shake it so that you can hear the milk sloshing about. A "dry" coconut will almost certainly have rancid flesh. You can simply crack the shell with a hammer, preferably with the nut inside a plastic bag, but it may be better to pierce the two ends with a sharp nail or skewer first in order to collect and save the coconut milk. An alternative method is to drain the milk first and then heat the nut briefly in the oven until it cracks. Whichever method you choose to open the coconut, it is then easy to extract the flesh and chop or shave it.

Tea and Fruit Punch

This delicious punch can be served hot or cold. White wine or brandy may be added to taste.

INGREDIENTS

Serves 4
2½ cups water
1 cinnamon stick
4 cloves
½ teaspoon Earl Grey tea leaves
¾ cup sugar
1½ cups tropical soft drink concentrate
1 lemon, sliced
1 small orange, sliced
½ cucumber, sliced

1 Bring the water to a boil in a pan with the cinnamon stick and cloves. Remove from the heat and add the tea leaves. Let brew for about 5 minutes. Stir and strain into a large bowl and chill in the refrigerator for 2–3 hours.

NUTRITIONAL NOTES	
Per Portion	
Energy	1,108cal
Fat	0g
Saturated Fat	0g
Carbohydrate	294.5g
Fiber	0g

2 Add the sugar and the soft drink concentrate and let rest until the sugar has dissolved and the mixture cooled. Place the fruit and cucumber in a chilled punch bowl and pour over the tea mix. Chill for another 24 hours before serving.

Spiced Lassi

Lassi or buttermilk is prepared by churning yogurt with water and then removing the fat. To make this refreshing drink without churning, use low-fat plain yogurt.

INGREDIENTS

Serves 4
scant 2 cups plain yogurt
1¼ cups water
1-inch piece fresh ginger root, finely crushed
2 fresh green chiles, finely chopped
½ teaspoon ground cumin
salt and black pepper, to taste
few fresh cilantro leaves, chopped, to garnish

1 In a bowl, whisk the yogurt and water until well blended. The consistency should be that of whole milk. Adjust by adding more water if necessary.

2 Add the ginger, chiles, and ground cumin, season with the salt and black pepper, and mix well. Pour into four serving glasses and chill. Garnish with chopped cilantro before serving.

VARIATION
For a sweet version of this refreshing drink, omit the spices and add sugar to taste. A little rose water or orange flower water can also be added.

NUTRITIONAL NOTES	
Per Portion	
Energy	63cal
Fat	1.1g
Saturated Fat	0.6g
Carbohydrate	8.5g
Fiber	0g

Pistachio Lassi

In India, lassi is not only made at home, but is also sold at roadside cafés, restaurants, and hotels. There is no substitute for this drink, especially on a hot day. It is particularly good served with curries and similar hot dishes because it helps the body to digest spicy food.

INGREDIENTS

Serves 4

1¼ cups plain low-fat yogurt
1 teaspoon sugar, or to taste
1¼ cups water
2 tablespoons puréed fruit, (optional)
1 tablespoon crushed pistachio nuts, to decorate

1 Place the yogurt in a pitcher; whisk until frothy. Add the sugar.

NUTRITIONAL NOTES	
Per Portion	
Energy	70cal
Fat	2.60g
Saturated Fat	0.63g
Carbohydrate	7.50g
Fiber	0g

2 Pour in the water and the puréed fruit, if using, and continue to whisk for 2 minutes. Pour the lassi into serving glasses and serve chilled, decorated with crushed pistachio nuts.

VARIATION
To make a simple savory lassi, omit the sugar and fruit and add lemon juice, ground cumin, and salt. Garnish with mint.

Almond Sherbet

Traditionally, this drink was always made in the month of Ramadan to break the fast. It should be served chilled.

INGREDIENTS

Serves 4

½ cup ground almonds
2½ cups low-fat milk
2 teaspoons sugar, or to taste

NUTRITIONAL NOTES	
Per Portion	
Energy	155cal
Fat	9.40g
Saturated Fat	2.04g
Carbohydrate	11.00g
Fiber	0.90g

1 Put the ground almonds into a serving pitcher.

COOK'S TIP
Refreshing, cooling drinks are the perfect accompaniment for spicy Indian dishes. Similar drinks are made with fruit juices flavored with chopped fresh mint.

2 Pour in the low-fat milk and add the sugar; stir to mix. Taste for sweetness and serve very cold in tall glasses. Chilling the glasses first helps to keep the drink cold and adds a sense of occasion.

Glossary

Almonds Available whole, sliced (or slivered), and ground, these sweet nuts impart a sumptuous richness to curries. They are considered a great delicacy in Pakistan and India, where they are extremely expensive and are generally only used for special occasion dishes.

Asafetida A resin added to dishes as an antiflatulent. It has an acrid, bitter taste and only a tiny amount should be used.

Banana Leaves Traditionally used in Indian and Asian cooking as containers to steam foods, banana leaves are sold in Indian and Asian food stores. If unavailable, squares of lightly oiled aluminum foil or buttered parchment paper can be used instead.

Basil One of the oldest herbs known to man, basil is thought to have originated in India, although it is much more widely used in Southeast Asia. Add basil to curries and salads as an ingredient and as a garnish. Avoid chopping the leaves, but tear them into pieces or add them to the dish whole.

Basmati rice A slender, long-grain rice grown in northern India, in the Punjab, Pakistan, and in the foothills of the Himalayas, basmati is famous for its distinctive and beautiful fragrance. It is widely used in Indian cooking, particularly in pilaus and biryanis; it has a cooling effect when eaten with hot, spicy curry dishes.

Bay leaves The large dried leaves of the bay laurel tree are one of the oldest herbs used in India. Bay leaves are used for the distinctive flavor they add to a dish.

Bean curd More commonly known in the West by its Japanese name, tofu. See *tofu*

Bengal gram One of the many legumes that are widely used in Indian cooking, this is related to the chickpea. The peas are often used whole in curries.

Besan flour Also known as gram flour, this is used to flavor and thicken Indian curries and other spicy dishes. Besan flour is also used as a stabilizer: when added to yogurt it helps to prevent it from curdling in hot food.

Bitter gourds One of the many bitter vegetables often used in Indian cooking, this long, knobbly green vegetable has a strong, distinct taste. To prepare a gourd, wash it, slice it in half lengthwise, remove and discard the seeds, then cut into slices.

Bottle gourds As the name suggests, these gourds have a distinctive shape. Young gourds can be eaten, but taste extremely bitter, so are generally reserved for highly spiced dishes, such as curries.

Cardamom pods This spice is native to India, where it is almost as highly prized as saffron. The pale green and beige pods have a finer flavor than the coarse brown or black ones. The pods can be used whole or husked to remove the seeds. They have a slightly pungent, very aromatic taste.

Chapati flour A type of whole-wheat flour, often sold under its Indian name, atta, in Indian food stores. It is used to make chapatis and other breads. Well-sifted whole-wheat flour is an acceptable substitute.

Chiles All chile varieties are native to the tropical parts of the Americas and were introduced to Asia by European traders after Christopher Columbus brought them to Spain. They soon became an integral part of Asian cuisine. Fresh and dried chiles are used in India to add heat and flavor to sauces, sambals, and salads, and to cooked dishes, such as stocks, soups, curries, stir-fries, and braised dishes.

Cilantro The leaves from the same plant that provides coriander seeds, cilantro is a favorite ingredient in all Asian countries, and its unique delicate flavor and bright green color make it a popular garnish for curries.

Coconut milk An essential ingredient in south and east Indian and Southeast Asian cooking. Coconut milk can be made at home from dry unsweetened shredded coconut, but is also available in cans. If the milk is left to stand, coconut cream will rise to the surface as a separate layer.

Coriander The seeds from the same plant as cilantro leaves, they are used whole or ground.

Coconut cream is sold in solid blocks, created when the cream is left to solidify. In India, it is used to enrich spicy and sweet dishes. A small quantity can be cut off the block and stirred into a dish just before serving, or it can be diluted with boiling water to produce coconut milk, with the proportion of coconut cream to water being altered, according to required thickness.

Cuddapah nuts Known locally as chirongi nuts, these come from a tree that grows in the more arid regions of India. They are used as a substitute for almonds.

Cumin These seeds are oval, ridged, and, although described as white, are greenish brown in color. They have a strong aroma and flavor and can be used whole or freshly ground. Black cumin seeds are not as easy to find as the paler variety. They are dark and aromatic and are used to flavor curries and rice dishes. If you buy ground cumin, as with any other ground spice, keep it in a dry, cool place and use as soon as possible, because the flavor will deteriorate rapidly.

Curry leaves Fragrant, glossy green leaves that are produced by a hardwood tree indigenous to southern India. Curry leaves are used in curries and rice dishes all over Asia, but especially in India. The leaves are sold fresh or dried in Indian food stores.

Curry paste A wet blend of spices, herbs, and chiles that is used as the basis of a curry. The blending of the various components is an art; each curry paste is designed to produce a flavor that will harmonize with the main ingredients. Because they contain fresh ingredients, curry pastes must be stored in the refrigerator.

Curry powder A dry blend of spices and dried chiles. The spices chosen and the way in which they are roasted determine the flavor and strength.

Dhal See *Legumes*

Eggplant Numerous eggplant varieties exist in Asia, where the vegetable has been grown for more than 2,000 years. Eggplant absorbs the flavors of other ingredients like a sponge, and, therefore, benefits from being cooked with strongly flavored foods and seasonings.

Fenugreek Sold in bunches, this fresh herb has very small leaves and is used to flavor both meat and vegetable dishes. Always discard the stalks, which will make the dish taste bitter. Flat fenugreek seeds are pungent and slightly bitter. They are widely used in curries and rice dishes.

Garam masala A mild, sweet seasoning from north India, and a very popular curry powder. Recipes for garam masala vary, but all will contain cardamom, cinnamon, cloves, coriander, and black peppercorns. What distinguishes garam masala from other curry powders is that is often added toward the end of cooking, rather than at the start.

Garlic Prized for its pungent warmth, garlic is used whole, chopped, or crushed in curries.

Ghee The traditional Indian cooking fat, ghee is clarified butter than can be heated to higher temperatures than other oils without burning. Pure ghee is made from dairy milk, but vegetable ghee is also produced, and nowadays this is often used in place of dairy ghee because of its lower fat content. Many modern Indian households prefer to use vegetable oil as their chosen cooking fat.

Ginger Fresh ginger root is a basic ingredient in Indian cooking. Choose plump roots whose skin looks shiny and bright, not dry. When cut, the flesh should look moist and creamy. Ground ginger is seldom used.

Legumes Hundreds of different legumes are used in India. Dried beans, peas, and lentils are nutritious, easy to cook, and very versatile, making them ideal ingredients for vegetarian dishes. Those featured in this book include black-eyed peas; chickpeas; chana dhal, a yellow lentil for which yellow split peas can be substituted, although these two are not the same; mung beans, which can be eaten whole or split; mung dhal; and

masoor dhal, which is a split red-orange lentil. Tuvar dhal is a split bean that is commercially oiled and urad dhal is a black lentil with a dry texture when cooked.

Mango powder Sold as amchur, this is made from unripe green mangoes that have been sun-dried and then finely ground. The flavor is tart and the powder is used to add a tangy flavor to curries and other dishes.

Mangosteen A fragrant fruit that looks like a lychee, although they are not related. Mangosteens are dried, like mangoes, to produce a powder called kokum, which is used as a souring agent in India.

Mustard seeds Round in shape, with a sharp flavor, mustard seeds are most often used in Indian cooking to flavor curries and pickles.

Mustard oil Made from mustard seeds, this oil has a pungent taste when raw, but becomes sweeter when heated. It is widely used in India, especially in eastern regions, where mustard crops are grown.

Nigella seeds These come from a herbaceous annual. The bulk of the crop is grown in India and the seeds have a peppery, herblike taste. They are used in spice mixes, in dhal and vegetable dishes, pickles, and chutneys. Nigella seeds are often sprinkled on nan and other Indian breads. They are sometimes called wild onion seeds or kalonji.

Okra Also known as ladies' fingers, this is one of the most popular Indian vegetables. The small green five-sided pods have a distinctive flavor and a sticky, pulpy texture when cooked.

Onion seeds Black in color and triangular in shape, these seeds are used in pickles and to flavor vegetable curries.

Pandanus leaves Sometimes known as screwpine or bandan leaves, these are used in sweet and savory dishes. A green coloring obtained from the leaves is traditionally used to tint desserts, although

today, edible food coloring is often preferred for convenience.

Paneer A white, smooth-textured cheese from northern India, paneer is excellent with meat or fish, or on its own in vegetable dishes.

Pomegranate seeds Dried seeds from sour pomegranates are used in a number of Indian dishes to impart a tart flavor. Look for them in Indian food stores. They are often sold as anardana.

Red gram Also known as pigeon peas, arhar, or tur, this pea is widely grown in India.

Saffron The world's most expensive spice is produced from the dried stigmas of the saffron crocus. Only a tiny amount of saffron is needed to flavor or color a dish, whether sweet or savory. Saffron is sold as threads and in powder form.

Tamarind The dried black pods of the tamarind plant are sour in taste and very sticky. Tamarind is used for its flavor, which is refreshingly tart, without being bitter. Lemon juice can be used instead, but will not have the intensity of flavor.

Tofu Also known as bean curd, tofu is made from soybeans, is a rich source of protein in vegetarian dishes, and is a popular ingredient in India and Southeast Asia. Tofu is sold in supermarkets and health food stores as silken or soft tofu, and also in a firmer form. Yellow tofu is usually only available from Asian food stores, where it is sold cubed, ready to be deep-fried. Despite the bland taste of tofu, the porous texture will absorb the flavor of the ingredients with which it is cooked.

Turmeric This bright yellow, bitter-tasting spice is sold ground and fresh, with fresh turmeric being peeled and then grated or sliced in the same way as fresh ginger root. Turmeric is often used as a cheaper alternative to saffron, but the two do not compare in terms of flavor. Turmeric adds a more vibrant color. The aroma is harsher, being peppery and musky. Ground turmeric is often used in curry powders and it is this spice that is responsible for the characteristic yellow color.

Index

Suppliers

The following is intended as a useful list of online suppliers and information sites to help the reader source Indian groceries and cooking equipment. Their inclusion in this book does not necessarily warrant an endorsement by the publishers.

USA

www.indiavilas.com
An information site detailing products and resources available throughout the United States. Includes a comprehensive, nationwide list of grocers and restaurants, which visitors can search according to state.

www.mahabazaar.com
Online bazaar of Indian products, including dried fruits and nuts, oils, spice mixes, pastes, and marinades, plus a range of herbal and beauty products.

www.namaste.com
One of the largest retailers and brands of Indian products in the United States. Online store sells a range of groceries, books, and gifts, plus health, Ayurveda, and beauty products.

store.indianfoodsco.com
A selection of accompaniments, snack foods, beverages, and basics, plus a guide to Indian pantry essentials and meal ideas for barbecues, street food, and dinners.

www.tastybite.com
A U.S.-sponsored retailer stocking Indian-made foods, with specific lines in vegetarian, meat, and bread products. Provides information on vegan, kosher, and gluten-free products for customers.

UNITED KINGDOM

www.theasiancookshop.co.uk
A large range of Indian groceries available for delivery; includes spices, pastes, chutneys and breads. Also features cooking utensils, cookbooks and gifts.

www.sweetmart.co.uk
Online ordering service based in southwest England with a catalog featuring dhals, rice, pickles, spices, and sauces.

www.spicebox.co.uk
Online information about Rafi Fernandez's two UK spice outlets, Rafi's Spicebox, based in Sudbury, Suffolk, and York. Also includes recipe ideas, books, and special offers.

www.theindiangrocerystore.com
Offers a range of authentic Indian grocery products, plus a home delivery service covering Nottingham and the Midlands.

www.thespiceshop.co.uk
Information about the range of freshly ground, hand-mixed and additive-free spices sold at this West London outlet, which is based near Portobello Road in Notting Hill.

WORLDWIDE

www.ethnicgrocer.com
A world market covering various cuisines, which invites visitors to shop for products by country. The Indian category includes a wide range of cooking oils and vinegars, plus kitchenware, spices, sauces, confections, and baking products.

www.getspice.com
Specialist online culinary store featuring Indian spices, teas and kitchenware. Includes a selection of rare and organic spices.

www.indiamart.com
India-based suppliers of spices and condiments, which aims to export packed goods to businesses across the globe.

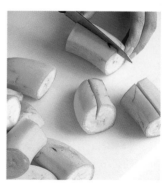

www.indiandownunder.com.au
Lists up to 60 Indian grocers trading throughout Australia, with the opportunity to search for outlets according to state. Also lists a selection of Indian restaurants.

www.natco-online.com
Extensive online store with perhaps the widest range of speciality Indian cooking ingredients available on the Web. Up to 800 authentic foods available for purchase.

www.valueindia.com
Online outlet with specific sites set up for customers in India, USA/Canada, UK, and Australia/New Zealand. Enables visitors to browse for a wide range of authentic groceries and condiments.

Publisher: Joanna Lorenz
Editorial Director: Helen Sudell
Project Editors: Ruth Baldwin, Lindsay Porter, Judith Simons and Catherine Stuart
Production Director: Ben Worley
Book Design: Sarah Kidd
Additional Design: Diane Pullen and Public Impact
Text Editor: Jenni Fleetwood
Recipes: Mridula Baljekar, Linda Doeser, Rafi Fernandez, Jenni Fleetwood, Brian Glover, Shehzad
Husain, Christine Ingram, Manisha Kanani, Lesley Mackley, Sallie Morris, Jennie Shapter, Ysanne
Spevak, Steven Wheeler and Jenny White
Photography: Edward Allwright, David Armstrong, Nicki Dowey, Amanda Heywood, Ferguson
Hill, Janine Hosegood, David Jordon, David King, Patrick McLeavey and Sam Stowell
Nutritional Data: Claire Brain and Wendy Doyle

Metro Books
122 Fifth Avenue
New York, NY 10011

ISBN-13: 978-1-4351-0611-6

Printed and bound in China

10 9 8 7 6 5 4 3 2

Previously published as *Complete Indian Cooking*

NOTES
Standard spoon and cup measures are level.

Large eggs are used unless otherwise stated.

Electric oven temperatures in this book are for conventional ovens. When using a fan oven, the
temperature will probably need to be reduced by about 20–40°F. Since ovens vary, you should
check with your manufacturer's instruction book for guidance.